Robert E. Park and the Chicago School

FRED H. MATTHEWS

Montreal and London   1977

301.0924

M43q

118835

July 1981

© McGill-Queen's University Press 1977
International Standard Book Number 0 7735 0243 2 (cloth)
International Standard Book Number 0 7735 0263 7 (paper)
Legal Deposit 1st Quarter 1977
Bibliothèque nationale du Québec

Design by Peter Dorn, RCA, MGDC

This book has been published with the help of a grant from the Social Science Research Council of Canada using funds provided by the Canada Council.

Printed in Canada

Contents

This study in the development of American social science, which has been under way sporadically throughout a traumatic decade, has accumulated many debts along the way. I am deeply grateful to librarians at Fisk University, the University of Chicago, and the Library of Congress, who guided me to a variety of manuscript and letter files pertaining to the career of Robert Park.

To the former colleagues, students, and friends of Robert Park who generously shared their memories and files with me, in letters, interviews, and the loan of documents which they had preserved, my debt is very great: the late Saul D.Alinsky, Nels Anderson, Albert Blumenthal, the late Emory S. Bogardus, Jessie Bernard, Herbert Blumer, the late Horace R.Cayton, Bingham Dai, H.Warren Dunham, Clarence Glick, Harold F.Gosnell, Bernhard L.Hörmann, Lewis W.Jones, Mrs. Charles S.Johnson, Guy B.Johnson, Harold D.Lasswell, Donald Pierson, Walter Reckless, Ernest H.Shideler, Edgar T.Thompson, Leslie A.White. Professor Norman Hayner of the University of Washington deserves a special place for allowing me to read and quote from his valuable diary of the Chicago years, and for freely answering my numerous and often obtuse questions.

Greatest thanks are due to two of Robert Park's children and to his closest surviving friends, his daughters, Mrs. Donald Breed and Margaret Park Redfield, his longtime assistant, Winifred Raushenbush, and his students and close friends Everett C.Hughes and Helen MacGill Hughes. Without the patience and free access to manuscript data which they were willing to extend, any penetration beyond the surface of published work which this study may have achieved would have been impossible.

Additional acknowledgment is due to the unselfish generosity of Park's children and intellectual heirs because to some degree this study is bound to disappoint them. While I have tried to describe Park's historical importance in the development of American social science, and the continuing vitality of some of his special theories, I cannot wholly share their admiration for him as a scholar. Still, I retain a vivid sense of their enduring enthusiasm, and the extent to which many of the people who shared their recollections with me had found their encounter with Robert Park to be one of the decisive events of their lives. Park was clearly a great Teacher, a compelling personality who offered one model of the scholar's vocation to a generation of students, the type of man whose absence or decline in power of conversion has exacerbated the tensions plaguing the University in recent years.

My thanks are due to Donald Fleming for the original idea of studying a social scientist in the context of general intellectual history, and for the model of enthusiastic but fastidious scholarship which he set for his students. He has probably suggested more of the ideas scattered through this work than I could now state, but no imputation of responsibility to him for their present form is intended. Two very old friends, John Finley Scott and Laurence R. Veysey, are expert in many of the areas touched upon here; I have long benefited from their conversation as well as their published works, especially Scott's *Internalization of Norms* and Veysey's *Emergence of the American University*, though neither would probably endorse altogether my effort to re-create and find the permanent value in an academic career that is far removed from the professional present. I am grateful to the editors of the *Canadian Journal of History* for permission to reprint, in slightly altered form in chapter 3, material which first appeared in that journal. My most profound debt is to my wife, Jean V. Matthews, also a student of American history, who has given inspiration, prodding, close criticism, and most other conceivable types of aid to this project, in unstinting quantity and unfailingly high quality.

The present mood of North American scholarship, with its positivist insistence on the definable and definitive, seems to require two exculpatory comments. This is an intellectual biography, not a chapter in the history of sociological theory or in the institutional history of academic departments. Given the eclectic nature of Park's own interests, it has perforce become a series of essays in intellectual biography rather than an exhaustive and definitive treatment of a single subject. It reflects Park's own position as a transition between the traditional idea of the universal scholar and the recently modern notion of the social scientist as possessor of precise, objective, and timeless truth. Park himself spoke for the second ideal, how seriously it is now hard to say, but he and his work seem to represent the earlier and more relaxed model. An attempt to understand and delineate the mind and resonance of a traditional scholar from the vantage point of a positivist era entails a good deal of deliberate alienation from one's own scholarly context. The most astringent of contemporary intellectual historians, Steven Lukes, noted the irreconcilability of understanding and assessment in his Introduction to *Emile Durkheim:* 'only by inducing oneself not to see certain things ... [can] one ... achieve a sympathetic understanding and only by seeing them that one can make a critical assessment.' Whether or not the two are ultimately irreconcilable, I have tried to weigh the scale in favor of understanding over judgment, of comprehension of a thinker in context and resonance over the facile fun of picking every nit illuminated in the hindsight of theoretical progression.

There is a deeper sense of 'assessment': the calm appraisal of the adequacy and utility of a theory from some consciously valuational viewpoint, in the historical context in which it could possibly have acted as an independent force. Even in this more complex context, I hope that the choice of understanding over assessment can be defended by the criterion of historical value that stresses the need for a 'usable past'. If we need to inform ourselves about the doings and thinkings of the now deceased, then it is worth trying to write a history that will do more than reinforce the natural complacent sense of superiority that every actual or potential Present has over every Past. Ultimately, judgment is essential and unavoidable; but it should be a serious judgment of mind in context and not the perfunctory judgment of semantic meaning that has become predictable in our present rush to premature dismissal. The current eclipse of intellectual history on this continent has many causes, but one seems to be the embarrassment that a sense of the past as living option might bring to the discussion of current issues. The history of obsolescent ideas seems useless only to those who have dedicated themselves to the distinct and contradictory propositions that ideas always deceive and never matter.

Note on Citation of Unpublished Sources

Citation of manuscript sources presents a special problem for this work. At the time that I studied the various Park papers, in 1963/65, many of them were not yet in final, clearly citable form. Those which were deposited in libraries present few problems, though the letters to and from Park during the Tuskegee years were scattered more widely throughout the Booker T. Washington Papers than a glance at the formal organization of these papers might suggest. There were two principal private archives, that of Professor Everett Hughes, then of Brandeis University and now of Boston College; and that of Mrs. Winifred Raushenbush Rorty of Columbia, New Jersey. These are cited as 'Park-Hughes' and 'Park Raushenbush' respectively. Both of these archives, along with the letters of reminiscence elicited for this study, will eventually be deposited in the University of Chicago Library.

Robert Ezra Park came late to the professional role for which he is remembered. Park's permanent association with the growing but amorphous discipline of sociology came from an accidental meeting while he was working as press agent for Booker T.Washington of Tuskegee Institute. One expression of Washington's unremitting drive for power via publicity was his desire to sponsor conferences – that characteristic activity of institutional self-advertisement. In 1911, his ambitious rival, W.E.B.Du Bois, had participated in a Universal Races Congress in London.[1] Sensitive to the prestige of scholarship, if distrustful of its practical efficacy, Washington organized in the spring of 1912 an International Conference on the Negro at Tuskegee. Among the speakers at a morning session on education were William I.Thomas, the University of Chicago sociologist, and Washington's press agent and general factotum, the former newspaperman and publicist, Robert Park.[2]

Thomas had never met Park before, but was so impressed with him that, by his own account, although he had planned to remain at Tuskegee only two days, 'he had found a man there, and remained two weeks to talk to him'.[3] After this extensive conversation, Thomas asked Park to go to Chicago and give some lectures on the Negro in America during the University's summer quarter.[4] Some years earlier, Park had received a similar invitation from Albion W.Small, the head of Chicago's sociology department, but had been so dissatisfied with the scholar's career that he never took it up.[5] Now, at the age of forty-eight, after a varied and restless career, he was once more anxious to break with an environment whose possibilities for self-instruction he seemed to have exhausted. After seven years as an agent for Booker T. Washington, Park chose another withdrawal from affairs, another retreat to reflect upon and draw conclusions from the mass of exotic, even shocking experiences he had accumulated.

This move, unlike the others in Park's varied life, was to be permanent. He remained at Chicago for more than twenty years, made a distinguished career for himself, and helped raise the status of sociology in America. Park's strong personality and wide experience helped to change the assumptions on which the academic discipline of sociology had been operating. In 1913, the growing academic field of sociology was a partly institutionalized alliance of three separate activities: formal speculation about the nature of society, Christian philanthropy and exhortation, and descriptive studies designed to display the magnitude of social problems to an educated and morally homogeneous citizenry. When Park left the scene of active sociological work in the late 1930s, sociology was a large and powerful, if intellectually insecure, academic discipline engaged in a permanent program of research, related on the one hand to the concrete description of society, and on the other to the development of a theory explaining social relations. Most important for its impact on general history, it was already challenging literature and popular culture for a share of the expanding educational market, answering the demand for both fact and value which was created by the decline of religion and routine patriotism in a specializing society.[6]

Clearly no one man was responsible for the transformation of sociology, which was interwoven with the entire process of professional specialization and the shifting center of ameliorative social action from voluntary organizations to government agencies. But Park came upon the scene just as forces within and without the profession made necessary a change of focus; he helped to shape the sociology of the 1920s and 30s by his special concerns and point of view. Park brought to this hitherto somewhat clerical and cloistered discipline the prestige of 'real life' and a wide acquaintance with practical affairs. From the standpoint of the self-consciously professional 1960s, his innovations were to seem incomplete, often elementary, and sometimes misleading. Nevertheless, his career spans the exciting period of transition from sociology as an area, or areas, of concern, to sociology as a discipline intent on proving itself a science capable of developing an integrated theoretical structure validated by self-testing empirical research. Much of the unique quality of Park's sociology came from the well-developed views which he brought to the field after thirty years of study and informal observation. After spending half his adult life in search of a believable and relevant career, Park came to the institution, the University of Chicago, and to that city above all others, Chicago itself, which would prove hospitable to the conversion of his personal quest for understanding into the theoretical foundations of a major social science, into what has become a major social institution and a formative influence in its own right on the American character.

A Child of the Middle border

In background and early environment, Park was a representative citizen of the old American stock of the Middle Border. His immediate family background was commercial, not clerical, and he was brought up to respect not only ideals but 'reality' in the sense of the external nature which man is duty-bound to subdue and develop.[7] He was born in Harveyville, Luzerne County, Pennsylvania, on 14 February 1864, while his father was serving in the Union Army.[8] When Hiram Asa Park returned from the war, the family moved to Red Wing, Minnesota, which Park recalled as a typical 'Main

Street' settled mainly by New Englanders.[9] His father was a 'big check-suited, boasting Westerner', who built up a prosperous business in Red Wing and later in Watertown, South Dakota.[10] His mother, Theodosia Warner Park, came from a Vermont family, and preserved a nostalgic affection for the mountainous and dignified New England of her memories. Unlike her husband, she had an interest in literature and art, some of which must have rubbed off on Robert. At first, this manifested itself only in a voracious taste for dime novels. Robert devoured them by the score and sank himself in the life of their characters, only giving up the 'vice' when a teacher made him promise to read no more 'trash'.[11]

During Robert's early childhood the family was not well off. Perhaps in reaction to Hiram Asa's concern with success and survival, Robert Park developed a revulsion from money and the quest for security. When his father died in 1911 and left him a considerable sum, he was reluctant to use it until his tiny salary at the University of Chicago made it necessary to fall back on the inheritance in order to support his family.[12] As a boy Park roamed with a neighborhood gang and regarded his early years as having been spent on 'the wrong side of the tracks'. This social handicap enabled him to observe 'the behavior of the town's "best families" with the detachment of the outsider and with an interest in the motive spring of human action rather than the obligation of conformity to the social code'.[13] Looking back on his childhood in later life, Park liked to associate his own youth with the symbols of mid-nineteenth century America, perhaps to unite it with the historical America of great events which to later ages symbolized the 1860s and 70s. He seemed to recall a vivid memory of Lincoln's death — even though he was just fourteen months old at the time — and liked to recount how, as a small boy, he had been stopped and asked the way by a stranger who turned out to be Jesse James.[14] Although he came from a state with a large Scandinavian population, Park's own recollections do not stress the conflict of Yankee and Outlander as a major force in his childhood. Park's significance as a transitional figure between the 'old' and 'new' America lies in the fact that he was a native-born son of the commercial classes, raised with a concept of American identity summed up in the contrasting figures of Lincoln and Jesse James, who came, through sociology, to understand the importance of cultural differences and the plurality of values in the urban nation of the twentieth century.[15]

At school Park was not particularly outstanding, although he was fascinated by geometry — an early interest in spatial relations which was to be reflected much later in his sociology. Outside class, however, he read a great deal and, like so many midwestern youth in the 1870s, imbibed the skeptical rationalism of the nationalist freethinker and orator, Robert Ingersoll. Park was particularly struck by Ingersoll's lectures on 'The Ten Mistakes of Moses', a satirical re-telling of Old Testament tales which emphasized their literal absurdity when judged by a common sense faith in material reality.[16] Red Wing too, had enough intellectual life to nourish a 'society of young radicals' – perhaps no more than a group of 'regulars' in a drugstore or tavern like the one where the great Ingersoll himself first expounded his materialistic views. Park recalled these free spirits carrying on a 'protracted series of rather ribald debates on the subject of evolution'; 'the debating society', he wrote later, 'seems to have played about the same role in my intellectual life that the debates of the Hell Fire Club did in that of Benjamin Franklin'.[17] During one of his periods in Minneapolis, first as student and later as a reporter, Park heard Robert Ingersoll lecture and met the great orator who so impressed him.[18] Ingersoll's combination of conventional morality with iconoclastic free thought and activist, yet often pessimistic, materialism found echoes in both the young reporter and the mature sociologist.

The College Years: Conformity and Awakening

At the age of eighteen Park ran away to the small University of Minnesota. A university in name only, Minnesota in 1882 was a tiny college of the sort which struggled for life throughout the midwest just before the period of massive development in higher education. Minnesota's campus had only two buildings in Park's time, and awarded nineteen diplomas in 1884.[19] Park's father wanted him to go into the family grocery business; however, since Robert was determined, the elder Park insisted that he should at least choose a 'real' university. Accordingly, a year later, 1883, at the age of nineteen, Park enrolled at the University of Michigan.[20]

The school which Park found in Ann Arbor in the fall of 1883 was near the height of its reputation as the outstanding state university in America; as one graduate later recalled, Michigan was regarded as tougher than any university except Harvard.[21] Park came to Michigan at a uniquely advantageous time, just when the university was on the verge of its rapid physical expansion, when it had close ties with political life and had begun to feel the influence of German scholarship, but before the impact of the university on its students had been diluted by sheer weight of numbers. The number of students had remained almost stationary for over a decade and in proportion to population had even declined, but the massive explosion of campus population was just ahead.[22] The campus was large, with eighteen buildings and eighty-six full-time teachers in 1890; a separate library building had just been finished when Park arrived, and opened with 44,000 volumes in 1884.[23]

The faculty contained men of recognized national stature, who validated their scholarship with practical activity. President James B. Angell, once a newspaper editor and recently on leave as minister to China, brought to the campus a sense of connection with world affairs. He was convinced, as he had said in his inaugural address in 1871, that every 'vigorous college' should take the lead in shaping public education – and his university had already made impressive progress in molding the public school system of the state.[24] Judge Thomas M. Cooley of the State Supreme Court, when not away on government assignments, was still offering a course in the 'Constitutional History of the United States'. There was a fair proportion of scholars who had been trained in Germany, including the Hegelian philosopher George Sylvester Morris, who spent half the year at Michigan as head of the philosophy department and the balance at Johns Hopkins, and Henry Carter Adams, fresh from training with the German historical economists, who taught 'Principles of Political Economy' and displayed his unorthodoxy by building a course around 'unsettled questions' of that discipline.[25] Although the goal of knowledge was still assumed to be both practical and ethical, the trained professional was rapidly replacing the traditional disciplinary teacher and the jack-of-all-trades who drifted into academic life. Park's own special subjects, philosophy and German, reflected the transition from generalized inspiration to categorized knowledge. Until 1883, for example, the courses in psychology and speculative philosophy were given by a popular, fatherly teacher, a businessman who entered the ministry and then teaching, to thank God for a miraculous escape from cannibals in the Fiji islands. On his death, he was replaced by a scholarly young Johns Hopkins PH.D. named John Dewey, who added courses in the philosophy of Herbert Spencer and in the new experimental psychology. Robert Park enrolled in several of Dewey's courses and formed a friendship which lasted at least a decade. Even more lasting was the concern with intelligent understanding of everyday 'reality' which Dewey urged on his students as the philosopher's duty in a democracy. Park took from Dewey a life-long interest in the role of communication as a force for integrating society and in devices for communication, especially the newspaper and the telephone.[26]

To speak of students being influenced by their courses, to assume that there was intellectual excitement in the classroom, violates the self-conception and much of the historical reconstruction of the American university in this period. As the student magazine which Park edited put it: 'Whenever you see a student particularly desirous of having a discussion with a professor you may put it down that the student is prepared to flunk if called upon to recite'; feigning interest was a gag, ancient and understood by all.[27] This was the heyday of Greek letter societies, of athletics, of extracurricular activities as surrogate for the adult world, or romanticized symbolic confrontations with 'real life' which challenged and trained students far more directly than the rote learning and arid discussions of the classroom. Thus football was physically satisfying — the antithesis of classroom restraint; it had no direct relation to the real life of commerce or the professions, yet was a paradigm of the peculiar mixture of team play and ruthless individual assertion which the youth would encounter later in his life 'in the world'. The fraternities, with their elaborate social affairs and byzantine politicking over trivial campus offices, were a play-world facsimile of real political life, at once parodying adult absurdities and training youth to the skills necessary to success in the adult world.

Robert Park certainly did not hold himself aloof; he jumped enthusiastically into this play-world, more real than the official curriculum. He joined a political alliance of fraternities and hangers-on which established its own weekly newspaper, the *Argonaut*, in rivalry to the older *Chronicle*, run by a rival fraternity cabal.[28] The struggle between the two newspapers and their supporting factions was a miniature of the great world of politics in the heyday of inherited loyalty and military-style campaigns. Student caucuses developed skill at political trading and bargaining; it was customary, said a contemporary historian, 'to use the machinery of a political campaign', including the purchase of votes by paying a man's membership dues.[29] The *Argonaut-Chronicle* feud showed how student desire defeated the faculty's hope of maintaining the campus as a paternal community where invidious exclusion did not separate the students. This 'democratic' sentiment among the teachers was strong enough to have outlawed Phi Beta Kappa as undesirably exclusive, but by the 1880s loyalty to secret societies had replaced class spirit, and social life was largely organized around the fraternities. Where complex social distinctions did not exist 'naturally', it was necessary to invent and elaborate them with enthusiasm sufficient to overcome their artificiality. Playful simulation of adult reality went beyond the creation of rival social fraternities; the battles of *Argonaut* and *Chronicle* enlisted both 'Greek' and 'Barbarian' on each side in a conflict waged for pleasure, prestige, and practical education.[30]

The squabbles of campus politics did not consume all of Park's efforts as editor of the *Argonaut*. Students retained a sense of sentimental loyalty toward *Alma Mater*, with the University as symbol of happy days and fraternal adventure. Park's proudest achievement as editor was organizing a monster torchlight parade to celebrate the fiftieth anniversary of the university and of Michigan's statehood. While exhorting the students not to let themselves be outdone by the faculty in a display of spirit, he failed to hand in a series of homework assignments in Greek, already his weakest subject, and did not pass the course. Failure in Greek imperilled graduation, but the faculty voted him the Bachelor of Philosophy degree, given to students who had assumed an extra load of modern subjects in lieu of the classical course. Despite the cost in formal prestige, Park recalled with pride this demonstration of power in the world of men and things.[31]

If the passions of most students were devoted solely to their extracurricular lives, as the most comprehensive study of the American university in the period asserts,[32] Park certainly belonged to the minority who found excitement within the classroom as well as outside it. While living a full campus life, he found no mental barrier between life and thought; as he recalled five decades later, the hard drinkers were hard workers as well.[33] Academic experience, as much as any other kind, was assimilated to his personal quest for understanding, for ultimate meaning in himself and the world. Reading *Faust* in the original was a profound personal experience, giving words to his own vaguer desires. Indeed, it was Park's young instructor in German, Calvin Thomas, who wakened him intellectually and gave a certain direction to his inarticulate dissatisfaction, his gropings toward understanding.[34] Calvin Thomas was a native of Michigan, only a decade older than Park; he had graduated from the state university as the youngest in his class, and spent a year studying classical literature at Leipzig. Then, in a transition typical of the embryonic era of the American university, he returned to Michigan to teach Greek and was then given full-time work in the German department. In the mid-eighties he was early in a distinguished scholarly career which eventually took him to Columbia University, where he wrote a biography of Goethe, and produced a great critical edition of *Faust*.[35] Thomas had a warm, pleasant personality, but he was not a classroom Barnum; when he lectured on Goethe to an adult audience, one of the St. Louis school of Hegelians noted disapprovingly that his approach was philosophical and historical, rather than enthusiastically appreciative of 'Goethe as a literary Bible'.[36] Park was not responding to a personality who happened also to be a scholar; it was precisely the scholarship which appealed to him. Thomas was 'the first real scholar' Park had met; at Michigan, 'the others were just teachers'. He wrote a sarcastic note on one of the youth's German papers, saying that even if he improved six times during the semester he still would not pass. The challenge of this note, Park said, changed his career:

I had been a football player and an outdoor boy. I became a student and a consistent burner of the midnight oil. My intention in going to college had not been, originally, intellectual but practical. I intended to be an engineer. I became instead a student of philosophy, and was presently possessed with a devouring curiosity to know about the world, and all that man had thought and done.[37]

With Thomas, Park studied German lyric poetry, Goethe's *Egmont* and *Hermann und Dorothea*, and above all, *Faust*. Philosophy, however, became his central interest and leading subject in the undergraduate curriculum. He took ten courses in the department, six of them with John Dewey — formal logic, empirical psychology, speculative psychology, the study of Kant's *Critique of Pure Reason*, Dewey's favorite seminar on the *Republic* of Plato, and a course on the philosophy of Herbert Spencer which Dewey had added at student request, to counterbalance undergraduate suspicion that the department emphasized German idealism in order to defend religion against scientific materialism.[38] Park discovered that Dewey was a dull lecturer but 'an inspiring leader'. Dewey was himself the type of teacher praised in his later manifestos, able to transmit the feeling that teacher and students were together in 'a common enterprise', an 'adventure into the realm of the problematic and unknown'. Unlike the majority of teachers who, Park felt, gave only definitions and set convictions which closed the students' minds, Dewey provided insights, ideas, and facts which re-oriented the mind; he made philosophy seem open-ended and relevant to life.[39]

Dewey transmitted to Park, both through his teaching of Spencer and his unstable personal mixture of Hegelian philosophy and scientific naturalism, the idea that society was not organized by a voluntary compact of rational individuals, but was a functioning organism, whose interrelated parts depended upon one another for sustenance and survived through the preservation of the whole.   Like other American scholars trained in German philosophy and social science, Dewey was anxious to stress the prior and higher claims of society over the individual. Yet this effort to introduce organicism into American thought was not, at least in the 1880s and 90s, a repudiation of individualism so much as an attempt to meet the challenge of laissez-faire by finding more compelling, novel intellectual justifications for the traditional ethical concern of the New England conscience, the reconciliation of individuality with the virtues of duty and responsibility.[40] The individual members of society, Dewey said, were bound together by common goals, and they achieved full realization of their personalities only when they co-operated with others to realize these collective ends. The true democratic individualism was moral, not numerical, 'an individualism of freedom, of responsibility, of initiative to and for the ethical idea, not an individualism of lawlessness'.[41] In his emphasis on the organization and *direction* given to society by the goals which moved its members to common action, Dewey gave Park intellectual support for what became one of the younger man's most passionate convictions. Park's life as a reporter was to give him vivid personal knowledge of the dangers of the purely private life.

Newspaper Days

Upon graduation, Park turned back with relief to the 'real world' of active life outside the ivied halls. His enthusiasm for Thomas's and Dewey's courses had not rested on a new-found passion for abstract ideas as an end in themselves; rather, these men inspired him because they showed how literature and philosophy were supremely relevant to his personal quest for understanding, both of himself and of the experience of daily life. Academic life could supply only part of the answer he sought, and so, like his cherished 'Faust', he turned back to the 'world of men'. But what to do? The family business was no more appealing than ever and Park apparently would not consider any sort of commercial career; yet school teaching, after a brief stint in Red Wing, seemed a dead end.[42] But Park was fortunate in entering the job market when intense competition among newspapers to attract readers through lively reporting offered a new escape from sterile respectability. Editors were anxious to secure well-educated reporters, and so bright young college men who wanted to experience life without succumbing to the choking discipline of an established profession, found in reporting the sanction of legitimate work without having to accept the shackles of respectable routine required by the church, the law, or teaching.[43]

Park began his career as a cub reporter on the *Minneapolis Journal* but after about three years he began to hanker for New York, 'the mecca of every ambitious newspaperman'. It took him a couple of years to reach there, and he spent some time in 1891 as a reporter on the *Detroit Tribune* and the *Denver Times*.[44] But by 1892 he had managed to get a job on the *New York Journal*, 'the dirtiest paper' he ever worked on, a paper which, Park said, specialized in titillating the resentments and desires of its working-class readers with tales of pure, poverty-striken maidens seduced by playboy millionaires.[45] At the same time Park wrote occasional pieces for the Sunday *New York World*. The 1880s and 90s were the great boom period for Sunday newspapers which devoted most of their pages to advertising and features rather than to yesterday's events. Park found that the Sunday paper was 'willing to publish anything so long as it concerned the local community and was interesting'.[46] Assigned by the *Journal* to the police beat of Essex Market Court House, Park also tried his hand at describing urban color for the Sunday supplements; he tramped the streets of the city looking for human interest copy. He recalled one of his reporting episodes, when the city editor sent him to find an opium den and gambling ring which the police declared could not be discovered:

I got into the opium den with good luck and I had a few pipefuls of the awful stuff. The place was crowded with the riff-raff of the town, and they were talking openly about the gambling house that I wanted to get into.

One of them, not knowing who I was, consented to take me to the place. We did get in, but we didn't get very far. One of the men who owned the "establishment" was well known at the police court, and in turn knew every reporter on the beat. He recognized me and I was hustled out of that place on the spot. Scared? You can answer that! But I did get the story.[47]

Park loved to wander through New York, drinking in its noise and visual variety; he loved especially the walk home at dawn when the city was just stirring to life.[48] The experience of Manhattan developed Park's sense of the large-scale organization and interdependence of the city's life. Like his hero, Walt Whitman, he reveled in the drama of the city's tidal ebb and flow. 'Walking on upper Broadway or down to the Battery on a bright afternoon, or watching the oncoming and outgoing human tide as it poured morning and evening over Brooklyn Bridge, was always for me an enthralling spectacle'.[49] This experience of the city as a complex of forces reinforced Dewey's lesson of society as an organism. 'Out of all this', he remembered later, 'I gained among other things, a conception of the city, the community, and the region, not as a geographical phenomenon merely but as a kind of social organism.'[50]

In spite of the fascination of New York as a city, Park was discouraged by the brief working life which a New York reporter could expect before being replaced by fresher, more energetic men. So he decided to head west.[51] He spent the next few years first as a reporter, then as city editor of the *Detroit Tribune*. Later, he moved to the *Detroit News* and finally, in 1897-98, closed this phase of his career as drama critic and reporter on James E.Scripps' paper, the *Chicago Journal*.[52]

Park's years as a newspaperman were spent in the heyday of the city beat reporter, before the reporter was ousted from first place by the feature writer and the rewrite man, before radio had deprived him of the pride of being first to bring the news to the public. Park became a reporter when the city beat was full of exotic glamor and the young Mencken decided that the best way to learn the ways of the world was to join the *Baltimore Herald* as a cub reporter.[53] The reporter was an institutionalized voyeur, rewarded with modest pay but considerable, if ambiguous, prestige for taking up as a professional duty in the specialized city the role of gossip filled by many citizens in the smaller community. The city beat reporter from the first fulfilled the role of informal and intuitive sociologist, acting as eyes, ears, and moral censor for the audience removed by size and distance from the direct exercise of these traditional communal roles. As the specialized crystallization of what had been a generalized means of social control, the reporter gave his readers information not only about singular happenings – murders, elections, stuffed ballot boxes – but also about the slower changes in environment which underlay these colorful events – the growth of new urban neighborhoods and institutions, the appearance of novel personality types, ways of making and spending money, modes of entertainment.[54] Furthermore, the reporter was considered by many to be trustworthy because he was *disinterested*. Free from conscious desire to exercise influence, at least in the interest of a political party or a corporation – the most obvious form of bias in that fortunate era before depth psychology – the reporter became the ideal of a man who gave the 'facts' without fear or favor.[55] As such, but also as a man with inside contacts, he was in an ideal position not only to communicate but to expose deviations from the conventional moral code, not yet itself assumed to be problematic or in need of 'exposure'.

This mixture of detachment and inside knowledge bred a certain cynicism in the reporter. He could not help noting the hypocrisy of everyday life, the discrepancy between moral profession and actual behavior; yet the crusading of the popular press was based on the moral drama of a virtuous public preyed upon by evil parasites. Much later Park recalled how a reporter grew cynical as he gradually discovered 'how feeble a bulwark the conventional mores are against the impact of the natural curiosity of human beings'.[56] For Park, natural curiosity was always the prime motive for becoming a journalist. He noted that a reporter, outwardly powerless, was in fact tremendously powerful in that merely by *reporting* he could help to change society.[57] However, Park was not a reformer by nature. His passion was for observing rather than changing. As a police reporter on the *New York Journal*, he often ran across 'the Pious Dane', Jacob Riis, who was doing a similar job for the *Sun*. But whereas Riis's experiences amidst the vice and misery of the East Side turned him into a crusader for tenement house reform, for Park the pure enjoyment of the various and exotic scene tended to stifle moral indignation. The assignment to lower Manhattan gave him 'wide acquaintances in the slum district', which developed, as he recalled, his 'interest in sociology'.[58] In a similar fashion, the first generation of practical sociologists developed an interest in human relations from the confrontation with slum variety and misery. But Park loved New York, warts and all, and enjoyed flirting with the criminal underworld and visiting opium dens. Park always brought to the observation of the city scene the wonder of the small-town dreamer, filled with 'vague thoughts' and the categories, at least, of nonconformist Protestant morality. He did not bring the traditional innocence or censoriousness of the small town; he set off Middle Border morality against slick city ways with a calm and ironic detachment, professionally fascinated by both, but as journalist or sociologist, committed to neither.

Conflict and Resolution: An American Faith

Late in 1892 Park met his future wife, Clara Cahill, the eldest daughter of Edward Cahill, a judge of the Michigan Supreme Court. She was then twenty-four, 'warm, cheerful, impulsive, quick-moving' and an amateur artist of some talent and youthful stirrings against conventional opinions.[59] Park approved her small rebellion. During their courtship they read together books on the French Revolution and Russian nihilism. Courting Clara, daughter of a prominent family, made Park acutely aware of his own deficiencies and slim prospects. Clara was an aristocrat, and knowing her made Park feel his lack of polish: 'a peasant! that is what I am at heart. I love the common things, earth, air — the song of the robin and the great herds of common people, simple and natural as cows. — Yes, that is possibly the contemptuous word that the French apply to them.' He was sure, however, that their qualities were complementary, not contradictory. A union in which he could 'mingle ... my strength with your sweetness' would obviously be fruitful.[60]

There remained the question of money and prospects. Park was already becoming disillusioned with newspaper life. He attempted to augment his income by teaching at night school; then, since Clara had no particular desire for him to stay in the newspaper world, he tried to secure an administrative job with the Detroit Board of Health. But Park put too high a price on himself and the board refused to pay. However, acting on the assumption that the best way to win success was to act as though successful, he was not daunted: 'I am trying to get myself an independent position here in this city by doing things better than anybody else which is not difficult, because I am older and more experienced. I will make a reputation as much by assuming that I am better than everybody else as any other way. It will not injure me to have it known that I refused a job that so many other men in town were trying to get.'

Clara, at least, believed in him; and her father eventually came round. As Park rather touchingly said, 'Everybody likes me at last because they see that I am doing my best.'[61] The couple were married in 1894. Park remained in journalism, first in Detroit and then in Chicago, for another three years; but the bloom had gone from it for him. Reporting could not offer the security and prestige which a proper husband ought to give Clara and the four children born during the next decade. Beyond this, Park clearly felt that the reporter's life could teach him nothing more; merely to watch, notice, and report could no longer fulfill his craving for understanding and for meaning.

By the time of his marriage at the age of thirty, Park's character and views of life had taken a shape which changed very little during the eventful half century of life ahead. Together with one of his newspaper interviews is a sketch of the young reporter during an interview: tall, heavily built, clean shaven, a face potentially sensitive yet disciplined into stern reserve, stamped with overt determination and resolution.[62] The features conform almost too well to the personal impression left by Park's few surviving letters of this period. Park at thirty appears in the letters to Clara a classic 'seeker', a troubled, self-divided soul for whom the bonds of convention could not bring satisfaction yet could not be broken. Business, with its easy validation of masculine identity, was boring and sterile; yet Park came from a business family, he lived in a ruthlessly commercial and competitive environment. He enjoyed abstract speculation, and the search for the ultimate nature of things; yet he had absorbed more than enough of the values of the Middle Border to be uneasy with abstract intellectuality and suspicious of self-conscious sophistication. The midwest, even in a sizeable, wealthy city like Detroit, offered neither a great variety of respectable roles, nor easy tolerance to men who did not find a recognized place. Thus Park found himself on the margin between practicality and intellect, between the life of business and things and the life of abstractions and the mind. His uneasiness with cultured, sophisticated people was reinforced by an awareness of his own slow, deliberate, and down-to-earth character. Contact with self-conscious elegance and dazzlingly articulate people made him feel boorish and inadequate. He complained to Clara of a society call he had made:

I have not the patience to chat with people at the distance of half a mile, not even if they have grey hairs and are society people. ...

... It was that indefinable something about Mrs. Smith, the delicate fragrance of aristocracy, that sort of reflection, mental reflection, you know, that this person is forever outside the circle of my interests in life and what he says and thinks I can not know nor do I care to know. It is not true. She is a woman of intelligence and I am interested in all things that intelligent people are interested in. I wish I could make her feel that.[63]

Park's thirst for knowledge was tied to another quest, frequently expressed in letters to his fiancée, a search for some great cause to catch hold of, a faith that would grasp him in turn and lift him above himself, sweep him along without self-doubt. Calvin Thomas, his teacher at Michigan, had been impressive because of his disciplined dedication to an ideal, yet pure scholarship both attracted and repelled Park. To grasp, to understand, was a profound satisfaction, but he did not fancy the encapsulation of scholarship in the insulated life of the campus. In the absence of a cause, Park was constantly plagued with doubts about his own abilities, about his capacity to make a favorable impression on people, his regrets for his life as a newspaperman. 'You cannot understand what torment it is to live in hell', he wrote to Clara, 'neither can you understand the delights of it − but I lived in it for many years − all the time I was in college and afterwards.'[64] Park asked Clara to explain to her father that 'I am not trying to do anything so very great, just trying to find something to do which will be profitable and interesting ... if we can find something that we like to do, then we will forget ourselves, our little selves in the enterprise.'[65]

This desire for purpose to absorb personal energy was central, not only to Park's personal search for definition, but to his whole perspective on life, on America, on the meaning of the age. Like other sensitive Americans of the 1880s and 90s he was profoundly nostalgic for the conviction and self-sacrificing purpose which the generation of the sixties had found in the Civil War.[66] Perhaps the most moving passage Park ever wrote is in a letter to Clara on Memorial Day, 1893, which sums up the dissatisfaction and nostalgia for purpose of his own generation. He had attended a Memorial Day ceremony in honor of the Civil War dead. 'I wandered through the long avenues until it seemed to me I was in some vast cathedral and this was a ceremony we were performing there in honor − not so much of the poor human souls whose bodies were buried there as in honor of the great cause of human freedom for which they fought.' One speech in particular moved him very much: it was built around the idea

that whatever we honestly strive for cannot perish. And suddenly there flashed up before me the whole vision of that army of men − rough, sullen, hungry, drunken, licentious − all the vices that men are heir to − yet all sanctified because it was human and it was part of the incidents of a great human struggle. I can't write it. But I went home and went into hysterics I know in my customary foolish fashion.

It wasn't anything in particular but it was the vision of marching men — vision typical of the whole human race — marching on to die for what it loves.[67]

Marching Men! Two decades later Sherwood Anderson gave this same title to a novel set in Chicago in the 1890s, a curious novel filled with inchoate intensity, describing the passionate, ugly enthusiasm and moral strength which the unorganized workers of the metropolis gained from drilling together in marching clubs, a strength based not on ideology but on the sheer community, the disciplined oneness of mass military maneuver. This was an ugly sentiment to mid-twentieth century intellectuals, conjuring up images of fascism — yet Anderson's marching men were clearly identified with the demoralized masses — the underdogs against the overlords of capital who were ruthlessly exploiting them.[68]

The image of 'Marching Men' suggests the lack of direction, the ideological variability, of this quest for faith which drove many young Americans in the 1880s and 90s. The new generation, listening to their fathers' tales of martial glory, sought to prove themselves not after all decadent, by discovering and living valid ideals larger than themselves which could equal in purity and self-sacrifice the finest achievements of Robert Gould Shaw, the Boston Brahmin who died with hundreds of his Negro soldiers while storming Fort Wagner in Charleston harbor.[69] But *fin de siècle* America offered few opportunities for transcendence; Park sometimes found the daily life of mere pleasure, mere vice, mere virtue to be almost intolerable. 'It seems to me sometimes', he wrote to Clara, 'that the most beautiful thing in the world after love for a woman is death for an Idea in which we believe. We waste our passion in licentiousness, we exhaust our strength in striving to keep pace with the fashions, in eating and drinking and trying to be merely good. There is so much that is strong and great in men that is wasted in mere vice because there is not something worth while to do.'[70]

A variety of possible loyalties presented themselves to young people seeking to fill the void. There were disparate and often contradictory causes, yet all seem to have had a common psychic center in the failure to find meaning in the orthodoxy of the age, the private pursuit of success. For a few, political radicalism was the answer. Others, identifying with a more defensive version of the native tradition, found their outlet in civic reform and even in nativism — in the fight to re-establish what they thought were traditional civic ideals against the corrupting force of jobbery, corruption, and sometimes 'lesser breeds' from beyond the gates who seemed the willing tools of corruption. For a large number there was something less precise than ideology, but more specific than yearning, a humanitarian identification with the cause of 'the people,' like the enthusiasm of John Dewey and his wife Alice for The Russian peasantry as portrayed by Turgenev and Tolstoy, which often inspired settlement-house work among the transplanted peasants in American city slums.[71]

Robert Park shared this enthusiasm of his old teacher and was also deeply moved by Tolstoy. Although in conventional political allegiance a Mugwump Republican, he identified passionately with anarchists. 'It seems to me that these Anarchists are wiser than we,' he told Clara. 'Think of the life these men and women lived. To feel that you are really part of a great Cause. To feel pulsing in your own veins the great intellectual life of a Nation. To feel that you are part of it — to feel that absolute conviction that you are a living vital part of a great historical drama.'[72] In the unheroic present, anarchists were the noblest representatives of the virtues celebrated by Tennyson's 'Ulysses', one of Park's favorite poems; these rebels at least were still determined 'to strive, to seek, to find and not to yield.'[73] He applauded not only the anarchists' passion and devotion as abstract qualities but he also approved of their goal — the creation of an honest society purged of hypocrisy and compulsion. Not surprisingly, therefore, Ibsen was another of Park's heroes. He admired the dramatist as the 'great apostle of Individualism, or Anarchy', gloried in Ibsen's 'uncompromising radicalism ... denying all existing things including the state', but saved from cynicism by 'faith in the fundamental spiritual purpose and destiny of the world'. Park noted laconically that Ibsen's desire to 'undermine the idea of the State; put in its place free will and spiritual affinity as the one decisive reason for union', although it 'would be the beginning of a freedom that would be worth something', offered 'little hope for the conservative and business interests of the community'. Yet he believed 'there might be great hope for the race. The mere conception that the whole visible form of government might be swept away with all the mental toys and material interests that are bound up in it, without seriously endangering the future of the race is of necessity based upon a faith in the spiritual life which they represent which is as sublime as it is unparalleled and original.' Park was obviously doubtful as to the workability of the idea, but he reveled in the faith that inspired it, the youthful faith that individualism could mean self-fulfilment as well as selfishness, that Truth and Justice could be realized in a harmonious existence that transcended the oppositions of conventional politics.[74]

Park was much affected by the romanticism of nature, the notion that what is 'natural' is good. Thus, he shared the exaltation of simple folk, those who had the fewest barriers to direct expression, who were unsophisticated and so revealed their real natures. A return to Nature was liberating, a casting off of artificial barriers. Park wanted frankness and openness in everyday life; he hoped for a coming liberation of thought and honest emotion, a time when the ladies of Detroit women's clubs would no longer be able to force the draping of nude statues.[75] He responded passionately to Whitman, thrilled by the note of insurgency in the 'Song of Myself' and 'The Children of Adam'. He waited for the time 'when thought and literature in America should be free, untrammeled by the traditonal forms and inherited conventions'. Whitman's poems were 'refreshing, like rain, or like the summer breezes on the prairie. ... They suggest a certain mystical joy in simply being alive and able to see and hear, touch and smell the natural world about one.'[76]

Yet for Park at thirty, romantic faith in simple honesty had not soured into the desire to escape from consciousness into the bliss of animal-like oblivi- ousness. His sentiment was more puritan, or perhaps Emersonian, than primitivist; the unique joy and glory of being human lay in self-conscious control and co-ordination of all one's faculties. It was the ability of the rational consciousness to understand the necessary laws of life and live in accordance with them, that was uniquely human. 'Strange and incomprehen- sible is the fate', he wrote of a visit to an asylum, 'that takes from man the mind that makes him human and leaves him a mere thing, governed by passions that he knows not the sources of ... out of all tune with his fellow- men, no longer a social being, but a mere fragment of spiritual force torn from the life of the race to which it belongs, and wandering about in indefinite space upon impulses quite its own, no longer a thing governed by the laws of ordinary human life.'[77] Similarly, 'naturalness' supported conventional Mid- dle Border morality in another way. For Park, as for D.H. Lawrence, return- ing to nature meant opposition to feminism. Physical differences between the sexes seemed to imply barriers and separate spheres which were part of the order of nature and therefore proper. Among the press clippings from his Detroit days are little fillers, satirizing the reversal of sexual roles — women playing baseball, watched by daintily dressed men, the husband putting the children to bed while his wife rejoiced 'there's none of this "new man" nonsense about him.'[78]

His search for 'honesty', and his Emersonian concern for aspiration led Park to draw a rigid distinction between rebellion and despair, satire and cynicism. Art or action which challenged the constricting convention of an artificial society was morally admirable; but men who surrendered to despair and wallowed in an undifferentiated disgust for life were contemptible: 'Satire laughs down foibles, hunts out insincerity and chases folly from the world. But cynicism is nothing less than a form of elegant sport. ... It saunters along through the world hurling its elegant shafts indiscriminately against friend and foe, pleased only if something falls.'[79]

Park's apparently contradictory views on politics rested also on the ideas of 'sincerity' and 'aspiration'. Anarchist on one level and mugwump Republican on another, he was sympathetic to revolution but contemptuous of the hypocrisies of dedicated idealists. Do-gooders were suspect both because of their conscious elitism, their arrogant assumption that they had the right to manipulate others, and because their characters and actions seemed less pure than their professed intentions. Reformers, to earn respect, must validate their cause by the proof of their personality. So Park took great joy in ridiculing the 'Women's Independent Voters Association of Detroit' who had been 'malicious in their slanders'.[80] As an obituary said, if Park was ever intolerant of anybody, it was reformers.[81] On the other hand, he did not therefore glamorize the professional boss and his cronies. He had no sympathy for the 'thugs, convicted thieves and gamblers', who, he thought, composed the Democratic Party in Michigan.[82]

Thus, although Park shared the desire for national rejuvenation through a return to 'the people', this compelling slogan had a meaning for him rather different from that which moved Jane Addams and many other dissatisfied spirits of the nineties. Clearly 'the people' is a vision as vague as it is magical in its power to inspire self-sacrifice; a social history of the American intelligentsia might well begin by tracing what sorts of men and women were included and excluded at different times. In the twentieth century, the phrase has usually implied a distinction between masters and slaves, privileged and underprivileged. To Park, however, 'the people' had a much more traditional meaning — not a clearly defined social stratum, peasantry or proletariat, but almost everyone who was not pretentious, everyone but the self-conscious intellectuals and social climbers who deliberately separated themselves from the majority. The merchant, as much as the artisan and farmer, belonged to 'the people'. Self-conscious withdrawal, not bourgeois vulgarity, was the primal sin against democracy. These socio-ethical categories were more than personal or even American; they were those of many bourgeois romantics before the late nineteenth century. Herder, for example, distinguished his *Volk* from *Pöbel* (rabble) on the one hand, and from aristocrats and intellectuals on the other. The core of the *Volk*, the *Bürger*, were people in traditional occupations, possessing such personal traits as 'spontaneity', 'earthiness', and the 'naturalness and simplicity found in children'. The bourgeois romanticism of Park's youth underlay many of his professional attitudes, and distinguishes him sharply from the later Americans analyzed by Christopher Lasch, whose attitude might be characterized as a combination of Herder's three excluded categories into a conceptual alliance, by intellectuals who admire and emulate the 'aristocratic' quality of the 'rabble'.[83]

Just as Park's admiration for anarchists could not possibly be described as 'un-American', since it was an archetypically American admiration for individual independence and heroism, so his passionate belief in democracy was also a traditional one; despite his Republican loyalties, his democratic faith was Jacksonian, if not 'populist'. He believed in the wisdom of the unsophisticated mass of people and the probable degradation of snobbish, self-isolating elites, priding themselves on the special tastes behind which they hid from the polluting mass. 'I like the people themselves just as they are. I would rather go among them than look at pictures of them — except when some man like Walt Whitman or the man who painted the *Angelus* pictures them,' he wrote to Clara.[84]

Similarly, though he loved symphonic music and was a passionate devotee of Wagnerian opera, Park detested the exclusiveness of professional musicians and critics who wanted to separate 'high' from popular art. 'Music has become a class interest ... the musician is different from other men. He belongs to a sect. Until you can accept his doctrine ... you cannot know the higher truth. ... ' With the usual note of ironic self-mockery which does not entirely destroy the conviction of his words, Park argued that elitism in music as elsewhere was undemocratic and therefore morally damaging:

The doctrine of democracy is that the individual and the class cannot rise over the great mass of the people — either in wealth, culture or their own estimation — without suffering for it. The democratic notion of art assumes that the greatest product of the human genius is that which has moved the largest number of people and moved them most strongly, the product of human genius that has brought the greatest revelation to man, added the largest area of knowledge and understanding to the conscious life of the race.

The democratic audience refuses to separate the technical qualities of art from its emotional content. 'It is not ashamed to be moved — even to tears — by the visions that the magic of music has conjured up before it. It is not ashamed of its emotions ... it believes that is what art is for. All music is music ... even though it is played on a hand organ or whistled in an alleyway'.[85]

For all Park's yearning for transcendence, he did not expect the heroic ages to come again in America. Moral virtue, in the age of matter, would consist in faithful service to one's calling, however lacking in danger and excitement it might be. Since the conditions of life were given, men must charge their everyday experience with loyalty. After demanding nobly in a letter to Clara, 'When the world gets a real belief again why should not men return again to nature and to God?' he concluded:

If a man believes, why should he not perform the simplest and most commonplace things of everyday life in that same joyous, heroic self-forgetful way again. Mr. Brown who sells us butter would then scour the country with the fervor of a fanatic to get us good butter and to run his business in a way that was most profitable to himself and serviceable to the public. Mr. Jones would take the pride of a warrior in the way he polished our shoes. If men could see the heroism and the beauty in doing well the common things of everyday life.[86]

It was a good mixture of Christianity, sound business practice, and Elbert Hubbard, whose *Message to Garcia* made a sensation in 1899.[87] There was a strong streak of fatalism in Park: to give oneself to life meant accepting everything as given, including disease, pain, poverty, insanity.[88] Under the pressure of an ambitious marriage on his own self-doubt, Park was led to a defiant acceptance of the universe in all its bloody imperfection — a defiant affirmation of the nobility inherent in man's very imperfection, its necessity almost, an attitude designed to repudiate the other-wordly perfectionism of genteel reform. 'I believe in fire,' he told Clara in a Whitmanesque apostrophe,

in rapine, in destruction just as I do in the comforts and the elegancies of life, because they are all parts of God's world, part of the means the world uses to work out its destiny. If I did otherwise I should be sitting a sad-eyed spectator in this great beautiful and terrible world, measuring my pain because the flowers had to die, mourning the destruction of this and that ideal, sighing over the bloodshed that won the battles for Freedom — sitting with my face continually turned toward the past instead of to the future, doubting the wisdom that governed the world because it permitted things that shocked my delicate feelings. But henceforth I shall measure things by a broader and deeper standard. I shall measure them by my own feelings still but I shall try to know and to feel with all the world at once. I am now convinced that the intoxicating pleasure of sharing consciously in the movement of the whole world, of making the whole world me, of feeling in my bosom all the joys and sorrows of it is the greatest pleasure, the supreme happiness of life.

And with a striking bluntness which vivifies the demand for practicality, for cash-value success or failure dominating the heartland of America, Park added 'Furthermore, I believe that this is a business principle. I believe that a man's success in life is dependent on the extent to which he shares in the life of the race. In the end I believe the man who is the greatest service to the world is the best paid.'[89]

Thus, Park's discontent did not lead to any kind of concrete radicalism, but rather to an abstract admiration for heroic individuals — world shakers, people who would mold the world and lead the people, or failing that, who could accommodate to the world and find something in it to give meaning to their own lives. He admired 'big and original men'[90] who could put their stamp on the universe in a benevolent way, just as Theodore Dreiser admired the traction magnate Charles T. Yerkes for his personal force and his power to mold matter to his own and society's benefit.[91] Park, like many of his generation, had learnt the complex interrelatedness of things from Herbert Spencer, as well as through the democratized Hegelianism of Dewey. In many ways the harsh Darwinian world of Spencer held more natural attraction for him than Dewey's flexible world of intelligent pragmatic accommodation and adjustment.

Conflict, for Spencer, was the way Nature weeded out the feeble in body and spirit for the overall good of the human race.[92] The struggle built character by inculcating self-discipline, courage, and initiative. Total commitment to the struggle gave meaning to life, and, most important perhaps for Park, was a barrier to the temptation of self-pity. His later involvement with and attraction to the Negro was associated with his feeling that Negroes were a *struggling* people, fighting their way up, developing self-consciousness, goals, and discipline.

The terms of the Darwinian struggle were hard because it had to be waged within the 'rules' laid down by one's environment. This meant in practice that the milieu tended to be validated against the dissenting individual. The Midwest, for example, was correct to value business rather than philosophy, for through profit the region would develop its resources. So the 'sport', like Park, had to endure the burden of guilt at not being able to achieve in the style valued by his milieu. Theory validated popular prejudice and made the burden of deviation all the harder. But this was something Park accepted; and when he later became involved in Negro affairs he advised his friends to struggle, but always within the rules, to beat whites at their own game, to achieve acceptance by excelling in 'white' skills, 'white' virtues.[93] Whatever the limitations of the Social Darwinist world view, it offered a challenge and it provided a comprehensive meaning to the apparent disorder of life. For all the withdrawal of God's presence that it implied, Darwin's famous image of the tangled bank, reminding man that the higher animals were produced by 'the war of nature ... famine and death', offered to the agnostic moralist like Park the emotional security of knowing there was an *order*, an objective structure which rationalized the apparent injustice of events.[94]

Thought News

Park's belief in a program of evolutionary change through understanding was best revealed in the episode which shaped his mind more than any experience until he met Booker T.Washington in 1904. This was the *Thought News* experiment: an attempt to publish a journal interpreting current events according to the insights of philosophy. This abortive venture, in which Park participated during his newspaper days, brought him into renewed contact with his old mentor, John Dewey, and with a reflective journalist named Franklin Ford, and crystallized his interest in the social significance of news. The affair is revealing and significant, not only for the touching naiveté of the whole venture and the clear and permanent mark it made on the young Park, but also for the light it casts on John Dewey and the development and meaning of his doctrines.

The whole affair began for Park, as he later recalled it, when a colleague, 'Hartley Davis went on to New York from St. Paul, and wanted me to come. I followed about a year later, and worked there for about a year. Then I started back West, disgusted, and was ready to go into the grocery business as my father had wanted me to do some years before. On the way West I stopped in Detroit, and heard of the project which Ford and John Dewey had for bringing about a revolutionary thing, a new kind of news. I stayed there and waited for it.'[95] After Park's graduation in 1887, Dewey had moved on to head the philosophy department at Minnesota, but the sudden death in 1889 of George S. Morris, Michigan's senior professor, brought him back to Michigan to head the department there. Here he was joined by James H.Tufts, Albert H. Lloyd, and George Herbert Mead, who were to become famous along with Dewey in the next two decades as forming the 'Chicago school' of social philosophy and social psychology. During this period Dewey had been undergoing a double development in intellectual position, in ethical outlook away from the Protestant faith of his youth toward a socialized but non-supernatural perspective, and in philosophy from formal idealism to an organicism rooted in Darwinian biology and scientific naturalism.[96] Dewey's socialized ethic was not identical with any variety of socialist orthodoxy, but rather was an effort to realize a 'psychic democracy' based upon the extension of consciousness to bring people into closer contact with one another. 'There is but one fact ... the more complete movement of man to his unity with his fellows through realizing the truth of life.' Democracy, Dewey said, was 'the loosening of bonds; the wearing away of restrictions, the breaking down of barriers, of middle walls, of partitions'.[97] Ethics must educate the individual as to his proper relation with society, the organism which exists for the 'fullest realization of individual personality'. This realization of individual powers 'becomes possible when the individual finds his proper place in the community and freely participates in the larger life of society, as he can most nearly do in a democratic social order'.[98] Rather than doctrinal socialism, Dewey's position was a lament for, and an effort to restore the values of, the natural sense of belonging and responsibility engendered in a face-to-face community. If the direct communication among men of different status and occupation that he thought had characterized the communal order could be re-established in a large-scale society, then the old sense of moral obligation resting on personal knowledge would also be restored. As his future friend and sympathizer, Jane Addams, put it, the young moralists of the late 1880s and 90s were anxious to re-establish and extend 'the obligation inherent in human relationships as such'.[99]

Dewey was encouraged to make his ethical concern more concrete, and to apply it in a scheme designed to remedy the lack of knowledge in modern society, by his meeting with the colorful but obscure brothers, Franklin and Corydon Ford. Franklin Ford's influence seems to have been second only to that of William Jame's *Psychology* in persuading Dewey to re-define his idealism in naturalistic terms. Writing in 1891, Dewey credited to Ford 'whatever freedom of sight and treatment there is in my ethics'. Personal interest, or 'instinct', had led Dewey to idealism, the 'conception of some organism comprehending both man's thought and the external world'. Then, Ford's concern with the 'social bearings of intelligence', his speculations on the effect of 'freedom of intelligence, that is, its movement in the world of social fact' gave Dewey the insight that philosophical doctrine must be validated through instrumental action: 'What I have got out of it is, first, the perception of true or practical bearing of idealism − that philosophy has been the assertion of the unity of intelligence and the external world *in idea* or subjectively, while, if true in idea it must finally secure the conditions of its objective expression.'[100]

Ford was a former newspaperman, who had been editor of *Bradstreet's* in New York for a time in the 1880s. He had become disillusioned with the ability of the existing commercial press to give insight to its readers, since they were inhibited by special interests as well as the pressure of the deadline. The solution, he thought, was a national journal of news and opinion, interpreting current events in the light of philosophical insight.[101] The paper would concentrate on what Ford called the Big News, the 'long-time trends which recorded what is actually going on rather than what on the surface of things merely seems to be going on'.[102] After trying vainly to enlist support among newsmen, Ford turned to the universities, and eventually met John Dewey, who, Ford said, 'having the sense of politics ... was able to comprehend the scope of the principle and its practical bearing on the publishing business'.[103] Dewey was overwhelmed by this sudden gust of real life. He regarded the meeting as 'a wonderful personal experience' and developed from Ford's program a vision of the coming kingdom, in which 'the intellectual forces which have been gathering since the Renaissance and Reformation, shall demand complete free movement, and by getting their physical leverage in the telegraph and printing press, shall, through free inquiry in a centralized way, demand the authority of all other social authorities'.[104]

Ford expected his projected paper to have revolutionary consequences, but the enterprise was hardly socialistic; it was rather a corrective mechanism within the competitive order of liberal capitalism. As Dewey explained it to James: 'with inquiry as a *business*, the selling of truth for money, the *whole* would have a representative as well as the various classes − a representative whose belly interest, moreover, is identical with its truth interest'.[105] The news agency would maintain itself as a private enterprise by selling truth, the common object of interest which united all men; truth would demonstrate its utility through cash profit like any other product offered on the market. The marriage of news and philosophy would help to make the movement of history intelligible, because only philosophy could transform 'happenings' into 'typical facts', and only the events of daily life could make philosophy 'real' and relevant.

The fact is the social organism. When philosophical ideas are not inculcated by themselves but used as tools to point out the meaning of phases of social life they begin to have some life and value. ... When it can be seen for example, that Walt Whitman's poetry, the development of short stories at present, the centralizing tendency in the railroads and the introduction of business methods into charity organizations are all parts of the organic social movement, then the philosophical ideas about organism begin to look like something definite.[106]

The *University Record* for April 1892 announced the publication of the first edition of *Thought News* for late that month; further issues would be published from time to time as the pressure of news demanded. The Journal was announced as one that

shall not go beyond the fact; which shall report thought rather than dress it up in the garments of the past; which instead of dwelling at length upon the merely individual processes that accompany the facts, shall set forth the facts themselves; which shall not discuss philosophical ideas *per se* but use them as tools in interpreting the movements of thought; which shall treat questions of science, letters, state, school and church as parts of the one moving life of man and hence of common interest, which shall report new investigations and discoveries in their net outcome instead of in their over-loaded gross bulk, which shall note new contributions to thought ... from the standpoint of the news in them and not from that of patron or censor.

The subscription price would be $1.50 per volume of twelve issues; the enterprise was under the responsibility of John Dewey and was 'prompted by an enquiry movement centering at Ann Arbor'.[107]

The project aroused considerable interest in the Michigan press but, as Park put it, 'we got out the copy for the first issue of the *Thought News*, but it was never published. It was set up, and then pied. My share in paying for it was about $15.'[108] Looking back on the affair, Dewey decided that 'it was an over-enthusiastic project which we had not the means nor the time ... and doubtless not the ability to carry through ... the *idea* was advanced for those days, but it was too advanced for the maturity of those who had the idea in mind'.[109]

His encounter with Franklin Ford provided Park with much of the fundamental theoretical framework through which he came to observe and interpret the flux of events. The personal influence of Ford and Dewey vivified the classical (and Spencerian) model of society as an organic whole of interrelated parts whose precise relations could be specified and within which the 'significance' of daily events would be revealed by connecting them to 'the movement of a whole' according to 'the social law'.[110] The *relations* between areas of study, like those between concrete events, were vital in understanding their significance; understanding would come from treating 'questions of science, letters, state, school and church as part of the one moving life of man'.[111] Ford also offered to both Dewey and Park as the principle of organization according to which the phenomena of society could be interrelated, the idea of the division of labor.[112] Park never gave up his allegiance to Aristotle's and Adam Smith's rationalistic principle as the 'key to the organic social'[113] as the principle by which social phenomena were interconnected, and also as the key to the process of historical change.

These two principles — the organismic model of society and the division of labor as the central mechanism of functional organization — were of course familiar ones. It would be easy to conclude from Park's use of them as general framework of his later theory that he was, in effect, a retarding, reactionary force in the history of sociological theory, a prisoner of his own intellectual generation who transplanted the social theodicy of the 1880s down to the 'empirical' sociology of the 1920s. There is some validity to this formulation, though it ignores much of Park's thought, and is based upon a one-dimensional and rigidly adaptive notion of the validity of ideas. Most important for our present purpose, it misses the psychological dimension of conceptual choice, the reason why one idea resonates in the mind of a man or generation while others are stillborn. Robert Nisbet and Maurice Stein have suggested that a social theory begins to lose its vitality once it no longer refracts and illuminates the lived experience of its users.[114]

This familiar theoretical structure was compelling for the young Park, and then for a generation of midwestern students in the 1920s, because it gave conceptual illumination to the central felt dilemma, first of Park's own identity and then, perhaps in lesser degree, of Chicago graduate students after the First World War. This was the problem of vocation-as-identity in a society that defined success in technical, specialized pursuits as the test of human value and perhaps even of human existence. Leo Lowenthal has noted the centrality of vocational choice and its tragic alternative in the plays of Ibsen: 'the specialist is an incomplete bore, the generalist is no longer Whole Man but Jack of All Trades, a kaleidoscope of incoherent, diffused roles'.[115] Much of the discontent that fills Park's letters and journalism seems to be a direct expression of his inability to find a vocation to satisfy his varied, and in this society at least, contradictory yearnings. Even the most familiar of his youthful hostilities, that toward the frustration of human frankness imposed by gentility, can be traced to the effect of technical specialization. The central theme of Victorian social criticism can be seen as a more alarmist restatement of the classical-whiggish psychology of the self-governing man, in which the division of labor erodes the communal support needed to develop rounded and autonomous personalities. If this lineage is accurate, then the characteristic dislike of 'gentility', of 'airs', and the excessive personal distance of exquisite politeness, so characteristic of younger generations since at least the 1880s, is ultimately directed at the effect of specialization on human relations. Gentility was in one dimension allowed by the divorce of the affluent from unpleasant reality made possible by technical progress; in another dimension it was an essential grease on the mechanism of complex society, allowing people to deal hastily but smoothly with a variety of human types beyond their own threshold of intimacy.[116]

Thus, the future sociologist had absorbed, in a vivid personal sense, the grand transformation that characterized the history of his era and the dichotomies within which social theory formulated it — rural/urban, community/society, the elaborating division of labor. His own theoretical work can often be seen as a very direct response of mature wisdom to the frustrations of his own youth. If the categories came later to seem trite or empty, that may be due to the passing of the generations for whom Park's experience and double vision were immediate reality, the domination of sociology by a wholly 'urbanized' consciousness in which classic social theory no longer resonated. Dewey's and Park's desire to validate intellect and abstract thought by 'proving' its relevance to 'practical' daily life was also far from unique. The utilitarian concept of education had become the principal justification of the great expansion in university size and scope which culminated, even as Dewey wrote, in the foundation of Stanford and the University of Chicago. Professors and presidents won appropriations and endowments, convinced opponents and quieted their own doubts with the double argument that the university could benefit society in two ways — by turning out trained graduates able to enrich the community as they enriched themselves through their vocational training, and by serving as a reservoir of expertise available to society when called upon by the state.[117]

Dewey's and Park's faith in *Thought News* as a model for realizing a liberal utopia through mass communication affords a rare glimpse not only of the simplicity of this faith in perfection through the communication of philosophical ideas, but also of the sense of guilt which underlay and energized it. Dewey and Park felt cut off from 'the people', the common life of the mass of men; they could bridge the gap between the democratic mass and the 'aristocratic' elite of scholars by proving the relevance of abstract thought in improving the common lot. At the same time, the ability to communicate with one's fellow men would restore the self-confidence sapped by pursuing a minority interest in an egalitarian society.[118]

The novelty in Dewey's passion for self-expiation through 'relevance' came from the *subject* which he offered to the public as servant of democratic values. Previous exponents of the utilitarian university had not often been philosophers, but rather representatives of the applied sciences or the new social sciences — engineering, medicine, political economy. Philosophers generally retained a genteel concern with developing in youth an aristocratic sensitivity to truths so complex that they resisted dissemination to the masses.[119] But now John Dewey, eager to clip the psychic dividends which utilitarian relevance offered in a democracy, presented philosophy too at the altar of practicality. If the result was a radical alteration in the subject matter and style of the enterprise, he did not reckon this a loss. Nor, indeed, did he shrink from the outcome in which philosophy would progress by the elimination of all its traditional concerns and become a discipline of scientific ethics, an organ for dealing with contemporary social problems and conflicts.[120] The evolution of Robert Park's career was an excellent demonstration of Dewey's goal — from abstract thought to 'real life' and back to a more concrete discipline whose findings would be useful to the common weal.

The principles of 'philosophical' interpretation which Ford and Dewey offered in the prospectus of *Thought News* had also become familiar to educated Americans by 1890 as a basis for social criticism, if not yet as an intuitive 'native' style of thought. Louis Hartz has suggested the importance of a 'Lockean', rational-individualist frame of reference for eighteenth and nineteenth century American social thought, in which social institutions were seen as rational constructions of human intelligence, created by the conscious will of the majority to solve specific problems.[121] By the last quarter of the nineteenth century this once radical doctrine had become a defense for entrenched economic power. Defenders of privilege employed the ethical priority of individual over society assumed in Lockean theory, as well as the utilitarian argument that a society based on individual competition had the greatest efficiency in the struggle for existence. But German idealism gave social critics a new weapon in the form of an organicist social theory. The influence of Hegel and Darwin became powerful in educated circles at the same time, in the 1860s. Despite the important difference in metaphysical basis between idealism and naturalism, and the fact that Darwinism was used to support the *utilitarian* argument for laissez-faire, they operated along parallel lines in offering a theory of social relations that stressed the priority of group over individual and the imperative quality of the social obligations which bound the individual.[122] Despite the important differences, Hegel and Darwin offered a common challenge to the rationalistic individualism of the American tradition, with its assumption of contract and consent as the basis of the social order. They joined in offering a 'functional' theory of society, in which the obligation of the individual to the collectivity rests not on consent but on involuntary participation in a common endeavour to survive, to surmount the challenge of external nature and human enemies, and to relate the variety of human talents to the common good through the division of labor in society.[123] Thus, human interdependence and obligation were founded in 'Nature' and the imperatives of the universal social situation; historical changes were not accidental and separate but bound together by their relation to the evolution of society. And, since society was a functionally differentiated but interrelated whole, a philosophical interpretation of 'news' meant placing each event in the determined 'social context' of institutional change and growing complexity.

Though the program which Dewey, Ford, and Park offered in *Thought News* was within the Hegelian/Darwinian world view, it also reflected the effort of Americans to find a place for social action within the bonds of Darwinian naturalistic theory and social science. The concept of 'Nature' in writers like Herbert Spencer filled the emotional role of a secularized Deity; it was an order of impersonal regularity whose interwoven complexity made conscious efforts to manipulate it appear to be impertinent presumptions.[124] Even without the notion that a scientific law was no mere descriptive statement but a moral command to conform to Nature's norms, the organicism of post-Darwinian science − its model of nature as an elaborate structure of functionally interrelated parts with competition as its mechanism — led to an exaltation of the superior wisdom of this impersonal process which maintained the equilibrium of nature. The limited intelligence and short time span of man could rarely produce results equal to it in scope or staying power. 'How fleeting are the wishes and efforts of man! how short his time', Darwin had concluded. 'Can we wonder then, that Nature's productions should be far "truer" in character than man's productions; that they should be infinitely better adapted to the most complex conditions of life, and should plainly bear the stamp of far higher workmanship?'[125]

Yet the naturalistic theory of social evolution did not necessarily dictate a laissez-faire position in politics; the philosophy behind *Thought News* points up the danger in over-simplified accounts of an antithesis between 'Social-Darwinism' and 'Reform-Darwinism' to organize the materials of late nineteenth century thought.[126] This approach may exaggerate the theoretical differences between such men as William Graham Sumner and John Dewey, and minimize the extent to which they share the overall framework of naturalistic evolution. Sumner once divided social problems into two classes. On the one hand were those that were due to the violation of natural laws, which were beyond the possibility of human intervention and could only be met by 'manly effort and energy' on the part of individuals in adjusting themselves to the objective conditions. On the other hand, entirely separate from these, was that class of social problems due to 'the malice of men and to the imperfections or errors of civil institutions'. These, he thought, were properly 'an object of agitation and a subject of discussion'.[127] Sumner's own allegiance to the laws of classical economics led him to place most of the causes of social misery in the first class, natural phenomena outside social control — but even he included a fair number of problems within the category of 'the imperfections or errors of civil institutions'. It was possible to introduce a greater degree of conscious social control within this framework simply by demonstrating empirically that a greater share of human misery and inequality than Sumner had thought was caused by human arrangements that could be altered without damaging the ability of the society to survive.[128]

Thought News represented an effort to perform this task by a democratic method — to enlighten the public as to the social laws producing what were conventionally defined as 'problems'. Thus, by supplying a greater understanding of the deeper forces, this higher journalism would give the knowledge which must precede effective action. And for John Dewey this always implied the ability to discriminate between what could and could not be changed. Dewey was not trying to show that science really made everything possible. He accepted thoroughly the broad theory of evolutionary change, from simple to complex, homogeneous to heterogeneous, rural to urban, agricultural to industrial, which was laid out before the eyes of his generation and codified by Herbert Spencer as an inevitable law of historical change.

Dewey was certainly concerned to restore communal values which, like so many other theorists of his generation, he found enshrined in the life of the small community. But social research and scientific theory were to show means of restoring these universal moral qualities within the framework of the modern society which technical change inevitably spread over the world. The progress of social science would reveal the natural laws which had operated unconsciously in the small community and which could be reinstated through conscious effort in the larger society.[129] While the broad contours of historical change were determined, intelligence could smooth sharp corners, make 'the rough places plain'.

The philosophy of *Thought News*, then, was a synthesis of the collectivism of organic social theory with the individualism and activism of the American tradition. The tradition of social organicism tended historically to be linked with conservatism; and the Comtean notion of the sociologist as a social priest-physician advising the Ruler left little room for democratic social participation. But *Thought News* was to communicate the organicist awareness of structure and functional interrelatedness to an educated citizenry which would seize the understanding given by this knowledge to make intelligent and viable changes in structure. A few years after the *Thought News* episode, Dewey told his class at Michigan (as recorded by the graduate student, Charles H.Cooley, later to extend and enrich Dewey's insights): 'Men as different as Comte, Mill and Carlyle agree that the problem of organizing intelligence so as to bring it to bear on the conduct of the state is the condition of political equilibrium ... all agree that the problem is to control public opinion by science. Comte simply makes an autocrat of his scientific intelligence. Mill and Carlyle say they are stuck'. But the key was to use the power of the press to impart the sense of *relation* – the relations between facts, and more generally, 'their own relations to the movement of life', which 'changes opinion to intelligence and gives a scientific axis to social action. Interpretation is the aim of social science. A proper daily newspaper would be the only possible social science'.[130]

Park gave his intellectual allegiance to Dewey, but he had a strong temperamental affinity for Sumner. There is no clear statement in any of Park's writings that he had a 'moralistic' view of social law; but he thought that social action, though possible, would usually fail through lack of knowledge of the complexity of situations and through the moral corruption of reformers who contaminated their own attempts to purify the world. Nonetheless, he never gave up Dewey's early vision of a democratic but unbiased social science, giving the public a deeper understanding of events as the basis for political action. Throughout his life Park stressed the need to communicate to the public, and at the end of his career he found the ideal of *Thought News* embodied in the Luce newsmagazine, *Time*.[131] This conclusion suggests that Park's and Dewey's vision of *Thought News* cannot be judged apart from the observer's opinion of the modern newsmagazine as a force for democratic enlightenment.

His experience with *Thought News* left a permanent impression on Robert Park. He retained Franklin Ford's conviction that communication was the essential cohesive force in modern society, and that by improving the quality of news transmission the quality of the total society could be raised. He retained too, something of John Dewey's passion to relate abstract thought to the daily life of concrete human beings in order to validate the former and perfect the latter: 'popularization', in the sense of communicating knowledge in palatable form to an active public, was the *raison d'être* of the scholar. 'The solution of all the problems of our social life', he wrote to Clara, 'is the extension of the nervous system of the social body. It is this terrible chasm between knowledge and action, between the University and life that is the cause of all the present trouble'.[132] The failure of *Thought News* did not discourage his efforts to realize the fusion of academic and practical in the microcosm of his personal milieu. During the next three years, living in Detroit, working as reporter and city editor, involved in a passionate courtship, Park still found time to promote more modest projects toward the *Thought News* goal. Early in 1893 he was consulting with Dewey and George Herbert Mead about the foundation of a University Club in Detroit, an organization designed

To bring people who are outside of the University in closer connection with it and through them bring the University in closer connection with life. It will also encourage study and reading under the direction of the University but more particularly it will encourage investigation – the putting into practice for the solution of the practical business and social problems ... the 'theories' and ideas that have been worked at the University.[133]

On Dewey's advice Park narrowed the focus of his proposed organization into 'a Bureau of Criminology', as Dewey felt that 'the pathological side' of society, 'the crime and disorder are the easiest things to undertake to study'.[134] There is no further word of the 'Bureau of Criminology'; Park's work and impending marriage may have distracted his attention. Yet the passion to integrate the two sides of his existence – the intellectual and the daily round of a reporter's world – remained with Park to the end and underlies his restless search for a career which could offer both colorful experience and its integration with theoretical understanding.

So, entering his thirties, on the verge of making the break from journalism back towards theoretical reflection on his experiences, Park remained very much a 'seeker', a rebel against convention and hypocrisy, contemptuous of most 'reformers' because they seemed hypocritical, an 'affirmer' of the glory of violence and imperfection, because this affirmation stripped away the mask from genteel pretences. Some men turned to war, nativism, conserva-

tion, reform — Park sought his commitment in understanding the commitments of others. His assumption that value resides in psychic qualities rather
than specific ends foreshadows the therapeutic mentality characteristic of a
relativist age when unselfconscious commitment had become difficult.[135]
This vicarious search for faith is 'sociological' or 'functional', in that the
manifest content and overt goals of men's actions and symbolic systems fade
into the limbo of the forever uncertain, while psychic value and social
function take the center of the stage. Before meeting William James, who gave
the position permanent expression in 'The Will to Believe', Park had groped
toward the pragmatic justification of belief. Faith is a functional necessity,
good for the soul: people must believe because only through the concentration of energy on a single goal could they avoid disintegration of character.
The truth of this perception, later trivialized by over-exposure into a cliché of
mental hygiene, was fresh enough in the 1890s to seem inspiring. Indeed
much of the inspiration of early sociology was to isolate the common core of
loyalty among the deceptive convolutions of doctrine, so as to decant this
psycho-social essence and re-build a human brotherhood on the basis of this
universal idealism.[136] Park himself found such belief difficult, but he integrated his own character around the effort to understand the thread of life of
others. 'There is only one thing I can do', he wrote to his fiancée, 'understand'.[137]

Return to Formal Education: Harvard and Germany

The six years after leaving the *Chicago Journal* in 1898 involved the first of
the returns to the academy which marked the dialectical pattern of Park's
search for understanding. During this period Park completed his formal
higher education and acquired the concepts and the interpretative system
which he would later use to integrate the empirical work of his students at
Chicago.

By 1898 Park had become doubly dissatisfied with life as a reporter. He felt
that he was not providing his wife with sufficient security and status and,
perhaps even more discouraging, newspaperwork, intellectually as well as
socially, had come to seem a dead end. A way out opened when his father
offered to finance his further education and Park decided to return to the
formal study of philosophy and psychology.[1] He naturally gravitated towards the foremost center in the country, the department of philosophy at
Harvard, newly established as a separate entity, and enjoying its golden years
under William James, Josiah Royce, George Santayana, Hugo Munsterberg,
and George Herbert Palmer.[2] His formal intention was to study 'the
philosophical aspects of the effects of the printed facts on the public'.[3]
Significantly, Park still chose to approach his goal, the analysis of news and
public opinion, through philosophy and psychology rather than sociology.
By 1898 sociology departments existed in many newer American
universities;[4] Park's choice probably reflects not only his loyalty to Dewey
and his earlier training but also the relative lack of prestige which sociology so
far enjoyed. The new subject embraced applied betterment courses like
sanitary engineering and a hodgepodge of Protestant uplift and reform. In the
vague borderlines between disciplines Park had the example of John Dewey
that his answer lay broadly in philosophy more than in that applied discipline, sociology. According to his own account, 'I studied philosophy because I
hoped to gain insight into the nature and function of that kind of knowledge
we call news. Besides I wanted to gain a fundamental point of view from
which I could describe the behavior of society, under the influence of news, in
the precise and universal language of science'.[5]

The Harvard department was remarkable for richness and diversity of
talent. It included the divergent, but roughly neo-Hegelian Palmer and
Royce; William James, just making the·first announcements of pragmatism

as a method, and whose concern with the status of religious belief in a scientific age had already inspired 'The Will to Believe' and would culminate in the Gifford lectures of 1901; George Santayana, then principally known as an esthetician, and the experimental psychologist, Hugo Munsterberg. The fact that these men differed widely and attacked each other freely in class helped to contribute to a general air of vitality and friendliness. 'Truth was sacred; and criticism, the surest way of approaching it, was a friendly, not a hostile process', wrote Palmer. 'We wished our students to cultivate the critical habit, learn to be dispassionate, and not permit personal feeling to encroach on intellectual judgments'.[6]

Park was particularly impressed by William James, whose classes were informal discussions, bull sessions, in which James genuinely sought the opinions of his students and dispensed enlightenment with impromptu remarks. Park especially recalled his closing a discussion on progress with the casual but — in The Age of Spencer — startling observation that 'progress is a terrible thing'. James' capacity for an unfeigned and natural sympathy with all aspects of human life struck a responsive note in Park; he remembered the occasion when James took his seminar on abnormal psychology to visit an insane asylum. Among the inmates, James discovered an old friend who had the delusion that he was directing the universe. James 'took his arm and walking along in the most natural way, listened sympathetically and with real interest, as if he expected, as I believe he did, some new light from this insane man on this wild and irrational universe of ours'.[7]

James's most profound influence on Park came through his essay 'A Certain Blindness in Human Beings', which he read to the class in 1898 or 1899, before it was published. James himself felt that this was one of his most important essays; he insisted that 'it is more than the mere piece of sentimentalism which it may seem to some readers.'

It connects itself with a definite view of the world and of our moral relations to the same ... the pluralistic or individualistic philosophy. According to that philosophy, the truth is too great for any one actual mind, even though that mind be dubbed 'the Absolute', to know the whole of it. The facts and works of life need many cognizers to take them in. There is no point of view absolutely public and universal. ... The practical consequence of such a philosophy is the well-known democratic respect for the sacredness of individuality.[8]

The essay must have struck home to Park because it fitted so well with his own temperament and experience. Indeed, 'A Certain Blindness' became Park's habitual weapon against the prophets of a rigidly behavioral method in sociology, a method which did not preserve inviolate, as an essential causal element in any situation, the subjective perception of life by the actors. 'A Certain Blindness' insisted that the abundance of life was too varied and vital to be reduced to positivist categories of explanation; only by penetrating through the mask of phenomenal regularity to the subjective uniqueness and passion of the human individual could one understand the world, be able to do it justice without devaluing human variety. This essay gave Park prestigious support for his own dislike of 'scholastic' abstractions in social research. He agreed with James that 'wherever a process of life communicates an eagerness to him who lives it, there the life becomes genuinely significant ... that is the zest, the tingle, the excitement of reality'.[9] He always remembered, and used to repeat with approval, a remark he had once heard James make, 'that the most real thing is a thing that is most keenly felt rather than the thing that is most clearly conceived'.[10] James also gave Park a crucial modification of the reporter's outlook. The outsider who merely observed could only partially understand; any real understanding demanded an imaginative participation in the life of others; insight demanded empathy as well as observation. In later years Park always tried to impress this point on his own students, for, as he never tired of quoting, 'to miss the joy is to miss all'.[11]

James's most immediate effect on Park was to turn him away from philosophy. He reinforced not only Park's distaste for reductionist science, but more broadly his revulsion from all abstract, categorizing thought. A casual remark, that one of Royce's proofs of the attributes of God was 'infinitely old', had a profound effect on at least one of the students. Park recalled:

The remark banished once and for all so far as I was concerned, any further interest in the attributes of God ... it banished scholasticism. ... From that time on logic and formal knowledge of every sort, ceased to have for me that interest of authority they once had. Ideas were no longer to be anywhere or in any sense a substitute or a surrogate for reality and the world of things. Thenceforth my interest was in science rather than philosophy.[12]

With this shift in interest, and feeling still dissatisfied as to his understanding of news and communication, Park decided to move to the source of scientific knowledge about human life and society — Germany. Throughout the 1880s it had been accepted in American academic circles that 'Germany possessed the sole secret of scholarship' and any serious young scholar naturally desired to complete his education there.[13] In 1899 Park and his family, still financed by his father, journeyed to Berlin.[14] Although some of the magic had been dissipated, Berlin was still the most popular university with Americans and there were at least a hundred American students there in every term during the 1890s.[15] Although Park could, presumably, have gone to an American graduate school, Munsterberg at Harvard was always a powerful propagandist for the German universities and German philosophy,[16] and in any case Germany still remained the place *par excellence* for the philosophical analysis of history and contemporary events.

In Europe the Park family, which now included three small children, threw itself into German life.[17] A lecture Park gave many years later, describing the process of developing double vision which the typical American abroad undergoes, seems clearly based on his own experience at the turn of the century. At first to the innocent but good natured young man the formality of German life seemed merely quaint; then he began to enter into the German point of view, to share some of its attitudes. However, just to the extent that the American does begin to see with German eyes, he begins to have a basis for judging the native society on grounds more serious than quaintness. At the same time he becomes especially sensitive to criticism of his own country; he acquires a more sentimental and vigorous patriotism than he had ever had before, becomes self-conscious as an American and tries to define the meaning of American identity.[18] If Park's only published writing on Germany while he was actually there is any guide, his own immediate response was one of complete enthusiasm. He appears to have found the German army an example of that dedication, that will to victory and readiness for sacrifice which he had looked for in vain in modern America.[19] In an article for *Munsey's Magazine* on the German military machine he traced the over-whelming German victory of 1870 to a triumph of the national will 'founded in an ancient conviction inherent in the Teutonic race, the conviction that the man or nation that is not willing to fight for its own does not deserve to live'. Like many American progressives he felt that war for all its horrors provided a stiffening of the spirit necessary to prevent national decadence. Approvingly he quoted Von Moltke's opinion that 'without war the world would fall into decay and lose itself in materialism'.[20]

The University of Berlin, where Park first enrolled in the autumn of 1899, had been the great intellectual center of Germany, indeed of Europe. In the late 1890s however, the University 'seemed in partial eclipse'.[21] Park remained for only one semester, attending the lectures of Professor Friedrich Paulsen and Georg Simmel, then a *Privatdocent* lecturing at the university without an official salary beyond the students' fees. The neo-Kantian Paulsen was primarily a moral philosopher whose own ethics somewhat resembled those of James: he defined 'the good' as the many good things which people make the end of their action.[22] Georg Simmel, forty-one in 1899, was to become probably the most important single influence on Park's substantive sociological theories. Indeed, Simmel's lectures were the only formal instruction in sociology, so designated, that Park ever received.[23] The two men shared a career-line; Simmel had gone from journalism through philosophy to sociology. George Santayana, who had heard Simmel lecture a decade earlier, described him as 'a young man of sallow and ascetic look who lectures on pessimism and on contemporary philosophy in its relation with the natural sciences. He knows his subject like a German and likes to go into the fine points'.[24] By 1899 Simmel had passed on to the development of his own sociology, in which his passion for fine points was given free play.

While in Berlin, Park 'ran across a little treatise on the logic of the social sciences by a Russian, Kistiakovski'. It was the first thing that he had found anywhere that 'dealt with the problem with which I was concerned in the terms in which I had come to think of it'.[25] Bogdan A. Kistiakovski had been a student of the neo-Kantian philosopher, Wilhelm Windelband. He took over from Windelband and his student, Heinrich Rickert, their methodological distinction between the 'nomothetic' realm of science, which included sociology, as the analysis of nature determined according to general laws of causation, and the 'ideographic' realm of history, which dealt with unique sequences of events interpreted in the light of cultural values.[26] To track down these ideas to their source, Park went to Strassburg to study with Windelband and then in the spring of 1903 followed him to Heidelberg.

At Strassburg, besides studying philosophy with Windelband, Park also took political economy and geography as minor specialities. The lecturer on political economy, Georg Friedrich Knapp, a statistician and historian, had a lasting influence upon him. Knapp's lectures gave Park an insight into a way of life alien to the Middle Border, yet congenial to Park's emotional identification with 'the people' — the life of the German peasant. 'I gained from his lectures', wrote Park later, 'a knowledge of peasant life so complete and intimate as I would never have believed it possible to have of any people with whom one had not lived'.[27] Although a rigorous statistician who had made his name with a study of mortality rates, Knapp believed in the value of literature to bring home a real understanding of the lives of others.[28] He recommended to his class the novel by Wilhelm von Polenz, *Der Büttnerbauer*, a story of peasant life disrupted by Jewish finance and industrial capital, among whose many German-speaking admirers was Adolf Hitler.[29] Park drew the lesson that realistic fiction was basic to the understanding of 'the more intimate and human aspects of life' for it provided 'an acquaintance with' the subject 'as indispensable to the sociologist as to the historian'. The study of peasant life gave Park unusual comparative knowledge which he employed in the later work with Negroes in the American South, and with European immigrants in Northern cities. At the same time, Knapp and von Polenz heightened the color of the moral lenses through which Park would view the people he met. The East European peasant, like the Southern Negro later, seemed to Park a more perfect embodiment of the romantic doctrine of simple, unassuming human nature than any other types of mankind to be found in America.[30]

Park's Education in Sociology

During the four years spent in Germany and working on his Ph.D. dissertation, *Masse und Publikum*,[31] Park absorbed the persepctive and many of the specific concepts he would later employ and pass on to his students in the sociology department at Chicago. Very little of his instruction in Germany was formally in sociology, and his thesis was written for the philosophy department at Heidelberg, but his studies and his own analytical work provided him with his education in the sociological speculation and system building which had accumulated over the last hundred years.

Robert Park read deeply in the work of the founders of sociology as a discipline, especially in that of Auguste Comte and Herbert Spencer, and drew from them not only a general orientation, but specific interpretations of social life. Hence, a brief account of the emergence of sociology as a field of study is more than pious prehistory in this case; the 'founders' were living intellectual influences for Park throughout his career.

As a discipline, sociology was an offshoot of philosophy and history, an attempt to apply the insights of philosophy more particularly to the needs of society, and an attempt to draw valid, scientific generalizations about the laws of human social organization from history. Yet the stimulus to these efforts to create a generalized science of society had powerful roots in political ideology: the standard sociological insights were developed by conservative theorists in the early nineteenth century to analyze the central event of the age – the French Revolution – and, along the way, to discredit its ideology by diverting attention away from formal rights and liberties, and focusing instead on the abstract conditions of social stability required before any social program could be realized. The Revolution was felt as a great disorienting force whose baleful effects were extended by the modern forces of rationalism and industrialism to atomize the traditional taken-for-granted social order.[32] The political and economic forces hailed by liberals as progressive seemed to be producing a mass population, atomized, insecure, and morally degraded by its 'liberation' from the bonds of subservience to traditional authority. This rootless and desperate mass, according to classical political theory, was easy prey for ruthless men and could lead only to general anarchy and a new radical tyranny. This concern led naturally to a focus on what had customarily stood between the individual and the state, but had been neglected by eighteenth-century theorists – traditional society in its unique historical development, which by its customs, traditions, hierarchy of order, and deference had disguised and blunted naked power and had preserved a functioning order without violence. Now that its very existence seemed to be threatened society became an object of study: What were the necessary conditions of social stability and social cohesion?[33]

The new study centered around the problem of order in social life, upon the conitions required to produce the identification or balance of interests necessary for social stability. Although a theory of social equilibrium based upon a rational, utilitarian concept of human nature was possible, the great proto-sociologists were driven by polemical necessity to an organicist position.[34] Burke in England, Hegel in Germany, Bonald in France, all asserted the historical, logical, and therefore ethical, primacy of society to the individual.

Only through society was the human individual created from a mass of animal instincts, and only in society was there morality. The isolated individual was an abstraction; in reality the irreducible unit was the individual embedded in a network of relationships and statuses — fathers, sons, masters, workers, burghers, peasants. In reply to the ideologies of the Revolution, the sociological conservatives countered that society is not a machine and cannot lightly be tinkered with; it is a natural growth and efforts to tamper with one institution would violate the larger system of coherence. Society existed less to maintain the rights of man than to serve the basic needs which he took for granted. All its aspects, however 'irrational' they might seem, in fact did function to serve some such need or to preserve the whole structure — hence Burke's famous defense of prejudice as stored wisdom, enabling men to act more rapidly than conscious reflection would permit.[35]

The Revolution had attacked all the 'irrational' buttresses of the old social order in the name of equality as well as reason, but even at the height of the revolution the theoretical basis of egalitarianism was coming under attack. As the eighteenth century gave way to the nineteenth, the philosophers' emphasis on the basic sameness of men gave way, especially among physiologists, to an insistence on their fundamental and natural differences in capacities, desires, and needs. But it was these very differences which made a harmonious social order possible. 'Inequalities in a state of harmony, that is the order of the universe', declared Jacques Necker.[36] While these differences were naturally emphasized by ideological conservatives like de Maistre and de Bonald, they were also taken up by the more 'radical' reformer, Henri de Saint Simon, and through him passed down to Auguste Comte and the beginnings of sociology as a self-conscious discipline. St. Simon wanted to found the ideal society upon the fundamental nature of man, to make it answer to the most natural needs of men. But from reading the physiologists, he decided that the 'natural was inequality'; the good society therefore, must be a harmonious, interrelated organism of dissimilar men, organized so that each fulfilled his own natural propensities while contributing to the efficient functioning of the whole. Inequality, however, would not be invidious, nor lead to resentment since power was 'transformed into function and privilege into responsibility'.[37]

Thus, at its origin, sociology was given a theoretical center which rested on a fear of historical processes dissolving the bonds of stability — libertarian ideology, commerce and industry, the aggregation of strangers in cities. The significance, and often the hidden bias, of a scholarly endeavor is best revealed by discovering what it considers problematic and worthy of study, and what it takes for granted. The fathers of sociology bequeathed a two-fold heritage. First, a concern that order was being undermined, and therefore, that science must strive to isolate and describe the conditions of stability. Second, a belief that the forces undermining order were set in motion by social change and had in common a concept of 'rationality' which abstracted men from the envelope of the traditional milieu and faith. These concerns came together in the father of modern sociology, Auguste Comte, who sought to establish sociology as a positive, predictive and meliorative science – 'savoir pour prévoir pour pouvoir'. The purpose of science — of all kinds — was to bring *order*, to determine the relationship between facts and thus discover the laws governing them; progress depended first of all upon the right ordering of knowledge so as to apprehend these laws. The most important of the sciences was that which discovers and relates the facts of society itself, which investigates 'the effects and counter-effects which all parts of the system ceaselessly have on each other'.[38]

Society could be analyzed scientifically because it was an organic whole, whose organs were institutions, the most basic of which was the family, the fundamental organ of social control and the fount and origin of greater societies.[39] Society rests upon the division of labor; it is this which enables it to grow in complexity and which integrates it, since each man is dependent on every other; it lies too, at the base of the complex relations of subordination and responsibility which make government and order possible. This complex organism does not depend upon complete inertia for its maintenance, but change could not be produced by the naive and wanton interference of men according to their own 'rational' calculations. Such intervention merely destroys the integral life of the organism without being able to supply anything equally natural and men are impelled into formlessness and anomie.[40]

The progress of society was dependent on the immanent development within the organism itself; the task of the sociologist was to discover the laws of this development and ease its progress.[41] The final stage of evolutionary development would have thrown off the irrationalities of previous stages and be in tune with the teaching of science. To Comte, what really kept society together and made it function healthily was a moral order; 'Institutions depend on morals and morals in their turn depend on beliefs. Every scheme of new institutions will, therefore, be useless, so long as morals have not been "reorganized", and so long as ... a general system of opinions has not been founded which is accepted by all minds as true'.[42] Opinion governed the world; 'the great political and moral crisis that societies are now undergoing is shown by a rigid analysis to arise out of intellectual anarchy. While stability in fundamental maxims is the first condition of genuine social order, we are suffering under an utter disagreement which may be called universal'.[43]

Unity and subordination in society, both basic to its healthy functioning, were then dependent on a wide consensus on certain basic values. The medieval church had once produced this consensus but after the disrupting effects of revolutionary rationalism it could no longer do so. The details of Comte's attempt to found a new religion of humanity to recreate moral consensus met with little but derision, but the problem he stated remained valid for later sociologists: how can society remain healthy if there is not some basic value consensus, and how is such a consensus produced? The answer he offered, that 'opinion', or uniformity of belief, was the real integrating factor, reinforced the developing interest in the media of communication. Comte's stress on 'opinion' was naturally appealing to Park, given his fascination with 'news'. However, along with his concern with communication, Park always retained a strong sense of the pre-ideological sources of cohesion, the extent to which society hangs together not because of conformity but because of mutual utility.

The first sociologist whose work Park studied in detail was not Comte, but Herbert Spencer, the putative prophet of post-bellum America whose prestige had earned him an entire course at Michigan by student demand. While Comte attempted to organize all the sciences into one great hierarchy, Spencer was also erecting a synthetic philosophy which would integrate the study of human society with the natural sciences. Like Comte he asserted that society was an organism — although he had to admit that society could not be compared exactly to any particular type of individual organism, and that the social organism, unlike the human, does not have a directing brain. Nonetheless, society could be considered as an organism because of the functional interdependence of its parts. Like a biological organism society grows by increasing differentiation and integration. Like Comte, Spencer made the division of labor basic to the structure of society, for it was this 'which in the social, as in the animal, makes it a living whole'.[44] However, whereas Comte emphasized the dangers for social unity inherent in the division of labor, for Spencer, with his biological analogy always in mind, increasing differentiation was a sign of progress signifying an increase in mutual co-operation and integration.

Evolution established in both [body physical and body social] not differences simply, but definitely connected differences. ... The parts of an inorganic aggregate are so related that one may change greatly without appreciably affecting the rest. It is otherwise with the parts of an organic aggregate or of a social aggregate. In either of these the changes in the parts are mutually determined, and the changed actions of the parts are mutually dependent. In both, too, this mutuality increases as the evolution advances.[45]

Nonetheless, for Spencer, there was a major difference between an individual biological organism and the social organism: in the former, the parts existed for the good of the whole, in the latter 'society exists for the benefit of its members.' In society, unlike a biological organism, feeling and intelligence was diffused throughout the society, whereas society itself, as distinct from its members had no sensations, no perceptions, no intelligence.[46] This individualistic interpretation allowed Spencer to reach ethical conclusions opposite to those of Comte: if each man followed his own rational self-interest, the operation of natural law would tend to produce an increasing degree of harmony. He did not, like Comte and most later sociologists, believe that the health of society depended on producing a shared set of values among men: Comte, he thought, over-estimated the power of ideas.[47]

Though Spencer and Comte agreed that society was an organism subject to natural laws and therefore a proper subject for scientific study, their central explanations of social cohesion were diametrically opposed: to Comte, society was a relationship of consensus, to Spencer, a relationship of symbiosis. These polar types set the pattern for succeeding sociologists, who struggled to reconcile them without sinking into a vague affirmation of all possible alternatives. The most common schema was an evolutionary sequence from one polar type to another, such as Sir Henry Maine's progression from 'status' to 'contract' as the central principle of social systems of justice. The most celebrated of these contrasting typologies, perhaps because closest to common-sense nostalgia, was Ferdinand Tönnies' pair 'Gemeinschaft' and 'Gesellschaft', abstract, ideal types which were embodied to varying degrees in the values and institutions of historic societies. All human relationships could be classified either as communal, based on unreflecting tradition, like-mindedness, personal knowledge of the 'others', or as societal, based upon conscious utilitarian calculation of the means required to realize conscious goals. Most relationships have an element of both, all societies do, but in historical terms one can characterize societies by whichever type of association is dominant. Thus primitive and peasant societies are characterized by preponderance of Gemeinschaft or communal relations, whereas relations in modern societies are mainly Gesellschaft or associational.[48] The theories of Tönnies' French contemporary, Emile Durkheim, were not so suffused in a romantic mist, but used a formally similar typology. In De la Division du Travail Social (1893), Durkheim argued that modern society was more organic than the primitive because, instead of being based on mere similarity, it was a product of ever-increasing differentiation and thus of interdependence. In primitive societies men acted together because they were like-minded, but in modern societies their varied activities were co-ordinated by common goals imposed on them by society. A complex and differentiated society was not necessarily disorganized, since cohesion did not have to rest on the personal knowledge and limited variety of roles which characterized the traditional village. A modern society, with its 'organic solidarity', maintained unity by planting conscious values in the minds of its members. Because these values were more conscious, more closely tied to the individual's need to avoid guilt or humiliation than the vaguer common sentiments of the traditional community's 'mechanical solidarity', modern society could tolerate a wider variety of behavior and roles, a greater degree of individuality and impersonality than the traditional order could.[49]

Organicism, as a theory of society, did not necessarily dispose one to any particular political stand. In Comte, concern for order and stability led to a reactionary conservatism, but to Tönnies, the great celebrator of the German peasant, nostalgia for the stable fraternal community led to socialism. One might conclude that the sociological imagination could be conservative or socialist but never liberal; but Spencer used the organic functional analogy to validate an existing liberal competitive society. Durkheim's politics recognized the primacy of society over the individual and found formal expression in the idea of the corporate state. In spite of Spencer, the European tradition of sociology tended to concentrate on the group, rather than the individual and was most concerned with the order, stability, and solidarity of society as a whole. But while Park learned much from the organicists, his own acknowledged master, Georg Simmel, stood outside of this central tradition in the development of sociology.

If any one man could be called *the* sociologist for Park, it was cerainly Simmel. Park used his notes on Simmel's lectures, Simmel's *Soziologie*, and the translations of Simmel made by Albion W.Small,[50] in organizing the materials for his famous book of readings, *Introduction to the Science of Sociology*.[51] Simmel's celebrated essay on 'The Metropolis and Mental Life' seems to have provided many of the suggestions put forward in Park's essay 'The City',[52] and Simmel's speculations on a social geometry, on the importance of distance and position within social space in explaining the phenomena of social life, lay behind many of the formulations of Park's ecology. Not only the broad outlines of Park's theory, but his methodological premises and many of his interpretations, were developed from Simmel's speculative panorama of social life. To grasp the special quality of the theories with which Park and his students tried to interpret midwestern America in the 1920s, a brief characterization of Simmel's theories is essential.

Simmel might be characteriized as the 'phenomenologist of everyday life', his theory a social geometry of animate objects, an elaborate geography of subjective organisms, of the effect on individual consciousness and individual behavior of the 'forms' of sociation, the types of contact which each individual had with each other individual. The special perspective which Simmel brought to sociology may have resulted in part from his attempt to resolve through practical illustration the philosophical dispute − important to the German academic community where it was essential to achieve philosophical respectability for one's field of interest − over the precise status of sociology and its objects of attention. Much of Simmel's emphasis on what he called the formal aspects of society may have come from his need to carve out an area distinctly sociological, an area of objects and relations with which none of the established human studies had concerned themselves.[53]

Like early social historians, Simmel focused upon just those elements which had been neglected by the economists and students of politics because they did not fit neatly into the categories of significant social institutions seen by the educated public as determinative – the economy, the polity, the individual psyche. Simmel was inspired to show how important these 'trivial' aspects actually were in influencing behavior; he set himself the challenge of proving the necessity of sociology by demonstrating how powerful an influence such things as sociability or the abstract size of a group had upon the behavior of men who thought themselves acting on conscious motives in recognized, dignified channels of activity. Like Freud in *The Psychopathology of Everyday Life*, Simmel seized upon the neglected and 'trivial' to show up the inadequacy of accepted categories. The analysis of 'trivia' could show most impressively how important was the fact of sociability, of relatedness, in shaping action; Simmel scorned the mere assertion or theoretical elaboration of the notion that society was an organism which molded its members; he demonstrated the profound effect on human behavior of the 'formal' process of association with other men in varying patterns, to show beyond doubt that relatedness itself altered the behavior of men away from the channel determined for it by utilitarian judgment of means and ends.[54]

There was for Simmel an 'intermediate' realm of life, the 'social', which added another dimension to the study of the older subjects, and explained why rationalistic accounts of human behavior were inadequate because they ignored this invisible web of social relations, binding men together in all their activities. In his descriptive essays, Simmel emphasized just those types of social relations which seemed trivial to the older disciplines, relations which seemed to lack the power to determine the direction of human action. He chose the types of 'sociation' which reflected most clearly the abstraction of the 'form' of interaction from the 'content' or conscious utilitarian motives of action. Sociability, play, conversation best revealed the fine spider web of human relations conducted for sheer pleasure, for their own sake rather than rational goals. In 'sociable' relations, men communicated little except their own skill at the formal process of communication, their power to 'relate' abstractly.[55]

Simmel defined his sociology as one concerned primarily with the 'forms' of sociation, the active or interactive aspects of institutions or processes, as against the 'content' studied by the older disciplines. This obscure distinction led to many attacks on it as ridiculous and untenable.[56] But the distinction becomes less ridiculous if we note the other term Simmel used as a synonym for ' content': the concrete disciplines studied activity from the standpoint of the 'interests' expressed therein, while the sociologist studied the influence upon action of the 'forms' of interaction through which actors attempted to realize their interests. In Simmel's system, 'forms' were relatively constant types of association or relation, which appear in a wide variety of specific social contexts, and which are thus not merely aspects of any particular form of society. A form was a relatively fixed mode of relationship, considered and enumerated in its possible variations apart from any specific context. The analysis of each 'form', in the variety of contexts which reflected it, then afforded light on the sociological determinants of action. Thus conflict could be discussed in different situations and degrees of acuteness, in the aspects it revealed when conflict was among groups of two, of three, of varying larger sizes, or among groups whose bond of cohesion was political, religious, or personal.[57]

A characteristic example of Simmel's sociology is his discussion of 'the significance of numbers for social life'. 'It will immediately be conceded on the basis of every day experience',[58] Simmel noted, 'that a group upon reaching a certain size must develop forms and organs which serve its maintenance and promotion, but which a smaller group does not need. On the other hand ... smaller groups have qualities, including types of interaction among the members, which inevitably disappear when the groups grow larger'.[59] Simmel calls this the 'quantitative determinant of the group'. He applies this general insight to varying types of groups, classifying them by their function or commonsense appellation: socialistic groups, religious sects, aristocracies.

Up to this day, at least, socialistic ... societies have been possible only in very small groups and have always failed in larger ones. The principle of socialism ... can easily be realized in a small group, and what is surely quite as important, can be safeguarded there by its members. The contribution of each to the whole and the group's reward to him are visible at close range. Comparison and compensation are easy. In the large group they are difficult, especially because of the inevitable differentiation of its members, of their function, and claims. A very large number of people can constitute a unit only if there is a complex division of labor.[60]

Similarly, religious sects like the Waldensians, and the Mennonites, impose such intense restrictions upon action that they limit the effective size of the sect, reinforcing the strength of religious feeling by this very smallness and exclusiveness. The demand for distinctness entails exclusiveness to maintain purity. Exclusiveness means close ties to avoid loneliness.

Where dogma forbids oath, military service and occupancy of offices; where very personal affairs such as occupation ... are regulated by the community; where specific dress separates the faithful from the others and symbolizes their belonging together; where the subjective experience of immediate rapport with Christ constitutes the real cohesion of the community — in such situations extension to large groups would evidently break the tie of solidarity which consists to a large degree precisely in the position of being singled out of larger groups and being in contrast with them.[61]

The centrality of interactional 'form' rather than what later sociologists have seen as more objective and historically repetitive types of organization – social class, bureaucracy, etc. – had important effects on Simmel's system. It was both dynamic and classificatory, it used a multiplicity of historical examples without basing itself specifically on any theory of historical evolution; and it meant that the sociologist did not try to build an exclusive, total science which subsumed the material of the older disciplines into its own concepts.

Simmel granted that interaction, the specifically sociological field, was one perspective from which behavior must be approached; but the very conscious limitation of his approach implied also that the same data must be worked through from the standpoint of 'interest', of conscious goals, in order to give a complete account. Thus, while his interest in economics or political science was not great, it does not follow that he thought wealth or power immaterial to the study of society. Still, his particular method of carving out a unique sociological field made it all too easy for his followers to build a complete sociology upon formal interaction, one which would describe phenomena through the categories of interaction, while neglecting the element of 'interest', the degree to which all social life is affected by inequalities of political power and wealth. The divorce of 'form' from 'content' may not be logically absurd, but it raises the specter of a sociology which forgets its own partial nature, and tries to reduce all of social life to the result of formal interaction.

'Interaction', that is the behavior of individuals in which they are aware of others, and are modifying their behavior to take account of others and their expectations, became a popular sociological term in the United States, in no small part due to its central place in the Park and Burgess text and book of readings.[62] 'Interaction' was another of those new terms, like William Graham Sumner's 'folkways' and 'mores' and Albion Small's 'social process', whose popular diffusion has symbolized the growth of self-consciousness about one's social relations which accompanies the spread of the sociological perspective. For Simmel, the term embraced a variety of more precise mutual relations whose counters were usually common-sense terms; subordination and superordination, competition, dominance, secrecy, reconciliation, conflict. His method of analyzing, or discussing, each of these subjects was to approach it as a process involving the combination and reconciliation of opposites, describable implicitly as a graph along which the intensity of 'competition' or 'secrecy' could be located for each case. Examples of each formal process, drawn from a variety of situations, would reveal the manifold forms and degrees of intensity it could assume. Each process could be discussed in terms of the component objects and processes whose interweaving composed it.[63]

Along with the analysis of the category of social forms best described as 'processes' went the isolation and analysis of 'social types', or characteristic varieties of social character developed in human beings by their repeated participation in relatively ritualized forms of social action. The standard social processes, acting through the establishment of habits in the individual, imposed a predictable pattern of response which would be evoked when he found himself in a similar situation – one of subordination or conflict, for example. The miser, the cynic, the poor man, the non-partisan, the stranger, the aristocrat – these were treated by Simmel as complex behavior patterns, compounds of contradictory influences, which the situation established in the individual through repeated encounters. The point of view was that of the subject, responding to these influences; not that of the scientific observer, concerned to delineate the 'objective' structure of class and power relations molding the individual.[64]

Simmel anticipated much later role theory in this explanation of the relations between individual and society. The individual became *part* of society by playing a role which society delimited for him. It was only by having his personality 'generalized' in this way that the individual could interact with the larger whole; but the particular role he took was not determined solely by society; rather, his own inner qualities and desires, his 'vocation', propelled him towards a particular role. Thus, the inner motives and drives of the individual are fused with the requirements of society.[65]

The third major type of formal analysis for Simmel was the evolution of one social form into another, what one commentator calls the 'developmental pattern'. This was not the grand evolutionary pattern of total societies beloved of the previous generation, but in a sense the same process of explanation applied in microcosmic detail, the historical process of genesis and transformation applied now to a single institution which seemed typical of a class, for example the process by which religious sects develop. Robert Park found this method ideally suited to the sociological elucidation of the microcosmic social changes his students found in their studies of local communities and institutions; the work of the 'Chicago school' abounds in 'natural histories' of institutions, in which the observable changes are traced to necessities imposed either by changes in inner structure or in the environment which made demands upon them.[66]

Simmel was always aware of the historical process of growth in all existence and his emphasis on function and movement led to a philosophical position rather like pragmatism. Truth was always relative: any single idea could only be true in relation to another and a whole corpus of knowledge could only be true in relation to the outside world. Thus truth, like society, consists in relationships. There were as many valid perspectives as there were experiencing individuals, although men of a particular age and culture would tend to share a describably common outlook. And for each age and area, there was a single broad perspective which could be considered normatively valid, since it had allowed the men who possessed it to meet the challenge of existence and survive the Darwinian test. The student of human life did not, however, have to content himself with describing the mosaic of world views which social man had developed; since ideas could be manipulated to meet the ends which the thinker sought, the social scientist was free to abstract data and build concepts from the mass of raw material spread before him. The truth value of his hypotheses came in the coherence of each concept with the total theoretical structure he built, and the 'truth' of the whole derived from its adequacy in explaining the problem selected by the thinker. The method of science is the final judge of the truth, or better, the utility, of an idea, first by assessing its coherence with the total system, then its utility in bringing the system of ideas into relation with the external world.[67]

Despite his proposals for a relativist, quasi-pragmatic scientific method, Simmel's preferred mode of describing social behavior — in modern terms, the model he found most useful as a simplified picture of social relations — bears a striking resemblance to the physical universe as visualized in classical physics. Following Kant's insistence that phenomena, the experimental objects available to the natural sciences, can be thought of only in the context of their spatial relation, Simmel found it most useful to visualize society as a field of force within which individual particles moved, combined, reacted against each other, moving in accordance with laws of social physics which could be specified with some precision. However, this was a social physics which assumed its particles were conscious, in which the subjective awareness of the situation for each individual was a crucial part of the whole situation; the sociologist had to investigate to discover the plurality of subjective meanings which were one component of the resultant of forces pushing the individual. Simmel used 'play' to mean not only the common-sense category of actions pursued for the enjoyment afforded by performing them; it also implied the play of forces over a physical field, where atoms interwove in response to the complex of social energies released by previous interaction. This complex of energies was then shaped in expression into varieties of those social forms which Simmel specialized in delineating. Thus, he postulated a 'social space' in which various human energies and social imperatives determined the 'position' of individuals in relation to each other. Interaction and its results could be studied through observation of the social space between individuals since this space was 'energized' by the particular forms of interaction which took place between the individuals. Thus sociology might also be defined as the science of 'betweens', the apparently empty space between the concrete individuals and formal institutions which to the rationalistic viewer seemed to make up all of society.[68] Space implied boundaries; and Simmel was concerned to develop the position of people in groups in social space as an expression of the social relations existing between them. Ths concern of Simmel's seems to have left a permanent impression on Park; when the latter sought in the 1910s and 1920s for a theory to explain the observed regularities in geographical location and specific types of use, he found enlightenment not only in the work of plant ecologists but also in his old teacher's ideas about the symbolic meaning of space, position, and distance.[69]

Simmel's analogy of human beings as physical atoms suggests another important characteristic of his perspective, one which Park carried on and tried to blend with the more differentiated social psychology which he had absorbed from Dewey and James and which his future colleagues at the University of Chicago would be carrying on. Simmel postulated the ontological reality of individuals as discrete human organisms, and to an extent separate from the social organism which they comprised. Individuals, and their psychological drives, their 'wills', were fundamental units; the sociologist described the modification in behavior, and perhaps in more fundamental 'will', which social interaction produced; but he did not try to reduce human nature to a mere reflection of social forces. Personality, for Simmel, was not wholly 'the subjective aspect of culture'. The individual as he exists at the beginning of each social adventure is a 'given' bundle of interests, subject to modification by the immediate experience he will undergo.[70]

Simmel's concept of society was designed to balance the independent existence both of the individual and the collectivity. Society had an objective quality which allowed it to be analyzed by the abstraction of its repetitive aspects − its characteristic types of behavior and processes of interaction. Yet Simmel also preserved the analytic − and by implication, moral − independence of the individuals who compose society, by locating 'society' in these patterns of relationship among individuals. Although individuals define their own uniqueness through social contact, and are affected by their relation to social groups even when that relation is one of rejection, they still retain a fundamental 'core' not created by belonging.[71] The 'old conflict over the nature of society', he wrote, had plagued scholars too long. 'One side mystically exaggerates its significance contending that only through society is human life endowed with reality. The other regards it as a mere abstract concept, by means of which the observer draws the realities, which are individual human beings, into a whole, as one calls trees and brooks, houses and meadows, a landscape'. This dispute, Simmel argued, was beside the point. The solution was to regard society as

a reality in a double sense. On the one hand are the individuals in their directly perceptible existence, the bearers of the processes of association, who are united by these processes into the higher unity which one calls 'society'; on the other hand, the interests which, living in the individuals, motivate such union: economic and ideal interests, warlike and erotic, religious and charitable. To satisfy such urges and to attain such purposes, arise the unnumerable forms of social life, all the with-one-another, for-one-another, in-one-another, against-one-another, and through-one-another, in state and commune, in church and economic associations, in family and clubs.[72]

For Simmel there was always a certain dualism between the individual and the group; he was always aware that the individual who plays the role is not the *whole* individual; that every man has a secret self never entirely graspable, there is always something that escapes society and the sociologist. However, Simmel's 'individualism' was joined to a determinism, which gave his theory a fatalistic view of human destiny which Park found congenial. Since he conceived of the individual as being somehow drawn to the role in which he finds himself by his own inner qualities and drives, then everyone is, in a sense, in the 'right place'.[73]

Robert Park also found Simmel's subjectivist perspective sympathetic. His point of view was usually that of the individual participating in social relations, rather than the standpoint of social structures assumed to be objective, external, and exerting a coercive power over their members' consciousness and behavior. The subjective approach to the effects of interaction stressed by Simmel harmonized not only with the reporter's natural tendency to see each situation as discrete, unique; it also reinforced the moral lesson of William James's 'A Certain Blindness', with its injunction that each life is unique and must be approached through empathy if human dignity were not to be violated in the name of categorizing, reductionist science. The crucial task was to exemplify, convey inner meaning, express the unique effect of a social force through its reflection in a particular consciousness. While Park never regarded this ethically-charged empathy as the *only* task of a scientific sociology, he certainly considered it the first requirement of any descriptive work in the field. Despite the differences in philosophical background between Simmel and William James, their influence on Park merged at this point to validate the method of 'depth reporting' which Park was later to embody. Simmel seemed to provide a means of making a science, or at least building a classification of types of human action, which would satisfy the scientific demand for generality without sacrificing the sense of uniqueness demanded by James's moral philosophy.[74]

Although Simmel's concern with common forms of reciprocal action could be taken as a flexible, varied attempt to describe the ways in which societies actually manage to remain coherent, the driving passion of his work was not, to the degree which it had been for the classic sociologists, the problem of the conditions of social stability. He did not make a consensus on moral values central, nor begin his analysis with the assumption that society is a fixed structure of clearly delimited, functionally essential relationships. In fact, for Simmel, the central question tended to be not so much order, as freedom. Simmel was always trying to assess how free the individual was in any particular state of social development and how the conditions of freedom changed and developed with the evolution of society.[75]

This concern with the freedom of the individual rather than his security gave Simmel a different perspective from that of the *Gemeinschaft* school and made him much more kindly disposed towards the modern world. Many conceptual elements of the *Gemeinschaft* perspective are scattered through Simmel's work, notably in his essay, 'The Metropolis and Mental Life'. But for Simmel, the concern with evolutionary change from small organic community to large impersonal society limited itself to a selection of topics for discussion which would illuminate the dominant traits of the modern order. Thus he discussed the effect of money as a universal standard of value, the relation of complex differentiation to individual liberty. And Simmel's conclusions were generally favorable to the emergent modern order: whatever had been lost of moral certainty and effective social control had led directly to an emancipation of individual energies which might bring a greater degree of personal satisfaction, self-realization, and creativity.[76]

Simmel picked on two aspects of the modern social order, which had seemed most deplorable to the *Gemeinschaft* theorists, as particularly favorable to the freedom of the individual: the growth of a money economy and the development of a social organization from one based on propinquity to one based on interest. The single, public standard of value offered by the use of money was a tool of emancipation for large numbers of people formerly frozen in subordination to traditional authority. The process of social differentiation meant the creation of a multiplicity of social circles (modern scholars would say 'reference groups'); each individual belonged to a number of these and the overlap of membership meant that no one group could exercise as coercive a hold as the sealed moral envelope of the traditional community. Further, by escaping when necessary from one group to another, the individual could withhold his private personality from exposure and censure. This escape was possible, Simmel thought, because each organization in a pluralistic society demanded a specialized commitment, involving the performance of specialized roles, but none of them demanded the close moral scrutiny designed to weed out reserve or doubt, which lay at the heart of the unified moral community. The increase in the number of obligations reduced their *intensity*. The mobility of modern society allowed the individual a parallel increase in the range of choice, and thus the ability to escape a social situation which he found stultifying. A money economy increased the impersonality of society and this involved a corresponding increase in individuality.[77]

Thus, Simmel's qualified loyalty to the older liberal tradition which visualized society as a collection of independent rational individuals, was related to his preference for the *liberating* quality of that society whose ideology had conceived of man as capable of autonomous action. The contrast in moral concern between Simmel and Tönnies is striking. Leon Bramson has suggested that the early American sociologists were unusual in their inability to develop a fully organismic and determinist theory of personality, in their refusal to reduce the individual to a puppet of his group. But Simmel affords the case of a major European theorist of a similar persuasion. Unless admission to the sacred groves of sociology depends on accepting an organismic view of society and Simmel is thus placed outside, any *absolute* distinction between 'organicist' Europeans and 'individualist' Americans is weakened,[78] though Simmel's great early popularity in America (and the later decline in his influence) suggest that his work was popular because it incorporated sociological insights without forcing a violent break with American confidence in the benevolent effect of a marketplace of liberated individual atoms.

The Crowd and the Public

Park's doctoral dissertation was completed after his return to Boston in the fall of 1903.[79] The result was submitted to the philosophical faculty at Heidelberg in 1904 under the title *Masse und Publikum. Eine Methodologische und Soziologische Untersuchung*.[80] Its plan followed the subtitle closely, working through a 'methodological and sociological examination' of the concept of the crowd in an attempt to derive some understanding of the subject which Park was later to christen 'collective behavior'.[81] Park drew together recent European work on the psychology of crowds and American work on social psychology to illuminate the process by which individuals are drawn into associations of one kind or another, and to distinguish between those two characteristic social phenomena of the modern world — the crowd and the public. Like legions of frustrated scholars, Park was dissatisfied with this 'little book' which was all he had to show for the work of a full half decade.[82] Nevertheless, the book is a striking summary of, and memorial to, the philosophical and psychological background of sociology on the verge of its separation from the older disciplines. *Masse und Publikum* also summarizes the theoretical equipment which Park brought to his professional career in sociology a decade later. Several of the concepts re-appeared, a little altered, as the theoretical underpinning to his own work and that of several of his students in the 1920s and even later.[83]

Masse und Publikum was based on wide reading in political philosophy as well as European and American sociology and psychology. The literature on crowd psychology seemed the obvious starting point for Park's quest to understand the modern world, since the vogue for the subject had arisen as an attempt to discern the special qualities of the contemporary social order: its instability, the important role played by large groups of people brought into close but transitory proximity by city life, the lack of 'primary' bonds to restrain them from acting on the impulse transmitted from their fellows. As a recognized field of study, crowd psychology stemmed from the alarm felt by educated observers at what Le Bon called the 'entry of the popular classes into political life ... one of the most striking characteristics of our epoch of transition'.[84]

The nineteenth-century vogue of crowd psychology began with Hippolyte Taine's *Origins of Contemporary France*, in 1868, which had focused on the crucial role of the mob during the French Revolution. Taine blamed the crowd for foiling any chance of compromise and insuring further disorder without any apparent rational goal informing its behavior. Liberalism had torn society apart and isolated individuals now merely congregated in crowds.[85] But Taine's treatment of the crowd seemed inadequate to the theorists of the 1890s, the French physician, Gustave Le Bon, and the Italian, Scipio Sighele, whose reputations rest almost entirely on their work in this subject, and the more influential sociologist, Gabriel Tarde.[86] As Le Bon said, Taine never studied 'the genius of crowds. He took as his guide ... the descriptive method resorted to by naturalists; but the moral forces are almost absent in the case of the phenomena which naturalists have to study. Yet it is precisely these forces that constitute the true mainsprings of history.'[87]

This was the central task of the crowd theorists as they saw it — to bring within the ken of historians and philosophers the 'moral' or psychic influences which caused men to act in ways puzzling and distasteful to the rational thinker. Like other and more celebrated theorists of the decade, they were attempting to bring the sources of non-rational behavior under rational scrutiny, in obedience to Comte's dictum, *'savoir pour prévoir pour pouvoir'*. Viewed from the position of a twentieth-century social democrat, this interest represented a 'conservative' movement: men of prestige and power were disturbed by the upwelling of the masses which destroyed the genteel, club-like atmosphere with which they furnished their retrospective utopia of public life. To study the crowd was to analyze the conditions of modern democratic existence to find means of re-asserting the power of education and wealth. This retrospective interpretation, however, is only part of the story. 'Conservative', as a label for the crowd psychology school, seems misleading unless carefully specified. The standpoint of the crowd theorists was less that of medievalist organicism than of utilitarian rationalism newly aware that its account of human behavior was dangerously inadequate and trying to make amends by understanding — in terms capable of precise verbal statement — the sources and means of non-rational behavior.

Indeed, the characterization of Le Bon and Tarde as 'conservative' suggests the grave difficulties in terminology involved in clarifying the political connections of sociological theory. Certainly, social theory has had close ties to a variety of political programs, although it is less easy to specify one to one binding relations between a social theory and a political program. Comte and Spencer, for example, were both organicists, yet the one was an exponent of a planned society equilibrated by *cientificos*, the other a laissez-faire liberal in the classical style. Though in Germany the *Gemeinschaft* theorists were incorporated into the conservative political outlook, Tönnies, its most famous exponent, was a socialist, and in the United States, the *Gemeinschaft* theory had had quite different political ties and connotations than in Germany. Crowd psychology might legitimately be described as 'conservative' in an existential sense — i.e., by neglecting the concrete injustices which led crowds to act, it tended to discredit their action; it had the same reductionist, denaturing effect that psychoanalysis has when used by historians. However, by carrying this legitimate objection to its conclusion, one tends to reach the argument that all social science is necessarily an act of timid 'conservatism', since it entails the forging of intellectual bonds with which to contain the spontaneous variety of human playfulness. The scientist must reduce and classify; hence he destroys the richness of existence and defends his theories against existential challenges to their universal validity.[88]

The crowd psychologists, and Park with them, departed from a picture of the normal human being as rational, utilitarian, reflective, restraining random impulses in the name of reason so as to calculate the relations of means and ends more clearly. The crowd was fascinating just because it showed the limits of this theory. Most important, crowd study seemed to be a means of showing the limits on the utilitarian account of human behavior without discarding it altogether. The crowd was the exceptional, limiting case; but rational, reflecting man remained the norm. Certainly, this motive was strong for Park, as shown by his contrast of the crowd with the public, in which he described the crowd as ruled by instinct, the public by reason.[89]

The definition of 'crowd' in Le Bon and Sighele was broad; the term was virtually a synonym for 'social group', including not only 'heterogeneous crowds', like mobs, juries, parliamentary assemblies, but also 'homogeneous crowds', such as sects, castes, and classes. But the central concern was the apparently spontaneous, unorganized street crowd. Sighele tended to dwell on the dangerous and criminal nature of the crowd, but Le Bon stressed that the crowd was capable of great heroism as well as great crimes.[90] Park leant heavily on Le Bon and Sighele in his thesis but his concern for political stability in modern society was not so strong and he stressed the creative potential of the crowd to produce new institutions, a new order.

One of the principal attractions of the crowd as an object of study was that it promised to reveal the secret of the social, the *general* influence of human contagion on rational behavior which was everywhere present but disguised in more formal institutions by the weight of historical fixity which channeled action into accepted patterns − neither rational nor non-rational, but predictable because traditional.[91] All the crowd psychologists insisted that the individual was in some way transformed by joining a crowd, becoming both less and more than himself. Le Bon, under the influence of Durkheim, declared that a new collective mentality is created out of the crowd which then determines its behavior.[92] *Masse und Publikum* reflected Park's attempt to generalize crowd theory into an adequate social psychology, which would demonstrate in specific detail the way men were influenced by the contagion of their fellows, and the psychic mechanisms in individuals which conditioned their social behavior. As he said later in his course on 'The Crowd and The Public' at Chicago, 'sociology is necessarily social psychology'.[93]

In 1904 sociology had not yet developed a 'canon', a convention of disciplinary relevance to dictate those writers who had made a significant contribution and needed to be considered. Therefore, in a manner both refreshingly broad-minded and inevitably inconclusive, Park ranged widely in the material he used, from technical psychologists, such as William James and George Frederick Stout, through social psychologists like Le Bon, Tarde, and Sighele, back to the philosophers Rousseau, Hume, and Adam Smith. *Masse und Publikum* concentrated on two subjects: the social genesis of the individual personality and those aspects of individual psychology which lead men into closer association with one another. Park drew together, from varied sources, the emerging theory of the social genesis of personality, which was developing from the work of neoidealist philosophers and pragmatic psychologists. In England, the idealist school of F.H.Bradley, Bernard Bosanquet, and T.H.Green, dissatisfied with British empiricism and the individualism of Bentham and James Mill, stressed the interdependence of individual and society and the finding of the 'true self' only by participation in a larger whole.[94] William James's conception of the 'social self' reinforced this whole train of thought. For James, the influences forming the self included the images carried by other people, so that a man would have as many selves as there were individuals or groups who knew him.[95] Josiah Royce stressed that man's conception of himself, his self-consciousness, is a product of social experience; the child gains an awareness of himself as a separate person by his attemps to imitate the words and actions of others.[96]

Like many American academics, Park was drawn to Gabriel Tarde's concept of 'imitation' as the way in which social forms, traditions, and new ideas are spread and accepted throughout society.

This minute inter-agreement of minds and wills, which forms the basis of social life, even in troublous times – this presence of so many common ideas, ends, and means, in the minds and wills of all members of the same society at any given moment ... is ... the effect of that suggestion-imitation process which, starting from one primitive creature possessed of a single idea or act, passed this copy on to one of its neighbors, then to another, and so on. Organic needs and spiritual tendencies exist in us only as potentialities which are realizable under the most diverse forms, in spite of their primitive similarity; and, among all these possible realizations, the indications furnished by some first initiator who is imitated determine which one is actually chosen.[97]

The idea of imitation, like so many other popular doctrines of this period, was an attempt to specify the post-Calvinist truism that human nature is originally plastic but quickly becomes fixed. Tarde's idea is a less fruitful parallel to the theories of child development which Freud was evolving at the same time.

On the relationship of the individual to social influences Park borrowed from the work of the American psychologist, James Mark Baldwin. Baldwin was one of the most frequently cited men in Park's book and was very widely influential among American sociologists in encouraging an approach to society through the psychological analysis of individuals.[98] He insisted that the rigid dualist concepts like *ego* and *alter*, the individual and the social, were unfortunate abstractions, clouding the central core of any true social psychology — that the development of the individual and society are closely interwoven. 'We can get no doctrine of society but by getting the psychology of the "socius" with all his natural history; and on the other hand, we can get no true view of the "socius" at any time without describing the social conditions under which he normally lives, with the history of their action and reaction upon him'.[99] Through the socializing process of 'imitation' the individual and the social are integrated as mutually interacting factors in a common process of personal and social development. The child acquires a sense of himself by imitating others, and his sense of those others grows in terms of his sense of himself; 'ego and alter are thus essentially social; each is a *socius* and each is an imitative creation'.[100] Beyond this process of socialization, imitation became for Baldwin, and for Park, the more general process by which the individual is gently coerced and kept within bounds by society without violence — the prime element of social cohesion. Through imitation tradition was transmitted. Tradition is not only an external compulsion, but by becoming internalized as a norm it compelled the individual conscience as well.[101]

Baldwin's extended use of 'imitation' led Park to the definition of society. Individuals become a society when they have internalized customs, beliefs, norms, and accept them as ethically binding. In this way, a General Will — Park used Rousseau's term — is generated, which is more than the sum of the individual wills constituting the society. Just as the 'will' of the individual is not merely the sum of his impulses and drives at any one moment, but a more general tendency which constitutes the continuity of his personality, so the General Will of a society is that principle of continuity which enables us to see the *same* society at different stages in its history, as a continuous thing. This General Will expresses itself in custom, and then in ethical norms.[102] Park noted the tradition which ascribed the essence of society to a consciousness of fellow feeling — what the American sociologist Franklin H.Giddings called 'consciousness of kind'. Giddings had derived this idea from Adam Smith's *Theory of the Moral Sentiments* and Park used both Smith and David Hume as well as Giddings to show that the 'natural faculty' of sympathy in man awakes in him a fellow feeling with and understanding of the sentiments of others and thus makes society possible. However, Park insisted that more than sympathy was needed to make and maintain a society. The crucial bond was a normative General Will which enables men to act in concert. This General Will is often in opposition not only to individual desires, but also to the course of conduct suggested by sympathy. It is a slowly developed code of conduct, enforced by the recognition of the utility of common action.[103]

Park used his discussion of the General Will to illuminate by contrast the nature of the crowd and the public. These are both transitional social group-ings, fluid masses formed out of the dissolution or merging of older, stable groups, sects, and classes. New sects and classes will ultimately emerge from the volatile crowds and publics of the present. Crowd and public are ahistori-cal, with no past, no tradition, and no permanence. Once, however, a group separates itself from others and becomes self-conscious, it begins to build up a tradition, which becomes in turn the material from which a norm will be generated. In this way, the transitory will of all, which arises in moments of crisis, is converted into a General Will. Neither crowd nor public, however, are ruled by a normative General Will. Thus, they are vehicles of change, the embryonic expression of new interest groups. To Park, crowd and public were not merely symptomatic of the breakdown of an old order, they were the crucible of a new: the social unrest expressed by the crowd would eventually express itself in an organized movement, and when the movement died it would leave behind its essence crystalized in the forms of institutions. In Park, if not in Le Bon, crowd theory was formalized into a value-free explanation of social change.[104]

Park completed his thesis by elaborating the distinction between crowd and public. Tarde had also made such a distinction, but in rather more simple terms than Park. To Tarde, the public was a product of the printing press: the limits of a crowd were defined by the limits to which a human voice could carry, but a public arose in a higher stage of civilization in which suggestions are transmitted in the form of ideas and there is 'contagion without contact'.[105] Park, on the other hand, defined the difference between crowd and public in terms of the forms and effects of the interactions they embody. In the public this interaction takes the form of discussion, individuals act upon one another critically, opinions clash, parties are formed, the opposing opinions modify one another. The crowd, on the other hand, does not discuss or reflect, but simply 'mills', seeking an outlet for its discontent. From this restless milling, a collective impulse is formed which dominates all the mem-bers of the crowd. While sects, parties, or ordinary friendly society impose a 'moral' entry test on aspiring members — one has to abide by the norms of that particular group — the crowd and the public impose only psychological requirements. To be a member of the crowd one needs to be able to feel, to empathize with others; to be a member of the public one needs to be able to think, to participate in a rational discussion. This is the main distinction between crowd and public: the public is critical, opinions in it are split. 'If it stops being critical it breaks apart or changes into a crowd'.[106]

The ethical implication of Park's distinction between 'Crowd' and 'Public' was optimistic, characteristically 'progressive'. Crowd and public were alike in the sense that both were individualistic forms of organization, whose members were not controlled by tradition or custom but largely by the human stimuli of the moment; but only the crowd could rightly be considered anarchistic because of this emancipation from control. The public, although not ruled by any customary norm, not accepting any traditional set of beliefs, was nonetheless under 'the rule of reason', that is, characterized by the ethical norm enjoining rational discussion and adjustment of problems. Park protested that he was making no value judgment between crowd and public but only a formal, Simmelian distinction.[107] Nevertheless, his whole discussion seems to offer a reply to the conservatives of the *Gemeinschaft* tradition. The modern world, Park said, offers *two* alternatives to traditional society, not only the crowd, swayed by the emotion of the moment, but also the public, emanicapated from customary beliefs but not from the capacity for rational discussion of means and ends: the enlightened public in which Dewey and the progressives put their faith was a real possibility. Thus, as he prepared to return to the world of men and things, Park had arrived at a theoretical position which gave meaning and validity to the publicity work in which he would spend the coming decade.

For a decade after their return from Germany in the autumn of 1903, Robert Park and his family made their permanent home in Wollaston, Massachusetts, across the Neponset River from Boston on the Old Colony Railway.[1] While he wrote *Masse und Publikum,* Park served as course assistant to Munsterberg and Royce at Harvard. Park's feeling upon completing his work was probably similar to that of innumerable scholars: he was profoundly dissatisfied with it, and indeed with his professional life as a whole. He was forty years old, yet 'all I had to show was that little book and I was ashamed of it'.[2] Once again, the problem of choosing a meaningful career arose. The obvious choice would have been to teach philosophy or sociology in a college or university. But there were serious obstacles. Park was on the verge of middle age; his personal dignity and charm were offset by his lack of previous teaching experience and of the quick wit, self-assurance, and impeccable grooming which an institution was likely to demand of a mature candidate. Philosophy seemed to offer little hope; William James had warned Park before he left for Germany that he was not intelligent enough to make a contribution in that field.[3] There remained sociology, where the stimulus of the concrete might move Park's deliberate but reflective mind to distinguished effort. But even this field of study seemed barren, after the tedious grind of graduate work. One summer shortly after 1904, at his father-in-law's summer home in Michigan, Park met Albion W. Small, chairman of the sociology department at the University of Chicago. Small offered Park a summer term's teaching job, as an experiment, but Park was not interested;[4] he had become disenchanted with the life of scholarship as he had earlier lost interest in newspaper work.

So, after five years devoted exclusively to study and reflection, Park turned away from the academy for the second time. Always a 'seeker', he now sought a new commitment to 'real life', something that would give him a solid sense of achievement.[5] For a time, Park seriously considered going to South Africa to offer his services to Cecil Rhodes. The empire builder, he thought, was clearly an achiever, and seemed to offer a cause of sufficient scope and value to maintain the identity of a man still determined to overcome his sense of futility.[6] Before he decided for or against the imperial role, however, an accidental meeting with the secretary of the Baptist Missionary Society in Boston deflected Park into a rather different path. Through the missionary, he met other officers of the Congo Reform Association, and soon put his journalistic ties to work as secretary and chief publicity agent.[7] Since the 1890s there had been some disquiet in Europe and the United States about the state of brutality and exploitation in the Congo Free State, controlled by Leopold II of Belgium; feelings were especially aroused by the campaign led by E.D. Morel in England, and by the disclosures of William Morrison, an American Presbyterian missionary in the Kasai region, about the use of forced labor. On his return to the United States in 1903, Morrison began a · campaign to stir the Protestant mission boards to action, and to arouse public opinion. As a result of the agitation, the Congo Reform Association was formed and led an active life for the next few years, keeping the Congo continuously in the news and flooding Congress with petitions.[8] Park's job as secretary and press agent for the Boston branch was principally to publicize the whole Congo situation and stir up indignation, which he did by enlisting the aid of prominent figures, lobbying with congressmen for United States pressure on the Congo government, and writing a series of articles to be signed by notables. Park also produced three articles published under his own name in *Everybody's* magazine, a muckraking journal which compensated for its lack of *McClure's* solid content by a breathless, excited style.[9]

When Park's own Congo articles finally appeared in December 1906 and January 1907, they were well-timed to intensify the public petition campaign in support of the Lodge Resolution authorizing diplomatic pressure on Leopold and the Congo government.[10] But the author himself had lost interest in the moral, activist approach, typified by the Congo Reform Association. Park's personal response to imperialism was epitomized by his rapid conversion from disciple of Cecil Rhodes to hammer of King Leopold: the westernization of Africa was inevitable, and a sublime exercise of the will, yet inevitability did not rob the attendant cruelty of its horror. A few months at close quarters with the avenging ministers, however, sapped Park's indignation, and convinced him that the CRA offered no effective solution. Their agitation for improved administration barely scratched the surface of a problem which was basically political − the need to reestablish authority in a power vacuum created by European penetration and exploitation, and, more deeply, to recreate a social order completely shattered by the great historical process of European expansion. 'The Congo, like some other parts of Africa, was suffering from a kind of political disease which...seems to have been endemic everywhere the Europeans have attempted to uplift and civilize the peoples they call natives; civilize by incorporating them in the growing world economy which the expansion of the European peoples has created.'[11]

Expansion would continue, would complete the destruction of native institutions and leave Europeans with the duty of constructing an alternative life for the victims of progress. Political agitation against cruelty was grossly inadequate, and the Christian missions, so long as they confined themselves to religious instruction, were little more useful. Park's revulsion from the CRA was deep and lasting. The suspicion and contempt for 'reformers' which this experience reinforced never left him. Recalling the episode almost four decades later, he remarked that the secretary of the Baptist Mission Society was angry mainly because 'the Congo Free State favored the Belgian Catholic Missions rather than the Protestant missions. I didn't take much stock in their atrocity stories. This man got in returned missionaries and dragged stuff out of them. He made them sweat under his questions and would finally force stuff out of them. I certainly got the low-down on missionaries from this experience.'[12]

The comment reflects a naïveté which infected Park despite his broad experience, and is of great interest since it illuminates the emotional attitudes of so many Americans toward 'reform' and achievement. There can be no doubt that atrocities were committed on a vast scale in the Congo. But Park was hypersensitive to the problem of 'sincerity' and 'honesty' of method and intention in the reformers themselves, the moralistic nay-sayers who wished to intervene and save the world from its men of constructive vision and action. It did not seem to occur to him that the missionaries were reluctant to tell the truth because they feared the loss of privileges granted by the Congo government. Park's attitude illustrates the moral disadvantage faced by the critic and 'negative thinker' in a system that exalts activity. Criticism, however justified by the facts, is rejected because of its roots in anger; and the lesser psychic corruption of the reformer is rejected as an evil greater than the physical damage done by the Rhodes and King Leopolds, men of imperial vision and executive ability.

Despite his cynicism, or perhaps before it hardened, Park managed to turn out a lurid denunciation of Leopold's régime for *Everybody's*. The Congo was run as a capitalist enterprise, with profit as the only consideration; the souls and lives of men were subordinated to the overriding goal of efficiency. Park emphasized the personality and role of Leopold II, describing him as a brilliant man, forceful and emancipated from moral scruples. The lurid prose made Leopold a mythic figure, an archetype of the sublime, awful superman using his own freedom from tradition to exploit the conventional morality of ordinary men. 'A new figure looms large on the horizon of Europe! A figure strange, fantastic, and ominous − the King who is capitalist, *le roi d'affaires*; the man who unites in himself the political and social prestige of a reigning monarch with the vast material power of a multimillionaire.'[13]

Most fascinating of all was Leopold's press machine, 'a machine grinding tirelessly night and day, that its owner may pose as a Philanthropist and not be exposed as the Vampire. ...Nothing reveals him as the modern business king so plainly as does this mechanism, which involves the most highly perfected business methods of the twentieth century.'[14] The existence of this huge organization demonstrated Leopold's awareness of the power of public opinion; and its success showed how easily that opinion could be manipulated.

These articles interpreted Leopold II in terms familiar to the regular readers of *McClure's* and *Everybody's*, but it is not clear how much they reflected Park's own attitude. They were written in a tone of suppressed, sustained hysteria quite different from Park's deliberate, ruminative style, and they embodied an interpretation of events in terms of personal volition which Park later came to regard as superficial and unscientific. The two themes which stand out so strongly in these articles — Leopold as corrupting capitalist superman, and the *manipulation*, as distinguished from the *importance*, of public opinion — were not major concerns in Park's later work. Whether or not exaggerated in the case of the Congo, both themes expressed a personalized, devil-figure theory of history which Park found less and less congenial. Certainly, he later regarded his whole position in the Congo Reform Association as a false one. Park thought of himself as a scientific observer, not as a muckraker. Muckraking journalists, of course, covered a wide spectrum of topics, from vivid descriptions of the exotic to fervent moral indignation at remediable evil — a spectrum which represents the contrasting styles of American liberalism as a whole, ranging from activist, moral denunciation to a tolerant, passive appreciation of ways of life beyond the pale of Protestant, middle-class America. The exigencies of drumming up public fury over Congo atrocities necessarily drove Park into the first style of response, but his own predilections lay with the second. Careful, sympathetic accounts of immigrant life, such as those in Hutchins Hapgood's *Spirit of the Ghetto* (1903) were closer to Park's natural style of sublimating discontent into understanding.[15]

Park's years with the Congo Reform Association added more to his continuing education than disillusion with popular reform. The Congo Reform Association experience supplied him with another of the permanent concerns which would later become specialties of Chicago sociology. His fascinated study of race relations and cultural contacts on a world-wide basis, and his insistence on the historical and cross cultural perspective, certainly reflect the Congo Reform period. Because Park approached Tuskegee and Chicago through vicarious contact with the Congo, he 'discovered' race relations in a novel manner. The Congo was not an apparently stable situation, where the established pattern of inequality seemed a reflection of innate racial traits. Instead, it was a setting in which the process of European political control and commercial exploitation was compressed into a single generation, where the close historical ties of 'the race question' to human migration and economies were vividly displayed. His knowledge of the Congo conditioned Park to see the 'Negro problem' in the U.S. 'as an aspect or a phase of the native problem in Africa; it was ... a problem which, like slavery, had arisen as an incident in an historical process and as a phase of the natural history of civilization.'[16]

The link between Park's interest in the Congo and the continuing 'Chicago' tradition in the study of race relations can be traced down to the two symposia published by his students after the Second World War. Both volumes reflect the Park influence in their comparative, historical orientation, their concern to identify the processes of race relations by analyzing ethnic contact in a wide variety of situations, rather than through close analysis either of alleged 'racial' traits of behavior or through constructing psychological theories of the motives for racial discrimination in 'majority' groups.[17]

One aspect of the Congo situation impressed Park as more useful than political agitation and led him directly to the next and most important stage of his half century's preparation for sociology. While studying Christian missionary work in the Congo, he came across the efforts of some missionaries to teach European trades and methods of work to their converts, to provide them not only with spiritual but material aids for absorption into white civilization. 'As there was, however, no possibility of reversing this civilizing process, and very little hope of slowing it up, the only effective remedy that suggested itself to me was some form of education...that would prepare not merely the natives but the European invaders, as well, for the kind of world in which they were both inescapably destined to live.'[18]

Education Completed: Tuskegee and Booker T. Washington

While seeking support for the agitation to persuade Congress to discuss the Congo, Park met the last and most important of his teachers — Booker T. Washington of Tuskegee Institute, who in 1905 was at the height of his fame and influence as the Negro spokesman recognized by white benevolent and political elites. Washington devoted a good deal of attention to African affairs, both as educator and as a mediator between Africa and the white powers. Early in the new century, he had sent Tuskegee graduates to Togo where they were to co-operate with German officials in training the natives to grow cotton.[19] Washington became a vice-president of the CRA and made personal efforts to persuade President Theodore Roosevelt to put diplomatic pressure on the Belgian government.[20] In several conversations, Park discussed with Washington his idea that the Congo needed a system of education on the Tuskegee pattern.[21] As a result, he received an invitation to visit Tuskegee to study practical education for Negroes at first-hand. Even before Park made the trip, Washington had offered him a position as press agent, which was accepted tentatively. Here, at last, seemed something worth doing. Park's first publicity work for Tuskegee was done early in 1905, while still working for the CRA. His visit to the South did not take place until the autumn of that year. Until the trip, Park remained uncertain whether to associate himself with Tuskegee, and unsure as to what his relations to Washington and the other employees would be. He still toyed with the idea of travelling to Africa, now to study Christian missions, after preparing himself with first-hand know-ledge of the American South. But Tuskegee proved fascinating, and Park did not set foot in Africa until the 1930s, when after retiring from the University of Chicago he toured South Africa and observed the westernization of the Bantu via labor in the mines, and relaxation in night clubs and at Hollywood films.[22]

Until 1905, Park had known the South and the Southern Negro only through books, so that his leisurely journey to Tuskegee became 'a voyage of exploration and discovery'. He read all the local newspapers and talked to everyone he met, discovering 'the extent to which the lives of colored folk and white had been articulated if not integrated into a common pattern of life'.[23] The fascination of this pattern, and the joy of participating in a great experi-ment, held him at Tuskegee for the next seven years.

Association with Tuskegee had a special attraction for Robert Park, since it managed to overcome his sense of irrelevance without involving him in the sort of genteel reform activity which was the typical outlet for superfluous men and women, but distasteful to Park. He made clear that he did not wish to be engaged in 'philanthropic' or 'unselfish' work, perhaps because these roles implied both condescension and a confident certainty which Park did not possess. The Tuskegee program of 'industrial' education, a cause both practical and relevant, was a gentler surrogate for the 'civilizing' work which Cecil Rhodes embodied in Africa. Park himself knew how vital it was that he find a compelling role; as his earlier ambitions faded, he recalled, he felt the 'shades of prison walls descend' and faced the melancholy truth of maturity, that he would never 'disturb the course of history'. But he might still be able to serve in the ranks of some cause; and Washington, 'a man engaged in a fundamental task who has a sense of reality...who knows what should be done, and how to do it', offered the cause.[24] 'I was disgusted with what I had done in the University and had come to the conclusion that I couldn't do anything first rate on my own account. I decided the best thing to do was to attach myself to someone who was doing something first rate. Washington was not a brilliant man or an intellectual, but he seemed to me to be doing something real. So I went'.[25] At Tuskegee, then, Park found a 'task and a vocation', and finally completed his education.[26]

Park began his tenure at Tuskegee just as the Institute reached the crest of its fame as the center of Southern Negro life, the leader in the task of assimilating Negroes to the American ethic of self-discipline, through a program of 'industrial' or vocational education. The Institute now spread over a sizeable campus outside the county seat town of Tuskegee, Macon County, Alabama; its total enrollment was nearly 1,500 students, divided into five departments — Agricultural, Mechanical, Health, Girls' Industries, Academic. When Theodore Roosevelt recognized Tuskegee's symbolic value with a visit, on 24 October 1905, the school mustered '984 Young Men, in

Institute Uniform...made by students of the Tailoring Division, ...519 Young Women, in Institute Uniform...made in the Millinery and Dressmaking Divisions...Each of the young men and young women bearing a stalk of sugar cane, tipped with cotton boll, both raised in the school's Agricultural Experiment Stations'[27] to march before the president. The facade of prosperity masked serious problems, however, notably a very high rate of turnover. Of 1,621 students enrolled in the Spring of 1906, more than 200 dropped out during the term.[28]

The second Theodore Roosevelt administration marked the zenith of Booker T. Washington's political influence. He had a number of offices at his disposal and all of Roosevelt's Negro appointments were made on his recommendation.[29] Approaching the age of fifty, the stocky former slave was a figure of international repute. Washington's web of influence in government and business was so complex by 1905 that he was frequently absent from the Institute and day-to-day administration had largely passed from his hands. Tuskegee was the center of his power, his little kingdom where, as Park recalled, he acted the little Napoleon, but his personal oversight was no longer thorough.[30]

Park performed a variety of duties for Washington during his six to nine months away from Boston each year. Summers were passed with his own family in Wollaston, Mass., with time out for visits to Washington's summer estate on Long Island; but Park was considered a full-time employee of Tuskegee, and much of his summer time was taken up with the writing and revision of articles for Washington's signature – the prime task he had agreed to undertake, but often crowded out at Tuskagee by lectures, routine administration, special investigations, and other assignments. The letters of the early years at Tuskegee especially, reveal Park as eager to assume as many difficult tasks as Washington would allow, to make himself useful, and at the same time to explore thoroughly Negro life in the South.[31]

At various times Park investigated riots and lynchings, inventoried the Institute library, and acted as an intermediary between Washington and 'respectable' Southern whites who wanted Tuskegee's support for a vigilant committee designed to protect Southern womanhood. Most important, however, was Park's work as ghost writer and public relations man. The prestige of Tuskegee, and of Booker Washington, rested not only on political influence and ties with wealthy philanthropists, but also upon their publicity value: the Institute and Negro education in general, and Booker T. Washington's opinion on a wide variety of subjects, were marketable products. Tuskegee's program embodied the aspiration and activism which audiences expected of their entertainment, and editors welcomed Washington's signature as an acceptable by-line for spacefillers. Similarly, publicity was an essential element in the Tuskegee campaign for improving Negro morals and morale via practical education, and for building closer ties between Negroes and whites in the South: the results of Tuskegee education must be publicized to destroy the harmful stereotype of the lazy Negro.

Park's primary function was always to maintain the flow of articles, books, and press releases.[32] He thought of new subjects to appear over Washington's signature — the sequel to *Up from Slavery*, a series of sketches of prominent businessmen and their relations to Tuskegee called *My Larger Education*, was conceived and largely executed by Park, who saw it as an account of Washington's moral development through association with 'big men'.[33]

Park also did a great deal of work for Washington's two volume *Story of the Negro*,[34] in which he anticipated the 'life-history' method he later used in sociology, making extensive use of interviews with Negroes to give both solidity and human depth to his narrative.[35] While *The Story of the Negro* has long been superseded as a scholarly account of slave law or the origins of slavery in America, the special Tuskegee perspective gave it permanent value as an account of Negro life at the turn of the century. Washington and Park were concerned to present data on the material achievements of Negro businessmen, farmers, artisans in the 1880s and 90s, and also on the apparent growth of Negro crime, which other historians, projecting different biases, have discussed less fully.[36]

The process of composing *The Story of the Negro* was typical of Park's writing tasks for Tuskegee. Washington and his staff had gathered a mass of material culled from the press, their own interviews, and standard histories. Working from these, Park submitted for Washington's approval, in the summer of 1906, an outline of the first chapter — 'the ideas and the order in which they should be stated. If you approve of this I will write it out in full, incorporating the parts of your Ms that fit. ...'[37] Two years, as many books, and a half dozen articles later, Park outlined the concluding chapters of volume two, which would incorporate the Tuskegee line on racial self-help and supply examples of its success. The method of composition seems again to anticipate Park's own theoretical essays and some of the Chicago sociology series twenty years later. Park would sketch the chapters, then 'distribute through these chapters some personal anecdotes that I have gathered which are interesting and illustrate the work that colored individuals have done, and the progress they have made'.[38] Park's public relations work has ironic fascination for later observers. It is the first of many ways in which Park's career seems an anticipation of the anonymous corporate quality of work in the social sciences. In the work he did for Washington it is difficult to know exactly what ideas and phrases are his, which those of Washington or his secretary Emmett Scott. Washington himself confessed that he could often not distinguish 'how much what I have written is based upon my own personal observations and what is based upon those of Dr. Park'.[39]

Meanwhile, Park's own education continued, along with his toil over books to be signed by another. Not only direct contact in the South, but reading on race relations the world over, was building the comparative perspective which Park would later plant at the University of Chicago. 'One surprising fact I have learned is that there are more than 11,000,000 Negroes and people of African blood in the West Indies and S. America.' More attention should be paid to these people, 'especially as in many parts of the world they are doing very well'. In a manner foreshadowing the later work, Park tried to gather episodes reflecting the 'human nature side of the story' from local histories and plant them in an interpretative structure based on 'the economic side of the question, because that is the controlling factor: the thing that made slavery and is unmaking it'.[40]

Park's contribution was especially large, and was overtly acknowledged, in the planning and writing of *The Man Farthest Down*, a description of the peasantry, the urban working class, and the sub-proletarian drifters of Europe, from material gathered on a tour which Washington and Park made in 1910. Park crossed the Atlantic some months in advance — on a slow boat to save half the fare — while Washington followed later on the *Lusitania*.[41] In Europe, Park made the plans for the trip and searched out the situations that Washington would want to see. When Washington arrived they travelled around together, jotting down notes on anything that took their interest and comparing and sifting them during the long railway journeys between cities. Then Washington would dictate an account to a stenographer based on both his and Park's observations. Park would then hunt up documentation for their generalizations and bring the whole manuscript into shape.[42]

On the trip Park learned a good deal more about Booker Washington. He noted that Washington was always cautious, unconsciously on his guard when away from the controlled environment of Tuskegee. In Europe as in America, he got on well with most people he met, although never 'quite as humble as white folks like Negroes to be'. Wherever they went in Europe, Washington was interested in the pattern of land holding and methods of farming — 'the relationship of the man to the land was basic in his philosophy'. Park too, was interested in the way that 'tribal lands get into the hands, as they invariably do, of a landlord who transforms the man on the soil from an owner to a tenant'. Understandably enough, when asked questions about this process at a dinner given by Andrew Carnegie for Washington at Skibo Castle in the Scottish Highlands, he produced general embarrassment and received no clear answer.[43]

Washington's avowed intention on the trip was to see the real working people of Europe, not the palaces or cathedrals or museums: 'I have never been greatly interested in the past, for the past is something that you cannot change. I like the new, the unfinished and the problematic. My experience is that the man who is interested in living things must seek them in the grime and dirt of everyday life.'[44] In pursuit of populist reality, Park and Washington journeyed through England, Scotland, Germany, Austria, Hungary, Italy,

Sicily, Poland, and Denmark, talking to Polish peasants, London derelicts, and Sicilian miners. In Sicily, hundreds of feet down in a sulphur mine, Washington met a man who, like himself, had once worked in the coal mines of West Virginia, and reflected that 'there seemed to be no part of Europe so distant or so remote that the legend of America had not penetrated to it.' Everywhere, Washington stressed, he found the lot of the poorest classes in Europe to be worse than that of Negroes in the U.S. At least, 'The Negro is not as a rule a degenerate. If he is at the bottom of America, it is not because he has gone backward and sunk down, but because he has never risen...although he is frequently poor, he is never without hope and a certain joy in living.'[45] Throughout the tour, Washington's reactions were so chauvinistic that Park doubted later how much he really learned. 'When he was abroad he was not interested in the common people as I thought he would be. They were just foreigners. He was an American and thought everything in America surpassed anything in Europe. He just wanted to get the dirt on them that was all, to discover for himself that the man farthest down in Europe had nothing on the man farthest down in the U.S.'[46]

In writing *The Man Farthest Down*, Park struggled to strike a balance between Washington's eagerness to prove how much better off American Negroes were than European peasants and proletarians, the demand of *The Outlook* (in which the book was serialized) for colorful anecdotes, and his own concern for accuracy and balance. *The Outlook* demanded that the 'human side' be stressed in a 'simple, straightforward way'. Washington complained that Park had not made 'vivid enough' the contrast between the European city workers and the urban Negro in America — with the latter being 'many per cent better'.[47]

Between the larger assignments came the preparation of numerous articles on themes which might interest editors. Orison Swett Marden of *Success* was interested in the biographies of successful Negroes; the *Ladies' Home Journal* might respond to a description of Mrs. Washington's Mothers' Meetings at Tuskegee; Walter Hines Page might take a photo story on industrial education at Tuskegee for *World's Work*; Oswald Villard's *New York Evening Post* received an account by Park of Booker T. Washington's visit to his birthplace in Franklin County, Virginia; the *Independent* might like a brief sketch of a Negro-operated knitting mill at Weldon, North Carolina.[48] All were grist for the Tuskegee publicity mill. Some of the articles on which Park labored, together with Emmett J. Scott, were more directly intended to counteract unfair publicity given to Negroes. When the *American Magazine* published a story derogatory to Negro women, Washington's protests to the editor earned the promise of a 'balancing' true tale of some Tuskegee girl graduate who had gone on to good work in the world.[49] Exploiting more directly his old newspaper contacts, Park worked at the classic public relations job, planting stories and references favorable to Tuskegee in the daily press. Park followed up formal news items with editorials discussing the valuable work done at Tuskegee, writing them himself or supplying information for them, as the editors chose.[50]

A characteristic example of Park's work was a news item which he wrote for the *Springfield Republican* in 1909, whose title faithfully summarized the tone and content of at least the published portion: 'The Negroes of Tennessee. Booker Washington's Campaign for Education and Racial Peace. ...What was Found of Negro Progress. ...An Encouraging Situation.' The article recounted a tour by Washington and a party of Negro businessmen through the state. The party included the most prosperous businessmen in the Negro community and the article emphasized their savings and investments, their prosperous businesses and homes, their respectability of estate and tone. Conflict was glossed over; Washington himself was quoted as saying that 'A large part of our race troubles in the South are in the newspapers. When a man is running for office he will say almost anything. Frequently I have found that the persons who talk the loudest in public against the Negro are in private, when at home, his best friends.' Southerners were still unconvinced of the capacity of the Negro to profit by education, but the onus lay on the Negro to prove that once educated 'he becomes a better and more useful citizen'. The article concluded with Washington's oft repeated idea that in all fundamental things the interests of the two races were one.[51]

Much of Park's time during the winter months was spent in residence at Tuskegee and he took an active, if irregular, part in the school's program of teaching. He spoke on such subjects as 'How to Read a Book' to the Literary Scouts, an organization of Tuskegee graduates living near the school, and on 'Natural Science, History and the Negro' to the Science Club of the Agricultural Department, and he drew up an annotated list of books for students who wished to continue their reading privately.[52]

Park was fascinated by Washington's program of industrial education, of which the goal was not only to teach specific skills but to encourage self-respect through the sense of proficiency given by mastery of a trade. Washington had been stamped permanently with the rigid moral training he received from Samuel C. Armstrong at Hampton Institute in Virginia. Armstrong, the child of a missionary family in Hawaii, was anxious to apply in the South the lesson of the schools he had seen at home: the inculcation of personal discipline and social morality through vocational education. Along with specific skills, Armstrong taught the student 'that labor was a spiritual force, that physical work not only increased wage-earning capacity but promoted fidelity, accuracy, honesty, persistence and intelligence'.[53] Washington added to this moral concern an emphasis on direct confrontation with 'things', with 'real life'. As a young teacher, Washington had discovered that even unbookish children learned geography with pleasure when it was taught through an appeal to the play impulse by personal exploration of the countryside. Pupils must study 'actual things' and the situations of 'real life' first hand, rather than theorize about them in abstraction.[54]

Clearly this program was appealing to Park, after his education by Dewey, James, and the hard school of police-court reporting. However much his own sociological theorizing may have reflected the concepts he had studied in Germany more than the problem at hand, Park never tired of stressing in later years that theory must emerge from the practical problems of interpreting social reality, a first-hand acquaintance with the materials: 'sociologists cannot solve their problems by dialectics merely.'[55] In his letters and discussions of the Tuskegee educational program, Park stressed again and again its conformity to the canon of progressive education: the youth was taught moral lessons in accuracy and honesty by learning a skill, and he was encouraged to understand the relation of his own job to the larger economy by classroom teaching and by participation in joint work projects on campus. The teacher made arithmetic 'relevant' by assigning problems arising from the student's workshop projects. In the classroom, students reported on their manual work and what it meant. English compositions were made meaningful to the culturally impoverished student because they were about the actual stuff of his life: they were exercises in communication, in which he must explain in non-technical language the detailed processes involved in his job.[56] At the frequent conferences through which Tuskegee publicized its methods and achievements to local Negroes and Northern philanthropists, the students acted out their job routines — for example, the making of bricks or the daily work of the campus post office — while a teacher read out statistics about the number of bricks or letters. Park was deeply impressed by the value of these exercises in contrast 'with the Friday afternoon rhetoricals with their frigid little essays that I remembered from my own school days', and tried to defend the Tuskegee program against the charges of anti-intellectualism made by its critics among the Negro 'radicals.'[57]

Given the great isolation in which the children of sharecroppers grew up, Park felt it was difficult to make them appreciate the value of verbal or symbolic material. Speaking to G. Stanley Hall's Pedagogical Seminary at Clark University on 'the feeling of reality and its relation to education', Park stressed his conviction 'that only by doing things could the average colored boy get the idea that education had any relation to real life'.[58] Libraries and books were strange and fearful to the children of the plantation, even more than to those of the corner drugstore and the branch bank. The students at Tuskegee lacked a tradition of written literature, as well as the minimum knowledge of the civilized world needed to understand many books easily available to the 'ordinary schoolboy', like *Mother Goose* or the fairy stories of Hans Christian Andersen. The Negro students, Park found, responded best to the great Western myths, based on oral tradition, like the *Iliad, Odyssey*, and tales of King Arthur, which were 'large and simple in outline'.[59]

Since the goal of Tuskegee education was self-improvement and the development of group consciousness, programs for continuing study and for keeping the graduates involved in the life of the Institute were important. The conferences on which Washington placed so much emphasis were secularized revival meetings, where individual farmers came forward to bear witness to their self-sacrifice and success in gaining control of property.[60] At the twenty-first annual Tuskegee Negro Conference in 1912, 'the general subject of discussion was "How I have improved my farm," subdivided into sections on "the house I used to live in and the house I now live in"; "the conveniences I have provided in and around my house, especially the water supply"; "How I used to farm my land and how I now farm it"; "The farm tools I once used and the farm machinery I now use"; "The livestock I once owned and the livestock I now own." '

The walls of the Institute chapel were decorated with mottoes designed to impress the Tuskegee philosophy of self-help, self-discipline, and the parallel improvement of moral and material standards.

Every farmer should own and improve his home because he owes it to his family; he owes it to his neighbor; he owes it to his country; he owes it to his God. See that the school in your community runs eight months during the year. Go down in your pocket and support your school. ...Get rid of the immoral ministers in your community. Have a painted, seated and comfortable church. ...When you bring your wives and children to town do not leave them to loaf about the streets and in public places. ...Now is the time to begin to save something. ...Spend every moment that you can putting trash on the compost heap. ...Send your children regularly to school.[61]

The program was spread beyond the immediate hinterland of Tuskegee by graduates who taught in rural schools, and by a Negro demonstration farm program based on the Institute.[62] Park himself contributed to the goal of continuing education by preparing an annotated list of 'Books every Tuskegee graduate should know', together with rules for reading them profitably and not just for pleasure. 'Read every night, before going to bed, at least one good sentence; think what it means as you are going to sleep, and try to remember it first thing next morning. ...Never read any but Good Books. A good book is one that you will desire to read two or three times, one that leaves a cheerful, hopeful flavor in your memory or that gives you a helpful thought.'

Park's list, graded according to difficulty, began with *Alice in Wonderland* and the Grimm's *German Household Tales* and worked up to Emerson's *Essays* and the Washington-Park *Story of the Negro*. The emphasis on self-discipline was strong; George Washington's *Rules of Conduct*, Booker T. Washington's *Up From Slavery*, which 'illustrates the way in which the Negro masses are winning for themselves their moral independence in a kind of freedom not granted by the Emancipation Proclamation', and Samuel

Smiles' *Self Help*, which showed 'how the average man by patience, industry and thrift may succeed'. The Northern view of slavery and Reconstruction, as embodied in *Uncle Tom's Cabin* and Albion Tourgée's novel *A Fool's Errand*, was included with the note that these books represented a special, outside point of view. Park included two biographies of Lincoln, one a child's life and the other by Carl Schurz, since Lincoln was 'the one American in regard to whom colored students should know most'.[63]

Reflecting on the Tuskegee program as an 'evolutionary' solution to the racial problem, Park recalled later that Washington's central goal was improvement — economic, intellectual, and moral. The student was to be inspired to develop 'character and a career. This sort of struggle...lifts human life above...mere animal existence... an existence controlled by impulse merely, rather than ideas and ideals. ...Dr. Washington believed that...the most fundamental way to solve a race problem is to encourage individuals to solve their own problems ... getting a job, learning a trade or a profession was not a way of making a living but a way of making a life.'[64]

Washington was anxious to inculcate a sense of optimism and progress which would insulate the Negro against despair, and a sense of mutual responsibility, so that every Negro would try to contribute to the good repute of the race. It was better not to brood about present disabilities, but rather to identify with the future greatness of the race — 'happiness was not for the man at the top but rather for the man on the way up.' Negroes were to be the 'self-made race', the 'uptreading race', overcoming prejudice by their triumph over poverty, ignorance, and discrimination. In the long run, common interests would bring the two races together once the suspicion of Negro inferiority was overcome by the evidence of achievement. To speed up the evolutionary machine of reconciliation, publicity should bring home this lesson to whites and Negroes. Thus Park regarded *My Larger Education* as a valuable lesson to white Southerners, showing by implication the opportunities they had missed by failing to grasp 'this matter of the Negro in the wholesouled manner of men in the North'. At the same time the book would show the Negro how to get ahead via 'service' to society.[65] The underlying assumption was that self-interest and not sentiment, symbiosis not sociation as Park would later have put it, ruled the relations between men, and that Negroes could therefore coerce respect by making themselves essential to the American economy, South and North, since 'the economic side of the question...is the controlling factor.'[66] Two of Washington's favorite aphorisms reflect his utilitarian utopianism, his faith in the ultimate justice to be achieved by self-interest: 'disease draws no color line', and 'one man cannot hold another down in the gutter without staying down there with him.'[67]

Viewed with the knowledge of racial irrationality taught by the twentieth century, Washington's unheroic, evolutionary position clearly betrayed an excessive faith in the rational selfishness of human nature. However, it did have the great virtue of offering specific skills and psychic succor to the mass of Southern Negroes at a time when the white majority in a democratic polity was not willing to grant them power or justice before the law. Whether Washington could have helped the mass of Southern Negroes to achieve greater self-respect by setting an example of heroic defiance rather than one of shrewd compromise remains a hotly debated question. One footnote to this debate can be supplied from Park's records, which suggests that even Washington's moderate position went beyond the limits which 'responsible' Northern whites would sanction. The manuscript of Park's article for the *Springfield Daily Republican*, describing Washington's tour through Tennessee, had emphasized what Park called the Negro leader's most telling argument on behalf of Negro education — that a Negro was subjected to egalitarian treatment only when equality was to his disadvantage; he was expected to do a job as well as a white man and held responsible to the same law for a crime. ' "If at the finishing end of life," as Mr. Washington quaintly put it, "the Negro is expected to be equal of the white man, he ought to be his equal in the preparing end. He ought to have the same preparation for life that the white man does".' When the article was printed, however, the editor chose to omit even this tactful exposure of racial injustice.[68]

The Negro as Peasant

Park's personal experience of rural Negro life, together with his personal philosophy and his training in German sociology, led him to visualize — with a perhaps condescending idealization — the Southern Negro as the New World equivalent of that theoretical Adam, the European peasant. Park saw far more of Negro life than most whites could; much of his time during the Tuskegee years was spent travelling through the South on a variety of errands, sometimes as Washington's delegate, sometimes in his company. Many of the trips were devoted to specific projects — studying the causes of the Atlanta race riots in 1906, helping to plan a conference of the National Negro Business League, travelling with Washington and groups of Negro businessmen to publicize the progress of the race. On one of the speaking tours by which Washington spread his gospel of self-help and accommodation, Park encountered the brute reality of white violence. In Jacksonville, before his scheduled speech, Washington sent word to Park that a mob seemed to be forming outside. Park stepped out to hear 'the ominous tramp, tramp of men marching, in silence, except for an occasional cry, which betrayed the rising tide of excitement in a crowd which was not yet a mob'. Washington could hear everything, as the stage from which he spoke opened on the street, but continued as if nothing were wrong. After his meeting concluded, the streets were deserted; no violence had taken place.[69] For Park, the incident afforded direct experience of the Crowd which he had studied abstractly in Le Bon's writings, and whose inchoate power he was to stress as the new energy of social change in his course on 'collective behaviour' at Chicago and Fisk.

On other journeys, Park roamed the South without specific assignment, feeling his way into a personal 'acquaintance with' Negro life which probably surpassed that of most other white men of his generation. Trips to meet Negro businessmen, to inspect industrial schools, and discuss their problems, to track down Tuskegee graduates and other 'achieving' Negroes who might be useful as material for publicity — these gave him the chance to view Negro life from the very special perspective of a Tuskegee representative, associating largely with Negroes, yet himself white. On these journeys Park's contacts were principally with the 'upper levels of the Negro world'; he saw very little of 'that nether world of Negro life' known to Southern white men raised on plantations.[70] He also saw little of white life, keeping mainly within the confines of the Negro community — and almost becoming part of it. Once, when staying at a Negro hotel in Chicago, a man in line behind him for the bathroom remarked, 'Say, boss, you could easily pass in this town.'[71] Park later recalled the initial feeling of strangeness, when, staying with Washington in a small European hotel he found himself sleeping for the first time in the same bed with a Negro.[72]

Park did manage to meet a wide range of 'achieving' Negro citizens. Washington encouraged him to roam freely, seeking out interesting characters — hotel keepers, craftsmen, prosperous farmers, but especially 'the common man, particularly the small farmer in "the sticks" who because he was the first to purchase a piece of land or a mule or even a pig, had set the pace for other Negro farmers in this Community.'[73]

Park's white middle-class background and vague discontent with respectability, together with his exposure to the German sociological romanticism centered around peasant life, made him receptive to the mystique which Booker T. Washington wove around the special qualities engendered in the Southern Negro by his rural environment. While he was anxious to convert the sharecropper into an independent yeoman, Washington was also a convinced believer in the superior moral qualities of rural life; the small independent landholder was for him the Jeffersonian *via media* between backward primitivism and civilized decadence. He used symbols of Negro folk life quite consciously to soften the hearts of Northern philanthropists. Writing to George Foster Peabody of a tour through South Carolina in 1909, he noted that Major Robert R. Moton of Hampton Institute had led the crowds in community singing when the train paused at wayside stations. 'It was a great thing to have Major Moton along and have him lead in the revival of the old plantation singing among the masses. In many cases people came by the thousands at the various railroad stations where we stopped and sang the songs under his leadership. It was a weird and interesting sight.'[74] Similarly,

Washington instructed Park to stress that 'there will be plantation songs by a company of colored singers' during a meeting which Park was publicizing in New York.[75]

This was more than cynical manipulation of sentimental capitalists seeking a connection through their philanthropy with the virtue of the folk. Washington's willingness to exploit the Negro folk past — to embody moral homilies in dialect stories, for example — came partly, one suspects, from the realization that this 'color' pleased both of his principal audiences, the white Northerners who enjoyed its sentimental nostalgia, and the Southern Negroes whose natural speech it was. Further, the use of folk speech and of folk symbols reinforced the Negroes' sense of a shared culture separate from that of white Americans.[76] But beyond this manipulative utility, there is little doubt that Booker T. Washington himself was convinced that most Negroes lacked the self-discipline and independence to maintain themselves as respectable citizens in an urban setting. In the country, where the Negro saw himself visibly as a producer, he was kept from the fatal temptations of city life, where it was so easy to become a parasite.[77] 'Another point of great danger for the colored man who goes North is in the matter of morals, owing to the numerous temptations by which he finds himself surrounded. He has more ways in which he can spend money than in the South, but fewer avenues of employment are open to him.'[78] Similarly, he agreed with the philanthropist Peabody, that the collective rituals of the folk past, like community singing of spirituals, served a more serious function than merely satisfying sentimental observers; they were a means of generating loyalty to the Negro community.[79]

Robert Park was receptive to Washington's interpretation of the Negro's position in rural and urban society, and his sociological training enabled him to relate Washington's intuitive account to the corpus of German and American theory which emphasized the moral virtue of rural and small town life. Rousseau was far from the first, though perhaps the most systematic, thinker to use the stereotype of the simple, virtuous peasant as a moral alternative to the existing decadent and sophisticated society. There were numerous literary expressions of this eternal theme for self-doubting sophisticates in the eighteenth and nineteenth centuries. Steele in 1713 spoke of the 'innocence and simplicity of country life'; the 'incorrupted life' was more likely to be realized in rural surroundings — a sentiment enshrined by Cowper in 'God made the country; man made the town.'[80] The work of Johann Gottfried Herder reinforced this literary attitude and related it to a substantial body of doctrine arguing the relation of human culture to the geographical and historical environment. By his stress on the need for roots, the existence of 'natural' types of human kind conforming to the special geographical environment and historical tradition of each particular people or folk, Herder particularized what had been a generalized revulsion against sophistication and hypocrisy into one of the most powerful supports of the nascent nationalism of the nineteenth century. The natural virtue of the peasant community, the spontaneous anonymous folk culture which it had produced, were developed by romantic ideologists as proof of the deep historical roots and creative vitality which each particular national group possessed.[81]

The fascination with peasant society and culture, closely tied as it was to a concern for national tradition, became a useful vehicle of protest against the growth of industrialism and its effects on the human personality and community. The particular term which came to symbolize this whole *Gestalt* of attitudes and propositions received its ideological significance when it was used by Friedrich Gentz in the translation of Edmund Burke's *Reflections on the French Revolution*. In this translation, 'partnership,' in the famous phrase 'partnership between past, present and future generations', became *Gemeinschaft*.[82] This nostalgia for the simpler past of relationships characterized by tradition, sentiment, and piety, rather than the cold cash nexus, was not confined to ideologic conservatives like Gentz. As noted earlier, a wide varitey of political faiths could find utility in this stereotype of the peasant living happily within his seemingly eternal and organically bound community.[83] The peasant became in a sense the universal Adam from whom the human race had sprung and the diverse cultures of the present all found their roots and in many ways their purest expression in these early communities. As Horace Kallen put it, speaking of the peasants who had emigrated to America, they were the 'elementals' of human nature, 'the proletarian foundation material of all forms of civilization'.[84]

Park had absorbed much of this tradition of thought which contained elements of both 'pastoral' and 'primitivist' modes during his years in Germany; and when he came to study the Negro in America he instinctively regarded him as the American peasant still living, in the rural South, in a world of primary personal relations which imposed the local morality on the individual through face to face contacts with family and friends.[85] Like so many other white American intellectuals who sought a relief from civilized monotony in the study of exotics, Park found the color and simplicity of rural Negro Life powerfully attractive.[86] In an unpublished sketch, 'The Land of Darkness', he recorded his impressions of the 'places untouched by the influence of Tuskegee', the backlands occupied by sharecroppers distant from urban influence. His description cleverly employed the '*Gemeinschaft*' imagery which linked rational with urban, natural with rural.

As the town recedes the look of things changes. The well kept barns and fences give place by imperceptible gradations of difference to buildings that...seem to support themselves with difficulty...the fences begin to stagger, the lines in the fields wander. Energy, system, order are in retreat...against the most irrational forces of nature around them. ...And just across these grey-brown furrows, not 100 yards away from this unnatural life of toil, back to the lighthearted freedom of growing things, the paradise of the natural man. ...When the German people a few hundred years ago were struggling out of barbarism into civilization, they symbolized this call of the wild...in beautiful legends, like that of Melusina.[87]

Park, like Washington, never succumbed overtly to the passive pleasure of primitivism. The life of the plantation sharecropper was appealing but incomplete: 'these people need guidance — need inspiration — they are merely *primitive*.' Park wondered at the indifference of the cropper to his own poverty — 'or is it merely a mask in which (to) hide a voiceless sorrow?'[88] The land was rich, the cause was the apathy induced by dependence on the one-crop tenant system. As Park said in another essay, the Negro farmer was created by the agrarian system and improving methods of farming would help to instill ambition, intelligence, and independence in the farmer himself.[89] Tuskegee had an important task of civilizing and self-discipline to accomplish. And yet, there was a powerful note of unresolved sympathy for backwoods life in Park's account of 'The Land of Darkness': 'There was something irresistibly attractive in this untamed wilderness, with its rank and vigorous undergrowth, this bit of the untrammeled wilderness so full of vigorous and various life. ...I threw my categories to the winds...and devoted myself simply and in all humility to getting acquainted with this people and learning from them their wisdom of life.'[90]

He gave up the idea of trying to 'catechize and categorize' the local croppers or fire them with the Tuskegee spirit of improvement 'for the betterment of the race'. In its isolation and lack of self-conscious competitive spirit, the 'land of darkness' embodied 'all the elements of the human comedy — struggle and strife, love and hate, aspiration and despair', the pride in small things — cottage gardens, pigs and chickens — 'for these are the symbols in which the realities of life have embodied themselves'. The familiar turns of phrase reflected a frame of mind common to the sophisticated and disillusioned in all ages, but perhaps especially strong among educated Americans of Park's and later generations. Freedom was in the second-growth forest of the plantation gone back to nature — 'untrammeled', 'untamed'; true freedom from constraint lay in adjustment, in accepting the chains imposed by existence and learning to be happy with the small pleasures of everyday life, not in striving for an illusory material happiness.[91] Park noted elsewhere that in the rural South of the black belt there was 'a great deal of immorality, or unmorality, but these people are in no way vicious or degenerate; they are merely primitive'; not yet having eaten the apple of moral selfconsciousness, they retained primal innocence.[92]

For Park, as for other intellectuals, there was a serious conflict between his sentimental appreciation of 'natural' or 'simple' peoples and his desire to see that they enjoyed the advantages of American life. Perhaps they were better off in the backwoods, relaxed and unselfconscious? On the whole, Park would seem to have answered this question in the negative, or rather, dismissed it as irrelevant; the historical process exposed all men to the lure of western technology, and sooner or later, with more or less pain and friction, they would enter the arena of modern life to prove their worth in the competitive struggle. Yet, as the 'Land of Darkness' shows, Park's evolutionary fatalism did not entirely submerge a strong sense of the charm of primitive, isolated life.

In 1913, as he prepared to begin his lecturing at the University of Chicago, Park summed up his conviction that urban life, with its 'secondary' or impersonal relationships, had an evil influence on Negro youth. One of the last duties Park performed for Washington was a tour of Negro schools in the South in the spring of 1913, gathering material for a report to the Phelps Stokes foundation.[93] His letters to Washington show that Park's distinction between rural and urban character types rested on personal experience as mediated through Protestant moral categories and '*Gemeinschaft/Gesellschaft*' theory.

No-one can know much about the Negro race...until he has become acquainted with the masses of the people as they are in the black belt counties of the South. They are strong, vigorous, kindly and industrious people; simple minded, wholesome and good as God made them. They are very different from the people of the cities. As yet they have been very little affected with either disease or vice. The boys and girls that come from the country are usually earnest and ambitious. The young folk from the cities on the other hand are very likely to be indifferent and frivolous, and disposed to live by their wits. I noticed the difference as soon as I entered a school where a majority of the students were drawn from the sophisticated classes in the cities. Fortunately the great majority of the race still live in the country and if they can be educated there, where they can grow up slowly and naturally, and be kept out of the cities where they will be forced along at a pace that will make them superficial and trifling, the race problem will eventually solve itself.[94]

Ironically, Park began his years of 'academic' study and teaching on Negroes in the midst of the great migration of Southern croppers to the cities of the North in search of industrial jobs. Already, between 1900 and 1910, the lure of prosperity increased the Negro population of Philadelphia and Chicago by over 30 percent, while that of New York increased by 57 percent. Washington and New York each had over 90,000 negroes. The numbers would rise more drastically during the next decade as wartime jobs lured more and more croppers from the exhausted land of the South.[95] History had begun to make Park's moral preferences anachronistic even as he brought them to the classroom.

Tuskegee and Park's Theory of Social Action

Park's years at Tuskegee extended and strengthened his flexible but generally pessimistic view of social action. His newspaper years had left a fondness for 'the people' and a dislike for self-conscious individuals who arrogantly asserted their special right to control the lives of others. The brief encounter with the Congo reformers convinced him that moral imperialism seemed to release many of its true believers from the necessity of avoiding dishonesty and hypocrisy in the means they employed. Now, Park's distaste for reforming intellectuals was confirmed, as he noted the contrast between the calm, unassuming, and outwardly confident, practical-minded Booker T. Washington, and the harsh, quarrelsome 'radicals' who preened themselves on their intellectual superiority.

As press agent and principal 'ghost', Park could not help but take an active part in the struggle between Washington and his 'radical' civil libertarian opponents, led by W.E.B.DuBois and William Monroe Trotter, who demanded a more activist role in claiming political and civil rights for Negroes and in defending them against the growth of legal segregation and mob violence.[96] There is no evidence that Park found this role unpleasant, since his experience at Tuskegee had reinforced his distaste for moral reformers who relied on the word, on political agitation, rather than the 'evolutionary' solution of concrete improvements in Negro education and community life. Tuskegee-sponsored publicity could be a valuable lever in exacting political support; on one occasion in 1907, he exulted that an admiring article on Wilberforce University, a Negro college run by the African Methodist Episcopal Church, would trap the college president into the Tuskegee orbit: 'we are going to have him bound hand and feet after the Wilberforce article appears.'[97]

Park's years at Tuskegee included the period when Oswald Garrison Villard, grandson of William Lloyd Garrison and now owner-editor of the *New York Evening Post*, and later of the *Nation*, became steadily more dissatisfied with Washington's conciliatory attitude toward the South, and finally turned to support DuBois and the newly founded NAACP. Villard's eloquent efforts to push the Tuskegeean into supporting the NAACP and a firmer public stand on Negro rights seemed to Park to epitomize the impertinence of the meddling intellectual reformer whose zeal blinded him to the 'realities' of Southern life.[98] Years later, Park recalled: 'Villard used to write the nastiest letters. Villard raised a large sum for the school but he seemed to think that gave him the right to command Washington. These benevolent people seem to have got the idea that they were God's chosen people and seemed to feel the Negro belonged to them.'[99]

In later years Park recognized the value of W.E.B.DuBois' insistence on political rights and the importance for Negro life of its 'talented tenth', but retained his conviction that the personal qualities of the 'radicals' doomed them to failure in practical affairs. 'The people who criticized Washington weren't politicians and they didn't know how to deal with human beings.' Washington, Park felt, attained political influence because he realized that politics was the art of the possible: 'he looked at the Negro situation realistically... could be relied upon to take a common-sense view.' The confidence of Theodore Roosevelt was founded in the president's faith that Booker T. Washington would not embarrass him by recommending unsound men for federal office. Further, Washington refused to succumb to bitterness and thus discourage his clientele of Negro artisans and peasants in the South. He gave them present activity to keep away despair, and the hope of gradual improvement at the end of tasks which began immediately and involved them personally. Washington 'was never frustrated as DuBois always was and he did have the faith in the common man that DuBois never seems to have had'.[100]

Park's view of race relations always followed the Washington doctrine closely. Neither of them was a 'Social Darwinist', strictly speaking, in the sense of denying any useful role in the process of social change to conscious reason or to the use of political agitation by organized, coherent elites. Both were qualified historical materialists, convinced that in the process of evolution man's economic life played the dominant role in shaping social life; both accepted the idea that evolution did not proceed by leaps, so that successful change was likely to come in small increments. But they certainly assumed, and tried to demonstrate, the value of conscious mind and of goals for human behavior and ultimately on the direction of historical change. The whole Tuskegee program was devoted to the improvement of self and environment, to inculcating in the young a personal dedication to transform conditions rather than to succumb to them. And Park emphasized that getting ahead must be done through solid achievement: 'I do not believe colored men have ever made any very great success either by fooling white people or by fooling themselves.'[101]

Nor did Washington really repudiate political action although he often used against his reformist opponents the argument that economic progress must precede and prepare for political change. His own action, his efforts to work behind the scenes to block schemes of disfranchisement, suggest that Washington's 'Social Darwinist' rejection of political action was not a principle but a tactic, valid for his time and situation but not for others.[102] Similarly, Robert Park rejected the possibility of consciously directed political change only in a special sense, one produced by his own experience of reform and reformers and from Booker Washington's stress on the Negro as a conscious, separate, self-sustaining minority, a 'nation within a nation'. Political and social action was not foredoomed to failure if it was the authentic expression of the people who would benefit from it. In a later essay, 'Negro Race Consciousness', Park compared the Negro radicalism of the 1920s to the nationalist movements of Europe and pointed out that these were secular revivals, intensifying and elevating the lives of the whole people.[103] Negroes and other ethnic minorities naturally developed group loyalties when subjected to discrimination and disadvantages; it was inevitable and perfectly correct that this selfconsciousness then manifested itself in nationalistic literature and political agitation. What Park did find foolish and arrogant was the attempt by a minority, especially a minority of 'do-gooders' without organic ties to the people they wished to aid, to coerce citizens who did not necessarily share their own sense of inevitability. There is a Darwinian notion underlying this attitude, which Park shared with many other Americans of his own and later generations and which was revived in the 1960s: since human activity is, or should be, fundamentally a functional response to the environment, to the immediate *milieu*, people who deviate from this maxim are subject to suspicion. Exotic concerns were a sign of maladjustment; meddling in alien milieux was a variety of evolutionary *hubris* which would usually have unexpected and unpleasant consequences.

Another idea which Park helped to plant in the tradition of American sociology was the notion of America as a plurality of ethnic communities, at least temporarily separate and self-conscious. This idea was also pre-figured for Park by his Tuskegee experience, in this case by Washington's conception of the Negroes as a 'nation among nations'. Park noted Washington's concern to develop pride of race and a sense of separate destiny (even if, still, by excelling at the tasks which the white majority named as the measure of achievement). Washington had the vision to see the situation of the Southern Negro

in a larger context and in a longer perspective...a new people, if not a new race; a people of African origin but compounded of all the blood of all the races with which, in this cosmopolitan country, it had come into contact. What made the Negro in America 'a nation within a nation'... was the dawning consciousness of a common destiny. Behind this emergent minority, struggling to achieve in America a status which insured its economic security and personal self-respect, he saw in Africa a race, of which the Negro people in America seemed to be an advance guard, seeking and finding...a place in this new world-wide civilization, in what Graham Wallas has called 'the Great Society.'[104]

At the time, Park did not realize how widely the Negro's situation could be generalized, but his studies of immigrant communities during and after World War I showed that Washington's conception of Negro separateness was a paradigm of the American situation. His later researchers showed Park 'the extent to which the U.S. in the great cities and outside, is made up of little racial and cultural units, existing in, but not wholly incorporated into, the life of the total community'.[105] And, Park made clear, it was natural and desirable that these communities struggle for selfconsciousness and political expression, even though the long-term outcome in the U.S. was likely to be not perpetual separation but cultural assimilation.[106] Thus, Park assimilated his journalist's scepticism to the Washington philosophy of racial separation, gradual change and hostility to intellectuals.

No matter how low Park's opinion of 'do-gooders' had sunk by 1905, however, it is clear that he did not bring to Tuskegee an attitude of fatalistic acceptance on race relations. On his first arrival in the South, he had been horrified.

The thing that impressed me most...was the tragic insecurity — as it seemed to me then — under which colored people lived. It appeared that Negroes at the time had nowhere any security even in the cities, in cases where the law did not conform to the local mores...any violation of the racial etiquette by which the distances...were maintained, was likely at any time to be punished by an outburst of mob violence.[107]

Park compared the situation to that in medieval Japan where the Samurai 'might kill a man of lower caste for merely "behaving in an unusual manner".' But when Park finally reached Tuskegee and informed Washington of his horror, the sage 'listened patiently for quite some time and then said, "Well, that makes it all the more interesting, doesn't it?"' 'I never told Booker Washington any heart-breaking stories after that', Park concluded, 'since he was not interested.'[108]

Park pondered the implications of Washington's remarks as he travelled more extensively, and observed the Tuskegee program in action. Things began to look different: 'not that I had more facts but I had more insight. What that insight revealed behind and beneath the superficial pattern and external aspect of Southern life was the working of a great historical process, a process which was slowly but inexorably changing traditional units in this, as in every other part of the U.S., including the traditional relations between the races.'[109] Thus indignation was replaced by sociology, or at least by the proto-sociological attitude of understanding irrational events in terms of a 'rational' pattern of connections which underlies the flux of experience. However, Park's 'acceptance' of the pattern of Southern racial relations never led to the assumption that its historical existence and temporary viability gave it *moral* validity. The mark of scientific neutrality, to Park, was not a total abstinence from moral judgment, or from social action, but rather the willingness to face the facts of social resistance to change. He employed the neo-Kantian dualism between the phenomenal sphere of scientific law and the noumenal realm of free will, in order to persuade Negro students not to be discouraged by scientific arguuments on the inferiority of Negroes. In a talk to the Scientific Society at Tuskegee in 1905, Park reassured his audience they should not despair in the face of so much current scientific activity which gathered statistics on Negro crime, Negro poverty, Negro death rates, and then predicted from these figures that the Negro was not fitted for freedom and equality. However true the facts may have been, said Park, one could *not* predict from them. The sheer 'orneriness' of human nature would destroy the most careful calculations, for 'just as soon as a human being or a society or a race finds out that someone has predicted that it is going to do something it is likely to turn around and do something entirely different'. Who would have predicted that the young Lincoln splitting rails would become president, or that the slave child, Booker T., would become the second emancipator of his race to complete the work Lincoln had begun, — or for that matter, the rise of Japan? This did not mean that social science was useless, but its use was instrumental rather than predictive. Knowledge is power, not because it tells us infallibly what will happen, but because it enables men to rouse themselves and avoid the predictable. 'As soon as the Negro finds out where he is supposed to be racially inferior he will rouse himself and prove that he is not. That is human nature.' Knowledge would give the Negro the means to overcome his weaknesses. Social science should not cramp men's freedom and destroy their hope; rather it was to be the learned servant of action. 'Now don't you see that this is just the reason we want knowledge. So we may dodge and get out of the way of catastrophe, so we may do the exceptional and unpredictable thing, which history will record.'[110] Park did not want sociology to be the ward of reformers, but he wanted it to aid rather than hinder those who were struggling to make their own way up.

Once credit is given for the complexity of Park's racial outlook, however, the ironic, even tragic result of his position cannot be denied. Booker Washington's gradualism, always despised by intellectuals, had relevance in the hideous South which confronted the Negro in 1905; it was, arguably, for the Negro masses in that context a more potent barrier against despair and degradation that would have been the right of darkskinned doctors of philosophy to ride in Pullman cars. Further, for Washington this was a public facade, not an absolute bar against all efforts to influence the course of events. However, when Park, admiring Washington's calm persistence and willingness to work within the givens of conventional politics, absorbed the Tuskegee philosophy, the long-term result was very different. The qualified fatalism which many commentators have noted in Park's later writings on race relations developed not only from his experience of the South at the zenith of the Jim Crow and lynch mob era, but also from his over-thorough absorption of the Washington position. The attitudes which Washington tried to inculcate as a shield against total despair in the Alabama of 1910 were absorbed by Park, and transmitted through him a generation later to an audience of white (and even Negro) social scientists who then preached to a very different audience the 'good news' that political action to protect civil liberties against community mores was futile. While the evolutionary view of race relations was widespread early in the century, Park's espousal of it was vital because of his role in training the 'experts' of the next generation in an increasingly specialized society. The doctrine produced by the exigencies of survival and political advantage became the scientific sociology of the 1920s and 1930s. As Park transmitted to the next generation of sociologists this hostility toward manipulated change imposed from outside, this respect for the existing social situation as the context within which to work, the result was to perpetuate the attitude of 'scholarly moderation' in a society which might or might not have yielded to a more militant position, and to elevate what had been a necessary accommodation, a public face, into a 'scientific' principle. The unintended effect of Park's teachings, as Gunnar Myrdal pointed out, was to give 'scientific' justification to the Southern racial system as it existed between 1920 and 1940.[111] While Park's conflict theory of race relations anticipated the later recognition that social justice is more likely to be achieved if fought for from below than engineered from above, in the short term it had the effect of discouraging a call for government intervention at a point in the race relations cycle when it might have proved beneficial. In this context, a scientific neutrality that balanced the conflicting viewpoints without reference to an external standard of justice implied fatalism and deified the object of study in its present state.

An End to Preparation

Despite Park's deep satisfaction with his life during the first half-dozen years in Washington's service, pressures were building up at home which would lead to another bout of restlessness, another search for the elusive vocation. While Park spent most of the year at Tuskegee, or travelling on Institute business, his wife and four growing children remained in Wollaston, enjoying his company at Christmas and during the summer, struggling to make ends meet on the slender allowance he was able to send them. Although a comfortable income became available after his father, Hiram Park, died in 1911, Robert at first refused to draw on it and so he had only his salary from Tuskegee, which was often in arrears and which was stretched to the limits by four children, including a son at Harvard.[112] His children's letters during this period reflect a wistful yearning that the bills might be paid, that 'Mamma' might 'spend money regardless just once', that they might have $25.00 to spend on a Victrola, to dance and 'just have fun'. Park apparently replied by urging the nobility of keeping down one's living expenses as far as possible, of the responsibilities of wealth and the pleasure of luxuries when they are rare. His daughters agreed bravely, but even more than the lack of money, they felt the lack of a father. 'You say you can work so much better away from us,' wrote his eldest daughter, 'but I hope some day you will just turn around and say "darn the work!" and live with us for a while. I expect while we are far away, and cannot bother you, you will make a name for yourself, but...don't you think it would be perfectly lovely for you to just settle down like an old English squire, and devote yourself to your family and your land.'[113] On the whole, the family seems to have acquiesced with half humorous resignation in taking second place to Park's work, but it did rankle. They summed up their feelings in a little birthday poem for Park;

Students of Humanity
In the raw
Hardly have the time to be
Just a Paw.
If I were a marginal
Black or tan
Then I might belong to your
Five year plan.
Tho I'm simply hopelessly
Purely white,
Still I hope you'll think of me
If not write.
For you see its very hard
To be happy,
Life is just a dusty road
Without Pappy![114]

During her husband's absence, Mrs. Park was active in Massachusetts politics; she was a fervent supporter of the Bull Moose party and was an influential member of a governor's commission to produce a widow's pension law for Massachusetts. Park encouraged her in all this but remained personally aloof; his wife always had a more lively interest in politics and reform programs than he.[115] Park did, of course spend some time in Massachusetts during the Tuskegee years, 'trying to get acquainted' with his family again, but he felt he was neglecting them, and this, together with a growing personal restlessness, led him to contemplate making a break with Tuskegee.[116] In April 1912, Park sent Washington his resignation: he would gladly have remained if he could have persuaded his family to come down South to live, but as he could not, he wanted 'to spend the next few years, while they are growing up with my children'. But he added: 'I have never been so happy in my life as I have since I have been associated with you in this work. Some of the best friends I have in the world are at Tuskegee. I feel and shall always feel that I belong , in a sort of way to the Negro race and shall continue to share, through good and evil, all its joys and sorrows. I want to help you in the future as in the past in any way I can.'[117]

Washington, however, persuaded him to remain on the Tuskegee payroll and the break was not yet final. But Park remained restless. He had already been branching out to some extent in outside lectures and addresses – the fees for which he often turned over to Tuskegee. He would have liked to have more freedom to devote to his own interests while continuing to work for Washington, turning over the more routine jobs of a press agent to someone else. Washington, however, decided that the school could not afford to employ another man and that Park must stick to the job for which he was hired.[118] This made the impending change inevitable, since Park felt that routine was replacing excitement at Tuskegee, just as in the newspaper world. He always recalled Tuskegee as his apprenticeship, but recalled too that 'my apprenticeship was too long. If learning is to be adventure it cannot be at the same time a vocation.'[119] Thus, by the spring of 1912, Park was eager to move on from Tuskegee to a new arena of experience. His meeting of that year with Professor W.I.Thomas of the University of Chicago crystallized his dissatisfaction, and offered a new cause in which to enlist.[120] Although he began teaching at Chicago in 1913, Park was reluctant to make a complete break with Tuskegee; he spent several months working there in the spring of 1914 and remained in friendly contact until and even after Washington's death in November 1915.[121] Until wartime insecurity cut Tuskegee's income drastically, he continued to draw a salary from the Institute for preparing articles and answering troublesome letters, tasks to which he devoted about half his time.[122] The Chicago connection gave the authority of scholarly status to his work as Tuskegee spokesman. His students at Chicago were telling Southerners that he was an expert on the Negro, with the result that Park began to receive letters requesting enlightenment on such questions as 'Do you think the Negro understands the Christian religion in its spiritual and practical bearings?' His new Chicago letterhead gave a certain authority to Park's tactful reply.[123] In 1915 he was looking for a 'place down South' where Mrs. Park could live for half the year and so he could keep in touch with Tuskegee and their Negro friends, and he continued to give Washington advice and publicity material until the latter's death.[124]

Transition to the Academy

In the fall of 1913, after one of the longest apprenticeships served by a scholar, Robert Park, at the age of forty-nine, began the quarter-century of teaching and leadership in research which was to span the transformation of American sociology. From the beginning, Park gave far more of his time and energy than demanded by his contract with Chicago; this was at last a chance to follow his interests, with institutional protection against his own fear of dilettantism or impractical time-wasting. Initially, Park's formal teaching duties were confined to a single quarter – the fall term in 1913, the summer term in later years. Thomas had arranged that he give a single course, 'The Negro in America', to a small group of graduate students for a stipend of $500.00. Park reported to Washington that he was assigning a heavy load of Tuskegee books – *Up from Slavery, My Larger Education*, and *The Story of the Negro* – and that his lectures should 'do a lot of good'.[1] The course was evidently a success, since when Park resumed teaching in June 1914, the number of students had doubled.[2] Not only was he doing well professionally, but he was enjoying himself immensely, finding a whole new life as his children grew up and left home. Chicago turned out to be an ideal center for the preliminary work on 'writing the books I have in my head.'[3] During the summer of 1913, he was busy preparing a paper for delivery at the annual meeting of the American Sociological Society in Minneapolis embodying the general conclusions of his Tuskegee years on the conditions under which racial assimilation takes place. The address 'Racial Assimilation in Secondary Groups', was published in the society's *Publications* for 1913.[4] At the meeting Park joined the society, effective January 1914. A decade later he was to become its president.

Gradually, on his own initiative, Park worked his way into a key position in the Chicago department. Without administrative approval he took on more and more teaching duties, adding a new course on 'The Crowd and the Public' in the summer of 1914, and, later in the decade, courses on the newspaper and the social survey as institutions.[5] He and Mrs. Park found a new home near the campus and, although he was still being paid only the $500.00 for a single term, he remained in residence, actively giving courses, for two and sometimes three quarters of the academic year. After several years of this unsanctioned benevolence, an administrative directive arrived in the sociology department office 'authorizing Dr. Park to give courses in the Winter quarter without salary'.[6] As years passed and Park continued to shoulder more of the department's work, especially after the forced resignation of his patron W.I.Thomas in 1918, and as he took over the lion's share of preparing the new textbook originally assigned to young Ernest Burgess, the ageing chairman, Albion W. Small, (only a decade senior to Park, but already losing vigor and descending into reminiscent old age) became more anxious not to lose this unexpected acquisition to his department. As Park's early articles on race relations and urban theory won him prominence in the profession, Small fretted that some other university might offer the prestige of a permanent professorship. In 1919, Small recommended that Park be given a full appointment as professiorial lecturer, instead of his temporary summer quarter tenure which had been renewed from year to year. President Judson, an irritable septuagenarian, grudged a year's appointment as professorial lecturer with a stipend of $1,000.00; the full professorship came only after a new president took office in 1923. When, after his first temporary promotion, Small told Park that his salary was to rise to $1,000.00 'with a quizzical smile he (Park) commented, "Well, that will help on my stenographer's bills." '[7]

In order to maintain his family adequately while pursuing his passion on the quarter-time appointment at Chicago, Park had decided to accept the income left him in Hiram Park's estate. Even after the bequest, the Park family was far from wealthy, and the income from Park and Grant Wholesale houses in Minneapolis and South Dakota fluctuated with the prosperity of the Dakota wheat belt. However, it was a comfortable sum for the period, given Park's modest standard of expenditure and casual attitude toward the stigmata of respectability. This attitude had been illustrated by his attire when appearing for his initial interview with Small; Park's clothes were so casual and unpressed that W.I.Thomas, had feared he must be poverty stricken and had offered to lend him money for a new suit before he met 'the bishop'.[8]

Park's financial independence deserves close attention, since it not only eased the strain on his family but very likely had important effects on his professional life and work, reinforcing his personal predilections by freeing him from the need for academic conformity. Park was doing what he wanted; he enjoyed the teaching and research at Chicago. He was not, however, dependent on his professional position for income, and less dependent on it for self-definition and self-respect than most scholars. Therefore, he could push hard against the constraints of his work, its expectations of proper methods and ideas, as much as against those of suitable attire. He did not have to publish except when he felt that something needed to be said; he was not compelled to polish or glamorize his lectures, to reach the uncommitted student through popularization, and he felt no need to follow faithfully the commands of his employers when involved on social research projects.[9] The effect was liberating and refreshing; certainly this unorthodox, uncommitted 'visitor' gave the University of Chicago far more in service and renown than most men employed full time. Yet, it can be argued, there was also a debit side to Park's independence fron the sanctions of money and status. These vulgar essentials can be a valuable spur to self-criticism, a bar to self-indulgent vagueness. The debit side of Park's independence would be revealed in his conduct of the Race Relations Survey in California a decade later, when his employers attempted to confine Park's impressionistic methods within tighter limits. The chains of dependence on a salary might have encouraged Park to develop and elaborate his insights more systematically, instead of throwing them out to students and colleagues who made of them what they could – often, one suspects, less than Park himself might have done had he been more responsive to the process of communal criticism and judgment which organized scholarship affords.

Park's home address during these years was an apartment shared with his artist wife near the campus. However, his travels were extensive: trips to academic meetings, to consult with students and former students in the wider field beyond Chicago, later to teach at a variety of universities. On one occasion Park rented a room in a Chicago slum to experience the urban jungle at first hand. By 1932 he had travelled and studied race relations on the Pacific coast, the West Indies, Hawaii, China, India, Africa, and Brazil and had taught at the University of Hawaii and Yenching University in Peiping.[10] He was an impresario of research, talking, listening, but above all helping other people to define and undertake research projects which seemed useful within the broad evolutionary boundaries of his interests. In Chicago itself he had numerous off campus contacts and interests: he belonged to the congregation of the University Church of Disciples of Christ, presided over by the liberal theologian, Edward Scribner Ames, a professor in the philosophy department and a pioneer in the psychology of religion.[11] Park was a close friend of the Ames family and often entertained members of the divinity school at his apartment; for a while he even taught Sunday School at the Church, using Gilbert Murray's *Rise of the Greek Epic* as text. According to one of his students, Park had a 'small streak of piety in him', but on the whole it seems that his connection with the Church was one of intellectual curiosity rather than traditional belief. He was fascinated by sects and cults and by the history of religion, and perhaps above all he enjoyed joining in the ceremonial life of a community.[12]

The University of Chicago and The Rise of American Sociology

Perhaps Albion Small worried too much about the chance of Park being lured away from the University of Chicago. John D. Rockefeller's magnificent benefaction offered unique advantages to a student of urban life and ethnic relations, not only by its location in the archetypical American metropolis, but because the philosophy underlying the young institution gave the adventurous social scientist an unusual degree of freedom, both from administrative restraint and from the sense of embattled inferiority engendered in older institutions by the entrenched humanistic scholars' contempt for the upstart discipline of sociology with its bastard name and barbarian terminology.[13]

From the day in 1892 when students invaded its muddy and unfinished campus, the University of Chicago prided itself on 'service', on its self-defined role of sniffling out social 'needs' and providing an institutional means of resolving, or at least describing in detail, these social problems. The major goal of President William Rainey Harper, the Baptist minister and Hebrew psychologist who led the university until his death in 1906, was to break down the barrier between the university and the life outside its walls. To prove that the university could 'do a great service to mankind', Harper was determined to build a graduate school which would combine original scholarship with community service.[14]

To demonstrate its utility in a more immediate and emotional way, during the second year the university founded a settlement house near the stockyards. Harper was anxious to make all aspects of the university's program reflect a Protestant ideal of effective moral earnestness. Thus, he instituted the four quarter system, which allowed a devoted student to complete his degree in less than four years, and also made it possible for teachers and others with seasonal jobs to gain degrees through a series of summer residences. Similarly, by scheduling degree convocations at the end of each quarter, he hoped to fragment class spirit, that frivolous reflection of the 'play' conception of the university as a training ground for aristocratic youth.[15]

The summer quarter and the graduate school were central to Harper's conception of the university as an agent of service. The full status given the summer terms attracted serious, mature students, men and women who by their earnest probing embarrassed teachers accustomed to the tolerant indifference of adolescent collegians. Committed faculty members began to take their vacations in the winter, having discovered that not only more students, but better and more serious ones, and a higher proportion of post graduates, came in the summer.[16] Chicago's traditional emphasis on the summer quarter and the part-time graduate student was to have an important effect on Park's career at the university, and indeed on the scope and direction of the sociological research program there in the 1910s and 20s. A high proportion of his Ph.D. candidates were mature men and women, often several years away from school, who returned to write up their unique experiences of the world much as Park himself had done. Others were professional social workers trying to formalize their understanding of the situations they faced in daily life. Thus, Nels Anderson wrote *The Hobo* in great part from his own recollections of life on the open road and skid row, and the social worker Frederic Thrasher recorded and systematized his observation of gang life on Chicago's South Side.[17] The university's extroversion brought them the chance of study combined with a career, just as it gave Park himself the opportunity to pursue his own quest for understanding through part-time teaching and direction of research.

The university's stress on community service led to the growth of strong departments in the emerging fields of social science. At its opening in 1892, Chicago established the first separate department of sociology; in political economy it boasted the classical rigor of J. Laurence Laughlin as well as the brilliant evolutionary satire of Thorstein Veblen. Since the university had been founded as a Baptist institution, the divinity school received great attention and under Shailer Matthews, and later Edward S. Ames, as well as Harper himself, the divinity school became a center for liberal Christianity, the higher criticism of the Bible, and efforts to spread the gospel of social service.[18]

This service-minded divinity school was closely tied to the sociology department, not only through a common interest in civic improvement and social justice, but because the two senior professors in sociology, Small and Charles R. Henderson, were themselves Baptist ministers.[19] The journalist Edwin Slosson, appraising the university in 1909, noted that these three closely linked departments, divinity, political economy, and sociology, were not only the most popular, but were also the outstanding centers of creative work, since they had been given a remarkable degree of freedom to criticize the social conditions of industrial America.[20]

Chicago's sociology department in 1913, and for almost two decades to come, was the outstanding center of the discipline in America. It was the oldest, the largest, with a hundred courses in sociology and anthropology, and probably the most prestigious. The official *American Journal of Sociology* was published by the department and edited by its chairman and the professional association had been founded on the inspiration of Chicago.[21] Like any periodization, the dating of sociology as an academic discipline in America from the foundation of the Chicago department in 1892 is partly a matter of convenience, but more one of magnitude, The first college course in 'Social Problems' was probably established at Oberlin as early at 1858; George Fitzhugh had employed the Comtean term 'sociology' in 1854 and William Graham Sumner was offering political and social science at Yale from 1873.[22] However, the development of sociology as a distinct discipline came rapidly in the late 1880s. The peculiar institution of the South had made intellectual Southerners susceptible very early to an Hegelian-Fichtean emphasis on the reality of the social organism in which the central principle was the function of individuals and groups in promoting social cohesion, rather than the theoretical rights of individual citizens. In the North, however, the immediate background to the development of sociology lay in the growing awareness of 'social problems' which resisted solution on liberal principles. Early social science courses in the universities in the 1880s dealt with the problem of poverty, charity administration, urban sanitation, and criminology. Gradually, during the 1880s courses identified as 'sociology' began to be introduced. The first department which included sociology in its title was founded at the University of Kansas in 1889, jointly with history; in the same year President Albion Small replaced the president's traditional moral philosophy course at Colby University with one in sociology, while Franklin H. Giddings introduced the subject at Bryn Mawr, and courses in social science, social ethics, and social problems spread rapidly during the 1890s. By the end of 1892, with the addition of Chicago, Columbia, and the Valley City Normal School in North Dakota, at least sixteen institutions offered some form of sociology course. By 1909, at least eighty colleges and universities had departments which included sociology in their title, while another 139 had at least one course with sociological content in another department — usually economics, history, or political science.[23]

The rapid spread of sociology as an academic 'subject' reflects the convergence of several factors in the university world in the late 1880s and early 1890s. First was the ascendancy of 'utilitarian' education and the conversion of many teachers and administrators, especially in the newly founded and rapidly growing institutions in the West and Midwest, to the doctrine that the college best served 'life' by teaching the student directly about conditions outside the ivied walls, rather than by inculcating formal skills of analysis.[24] And when the college administrators inspected the 'reality' of American life about which students should be informed, the most striking phenomena were chiefly those of the emerging urban-industrial society taking form clearly from the early 1880s.

Indeed, it is remarkable how short was the 'conceptual lag' between the rise to statistical dominance of an urban-industrial order in the mid-1880s, and the academic response, which followed by only half a decade. This rapid response in turn reflects other factors: the fact that the large city emerged more clearly earlier than the 1880s in a few symptomatic instances; the dramatic episodes in the mid-1880s, the great strikes of 1885 and 1886, the Haymarket affair in 1886, and the Burlington strike of 1888.[25] The rapid response to social change also reflects the type of men recruited by the new discipline. Sociology lends support to Donald Fleming's hypothesis that the academic boom of the late nineteenth century represents in part a secularizing of moral concern and of the moral career, a displacement of personnel from clergy to academy. The young man of good family with a conscience too sensitive for business more often chose lectern to pulpit as a place from which to pass ethical judgment upon his fellows.[26]

One crucial cause of the 'separation out' of sociology in the late 1880s was to have lasting effect on the discipline. Sociology came into existence in great part by default, as the other zones of concern and research which until then had been fused with it in the portmanteau study of social science split off and differentiated themselves. History, political science, political economy each formulated official interpretations and techniques, and founded separate professional associations and university departments.[27] Thus, sociology at the beginning acquired that special character which dominated it for at least three decades, and still persists as its *raison d'être*. Its special subject matter was a residual category, or more exactly, two residual categories at extreme ends of a spectrum between concreteness and abstraction. At one extreme, the departments of sociology inherited the study of very specific 'social problems' — so christened by the common sense of right-thinking citizens — which were gladly excluded by the slightly older disciplines: charities and corrections, housing conditions, home economics, sanitation, delinquency. In particular sociology was to be preoccupied with the growth of 'the dependent, defective, and delinquent classes' and all those aspects of society which could be defined as pathological from the viewpoint of Social Gospel liberalism with its concern for physical and mental health, moral probity, and the construction of a more co-operative society.[28]

At the other extreme was the taxonomic problem of society as a whole, the endeavor to define and establish categories by which the total stucture and relations of a human population having common bonds could be described. Grand social theory could not be belittled as 'slumming' but its level of generality and abstraction was often so great that the other disciplines doubted its intellectual rigor as well as its relevance. The 'general sociologist' put faith in the proposition that there was a larger realm which included the spheres of political and economic behavior and institutions, but went beyond them to include all human interaction.[29] As Albion Small recalled, 'the Sociologists started out with the conviction that there was something for them to study, then went about to find it.'[30] Thus, American sociology, at least until the 1920s, was dominated by these two polar definitions of the subject — the macrocosmic concern with 'society' and its fundamental analytic components, and the microscopic focus upon strata of pathological tissue in the body social.

Both these emphases, however, were enclosed within the strategic assumption that sociology, even in its most theoretical moods, was a practical science oriented towards action and reform. The emerging discipline shared this assumption with other, related movements between the middle 1880s and the early 1920s. The imposing conservative edifice of laissez faire economics and Social Darwinism was under attack at the turn of the century from both the primarily humanitarian and religious viewpoint of the Social Gospel and Christian Socialism and from the 'scientific' standpoint of evolutionary sociologists like Lester Ward who found the moral prohibitions of social

Darwinism intellectually untenable. The social gospellers were essentially in the Puritan tradition of concern for the condition, both physical and moral, of fellow members of the Christian community, attempting to recreate in the vastly expanded America of the nineteenth century the cherished image of a 'city on a hill', a unified society in which the common morality of self-disciplined restraint and achievement in the world would be supported, and enforced if need be, by community ties.[31] The Protestant reformers took on themselves the heavy burden of trying to preserve, in a society growing more diverse, norms developed from those of the early settlers and assumed to be universally valid and necessary to a free, virtuous society.[32] Lord Bryce implied that this American faith in her own virtue was a vital self-fulfilling prophecy. But by the time he wrote, the faith was becoming more difficult to hold since objective conditions seemed more and more to undermine these values, and Protestants found increasingly burdensome the effort of will required to force society back to the mold of Christian, republican virtue.[33]

Still, many young men answered the call sounded by evangelicals like Josiah Strong in *Our Country*. Strong reflected the traditional Protestant concern with home missions to enforce a strenuous morality against the temptations of frontier life and commercial greed; but Strong modernized this traditional missionary appeal to the laity by pointing to the *new* challenges to Christianity. The virtue of Protestant America was being menaced by the perils of immigration, Romanism, Mormonism, intemperance, secularism, socialism, and excessive wealth, and the great city seemed the natural center of these challenges. The imminent catastrophe would be fatal to the whole progress of civilization. 'We of this generation and nation, occupy the Gibraltar of the Ages which commands the world's future.' Much of the appeal of Strong's book lay in its clever combination of traditional moral attitudes with the latest modes of argument. His familiar warnings against corruption and immigration were supported with statistics compiled by economists, geographers, demographers and sociologists, thus 'masculinizing' the 'feminine' field of moral exhortation with a battery of hard facts.[34]

For some of the Americans who felt the sharpening conflict between 'conditions' and traditional ideals, the resulting state of mind was one of resigned despair: Henry Adams, for example, simply admitted that science and the liberated commercial greed of the years after Appomattox had destroyed the faith which his own family had robustly embodied.[35] But many other admirers of the early republic and republican virtue refused to despair. They found the glory of the industrial age to be just in its challenge to a complacent acceptance of the older verities, but were convinced that now more than ever before, modern science and material prosperity made it possible to *realize* these traditional goals of American democracy — the equality of all men, and a share for all citizens in the processes of government.[36]

It was amid this growing stream of thought, or exhortation, that the discipline of sociology emerged in its characteristically American form – no less anxious than Spencer or Sumner to create a scientific description of society, but driven by a conviction that science not only liberated by giving understanding, but provided the practical tools with which to realize the just and virtuous society. These meliorists, who probably formed the majority of American sociologists by 1910, did not repudiate the teachings of Comte and Spencer that society was a complex interrelationship of forces which it was the sociologist's duty to describe. However, they agreed with Comte, rather than Spencer, that the sociologist's description and analysis of reality was a preparation for action, that science was the great enabling force which, by disciplining the mind and teaching the complexity of life, gave the vision and self-critical depth necessary to control reality. As Small said in 1907, 'sociology in its largest scope and on its methodological side is merely a moral philosophy conscious of its task.'[37] Nor did they fear that knowledge of complexity might paralyze the will to act. As Small's colleague at Chicago, Charles R. Henderson, exhorted the students of Chautauqua, 'For us the world is will before it is exact knowledge, for no one can ever know what is possible until the untried is attempted through faith.'[38]

The American pioneer of this 'liberal' or 'reform' sociology was Lester Frank Ward, the autodidact and polymath bureaucrat whose initial ambition to write a key to the universe called *The Great Panacea* was sublimated into a two volume *Dynamic Sociology*. For Ward, sociology was fundamentally a practical and melioristic science; it should be concerned not only with analyzing society, but 'with social ideals, with ethical considerations, with what ought to be'. He broke with the Malthusian fatalism of Spencer and Sumner and helped lay the foundation of American sociology as an activist, meliorist discipline; and his influence in the universities helped convince the rising generation of sociologists that it was their duty to minister to society, not from the pulpit but from the investigating commission and the administrative board.[39]

Within the new Chicago department of sociology, the meliorist assumptions of early American sociology were markedly embodied in its two oldest members, Albion W. Small and Charles Richmond Henderson. Henderson brought to sociology a committed Christian faith and a long experience of practical philanthropy. Born in Indiana in 1848, trained at the old denominational University of Chicago, Henderson had spent twenty years as pastor of Baptist churches in Terre Haute and Detroit before joining Rockefeller's new-minted University of Chicago in 1892 as recorder, chaplain, and assistant professor of sociology. He combined the chaplaincy with his work in sociology until his death in March, 1915, having become a full professor in 1897 and head of a separate, closely related department of practical sociology in 1904. As a student in Chicago he had served a church near the stockyards, and at Terre Haute helped to found the local Charity Organization Society — the British-influenced 'new departure' which promoted 'friendly visiting' by the well-to-do in order to encourage aspiration and gentility in the recipients of relief, and also, to make it more difficult for them to exploit the uncoordinated municipal and private relief funds, kept common records of recipients and grants. In Detroit he engaged in mediation of labor disputes and studied prison management, becoming a recognized expert in the field. His first book was an *Introduction to the Study of the Dependent, Defective and Delinquent Classes* (1893), followed by *The Social Spirit in America* (1897), and works on modern charity and insurance. Henderson developed close ties between the university and such special settlements as the Chicago Commons run by the Social Gospel minister, Graham Taylor, and Jane Addams' Hull House. In return, Taylor taught part-time in the university, giving such courses as 'Humanitarian Progress in Local Institutions'.[40]

From this practical side of the university's sociology department emerged the first program of organized research into the conditions of city life. Even before the university became active, Hull House residents had put out the celebrated *Hull House Maps and Papers*. At the Chicago School of Civics and Philanthropy founded by Graham Taylor, Sophonisba Breckenridge and Edith Abbott, experts in child welfare and labor legislation, were conducting numerous studies of Chicago social problems. In 1920 the school became a graduate department of the university with Breckenridge and Abbott as professor and dean. Meanwhile, the university itself had been working on parallel lines. Small's sociology department set up its own settlement house in Packingtown in 1894 with a former Hull House resident in charge.[41] Since the work being done in the sociology department and in the outside social work agencies was in many ways parallel and complementary, men and women like Taylor, Henderson, Breckenridge, and Abbott found little difficulty in working in both.

Small, Thomas, and the Development of a Chicago School of Sociology

While Charles R. Henderson remains interesting to the student only in the leaden sense of illustrating a characteristic career-line and common place ideas, two of Park's senior colleagues in the Chicago department, Albion W. Small and William I. Thomas, exerted considerable intellectual influence on Park and on the complex syndrome of interests and ideas which would later be known as the 'Chicago school of sociology'.[42] The other dimension of early American sociology, the drive towards a comprehensive theory of society, was represented at Chicago by Henderson's colleague, and chairman of the department, Albion Woodbury Small. Small was born in 1854 in Maine, the eldest son of a Baptist minister. After an A.B. from Colby University and two years at the Newton Theological Institute he spent another two years at Berlin and Leipzig, returning home in 1881 to teach history and political economy at Colby. He became president of Colby University in 1889, the same year that he took a ph.d. in history and political economy at Johns Hopkins. Small was rapidly becoming dissatisfied with the traditional fields: history seemed merely a chronicle of events and economics to neglect some of the most essential aspects of social life. To remedy this he started a new course in sociology at Colby and in 1892 moved to Chicago to become the head of the new sociology department.[43] His career is typical of the way in which well-trained students, unhappy with the fast hardening boundaries of the slightly older disciplines, settled upon sociology as a frontier field where professional ideology did not yet preclude experimentation. The intellectual 'imperialism' of sociology also appealed to Small: in the tradition which runs from Comte to Talcott Parsons he believed in the essential unity of the social sciences, and the role of sociology in providing the general principles upon which they would ultimately re-unite.[44]

Small's career influenced the development of American sociology both practically and theoretically. He built up the largest and most influential department in the country, collaborated with George E. Vincent on the first textbook in sociology, *Introduction to the Study of Society* (1894) and founded the *American Journal of Sociology* in 1895. Ten years later Small was one of the co-founders of the American Sociological Society, whose establishment marked the maturation of sociology as a profession seeking respectability.[45]

Small's attitude toward the ultimate goals of study illustrates the continuing shift of interest from moral philosophy to a professionalized discipline which would win the respect of believers in rigorous science. He hoped that sociology would discover the 'principles of societary relationships in such a way that they might assist all intelligent men in taking the largest possible view of their rights and duties as citizens'. While he believed that 'the ultimate Sociology must be essentially Christian', he distrusted the preachers of the Social Gospel. Emotional rather than empirical, they tended to 'quarrel with economic facts rather than to discover the real meaning of the facts'.[46] But a proper sociology, Small agreed with W.I.Thomas, aimed to substitute action based on knowledge for action based on feeling.[47] He argued that a professional organ was an essential means of screening the genuine from spurious sociology − apparently on the principle that editorial judgment would winnow out the work of the 'scientific' sociologist who displayed a chastened awareness of the difficulty of achieving reform in an interrelated situation when unintended consequences were likely to occur. Justifying the *Journal* to President Harper in 1895, Small claimed that 'every silly and mischievous doctrine which agitators advertize, claims sociology as its sponsor. A scientific journal of Sociology could be of practical social service in discrediting pseudo-sociology and in forcing social doctrinaires back to accredited facts and principles.'[48] Small thus tried to establish the tone of academic sociology as moderate, respectably meliorist, and at the same time scientifically valid. The denunciation of agitators, the stress on 'accredited facts and principles', also suggests another motive for Small's desire to establish professional credentials: it would make the field 'respectable' in the eyes of donors and university governors, by disproving the popular, and arguably perceptive, confusion of sociology with socialism.[49]

The theories which Small transmitted from Europe were intended to meet these multiple needs. He developed the ideas of the Austrian sociologist Ratzenhofer into a synthesis which had close ties with the pragmatism of James and Dewey. Although influenced by both Ward and Sumner, Small took most of his theory from the Rosencrantz and Guildenstern of sociology, those twin products of the Austrian imperial bureaucracy who were so impressed by the multi-racial character of the Austrian empire — Gustav Ratzenhofer and Ludwig Gumplowicz. Following them closely, Small concluded that social life must be understood as a constant formation, combination, conflict, and destruction of groups seeking to realize their interests. Sociology was to be a study, not of static social structures or of immutable institutions and functions, but a continuing and open-ended *social process*, whose motive power was the conflict of interest groups.[50]

Although later trivialized through repetition and acceptance, the idea of social process was one variant of 'the revolt against formalism' described by Morton White — one of the low-level ideas which help to transmit a new explanatory paradigm, but too sweeping and porous to be of much value once the paradigm is established. The broadly Darwinian idea of 'process,' derived immediately from Ratzenhofer and the German historical school, implied that since society was always in flux so too were social values.[51] Consequently, 'the human situation being always and everywhere, either actually or potentially, a becoming , human conduct is always good or bad according to the demands of the particular stage of the process to which it is referred or in which it must function. ...Our acts are all relative to a process which, so far as we know, may be infinite in all its dimensions.'[52] Thus, sociology could reveal no absolute social or ethical system; but a detailed study of a particular phase of the process could indicate proposals for reforms which could be 'scientifically derived from and directed towards a particular, clearly defined stage of the social process'.[53]

Small's ideas were rarely concrete and sometimes simple and vague; these qualities led some later sociologists to deny that he had any lasting, specific intellectual influence within the profession. However, when the growth of the discipline is viewed with an eye to broad perspectives and leading ideas, it can be seen that Small transmitted the general ideas of the group, of process, and of conflict sociology, not only to the political scientist Arthur F. Bentley but also to his colleagues, Thomas and Park. Certainly, his emphasis upon the group as 'the initial phenomenon of the social process' and the central unit of analysis for the sociologist has been a continuing factor in American sociology, and it jibed particularly well with the developing school of Chicago psychology with its conception of the individual as essentially a product of life within a group.[54]

A decade younger than Albion Small, his colleague, William Isaac Thomas, was one of the first American sociologists to blend theory with field research, forging a mold within which Robert Park would direct the Chicago sociology of the 1920s. Thomas brought Park into the profession; he was (with Simmel) one of the two major influences on Park's theories, and he transmitted to his colleague a conception of the proper relation of sociological theory to social research.

It is easy to understand the friendship and appreciation which sprang up so quickly between Park and Thomas. The two men shared similar backgrounds and training and both were sharply separated, in temperament and interests, from the Christian reformist tradition of Small and Henderson. Born in Tennessee in 1863, son of a Congregational minister, Thomas was raised in a relaxed small-town milieu similar to Park's. Thomas recalled that his childhood was 'of a strictly manual, perceptual-motor type, taking the direction of rifle shooting. ...I reckon that I passed not less than seven years of my youth in the woods along with a rifle, without a dog, shooting at a mark, and regretting the disappearance of large game and the passing of the Indian and pioneer life.'[55] An A.B. from the University of Tennessee in 1884 was followed by four years there teaching English and modern languages, a year studying philosophy in Germany and a post in English at Oberlin in 1889.

While in Germany, Thomas had studied 'folk psychology', the study of the group mind through language, myth, and custom, and at Oberlin he began to teach sociology as well as English. In 1895 he moved on to become a fellow in Small's new department at Chicago, taking one of the early doctorates in 1896 with a dissertation 'On a Difference of the Metabolism of the Sexes.' As the subject suggests, Thomas was influenced less by Albion Small than by the physiologist Jacques Loeb, but he read widely and gained first-hand knowledge of an alien milieu by tramping around Chicago. This practice made him invaluable to his colleague, Henderson, since he could report on his visits to a variety of saloons. (Henderson, Thomas claimed, had never visited a saloon or tasted beer.) By 1910 the prodigiously energetic Thomas had become a full professor and the center of the department's intellectual life.[56]

The intellectual development of W.I.Thomas was long and complex; his theories assimilated a vast range of material including evolutionary anthropology and the criticisms of it by Franz Boas, the German tradition of folk psychology, the functional psychology of John Dewey, the deterministic physiology of Jacques Loeb, and the conflict sociology of Ratzenhofer.[57] Thomas' theories of race relations had a great impact on Park's own work, discussed below in Chapter 6; aside from this special area, Park was influenced chiefly by Thomas' general theory of social change and the social psychology which, along with George Herbert Mead in Chicago's philosophy department, he was developing out of the start given by Dewey and Cooley.

Thomas' theory of social change was stated most succinctly in his *Source Book for Social Origins*, published in 1909, and was repeated and elaborated, with less dependence on evolutionary sociology and instinct or 'faculty' psychology, in *The Polish Peasant* of 1918. Years later, Park stated his own debt to the *Source Book*: it had lifted American sociology from concern for social problems to the study of theoretical problems. The ideas put forward in the *Source Book* found 'a consistent expression in most, if not all, of the subsequent published studies of the students and instructors in Sociology at Chicago'.[58]

For his general theory of change, Thomas drew upon the crowd psychology of Tarde, Le Bon, and their American interpreter E. A. Ross, and the *Folkways* of William Graham Sumner. To the common-sense framework of a pattern of stable institutions breaking down into 'crisis' situations and then the gradual recovery of stability through the acceptance of new institutions, Thomas added a social psychology, drawn from James, Dewey, Ratzenhofer, and Small, in which the stability of institutions depends on the observance of habit, the satisfaction of conditioned expectations, the maintenance of tradition, and the focusing of the individual's *attention* on traditional objects. Thomas' 'crisis' theory foreshadows the later work of Robert Park in many ways, not least of which is its effort to establish a parallel explanation of change at the microcosmic and macrocosmic levels — to link change in the individual with change in the total society. The same pattern of explanation was applied to the maintenance or disruption of patterns of personal life and of social institutions. Here was another re-inforcement of Park's conviction that 'all Sociology is social psychology.'[59]

Thomas' interpretation of stability and change in the individual and the larger unit was based on three psychological concepts — control, attention, and crisis. 'Control', for Thomas, was the central goal, or (in the case of non-conscious activity) function of human action; it was the pragmatic equivalent of Spencer's interpretation of human behavior in terms of adjustment to environment. Indeed, Thomas' discussion of 'control' as the central motive force in human behavior was essentially the evolutionary approach of Herbert Spencer, supplemented by an emphasis on spontaneity, creativity, mastery in human 'response', which both the American pragmatists and the German neo-Kantians had insisted upon. The goal of all activity was an extension of human control: 'The human mind is pre-eminently the organ of manipulation, of adjustment, of control. It operates through what we call knowledge...based on memory and the ability to compare a present situation with similar situations in the past and to revise our judgments and actions in view of that past experience. By this means the world at large is controlled more successfully as time goes on.'[60]

Thomas offered 'control' as a concept to replace the earlier interpretations of social process by such 'so-called elemental or dominant social forces' as Tarde's 'imitation', Gumplowicz's 'conflict', or Giddings' 'consciousness of kind'. Although his own proposed slogan seems just as vague and overloaded with multiple meaning as these earlier phrases, the *connotations* or metaphysical pathos of 'control' were clearly more congenial to a social science imbued with moralistic activism. 'Control', Thomas said, was the goal of the whole range of human activity — nutrition, reproduction, technology, religion, art, even play, which was 'an organic preparation and practice for control'.[61]

The second principle, 'attention', was a mental faculty, or power, drawn from James' *Psychology*, and closely related to the concept of 'control'. 'Control is the end to be secured and attention is the means of securing it. They are the objective and subjective sides of the same process.' Attention was 'the mental attitude which takes note of the outside world and manipulates it...the organ of accommodation'. It was closely linked to another of William James' fundamental categories, 'habit', the patterns of behavior which have become established and automatic through repetition: 'when habits are running smoothly, the attention is relaxed; it is not at work.'[62]

In the opposite relation to 'attention' was 'crisis' — the situation in which 'something happens to disturb the run of habit,' and the attention must be called into play to develop 'a new mode of behavior which will meet the crisis' created by the disruption of previously adequate habits of response to the environment.[63] The theory was thus a generalized restatement of Charles Peirce's Darwinian account of the conditions which produce thought, phrased in the terms of Jamesian psychology, with 'attention' as a broader term, so broad as to be vague, designed to cover the total repertory of human responses to unstable situations.[64] Thus rational reflection designed to solve problems was, for Thomas, only one special case of this fundamental human drive towards the recovery of equilibrium.[65]

Thomas went even farther, making this single psychic process support his entire theory of social organization in a manner strongly reminiscent of William Graham Sumner's *Folkways*. 'Crises' produce the specialized occupations: 'the medicine-man, the priest, the law-giver, the judge, the ruler, the physician, the teacher...represent classes of men who have or profess special skills in dealing with crises.' Differences in social organization reflect the varied crises which societies have faced in their early development, though once a framework of response is established, this pattern of culture then fixes limits within which later responses will be made. The parallel with Sumner's account of social change in *Folkways* is striking, though Thomas, as would be expected of a former colleague of Dewey, was anxious to grant to individuals a degree of creative power in originating novel adaptations: 'the individual

mind cannot rise much above the level of the group mind....The extraordinary individual works on the material and psychic fund already present, and if
the situation is not ripe neither is he ripe. ...The character of accommodation
already made affects the character of accommodation to the new crisis.'[66]
Thus Thomas offered an interpretative overview which gave full credit to the
coercive power of society while remaining firmly fixed on the individual, the
actual locus of social behavior, and mediating the power of collectives
through the psychic processes of the sentient individual.[67]

Thomas' crisis theory, with its implied normal or 'steady state' of individual and social adjustment through habit, was the basis of the celebrated
doctrine of 'social disorganization' later elaborated in *The Polish Peasant* and
employed to interpret most of the phenomena studied by the Chicago school
in the 1920s. Social disorganization was a self-contained theory on the cultural level, explaining stability and change in terms of the consistency and
vigor of the attitudes and values which cultures supply to their members, and
the ability of these values to satisfy the personal desires of individuals and give
meaningful outlets for action within the established rules of conduct. Social
disorganization referred not so much to the crises in individual behavior as to
conflicts which shattered the web of values which had helped men develop the
habits which protected them from the pain of taking thought.[68]

Thomas was careful to stress that all societies were 'disorganized' to a
degree since their norms were never entirely consistent, always undergoing
change. Further, with characteristic American distrust of a reified 'society',[69]
he stressed that a 'disorganization' of social norms did not automatically
mean that individual members of the society underwent a parallel personal
disorientation. Social norms meshed with individual 'temperament' and the
peculiar life-history which each man brought to the choices he must make;
while norms were important in shaping the personality, they were neither
omnipresent nor wholly consistent. Furthermore, for the individual to escape
from the norms of the group was not necessarily a disaster: 'an individual
who breaks some or even most of the social rules prevailing in his group may
indeed do this because he is losing the minimum capacity of life organization
required by social conformism; but he may also reject the schemes of behavior imposed by his milieu, because they hinder him in reaching a more
efficient and more comprehensive life-organization.'[70]

Thus, at the cost of introducing an additional vague and difficult to specify
concept, — 'temperament', the weight of past individual experience —
Thomas avoided the common vice of sociological organicism — the reduction of the individual to a series of attitudes pumped into him by forces in the
cultural environment. However, Thomas paid for this defense of human
uniqueness, since he needed to develop an adequate theory of psychology to
explain the motives which led men to deviate creatively from the patterns of

their culture. This attempt to arrive at a theory of motives, more concrete than the Jamesian psychology he offered in 1909, led Thomas to the first version of his celebrated 'four wishes', or universal human needs which will appear in all cultural situations — the desire for security, for new experience, for response, and for recognition.[71] Robert Park made less use of the 'four wishes' than did many of his students, who sought a simple classification of human motives to 'explain' the behavior they observed.

Thomas' most important contributions to Park's system were his conceptions of 'attitude' and the 'definition of the situation'. 'Attitude', which Thomas introduced in *Sex and Society* (1907) and elaborated in *The Polish Peasant*, was a complex of ideas and emotions which became an habitual disposition of the mind towards acting in a certain stereotyped way.[72] By 1923, in *The Unadjusted Girl*, Thomas had shifted emphasis away from attitude to what he called the 'definition of the situation', Before the individual acts, he sizes up the situation as it appears to him. This definition of each situation is the result of the individual's prior attitudes impinging on or acting as the filter through which the immediate perceptions flow and are interpreted. It is therefore the product of a process of social conditioning which included both common social elements and elements unique to the individual's life-history. In consequence, there is always 'a rivalry between the spontaneous definitions of the situation made by the member of an organized society and the definitions which his society has provided for him'.[73] The first steps towards understanding for the sociologist must be an attempt to grasp the actors' point of view in any situation through the gathering of attitude-revealing life histories, letters, and other biographical documents. Further, the sociologist must always remember that 'reality' lay just as much in the participants' *understanding* of any particular situation, as in the 'objective' measurable factors.[74]

The guides to interpretation which W.I.Thomas laid down became axioms for the research students whom Robert Park guided in the 1920s. Edmund Volkart has stressed the originality of Thomas' contribution viewed in the context of classificatory sociology and the search for original 'forces' which occupied sociologists before 1910. Thomas certainly did not escape from these earlier notions altogether, as the idea of 'four wishes' should show; however, he transformed the perspective in which they were treated, so as to make the concepts of 'general' or 'theoretical' sociology applicable to the study of concrete behavior, and thus at least potentially capable of empirical verification.[75]

Thomas' location of the crucial area of social change on the level of social psychology, in the attitudes and definitions of the situation of individuals and groups, had a political implication. No amount of legislative tinkering with external conditions would 'take', or persist, unless individual attitudes also changed to keep pace with them. An obvious deduction from Thomas' theory was that the truly 'natural' method of social evolution was a change of attitudes which then gradually produced change at the institutional and political levels. This explanation of change then reinforced, as it probably originated in, the Progressive assumption that 'education', or exposure to the 'facts' plus moral exhortation, was the major tool of the reformer. The assumption that lasting change could only proceed from a fundamental change of attitudes was to be central to Park's work on race relations.

This comprehensive theory of social equilibrium and change, a refinement of common sense through the social psychology of James and Cooley, was the general framework within which Park placed the particular facts which he and his students gathered and scrutinized. Thomas and especially George Herbert Mead of Chicago's philosophy department later developed and refined the concept of 'attitude' and its role in social change, but the 1909 statement was the simplest and most sweeping, and coming just before Park resumed his sociological work, it exercised the greatest influence on him. Park himself also attempted to make the concept more precise and sociologically useful by cautioning researchers to distinguish between 'attitudes' strictly defined, which were 'formed quite unconsciously, on the basis of experience', and 'opinions', which 'arise usually in discussion, in the effort of the individual to define and to justify an attitude already defined'.[76] He even toyed with the idea of developing methods of measuring social attitudes, but with his deeply entrenched distaste for statistical methods he went no further along this line.[77]

Park and Thomas remained colleagues for only five years. Thomas' formal academic career terminated in 1918, after he was arrested in a Chicago hotel room with a young woman on charges of disorderly conduct, false registration, and violation of the Mann Act. Public interest was fanned by the fact that the woman's soldier husband had just sailed for France, and that Thomas was a prominent defender of female emancipation. He had already evoked protests to the university from concerned citizens; an indignant Iowan for example, had found a talk by Thomas on American women so shocking that he complained to President Harry P. Judson, denouncing it as 'a vicious attack upon the social system of America', defending 'institutions not recognized by the moral code', and offering 'a psychological defense of the "moral evil"'.[78] Thomas denied that he was guilty as charged in the hotel incident, but affirmed that he was 'guilty of the whole general charge in the sense that I hold views and am capable of practices not approved by our social traditions'. The apparent progression from advocacy to action confirmed popular prejudice, and President Judson was anxious to purge this provocative personality. Thomas was suspended pending an inquiry into his case, and a day later he was dismissed by the university trustees on recommendation of the president.[79] Albion Small, though reported as bursting into tears, was also convinced that Thomas must depart. Robert Park, who had no great respect for propriety, defended Thomas without success. Later, however, according to his students' recollection, Park was instrumental in bringing his old friend back into the professional association and arranging for his election as president. As Everett Hughes recalled the incident, when Park became president of the American Sociological Society in 1925, he invited Thomas, who had been suspended from the society, to deliver a paper, then packed the business meeting with Chicago graduate students who elected Thomas a vice-president with automatic succession to the post of honor.[80]

The departure of William I. Thomas left a vacuum of leadership in the Chicago department, into which Park, as the colleague with the strongest personality and greatest experience, and the most sympathy with Thomas' concerns, naturally moved. So, partly by accident, Park found himself presiding over the institutionalization of social analysis, its movement into formal academic status.[81]

In 1921 Park wrote that sociology was only just being transformed from a philosophy of history into a science of society by entering into a period of investigation and research. The early flowering of social research took place largely outside the universities through numerous investigations by government and private agencies into 'social problems'. The increase in bureaucracy and the expanded role of government by the turn of the century gave rise to studies aimed at improving the efficiency of administration, such as the surveys conducted by the Bureau of Municipal Research of New York City.[82] At the same time, the overwhelming changes of the period led those concerned with the pathology of society to conclude that nothing could be done to solve social problems until they first studied the changes in detail. This felt need inspired the numerous social surveys carried out by settlements like Hull House, or by foundations, such as the Russell Sage Foundation which financed a pioneering survey of Pittsburgh in order to discover 'how human engineering had kept pace with mechanical in the American steel district'. By the early 1920s every state and major city had its surveys, some sponsored by local government, some by groups of concerned citizens.[83] The methods of the social survey were eclectic: as Paul U. Kellogg of the Pittsburgh survey put it, the surveyor

takes from the engineer his working conception of the structural relations of things...takes from the charity-organization movements the case-work method of bringing problems down to human terms...not in sweeping generalizations but in what Mr. Woods called 'piled-up actualities'...takes from the journalist the idea of the graphic portrayal...maps and charts and diagrams...photographs and enlargements, drawings, casts and three-dimensional exhibits.[84]

The overt aim of the surveys was always practical, to influence the policy of social institutions and of government; and the areas chosen for study were those aspects of social life which were malleable through government action — wages, hours, accidents, industrial relations, housing conditions, health, schools, and so on.[85] Park's colleague and collaborator, Ernest W. Burgess, called the survey 'a method of social introspection checked by statistical measurements and the comparative standards of the social expert...for the purpose of presenting a constructive program of social advance'.[86] The program of fact finding and publicity was based upon the Progressive assumption that there was an active public committed to a single moral vision of what is just and right, and that once the facts of any unjust situation were exposed, an outraged public would remedy it. The facts themselves would compel action because, as one worker in the field explained: 'there is something majestic in a fact. What is, is. This monumental character of facts can but make the deepest kind of impression. Contacts with these facts make a never-to-be forgotten dent upon our plastic minds'.[87]

For the academic sociologist, however, mere fact-gathering was not sufficient to create a social science: the facts were fruitless unless thoroughly integrated with theory. Albion Small himself, although his own 'mental patterns were of the pre-scientific and pre-methodological state of social science' recognized that sociology must be based on a research program founded on and directed by a sound theory. At present, he said in 1924, all social science was still 95 percent 'general discursiveness', 'pertinent and impertinent selections from the scrap heaps of human experience.'[88] Robert Park also attacked the theoretical aimlessness of the research that had been done so far. As he complained in 1921: 'a great deal of information has been collected merely for the purpose of determining what to do in a given case. Facts have not been collected to check social theories. Social problems have been collected, for the most part, to support this or that doctrine, not to test it. In very few instances have investigations been made, disinterestedly, to determine the validity of a hypothesis.'[89] The Chicago sociology of the 1920s hoped to integrate field research with general theory and produce, not philosophical systems, or random information, but a sound body of 'scientific' knowledge.

Already there had been some attempts within the sociological profession to marry close empirical study with theory. In particular, Franklin Giddings at Columbia had inspired a series of community studies whose aim was to describe the society of a delimited region and draw theoretical conclusions, without any overt plan for reform action.[90] Park at Chicago took over this kind of study and made it the center and hallmark of the Chicago school. The fact that so many Chicago studies focused on aspects of the local scene reflects not only convenience but the assumption which carried over from the Christian reformers like Josiah Strong to the sociologists — the city was 'problematic', both morally and etiologically: understand the city and you understand the central tendencies of modern society. Even though their intention was not overtly reformist, Park and his students seemed to gravitate naturally towards those aspects of city life which from the perspective of respectable smalltown norms could be called 'pathological' – the ghetto, the gang, the slum (*and* the Gold Coast), the taxi-dance hall, the residential hotel.

Park the Teacher

As the war's end ushered in the period of expansion and influence for Chicago sociology, the department's senior members in sociology consisted of Small, Park, and two new men, Ellsworth Faris (1874-1953) and Ernest W. Burgess (1886-1966). Faris, a social psychologist hired to replace Thomas, had trained initially as an engineer and then served for seven years as a missionary in Africa. He returned to America to teach theology and philosophy at Texas Christian University and then decided to go to Chicago to take his doctorate. Impressed by the psychology department there, but especially by the philosopher of consciousness, George H. Mead, he switched his interests from philosophy to psychology and after taking his Ph.D. in 1914 taught psychology at the State University of Iowa for several years. In 1919 he was invited to join the sociology department at Chicago.[91]

Ernest W. Burgess was a Canadian by birth, the son of a Congregational minister in the Southwestern Ontario town of Tilbury, but he had been educated entirely in the United States and received his Ph.D. from Chicago in 1913. He was brought back in 1916 to replace Charles R. Henderson. Slight, pale, harried, a prodigious worker, Burgess never married and lived with his father and sister in an apartment near the campus. With this personal experience, he made his specialty the sociology of family life.[92] Burgess had an exceptional talent for collaboration; he and Park shared an office and whole afternoons would be spent discussing 'both theoretical and practical aspects of sociology and social research'.[93] It turned out to be a very fruitful partnership; Burgess was not only a shrewd critic, sensitive to current canons of empirical verification, but also a very efficient manager. It was Burgess who set about getting funds for research projects, who read theses and reminded Park to read the theses lost in his messy desk. Park had the charisma to attract the braver students, but Burgess had the organizing ability to keep the research work and the teaching of the department running smoothly. Although they worked so well together their interests were sharply divergent: Burgess, a friend of Jane Addams, was closely involved with city politics and social service agencies – activities which held little interest for Park. Like Henderson whom he replaced, Burgess far more than Park was in the tradition of social science which studied society primarily to identify and solve problems, though for him this goal entailed a disinterested effort to understand social phenomena.[94]

Robert Park in his late fifties and sixties was an impressive figure, well-equipped to inspire the necessary mixture of affection, respect, and fear in the majority of his students. His future assistant, Winifred Raushenbush, recalled him about 1917 as a handsome, heavily-built man, with Roman head, ruddy skin and long brown hair which would soon turn a distinguished white. While his appearance suggested an athlete, he was forced by a mild heart condition to lead a quiet life and to eat only 'tea-room food', as he grumbled. With hair worn long and often untidy, and careless attire which became a student legend, Park appeared almost bohemian to some provincial students. This appearance was deceiving, however; despite his fascination with the unorthodox, Park seems to have led the life of an orthodox family man, dignified, quiet and reserved with strangers, but warm toward friends. His powerful, mask-like face would 'explode' with pleasure upon meeting an old friend. He was given to frequent, brief explosions of anger and frightened some students with his blunt, gruff manner. With an un-academic bluntness which probably stemmed from his humility and sincere belief that he could learn from anyone, Park did not hesitate to tell students before their peers that their ideas were worthless. While this emotional directness offended some students, it seems to have entranced many more, since Park's intense, explosive personality joined his interests to represent to students the 'real life' beyond the ivied walls of the genteel academy. Beyond this, Park's combination of enormous erudition and a wide range of personal experience with an ineradicable middle-western sense of wonder impressed students who came from a similar background. He was the classic doctor-father figure, the man who had read *Faust* in German, loved Wagner, had investigated lynchings in the South and racial conflict in California, yet found time to take students on walking tours of Chicago and spend hours with them speculating on their interests and academic goals. Sometimes there was an element of conscious contrivance in the Park reputation; skeptical graduate students puzzled by Park's verbosity and wooliness had to be convinced by exhortation. Norman Hayner noted in his *Diary* (the most revealing source for the inner quality of the Chicago school) that on 10 October 1921 he had an interview with Park, then on 11 October he had an interview with Ellsworth Faris, who told him that Park was one of the biggest men in sociology.[95] The implication is irresistible that Hayner had to be exhorted by one of Park's colleagues to be patient and learn from this Polonius figure what he could; however, it is my interpretation, not Professor Hayner's recollection. Still, however much initial indoctrination was needed, and whatever the precise sources of his power, Park was clearly for many of his students a great teacher of the type longed for in the 1960s and 70s, a man of passionate commitment and moral authority who could inspire serious students to realize and even transcend themselves in a joint quest for personal and professional understanding.

Park's qualities as a classroom teacher reflected his sincere, non-conforming personality. He was not a dynamic nor even a polished lecturer, perhaps not a lecturer at all by orthodox definition. He is recalled as brooding aloud to his students about the implications of whatever topic was formally scheduled, ruminating about problems of method and adequate definition of concepts and objects of attention. Harold D. Lasswell, who was a student at Chicago in the early 1920s, recalled that Park's oral style was 'rather clumsy' and that he 'sought to formulate the many general ideas that attracted his interest' in a 'rather inarticulate and mumbling fashion'.[96] Thus, some of his authority may have come from a desire to deny authority: his principal concern was to show how little was known, to inspire independent investigation and to guide his students to an adequate understanding of their topics. Park saw himself as a captain of inquiry with a company of men and women who must be directed to a worthwhile topic, then given the energy required to complete their work. The range of subjects which intrigued him was broad and shifting, including the urban field studies which made the department famous, but also many other topics, from witchcraft to revolutions, which might illuminate some facet of his central concern with the nature and processes of social change. Norman Hayner noted in his diary that Park 'would like to write a book on little-known forms of sport; drawing out the inside life of a person; theatre, saloon and Turkish bath; exploring a city park between 2 a.m. and 4 a.m.; visiting a Bohemian cemetery...'. To many of his students, and perhaps to Park himself on a deeper level, there was in all this the fascination of the saloon and Turkish bath to the innocent country boy; but to Park on the level of conscious reflection, these exotic, special, 'marginal' types of institution and behavior found in the city were of special significance because they helped to define the boundaries of broader categories.[97]

Park's involvement with students was unsystematic but often extensive, and contributed much to the great admiration with which many of them recalled him. If a student or a topic seemed promising, Park arranged long interviews in which the subject was defined, methods were discussed, and the student's own experience and concerns were integrated with his research topic.[98] Thus, while Park assumed objectivity as the ultimate goal, he seemed to have acted on the assumption that the student must be led toward professionalism through his own experience. Some students were treated to field trips, strolls through Chicago on which Park mused about the significance of what they saw; others recalled casual encounters on the street which became long discussions of the student's work. While a few recalled Park as vague, sententious, and unable to give clear substantive advice, most cherished their memories of his unstinting concern. Colleagues as well as students recalled the long conversations, sometimes continued from one day to another, in which Park, pacing the floor, tried to clarify his or their ideas. His assistant often listened to these talks, noting down the more promising ideas for further development. These conversations, or monologues, roved over concrete categories of investigations and the lives, interests, and peculiarities of people; but they also tried to connect the concrete data with coherent social theory. As Park said later,

When a student proposed a topic for a thesis, I invariably found myself asking the question: what is this thing you want to study? What is a gang? What is a public? What is a nationality? What is a race in the sociological sense? What is graft? etc. I did not see how we could have anything like scientific research unless we had a system of classification and a frame of reference into which we could sort out and describe in general terms the things we were attempting to investigate.[99]

Herbert Blumer considered that one of the most original aspects of Park's teaching was his insistence, which seemed to reflect his training in philosophy, that the student clarify 'the meaning of a concept by first identifying, as well as one could, the class of things to which the concept referred and then seeking very carefully to single out for distinction this class of things and other classes of things that lay in the margin between them.'[100] Norman Hayner recalled that Park once spent almost an entire seminar discussing the logical problems involved in defining a hotel.[101]

Recollections of Park tend to be divided between those who found him an impressionistic journalist or sociographer, and those who found his desire to generalize and compare case studies provocative and fruitful. The anthropologist, Leslie A. White, who found Park crusty and likeable, 'the most stimulating teacher I had at Chicago', defined Park's approach and its limits:

...I cannot tell you just what I learned from him...Park's genuine interests were in particulars, not generalizations. He was more of a journalist, or artist...concerned with individuals, pictures of the life of groups — immigrants, denizens of skid row, hoodlums, etc., much as Dreiser, Gorky, et al., were. ...I remember well his showing me a doctoral thesis written under his direction. ...It was an intimate account of a small town in the west. He had everything in it about all the characters, both respectable and otherwise. It was exactly the sort of thing that Sherwood Anderson and Dreiser wrote. Park was fascinated by it. This is what he was interested in.[102]

While Park clearly held a general theory of social change which the Chicago monographs were designed to illustrate, White's description does convey the brooding Dreiserian desire to understand the empirical given which was Park's principal gift to the majority of his disciples. They must become reporters-in-depth, so as to 'enter as fully as possible into the social worlds they studied, participating in them sufficiently to understand the attitudes and values of these worlds'.[103] Park spoke approvingly of the approach of the anthropologist, who studies not merely the institutions of a community but its 'mentality', who conceives of it not merely as a 'statistical aggergate' but as a 'cultural complex'.[104]

While Park gave his time lavishly, not only in interviews and tours of exploration but in dinners for students and extensive loans of books, his principal concern was the project and not the student. Although many students seem to have adopted him as Honorable Ancestor, his attitude was more that of the city editor — pushing, suggesting, inquiring, needling, re-writing, scolding — than that of a father or guidance counselor. The faith and energy he transmitted to his students through personal prodding may explain why so many of his disciples ceased writing substantive sociology once they passed beyond the Master's sphere of influence. Nels Anderson commented that 'Park has two kinds of student. Some he drains so dry, they never can piss another drop.'[105] The alternative explanation of the sterility of many Chicago doctors — that Park's theories did not lead anywhere, were not capable of development — seems to be refuted by the elaboration of the concepts of status and role by Everett Hughes and later Erving Goffman.[106] It may be true that Park's ideas were presented so aphoristically that they required an unusually perceptive student to grasp their implications, elaborate, and sur-pass them.

Park's absorption in the work to be done could also victimize an unwary student. Like a Sunday editor, he often became enthusiastic about the latest subject which caught his fancy, and reached for someone to write it up. The luckless or spineless graduate student who next wandered into Park's office was likely to find himself saddled with his latest and often transistory passion. One Chinese student emerged from the sanctum committed to a study of witchcraft in seventeenth century America, as Park had been reading a book on that subject when the student arrived.[107] Everett Hughes resisted Park's effort to assign him to a study of land values, and by persistent opposition secured permission to do a dissertation on the Chicago Real Estate Board studied as a 'secular institution'.[108]

Much of the vigor and productivity of the Chicago sociology department in its early days came from its close relations with other departments of the university — in particular, economics, geography, and political science. All these departments used the city of Chicago as their 'field' and turned out studies in human geography, patterns of land values, and urban politics which proved valuable to the sociologists. The close informal collaboration between these departments was formalized in 1923 by the creation of a Local Community Research Committee to stimulate interdisciplinary studies and to examine the social and cultural life of Chicago. The committee, which was drawn from the other departments with an immediate interest in the city, as well as sociology, co-ordinated the numerous studies of the local community being undertaken by members of the university, helped to organize the large numbers of graduate and some undergraduate students used as field agents, tabulators and investigators, and decided upon the allocation of funds. By 1929 the social sciences at Chicago had their own social science research building, so dedicated to pure empirical research that it was innocent not only of undergraduates but of books — although it did have a planimeter and an harmonic analyzer as well as a good many calculating machines.[109]

Within the sociology department itself, graduate and much undergraduate teaching was organized around field research. An army of students was let loose upon Chicago, making maps of every kind of distribution — Burgess, in particular, was fond of having his students make spot maps of the pattern of distribution of various social problems. From the winter term of 1918, Park and Burgess together offered a field-study course every quarter (taught by the other if one was absent), to initiate students into the Chicago method of social research at first hand. All of Park's courses were oriented towards research; he disliked textbooks and ran most of his teaching on the basis of mimeographed readings, special assignments, and directed field work. Every student was assigned a specialized topic for investigation, which usually entailed not only library research but going out into the streets of Chicago to ask questions, observe, and soak up real life.[110]

The Chicago School and Its Clients

The university's research program on life in Chicago was facilitated by the co-operation of various charity agencies and social service bureaux, such as the Juvenile Court, the Institute of Juvenile Research, the Health Department, and the Association of Commerce, which made their records available to sociologists and graduate students from the university. These proved useful sources of material, but ones which had their dangers since the type of data gathered, and the assumptions of approach, would inevitably influence the studies done by the sociologists. At the same time, the *cachet* of collaboration with outside agencies lent an air of purposefulness and solidity to the Chicago research program and countered the threat of appearing strictly academic. Useful though the aid of existing fact finding agencies was, however, what the university sociology department needed most was money to finance its own research projects. Until 1923 the Chicago department struggled along pretty much without outside funds, but from then on it received fairly sizeable amounts from city organizations and from foundations. The breakthrough came when Beardsley Ruml, who had been an instructor in psychology at Chicago, became director of the Laura Spelman Rockefeller Memorial Fund and persuaded the trustees to put a good deal of money into financing social science research in the universities. A grant and a promise of further funds enabled scholars in the social sciences at various universities to set up the National Social Science Research Council, but the foundation also decided to support research at individual universities directly. The first such grant, of $25,000, went to the social science group at Chicago.[111] For the next ten years the foundation continued to give Chicago $50,000 a year with an additional $25,000 if this sum could be matched with an equal sum from the community. It always was: the money came from numerous sources

— the Children's Bureau, the city of Chicago, various clubs, Rotary and the League of Women Voters, settlements and charities, the Urban League, the Advertising Association, the Institute of Meat Packing.[112] According to President Hutchins, the funds received from the foundation were relatively small (although in 1927 the University of Chicago got $2.225 m. out of $10.314 m.) but they came at a crucial moment and helped to transform the social sciences.[113]

The intentions of the Spelman Foundation were essentially practical. A review in 1932 of its earliest programs acknowledged that 'the Memorial had no interest in the promotion of scientific research as an end in itself; its motive was not sheer curiosity as to how various human and social phenomena came to be and are; the interest in science was an interest in one means to an end, and the end was explicitly recognized to be the advancement of human welfare.' On the other hand, the board of the foundation had also decided not to give too much money to agencies directly involved in social work or to engage actively in politics or reform projects.[114] Ruml, the director, urged on the trustees the proposition that all efforts at social improvement were at present hampered by the lack of a 'body of substantiated and widely accepted generalizations as to human capacities and motives and to the behavior of human beings as individuals and in groups'.[115] In providing these laws, the academic social sciences seemed an ideal vehicle for promotion — they would be, one may conjecture, an invaluable tool in the extension of the Progressive, meliorist norm of tention-reduction: 'Through the social sciences might come more intelligent measures of social control that would reduce such irrationalities as are represented by poverty, class conflict, and war between nations.'[116] Ruml pointed out that the universities were the best place for undertaking the kind of research needed and for training new men because they had developed, however inadequately in the social sciences, 'scholarly and scientific standards of work'. But at present the universities were too isolated and one purpose of the Rockefeller grants was to facilitate the direct involvement of the academic departments with the life of the city, since as Ruml observed, 'the impingement of the phenomenal world on the observer is the beginning of things scientific.' The foundation wanted to get the researcher out to his problem by providing funds for leaves of absence and travelling expenses, as well as statistical and clerical assistance.[117]

In spite of the welcome financial aid there were considerable difficulties in the relationship of the academic departments to the foundations and other clients. Tension often arose when a client agency used graduate students as research assistants and the requirements of the agency clashed with the demands of the thesis adviser who regarded the agency merely as a training ground for his student.[118] Furthermore, the academic mind was not used to working to very precise schedules; academic researchers were often tempted to go off in hot pursuit of an intriguing new development, to the despair of the administrative or business organization which had commissioned the study and expected results on time.[119] Even open-minded foundation like the Laura Spelman Memorial wanted to mold university sociology to their own purposes, in particular by insisting that academic sociology become both more precise and more visibly useful. Ruml's successor, Edmund E. Day, an ex-professor of economics at Harvard, complained: 'Practically all the sciences have sprung initially from philosophy. The introduction of laboratory methods enabled the natural sciences to make a rather complete separation, and the medical sciences made the same break later. The social sciences are still in the process of establishing their independence. We have thus virtually to break an academic pattern. We have to establish a new academic mold.'[120]

They did not immediately succeed, however, and after a while there grew up considerable skepticism about the cash value of many of the university projects they financed. By 1934 the trustee committee of the Laura Spelman Memorial was insisting that the foundation concentrate its funds on 'problem-oriented research for the immediate solution of pressing problems of human welfare'. Blanket grants to universities only led to money being wasted on exotic projects such as 'the study of the Constitution of Classic Greek Cities' and 'the Social Life of the Navaho Indian.'[121] Even Beardsley Ruml, by the end of the 1920s, seemed to repent of his policy of giving the universities their head and was complaining that

There exists at the present time a strong and an increasing emphasis on a point of view in social research that seeks to eliminate the motive of social reform and betterment, and that views social phenomena as a complex behavior of a naturalistic world. The interest of the investigator is centred simply on an understanding of social events and he attempts to eliminate judgments of value and as far as possible the presence of an ethical bias.[122]

He reiterated that research without application was barren and that it should lead in the 'direction of social technology — or social engineering — with its recognized divisions of business, law, public administration, and social work'.[123]

The 1920s were thus an interlude of tolerance. The major foundations had been established as organs of social service and reform and any research undertaken was incidental to this practical goal. But during the 1920s, contemplating the tangle of race and ethnic relations and the myriad problems of the cities, it became evident that many social problems were less clear cut than stamping out pellagra. The felt need for theoretical orientation led to the financing of university reserach projects with little control as to how the money was used, but with the optimistic assumption that what the academic researchers found out would eventually pay off. By the 1930s, with the insistent social problems of the depression, it was less clear that this was so.

It was fortunate, therefore, that Park, with his 'self-indulgent' curiosity and detachment, could make use of the foundations in their 'soft' period. Park's involvement with the survey of race relations on the Pacific coast in 1924 revealed many of the strains and tensions inherent in the relationship between client and academic researcher. The Institute of Social and Religious Research, in collaboration with regional committees on the Pacific coast, appointed Park to direct an investigation of 'the economic, religious, educational, civic, eugenic and other social conditions and tendencies prevailing among the Chinese, Japanese and British Indian residents in the Pacific Coast territories of the U.S.A. and Canada and their interrelations with the American and Canadian residents'.[124] The purpose was essentially the missionary one of improving the tense relations between whites and Orientals. Park spent some time on the coast, getting local people interested, and also doing some interviewing. The interviews were quite informal, just to get the feel of things, but he kept a note book covering some of them.[125] Emory Bogardus, who collaborated on the survey, said that Park came to the West coast with

as few preconceived notions as is humanly possible, and followed up one social contact after another in the main centers until rules of procedure began to emerge out of these experiences. The aim was not to find out who is right or wrong, but to learn, what IS and how it CAME TO BE. The passing of ethical judgments was in reality reserved for the public after the Survey should be completed and after the public had all the scientific data upon which to pass judgments.[126]

After surveying the scene and addressing the local workers, Park returned to Chicago to direct the survey at a distance. However, he kept up a stream of advice to his workers in the field, warning one researcher that questions should not be formulated so as to demand a direct answer but 'to stimulate a person to talk', insisting that a mere collection of prejudiced statements reveals nothing new, but must be explained by being related to external circumstances. He suggested that the local workers get a detailed map of their area, locate on it the various crops, grouping together those types of crops which employed the same kind of labor. Then they were to locate 'the name of every person interviewed, on the assumption that his opinion with regard to the oriental represented the attitude of that region'. Park assumed that opinions could be explained generally by two main variables: 'the character of the agriculture in the region and by the personal experiences of individuals'. Special attention was to be given to the personal histories of those people whose opinions differed from the norm of their region.[127]

From the beginning, there were cross purposes between the ISRR and Park. For Park, the value of the survey lay in its disinterestedness. As he wrote to Bogardus:

The unique trait of the Race Relations Survey is that it has sought from the beginning to accept existing public opinion as a fact, and then to understand it by studying the conditions under which it has arisen. Previous investigations on the Coast have sought primarily to determine the merits of the issues raised by the presence of the Oriental; that is, to arbitrate and adjudicate the disputed questions. This study...has sought primarily to learn — irrespective of their merits — how these issues actually arose, what were their sources in the social situations themselves, in the experiences of individual men and women, in human nature generally, and in the existing state of mind.[128]

Park knew quite well that the ISRR 'had a feeling that if the studies were carried on independently by the universities and colleges they would not serve, as intended they should, as a means of educating public opinion on the question', and that the ISRR suspected that 'the academic studies are not going to be of importance in modifying public opinion on Race Relations. I suspect also that "improving Race Relations" means something rather immediate and definite, and something that cannot possibly happen.'[129] However, Park assumed that he was naturally free as a scholar to do what he saw fit.

By early 1925 the Institute was beginning to doubt the wisdom of Park's 'indirect uncontroversial factual approach'.[130] In March 1925 a conference was held at Stanford University to help persuade the ISRR to continue its support for the survey.[131] However, a remark in the 'Tentative Findings' delivered at the conference to the effect that tension had dropped since the passage of the Immigration Act of 1924, excluding all Oriental laborers, shocked the liberals in the New York headquarters of the Institute. A telegram was dispatched to Park demanding that he remove the offending passage.[132] Park, of course, refused. The directors of the ISRR were 'Christians and liberals, sympathetic to the Oriental', as was Park himself, but they could not conceive that he 'might be equally interested in and sympathetic with the World War I veterans, etc., etc., that being the nature of a sociologist and journalist'.[133] Park certainly hoped that the survey would eventually be ameliorative, but indirectly, by making people understand each other better. He thought that the publication of life histories in particular and other intimate human documents would reveal the Asian immigrant to the American public and show the humanity behind the stereotype.[134] But he could not tolerate an approach which denied the right of understanding and full expression to the sentiments of any social group. Following the example of William James conversing with the asylum inmate, Park felt that this universal empathy was the first canon of the objective scholar.

Empathy combined with objectivity was the standard he held up to his students. Emory S. Bogardus, an earlier Chicago Ph.D. who worked with Park as junior and executive colleague on the California Race Relations Survey, recalled that 'Once he startled our research group by saying that sociology is not interested in facts...gathering facts is the work of the historian. Numbers of facts and their analysis is for the statistician. Sociology, he said, is interested in the *meanings* of the facts to the persons involved, hence in the study of attitudes and how they change.'[135] To Park himself, the self-understanding of the individual or milieu was the first step in a two-stage process of research: the student must combine empathy with ecology, and trace the evolution and significance of attitudes and values within a broader context of institution, position, and social utility. As Erle F. Young said: 'complete identification with the persons studied, however, was taboo, since the student was in danger of becoming an apologist or even a protagonist rather than remaining a research student. The student's warrant for studying presupposed that he had a broader point of view than that of the persons studied, that he had a richer background against which to reflect the data and a more adequate scheme for analyzing it.'[136] It is likely, however, that many of Park's students absorbed only the injunction to understand, to think oneself into an alien milieu. This invitation to *Verstehen* clearly excited many students, serving to liberate them at least partially from the limited perspective of middlewestern normality. However, the liberation could also be so complete as to defeat its original purpose when it affected an excitable, alienated young person. The student to whom Park assigned the bohemia of Chicago's Near North Side became so absorbed, and so sympathetic, that he finally refused to complete the project, on the ground that to report on and analyze his newfound friends would be a betrayal of their trust. Thus for some students, empathy could not be separated from sympathy, and Park's goal of value-free research turned out to be an unstable middle ground between one morality and another.[137]

How far objectivity is actually possible for the social scientist has always been as problematic as its exact meaning; in the intellectual climate of the 1970s its desirability or even 'healthfulness' is also under question. Alvin W. Gouldner, in an influential radical critique of the tradition of Western sociology, traces the value placed on detachment and objectivity to the 'pervasive anomie' in the middle-class culture in which sociology developed.

The objectivity of Sociological Positivism arose when men entertained the suspicion that the world in which they lived was passion-spent and had little in it worth living or dying for.

On this level, such objectivity is not neutrality, but alienation from self and society; it is an alienation from a society experienced as a hurtful and unlovable thing. Objectivity is the way one comes to terms and makes peace with a world one does not like but will not oppose; it arises when one is detached from the status quo but reluctant to be identified with its critics, detached from the dominant map of social reality as well as from meaningful alternative maps. 'Objectivity' transforms the nowhere of exile into a positive and valued social location; it transforms the weakness of the internal 'refuge' into the superiority of principled aloofness. Objectivity is the ideology of those who are alienated and politically homeless.[138]

Gouldner's analysis is a classic of that contemporary rhetorical mode, damnation through conjectural psychologizing, and in strict logic is probably irrelevant to the question of the meaning and possibility of objectivity, perhaps even to that of its desirability. Still, since the currency of this cornerstone of the scholarly vocation has fluctuated with the felt needs of scholars as citizens and sentient human beings as well as the dictates of logical analysis, it is worth pausing to ponder Gouldner's denunciation. Park himself had no doubt that a certain Olympian detachment was part of the essential make-up of a successful sociologist and that in deciding upon the role of sociologist, one consciously excluded certain kinds of behavior which might be desirable in others. He once told some students who wanted to be activists for civil rights that the 'world was full of crusaders' and that their role was to be 'the calm, detached scientist who investigates race relations with the same objectivity and detachment with which the zoologist dissects the potato bug'.[139] 'I do not belong to the evangelical school of sociology', he remarked to an acquaintance, and his answer to a student's question, What did he do for people? was a gruff 'Not a damn thing!'[140] This objectivity was a necessary component of his passionate concern for *Verstehen*: the sociologist could not get inside the skulls of the people he was studying, could not truly understand them, if his own political and moral commitments were so compulsive that they prevented empathy with all kinds and conditions of men. There was, perhaps, a certain element of voyeurism in Park's type of sociology, an attempt to suck the essence out of other people's experience, to savour it without committing oneself or getting hurt. Still, it also implied a willingness to accept a reality which existed independently of the observer's concerns or perspectives, and which it was the scholar's duty to interpret as sympathetically as possible, like a musician. Further, the masters of German romanticism who had insisted on this method of passionate re-creation, living-through, of experience, including Hegel and the Goethe whom the young Park had loved, thought of it as an ethical task, a prerequisite to the authentic reasoned life.[141]

However, while the rejection of objectivity common in the 1960s and 1970s seems too often an excuse for prejudice and lack of self-criticism, Gouldner's analysis does illuminate Robert Park's attitudes toward the particular loneliness of scholarship. Park himself, in an offhand comment, made the connection between the rationale of scholarship and the rationale of the market place. Trade fosters detachment because it is necessary to avoid any emotional involvement with those one sells to or buys from: 'one does not wish to know the other party and his necessity too well. ... One must, if possible, remain objective. It is for this reason among others, that trade has so frequently gotten into the hands of foreigners. It is easier to be objective if one maintains the normal distances. Detachment is the secret of the academic attitude.'[142] Thus the scholar is always in some sense a stranger and an alien in the world and among the peoples he studies, and so a natural object of suspicion. Remembering the passionate search for a cause 'worth living and dying for' of Park's youth, the rigorous demand for objectivity of his middle age seems not only a professional requirement, but the resting place of a man who never found the cause which could not only compel his will but also blunt the edge of a self-critical intellect. As a difficult stance, involving a degree of conscious ironic distance and perhaps masochism, objectivity must probably be congenial to the character and congruent with the experience of the scholar, and must also be bolstered by the prevailing climate of significant opinion. To simplify, the history of attitudes toward objectivity has taken dialectical form — a steady increase in sophistication in weighing the difficulties, persisting through an alternation of 'committed' and 'disinterested' eras, the former demanding focused research whose clear conclusions warrant surgery on diseased limbs, the latter preferring theoretical sophistication and profundity of understanding. James Q. Wilson seems to suggest that the most profound explanation in terms of social causes is likely to be the one that most discourages remedial action. This is likely true in the context of crime control of concern to Wilson, but an overall explanation may be complex but still encourage action.[143] Most even of harsh critics of Marxism would admit its claim to profundity as well as complexity. The difference lies in the incisive reduction of behavior to a single crucial factor: an action theory must discriminate between independent and dependent variables. Park's perspective was existentially 'conservative' because its pluralism of perspectives undercut both easy indignation and the sharp conceptual focus needed to find the offending tissue. In the sense that the natural state of man is youthful prejudice, Gouldner may be right to find this tolerant wisdom of maturity 'alienating', but from another viewpoint it represents one of Park's most important achievements, the transmission of this classic scholarly ideal from the German humanists to a generation of Americans. Park, in the disillusioned twenties, helped to mold a professional ideology which, though certainly challenged in the 1930s and redefined later with the rise of more rigid scientific method, survived largely intact into the 1960s. Its period of dominance may be passing in the 1970s, as the attrition of age alters faculties and younger scholars seem to return to the actively manipulative stance from which Park recoiled — though 'radical commitment' replaces 'Christian uplift'.

Park saw his own role in the ongoing research endeavor as modest. He organized, advised, criticized, and re-wrote; but his own published contribution was usually limited to a brief preface to a student's book which emphasized the interest of the work for a student of society, and to an occasional more theoretical essay which formulated theories of social change or of social types on the basis of monographs. His role as seen by an enthusiastic disciple is summed up in an anonymous poem found among the Park papers:

> *You are the writer of introductions:*
> *Like the architect of a building*
> *Who does not himself*

Lay the brick on the mortar,
But who knows the meaning
Of basic design or method,
So you present a study
Of friend or colleague
You write the introduction
Better, oft-times, than the book itself,
A finished essay,
Suggesting approach or direction!
Always expanding, not closing a subject.
To introduce;
That, in truth, is your function.[144]

However, in the process of introducing, or inducing others to write, Park sometimes made crucial suggestions, which, fully, developed by more patient and painstaking men, emerged as influential ideas or methods. Emory S. Bogardus recalled that 'Park was aware of the weaknesses of all social research methods. ...He wanted us to obtain subjective data and present them objectively. One day he drew some vertical lines and set me at work on developing a scale for measuring racial attitudes. This was the origin of my work in developing a Racial Distance Scale and in measuring racial and other social attitudes of groups of persons.' The resulting Bogardus Social Distance Scale, one of the first efforts to 'measure' the quality and strength of opinions, was familiar to at least two generations of graduate students.[145]

While Park's reluctance to write books stemmed in part from the very daring of his plan to document and analyze the crucial sectors of social change in the modern world, it is difficult to resist the surmise that more personal factors were involved. He seems to have been too impatient and unsystematic to organize ideas and evidence into a coherent whole. Two of the books he signed drew heavily on the labor of others: William I. Thomas was the principal author of 'Park and Miller's' *Old World Traits Transplanted* (1922) while the devoted Winifred Raushenbush wrote much of Park's *Immigrant Press and its Control* (1926).[146] Park's short essays often seem brilliant improvisations at best, random collections of tentative ideas at worst. And while he was devoted to the *idea* of empirical research, he did comparatively little field work or systematic documentary research himself; his essays tended to be a spinning out of ideas, generalizations, and observations around a fairly limited set of factual data.[147] The books published under his direction are often club sandwiches, with slices of theoretical suggestion surrounding thick slabs of direct quotation from newspapers, informants and public documents.

During the generation after the decline of Chicago dominance in American sociology, the judgment was offered that Chicago sociology was 'pure empiricism'. In Park's case, the charge as stated was close to the opposite of the truth. As Edward Shils said, though there was a strong tendency for the Chicago studies of ' "press while you wait" tailors in the Loop, dwellers in rented rooms, etc.' to become mere fact-gathering, within Park's own vision they were 'microphotographic illustrations of some significant aspect of modern life − something fundamental about human relations in modern society was documented by them.'[148] Even Shils hardly does Park sufficient justice − Park had an elaborate theory of social process, drawn in large part from his mentors Simmel and Thomas, but encrusted with the deposit of his readings over forty years. Park was if anything too theoretical, even scholastic, in his own individious use of the term: he had a strong desire to generalize from the most trivial instance, to entrap every datum in the spiderweb of his theory. What was lacking was a sense of representativeness and evidence, a desire to test his own interpretations against alternative models. Park tried to apply grand theory to concrete instances of the changing society, to build a bridge from theory to empirical research by focusing on small groups or communities or particular character types which would illustrate the operation of wide social forces. In the light of his own later experience with social theory, Harold D. Lasswell recalled that Park was searching for ' "generals", intermediate patterns that would provide a bridge between universals and particulars', 'concepts of intermediate generality between the universalism of traditional social philosophy and the particularities of concrete social circumstances.'[149] In the process, he worked out many specific theories which are deductions from his social psychology or his ecology as applied to concrete events. But the kind of research projects to which he set his students − the study of hotel dwellers, tramps, etc. − though they often provided a good deal of fascinating information, seldom meshed their concrete information into a satisfying and convincing theory of general explanation; too often both Park and his students juxtaposed rather than related data and theory. The monographs of the Chicago school, as one critic has pointed out, were illustrations of Park's preoccupations, 'first-hand reports of some process or inter-relation which appeared to Park to be of crucial significance in the modern world or in human behavior in general', rather than demonstrations of 'any explicitly formulated sociological hypothesis'.[150]

Modern critics, while acknowledging the power of many of Park's ideas, have been disturbed by his avoidance of thorough analysis, of 'formal and systematic testing'; they have been frustrated by what one critic called his 'kaleidoscopic intellectual style' which dazzled the reader into over-looking or swallowing a multitude of inconsistencies and contradictions.[151] The term kaleidoscopic is especially appropriate and may suggest one cause of Park's difficulty. For all his breadth of knowledge and his theoretical training, Park was cursed by a familiar combination of traits: a lack of clarity and logical power, and an over-strong, almost compulsive sense of the 'interrelatedness of practically everything', which abetted his vagueness and made it difficult for him to establish clear conceptual boundaries. In the seamless web of life, everything affects everything else, and logical categories are hopelessly artificial. Park had found the polemic aimed by pragmatists and others against conceptual 'formalism' all too convincing, with the result that his own theories as presented to the serious reader had an hallucinatory quality which could only be rectified by stringent clarification. Herbert Blumer has said that of all the people he has known, Park had 'the most profound understanding of human nature'.[152] But this kind of 'wisdom', while it may illuminate profoundly many aspects of human experience — indeed, perhaps because of its richness and insistence on multiple perspectives — cannot always be easily transmuted into a workable theory and method which can be carried on and developed by others. Perhaps the ultimate irony of his life was that he was an inspiring teacher, with a passion for understanding, who could not articulate his vision and erudition in clear abstract terms capable of transmission to the next generation. While a clever student might divine the coherence beneath the elaborate, eclectic surface, the mediocre tended to remain at the level of separate interests and could not integrate them into fully articulated general explanations.

On the whole, the critics are right: Park was not a great systematizer. His theory had gaps, much of it could not be easily meshed with the data and was highly 'scholastic' in the way Park himself had earlier denounced — it was an elaborate verbal system which, by collective scholarly judgment, turned out not to illuminate the data as well as other systems. But there *was* an elaborate underlying framework — perhaps more accurately, an underlying vision — to Park's aphoristic essays, which forms a dense texture, with all the areas interwoven and used to explain the other parts. Hence, it is very difficult to split up Park's theory for purposes of analysis.

The foundation of Park's theory lay in his own experience of relations between different races and of the complexities and excitements of city life as seen by a 'participant-observer'. His adult life spanned a period which witnessed the sudden and dynamic expansion of great American cities like Chicago, the high tide of foreign immigration into those cities, the steadily increasing trek of American Negroes from the rural South to the urban North, the proliferation of new modes of mass communication — not just the popular newspaper, but the telephone, radio, movies; and, two world wars. Perhaps Park's most basic perception of the world around him was the perception of change, movement, instability and conflict. The mystery of modern society was that it never quite fell apart; beneath the disorder lurked 'natural' principles of organization which kept it, if not healthy, at least functioning, and a certain natural vitality which kept it alive and lively, lurching from one state of disequilibrium to another. To elucidate this mystery was one of the prime tasks of the sociologist.

The City as Symbol

By choosing Chicago as his home and 'social laboratory', Robert Park
confirmed the interpretative judgment of a legion of poets, novelists, journalists, and clerics that the city was the natural home of human variety. The
fascinated love/hate relation of the European and American intelligentsia
with the metropolis, which produced a mass of literature both sublime and
vulgar, rested ultimately upon a sociological insight — that in the great City
the essential dynamics of human behavior became problematic, conscious,
and therefore visible. In more traditional communities, the network of social
relations was not a problem but a fact; the web of customary expectations
produced whatever common action was necessary to preserve order. But in
the great city of the industrial era, the constant condition of strangeness, the
fact that so many relationships were new, shifting, and impersonal, meant
that the processes of social control were no longer concealed under the cake
of custom, but laid bare for dissection.[1] 'In these great cities, where all the
passions, all the energies of mankind are released we are in position to
investigate the processes of civilization, as it were, under a microscope'.[2]

Further, the city represented the wave of the future, since the social processes typical of urbanism were increasingly becoming typical of the whole
world as local cultures crumbled under the advancing domination of metropolitan civilization. 'America', Park decided, 'and, perhaps, the rest of the
world, can be divided between two classes: those who reached the city and
those who have not yet arrived'.[3] It was those who had arrived, especially
those in the process of arriving, who interested Park.

Park brought to the study of urban life not only the compulsive curiosity of
the city beat reporter but the romantic sensibility developed among poets and
novelists by a century of observing with fascinated horror the growth of
industrial cities. He seemed to slip naturally into the modes of perception, the
categories of interpretation, offered by the moralistic and literary sensibility
of the nineteenth century, in which the city was seen as the habitat of the
anomic, atomistic crowd of Strangers, unknown to one another, barely
comprehended as human. 'How often in the overflowing Streets Have I gone
forward with the Crowd, and said Unto myself, the face of everyone That
passes by me is a mystery'.[4] The romantic reaction to the city assumed that it
was no longer a human artifact which facilitated civility, but a great natural

phenomenon beyond man's immediate control: Nature had in a sense re-claimed as her own man's most triumphant barrier against her, and the city had become 'wide wilderness'.[5] The threatening aspects of nature — nature red in tooth and claw, nature as irresistible power, nature as threat and decay — had been projected onto the city, while nature outside the city could be freed of its more savage connotations and remain gentle, nurturing, and inspiring.

The image of the industrial city was the focus of a variety of moral and aesthetic sentiments, especially those which reacted to social change with a sense of shock and threat, because the city seemed symbolic of the modern world order, with its union of opportunity, activity, normlessness, and vulgarity. Some European commentators had tended to define the salient traits of their own times in terms of national or political type, as particularly American or 'democratic', rather than as universal products of a mobile, heterogeneous, concentrated social order. However, Park's generation of journalists, novelists, and sociologists was drawn largely from the American-born *bourgeoisie* of the smaller cities and towns;[6] they had grown up in an American environment which emphasized individualist, competitive values, but in which communities were at the same time relatively stable and possessed some of the 'conservative' qualities of the face-to-face community. Thus, 'democracy' or 'Americanness' for them did not equal disorder and degeneration; they had personal experience of a society at once unified and individualistic. However, coming as they did from Protestant clerical or business backgrounds, they did share with European critics, as with the Jeffersonian tradition, a concern that democracy could degenerate into license and disorder, if the essential self-restraint and disinterestedness provided by 'Republican Virtue' and Protestant personal morality were ever dissolved.

Both European conservatives and American Jeffersonians feared the possibility of degeneration into license and then tyranny which classical political theory had suggested. To the Europeans, however, this was a foregone conclusion since only external restraint could check a vile human nature, while the Americans, on the whole, put their faith in the learned virtue of Protestant self-discipline, reinforced by the watchful eye of informal community discipline ranging from neighborliness to vigilanteism. Moreover, American liberal thinkers from Thomas Jefferson on had developed the Aristotelian argument that certain objective social conditions were necessary to the creation and maintenance of a self-governing political system. The good liberal life could be lived only in a special type of society — one of relative stability and equality of conditions, a fairly high diffusion of education, a high level of honesty among politicians, and common agreement on the importance of these conditions.[7]

Thinking in this tradition led to a distrust of the large city as an environment which swept away the bounds and controls necessary to produce a stable self-governing society. This 'Whig' theory of democratic stability has often been associated with a romantic appreciation of nature, both by its exponents and by its twentieth century historian-critics. Leo Marx, for example, seems to misunderstand this Jeffersonian sociology when he assumes that Jefferson linked civic virtue with the closeness of nature or the prevalence of farmland; rather, perhaps equally mistakenly, Jefferson linked it with economic independence, low population density, and physical and social distance.[8] This fear of modern city life and the processes it crystallized runs like a dark thread through post-Jeffersonian American thought, from the distaste of literary men like Thoreau and Cooper for commerce and competition, whose natural home was the city, to the denunciation of Christian critics in the 1880s and 90s, who argued that in the city commercial values replaced those of the Christian saint, the gap between social classes widened as the cities grew larger and more specialized, and the cash nexus replaced neighborly responsibility as the link between man and man. In a simpler fashion, this Victorian fear of the city was embodied in Algeresque novels in which the country or small town boy battled urban temptations and resisted a life of easy vice.[9]

This environmentalist theory of democracy entailed a theory of human personality. The individual personality also required certain environmental factors to grow straight and tall. The wholesome environment of the country or small town molded a stable personality because the stimuli it provided were low key, unified, and coherent; strength was a function of harmonious development. The 'American' theory of personality, of Cooley, Mead, and Thomas, with its emphasis on the environmental molding of human identity, was in a sense developing a sophisticated theory of social psychology out of the common-sense prejudice of the Middle West, which assumed the more perfect psychic unity and therefore moral superiority of the simple countryman over the sophisticated urbanite. W.I.Thomas, for example, believed that much of the 'moral unrest' of the modern world, 'the almost complete disappearance of the "strong and steady character" of old times', was due to the fact that the speed of change prevented groups from being 'permanent and stable enough to organize and maintain organized complexes of attitudes of their members which correspond to their common pursuits'.[10] One reason why the great modern cities were the locale for so many social problems was that there the individual was subjected to so many varied and contradictory stimuli, impinged on mainly by numerous secondary, and therefore partial, contacts, that he could hardly 'establish a character'. In this sense the old moral denunciation of the effect of city life was restated in secular terms — character became more 'shifting' or 'shifty' and thus the individual was more of an unknown quantity to himself and to others.

Another dimension of this broad perspective that classical theory afforded on the current scene stressed the division of labor more than the tempo of change. Extreme specialization made men less manly, less 'whole' as well as less 'holy'. The complex division of labor, basic to the modern city, stunted the individual through arid concentration on a particular narrow task. This was a fear shared by conservatives and radicals; Marx's vision of the ideal society, for example, would sweep away the division of labor as a permanent and rigid fusion of person and function and allow a man to 'hunt in the morning, fish in the afternoon, rear cattle in the evening, criticize after dinner ... without ever becoming hunter, fisherman, shepherd, or critic.'[11]

The object of attention called 'city' and the category 'urban' were used so broadly in the nineteenth century that they came to include almost every facet of social change which seemed novel, problematic, or threatening. In America, urbanism was probably the commonest of four distinct root metaphors of the contemporary situation available for selection by commentators seeking an interpretation: the political category, 'democracy', offered by aristocratic conservatives; the socio-economic category, 'industrial capitalism', offered by socialists; and the narrowly sociological categories, 'urbanism' and 'mobility'. 'Urbanism' was offered especially by an American intelligentsia which often seemed reluctant to accept a theory which made the distribution of political and economic power primary. To oversimplify a complex process of classification, American liberal thinkers tended to categorize as 'urban', as the result of the special functions and structures and the resulting special experience of the dense, heterogeneous, specialized city, the problems which socialists ascribed to 'capitalist exploitation' and conservatives to 'democracy'. This perceptual choice influenced the development of American sociology by diverting the early generations from the analysis of class structure toward a differentiation of human types expressed in spatial, ecological patterns. The fourth choice of explanatory metaphor, 'mobility' or 'locomotion' was less closely tied to an interpretative position. An ambiguous concept that could include movement in geographical or social space or both, the Victorians (including Park) usually used it to refer to physical movement and its psychic and cultural effects. It appeared as an important subsidiary trait of modern life in works as various as those of Toqueville, Park, and the survey of railway speeds published by the English commentators, Foxwell and Farrer, in 1889.[12]

With this choice of explanations, when observers began to delineate an apparent increase in the incidence of mental illness, it could be interpreted in more than one way, either broadly, as the inevitable penalty of a mobile, competitive, commercial society, or narrowly, as the particular vice of the fascinating but morbid city. A German theorist of the Restoration had linked the mercantile liberty of English society to its alleged higher rate of madness, and Tocqueville had described as 'American' or 'democratic' the tendency to preoccupation with 'business' and 'improvement', to frenzied perpetual activity directed toward immediate utilitarian goals.[13] The American physician

George M.Beard published a treatise on *American Nervousness*, noting the pathological tendency of the constant bustle which Tocqueville had described, and assigning it to the effects of 'steam power, the periodical press, the telegraph, the sciences, and the mental activity of women', which were more completely displayed in America than in Europe. However, those critics, including many American sociologists, who chose to define the problem as that of the city as such, narrowed the causes of modern 'neurasthenia' down to the 'disorganization' characteristic of urban life, which encapsulated the ills of commercialism and rapid change without designating them as such, and added to them the idea of urban impersonality producing lost, directionless individuals. Thus, the modern tensions which worried European conservatives and outraged socialists on both sides of the Atlantic were ascribed to 'the city' rather than to 'American democracy' or to the system of industrial capitalism. This evolutionary definition of sociology's prime object of attention as 'urban' thus had important if unconscious political implications, which would later hasten the supercession of Parkian theory by the more abstract and structural concepts which seemed necessary to later theoretical generations.[14]

While Robert Park accepted and developed the evolutionary sociology which made the city its locus of attention and explanation, he was not an uncritical adherent of the 'Whig' theory that the urban environment weakened character through an oversupply of stimuli. He employed the general categories of this nineteenth century response,[15] but not for purely jeremiad purposes. About the city, as about all things, he was ironic and ambivalent; certainly he felt a visceral delight in its kaleidoscopic variety, its mutability, and even its sordidness; he appreciated that 'the air of the city makes one free'. And, although he retained enough belief in original sin to realize that freedom did not necessarily produce virtue, health, or happiness, he was not struck with panic at the prospect of social disorganization, nor did he conceive of the human personality as being particularly fragile. While he saw the attraction of the great cities for the young as that of the flame for the moth, it was by no means inevitable that the moth be consumed. On the contrary, in an ironic reversal of Henry Thoreau's search for self-realization through nature, he felt that in the city the individual might find 'the moral climate in which his peculiar nature obtains the stimulus that brings his innate disposition to full and free expression'.[16] Even the urban crowd he regarded less as a hydra-headed monster than as a necessary way of renewing the springs of group sentiment and social solidarity. The 'stimulation and inspiration of great crowds is a form of excitement that human beings naturally seek', Park noted in his course on the 'Crowd and the Public'.

In such moments we live more intensely — there is more volume — so to speak to our feelings than in the calm joys of reflection and solitude. It is in this kind of crowd that the individual feels his part in the group. It is in these excitements that he becomes socially conscious. This kind of mass excitement is the first meaning of social consciousness. ... To live in, share in these big crowd excitements is part of human life ... to be shut off from them is not to live. This is why people come to the city.[17]

Few cities could have been more suitable than Chicago as a social laboratory for testing these perceptions against empirical reality. As one returning native noted, it was a city where all aspects of life were 'wide open. Wide streets, wide parks, wide slums, wide open tracts of the underworld, blatantly spread out for all to see'.[18] Adding to the image of Chicago as the ideal-typical city was its immediacy, the rapidity of its growth — it was the work not of ages but of a single lifetime. Chicago had driven 'through the whole cycle from frontier to metropolis within a single generation', and it continued to display the processes of urban growth in a raw, rapid form.[19] This compulsive growth took the population from 1.8 million in 1900 to 3.5 million in 1930, and the city's physical expansion was more than proportionate, gobbling up the flat prairie land surrounding it without much central control over the free play of market forces. It was the obviously 'unwilled' quality of Chicago's growth that suggested it to many people as the perfect example of 'natural' or 'market' forces, the resultant of human energies organized through competition for plentiful but not unlimited resources. When Dreiser's Sister Carrie came to Chicago in 1889 'its streets and houses were already scattered over an area of seventy-five square miles ... street-car lines had been extended far out into the open country in anticipation of rapid growth. The city had laid miles and miles of streets and sewers' out along the prairie 'where, perhaps, one solitary house stood out alone', in confidence that people and houses would soon follow. 'Narrow board walks extended out, passing here a house, and there a store, at far intervals, eventually ending on the open prairie.' Even as a city of 500,000, Dreiser noted, Chicago had 'the ambition, the daring, the activity of a metropolis of a million'.[20]

Perhaps the most striking of the metropolitan patterns revealed to the most casual observer of Chicago was its ethnic diversity and clustering. By 1900 Chicago had the largest number of Poles, Swedes, Bohemians, Norwegians, Dutch, Danes, Croatians, Slovakians, Lithuanians, and Greeks found in any American city, and visitors were noting how the fact that over half of the population was of foreign birth considerably complicated the process of administration and city government. By the time Park came to Chicago it was widely expected that the city would become the future metropolis of the U.S. By 1925, 7.4 percent of all manufactured goods in the U.S. were produced in Chicago, and the boosters confidently expected that banking and commerce would also follow the shift away from the East coast.[21] A city without strong natural features except for the lake which bounded it on the east, nor, in its earlier years with any interesting architecture, Chicago impressed visitors primarily with its commercial and industrial vitality. Chicago, noted William

T.Stead in 1894, 'knows only one common bond. Its members come here to make money.'[22] This was perceptive but incomplete — by the turn of the century there was sufficient established and educated wealth in the city to finance an architectural and artistic nascence. By the 1920s Chicago had a notable symphony orchestra and opera, and the number of teachers, actors, artists, musicians, authors, editors, and reporters was growing faster than the population as a whole. Still, the city's image did not become one of grace or charm. The symbol of Chicago for most outsiders was no longer the stockyards but the gangster; the wretchedness of the Chicago slums was thrown into glaring contrast by the opulence of the Gold Coast. But the atmosphere was electric with energy; Mary Borden in 1931 noted the exhilaration in the air that hit the visitor as he stepped out of the railway station.[23] The sense of vitality was a result of the same forces that had produced the city's problems. As Jean Gottmann has noted, urbanites have loved city life for the very reasons which have led so many sociologists to question its effects. Still, Park would certainly have understood one Chicagoan's explanation of his love for his city: 'No matter what goes on ... it goes on HERE'.[24] He would have understood, too, the ambivalence of many thoughtful urbanites towards their habitat. As one Chicago man explained to a Park student: 'Chicago "spoils life" for a person. While there he does not like it. When away he is not happy til he can get back'. One requirement for survival at the center of events, however, was a certain toughness of mind and spirit. 'There's a lot of room in Chicago', Mary Borden noted, 'but there's no room for doubt or hesitancy'.[25]

The theme of Chicago as a monster, devouring the feeble or hesitant, has been employed by novelists since at least the 1890s. Through this literary usage, Chicago had become for many observers not so much a concrete, idiosyncratic place as an abstraction, the type of the great commercial and industrial city. When in 1913 the young critic Floyd Dell appraised 'Chicago in Fiction', he noted of Robert Herrick that 'the Chicago with which he deals is a pervasive influence — a condition and not a place'. Dell noted that most Chicago novelists, like Herrick, had not shown much 'sense of place': 'Chicago writers have been obsessed with Chicago. It has appeared to them as a problem rather than as a vast and splendid collection of fictional materials'.[26] In one sense, the school of urban sociology which developed under the guidance of Park and Ernest Burgess sought to remove the blindfolds of the artist, and capture the particular texture and color of the neighborhood subcultures — the Gold Coast, the Ghetto, the slums and hobohemias of Chicago. Yet in another sense, Chicago sociology continued the novelists' drive toward extreme abstraction; Park and his followers, too, tended to view Chicago as the ideal-typical metropolis, the crystallization of pure urbanism. If one understood the social process and structural transformations in Chicago one would understand it everywhere; categories and explanatory models drawn from Chicago should be applicable to any metropolis. 'There is implicit in all these studies the notion that the city is a thing with a characteristic organization and a typical life history, and that individual cities are enough alike so that what one learns about one city, may, within limits, be assumed to be true of others.'[27]

Despite its tendency to generalize from Chicago data, there was also a concreteness about Park's urban sociology which came from its intensely visual, spatial quality. Park saw the sociologist as first (though not only) an observer, who must understand the empirical given, and there is a quality of sheer visual revelation in many Chicago writings. 'Many of the fundamental issues of urbanism', recalled Leonard White of the early days, 'of maladjustment, of the growth and interaction of institutions, of personality, were realized more sharply than ever before to spread themselves at our feet for inspection and analysis'.[28] A process like the 'succession' of ethnic groups in a particular neighborhood could be *seen* taking place; one suspects that Park's borrowing from ecology in an effort to build a general social theory was inspired not only by concern for change rather than structure, but also by his preference for concreteness, for remaining as close as possible to what could be seen by the average intelligent observer.

As many commentators have noted, the 'visual' quality of Park's sociology was often combined with a palpable sense of wonder, and sometimes of concern, at the variety and novelty of urban existence. Many of Park's students, like Park himself and other first and second generation scholars in the field, had grown up in less differentiated small towns; prowling the streets of Chicago under Park's stimulus, they were literally viewing for the first time the variety of human types and the tendency of subcultures to cluster together. Norman Hayner noted in his diary on 7 April 1921, that he had talked to a 'choice Irish character' who 'promised to bring two samples of moonshine to the settlement' where Hayner worked and played basketball. A year later, he visited Nels Anderson at the Vendome Hotel: 'Walked about and was shown the sights. Gave 10c to a "rounder" near the "mendicants' hotel." Saw a man on "a jolly jag" and two boy perverts. "Patty the Pig" was pointed out. Visited a gambling den.'[29]

The visual sensitivity of Chicago sociology was accentuated by and expressed through the heavy reliance on the use of maps, a method borrowed from earlier community studies and at Chicago made into the most typical method for isolating the incidence of distribution of some distinguishable group, trait, or practice. The huge social research base map which Erle F. Young drew up for the department

showed strikingly how the elevated railroad lines which crisscross the city and are generally flanked with industry constitute barriers which divide the city into many separate districts. The industrial and residential districts of Chicago when studied by this map are seen to be areas surrounded by a wall of elevated railroads and a ring of industrial establishments. In a similar fashion the better residential districts were typically surrounded by lake front, parks and boulevards.[30]

Thus the Chicago ecological theory of urban process could seem to be an irresistible deduction from the pattern of the city as revealed by personal inspection and verified by mapping. To a post-war generation of graduate students disillusioned by war propaganda, words had become suspect; they were skeptical of both theory and philosophy − much to the chagrin of Park himself, who tried hard to convince them that philosophy had liberalized his own studies. A map was 'hard', factual, and presumably could not be manipulated like words; at the same time it did not require the mathematical expertise of statistics. So for the Chicago department, map plotting became 'an indigenous variant of the quantitative method'.[31]

The Chicago department had produced a number of urban studies before 1913. The earliest Chicago dissertation in sociology was a study of 'American Municipal Government' (1895); in 1901 Charles J.Bushnell produced 'A Study of the Stock Yards Community at Chicago, as a Typical Example of the Bearing of Modern Industry upon Democracy with Constructive Suggestions', and in the next three years there was a dissertation on 'the Higher Life' of Chicago (1904), a study of juvenile delinquency (1906), and a treatise on 'The Social Significance of the Physical Development of Cities' (1907). The direction which this interest would take under Park's guidance was adumbrated in his article of 1915 on 'The City: suggestions for the investigation of human behavior in the urban environment'.[32]

Park's aims, and his significance in the development of the discipline, can be seen in his title: this widely read piece was a prospectus for a future research program, concerned to unify the 'applied' field of urban study with general theory. The article was in great part a synopsis of previous speculation on urban traits, with special emphasis on the ideas of Simmel, Thomas, and Sumner, together with a long series of questions designed to convert existing generalizations into the basis for empirical studies. These numerous questions can be divided into two major groups along the traditional distinction between unconscious/determined or external and conscious/volitional. The two categories were what Park would soon call the *ecological*, involving the effects of the division of labor and the distribution of population, and the *cultural*, involving the effects of human self-consciousness and choice upon behavior, and the particular character-types developed within the urban environment. The sociologist should seek to reveal those forces 'which tend to bring about an orderly and typical grouping of its population and institutions'. 'What are the sources of the city's population? ... What are the outstanding "natural" areas, i.e., areas of population segregation? How is the distribution of population within the city area affected?' The sociologist must also study the effect of the division of labor on human personality: 'To what extent is the grade of intelligence represented in the different trades and professions dependent upon natural ability? ... To what extent is intelligence determined by the character of occupation and the conditions under which it is practised? Is the choice of the occupation determined by temperamental, by economic or by sentimental considerations?'[33] Thus Park tried to explore the variety of ways in which human nature was influenced by the complexity and specialization of the urban environment, the consequences of metropolitan freedom from close customary control. In this concern for the psychological dimension of urban life, Park was following his master Georg Simmel quite closely, translating Simmel's insights into questions which might prove suitable for research. The city, Park noted in romantic vein, was 'of all places the one in which to discover the secrets of human hearts'.[34]

The range of questions raised in 'The City' was characteristic of the concerns which drove Park to sketch out a general theory of society and social change, as well as to stimulate dozens of students to apply his theories to some specific slice of urban life. For Park, the utility of the general theory lay in its ability to cast light upon the very concrete phenomena of daily life which aroused his interest. 'We focus our attention on a problem that seems interesting', he said, 'and from that we are led to other questions until we see the whole thing in some more or less systematic way'.[35]

The intensely personal nature of Park's quest, his drive to understand the fluid and varied world of the modern city, may help to explain the inchoate and sometimes casual condition of his theoretical writings. Although a complex, differentiated theory both of urban life and of social order in general does emerge from painful collation of Park's scattered essays and introductions, he never presented his theory in fully articulated form. The two relatively systematic works he published both came very early in his professional career; moreover, one of these , The Principles of Human Behavior (1915), was a pamphlet covering only one area, while the ambitious and influential Introduction to the Science of Sociology (1921) which Park wrote in collaboration with Ernest Burgess, was a combination of theoretical outline and collection of readings.[36]

The Park and Burgess Introduction was, along with the essay 'The City', probably the most influential of Park's writings, and for almost two generations of students at Chicago and many other universities came to symbolize the new discipline. Between 1921 and 1943 it had sold 30,000 copies, and for that period it was the 'Bible' of sociology for Chicago doctors who carried it into their own teaching.[37]

Ernest Burgess had begun the project which became the Introduction but, according to Albion Small, it would not have been finished by 1921 had not Park entered the collaboration. Once involved, Park seems to have taken upon himself the lion's share of the project; the theoretical framework, style, and wide variety of readings closely reflect his interests.[38] In 1921 Small still referred to the manuscript as 'Burgess and Park', but by the time of publication it had become 'Park and Burgess'. The resulting book was a highly sophisticated and eclectic compendium, reflecting a wide knowledge of European thought and aimed more at the advanced than the beginning student of sociology.[39] The work reflected a trait of Park's which was both blessing and curse — he was one of the most learned of American sociologists, widely read not only in the classical sociologists but in Western philosophy and literature, ready and willing to draw upon the whole range of Western thought for illustrations and insights. Thus, the *Introduction* included large chunks not only from Simmel, Sumner, Spencer, Durkheim, et al., but also drew from the realm of philosophy, literature, and natural science. However, Park's erudition exceeded his logical rigor, and the book suffered from his characteristic humility, by subordinating a clearly articulated argument to the presentation of a rich and varied set of 'materials' from which students might find nourishment.

The sheer scope and massiveness of the work, as well as its strategic source at Chicago, the largest and most prestigious department, ensured its status as a *summa* of previous sociological theory and made it one of those synoptic volumes which mark a plateau, a staging-area, in the movement of thought within a discipline. The ideas summarized in Park and Burgess were transmitted to most of the next generation of graduate students; those omitted, or transmitted in partial, limited form, were probably forgotten by the majority of American sociologists until the late 1930s at least. For its devout readers the book defined the proper territory of sociology and set forth the categories for examining and explaining social phenomena which would become the common currency of American sociology — competition, conflict, accommodation, assimilation, socialization, role, status, social change.[40] The heritage and repertory of sociology came to be defined for many Chicago doctors and their students by the contents of the *Introduction*, just as Ralph Linton's *Study of Man* (1936), and Talcott Parsons' *Structure of Social Action* (1937) would set new limits of knowledge for many in the generation of the 1940s and 1950s.

Park's theoretical framework was essentially present in *The Introduction* and in his essay on 'The City'; most of his subsequent work was refinement, explication, and specific application of ideas he had worked out by 1921. This discussion will therefore deal with Park's ideas thematically and draw upon the whole corpus of his works. It will also deal with his general and urban theories in conjunction, on the assumption that they are linked both formally and in their source in Park's personal world-view.

A Dualistic Vision and a Sociology of Process

As a theorist Park was transitional: he retained the evolutionary framework of the previous generation, but altered its implications and refined its application. Park still interpreted human history in broadly evolutionary terms: the progression from simple to complex, naive to sophisticated, rural to urban, static to dynamic, was the framework, if not the motor, of social change. His own sociological theory was built around the Spencerian concept of increasing complexity and differentiation, and the *Gemeinschaft/Gesellschaft*, simple/complex, static/dynamic contrast of Tönnies. Park termed his own version of this polarity 'sacred/secular'.[41]

However, if one ventures beyond the formal level of theory to its inspiration and implications, it becomes clear that the metaphysical pathos of Park's evolutionism was ambivalent and complex. He believed that 'progress' was inevitable, but was not naively optimistic about its effects. His own experience of modern cities had made him aware of the sheer human waste entailed by progress, the increasing numbers of people thrown into discard because they could not cope with the demands of a complex and technically sophisticated way of life. An inevitable part of every great city was an area of 'human junk' staffed by those men and women who had 'fallen out of the march of industrial progress, ... scrapped by the industrial organization of which they were once a part'.[42] Park agreed with William James that 'progress was a terrible thing' and that one could only develop an attitude of stoic resignation in the face of its exactions.

On the other hand, Park was not afflicted with any great sentimental nostalgia for a golden folk past, real or imagined. Whatever the costs of the urban lifestyle, he could not help but glory in the magnificent complexity and eccentricity of the metropolis. While he often paid dutiful tribute to the steadiness of character produced by traditional small-town upbringing he was obviously fascinated and entertained by the quick witted, ironic cockney; his sympathies, if not his unambiguous admiration, lay with the emancipated urbanite.[43] Park did not wish to return to Red Wing, and was sufficiently egalitarian not to expect the mass of his fellow citizens to lead a 'healthier' life than the one he preferred. Still, there was an implicit impeachment of the urban exotics close under the surface of his prose, which echoed the concern of classical theorists with the city: fully urbanized people were fascinating, because over-specialized, caricatures, not wholly or wholesomely developed human beings. The division of labor was essential to civilization yet its great cost was the fragmentation of the human personality. These were the terms of Park's ambivalence about progress and its end product, the city.[44]

On the level of theoretical structure the fundamental organizing principle of Park's work was dualism, a series of all-embracing polarities which Park tended to see as linked if not identical. To use other terms as well as Park's own in order to elucidate the unexpressed penumbra of his thought, the polarities would include these pairs: unconscious–conscious, ethically neutral–ethically charged, determined–volitional, 'hard'–'soft', forces which compel the actor regardless of his conscious wishes – conscious, willed efforts at control. Finally, in his own system, the major duality was expressed as ecology–social psychology. Park's dualism was the result of two major concerns. The first of these was his awareness of the classic concerns and doctrines of philosophy, and his dualistic sociology was an effort to translate them into sociological terms, in an apparent hope that they might thus be resolved, or side-stepped. For Park, with his broad reading and reflection in the classic disciplines, sociology could never simply cut itself off from its intellectual ancestors by declaring their problems irrelevant or meaningless.[45] The pervasive dualism of Park's theories also reflected an effort to create links among a variety of doctrines current in a confusing and overcrowded period in the history of social thought. Park tried to synthesize the plurality of interpretations of human behavior competing for attention in the early twentieth century, with the result that the excerpts, footnotes, and bibliography of the *Introduction to the Science of Sociology*, as well as the references in Park's later essays, are an anthology of the also-rans, the near-forgotten students of human behavior who enjoyed temporary currency in the two generations of Park's intellectual maturity, roughly the years from 1890 to 1930.

Park's dualism was formulated in terms adapted from one of his German mentors, Wilhelm Windelband, for whom *Masse und Publikum* had been written. Windelband had offered the distinction between history, the realm of 'pictures of men and of human life, with all the wealth of their individuality, reproduced in all their characteristic variety', and the realm of science, 'a system of abstract concepts ... a world of colorless and soundless atoms, despoiled of all their earthly sensuous qualities'.[46] The abstract sciences were instrumental in nature, allowing the prediction and control of those atomic systems amenable to scientific analysis, whereas it was the function of history to *interpret*, to give the emotionally colored 'meanings' which impelled human beings consciously to action: 'It is upon the interpretation of the facts of experience that we formulate our creeds and found our faiths. Our explanations of phenomena, on the other hand, are the basis for technique and practical devices for controlling nature and human nature, man and the physical world'.[47]

Park endorsed Windelband's distinction, separating sociology from history on the ground that the former sought to discover, not what happened and why, but 'on the basis of a study of other instances, the nature of the process involved'.[48] At the same time, however, he was determined to preserve the realm of subjective meanings, the 'wealth of individuality' and the 'sensuous qualities' of life as legitimate objects of sociological inquiry. Park's essential dualism, then, was an effort to embrace the range of methods and materials necessary to understand a working society. The existence of two analyzable 'orders' of social forces in the real world, the *ecological* order of unwilled, symbiotic interaction and the *moral* order of conscious meaning and willed institutions, which affected each other, meant that the student of society must employ both the analysis of consciousness and of external competitive forces. He must both explain social phenomena, in the sense of discovering the causal forces which mold them, and make them intelligible, in the sense of revealing their function for and conscious meaning to the people who live them.

Park's dualism carried over into his discussion of the individual and human nature. It was a mood as well as a doctrine, not only philosophical dualism but Dostoyevskian doubleness, a sense of the ambivalence and reversibility of human motives and feelings. He was most interested in those people who were 'double' in the sense of being caught between two worlds — black and white, old and new, rural and urban, static and dynamic — those marginal, interstitial people, who if unlucky might be ground between their conflicting subcultures, but if quick-witted might be able to thrive by playing off the elements of their complex environment against one another. While other Chicago sociologists might have had sharper and more precise minds, it is this sense of the subjectivity and relativity of human existence that sets Park off most sharply from most of his colleagues and students, indeed from most of his generation of working sociologists. Perhaps this sense of complexity and irony came from his age and the intellectual milieu of his youth — Social Darwinism was a better school for subtlety than the energetic Progressivism committed to the solution of sharply-defined 'problems' on which most other scholars of the 1920s were weaned.

The second fundamental trait of Park's thinking was its orientation towards process rather than structure. Park's sociology, unlike most American theories of the next two generations, was essentially concerned with the analysis and search for organizing principles of change through time — change at both microscopic and macroscopic levels. This concern with process stemmed both from the deep impact of Georg Simmel and from Park's absorption in the problems of early sociology. He was a Spencerian without complete confidence, an evolutionist who had absorbed enough of the Protestant and romantic critiques of the new order to find the Spencerian theodicy inadequate. Thus he approached the study of social structures with the assumption that their persistence was problematic, that one must account for stability by looking for patterns within change. Park once remarked to his class that society could be visualized as like a table, which was only a complex of atoms in motion;[49] on a larger scale, society too was a complex of small scale processes, which through their patterned sequence and interaction held it together through the changes forced on it by history. But Park's model for society was not one of equilibrium;[50] although states of equilibrium were the theoretical final stages of his patterned sequences of change, Park was perfectly aware that this equilibrium was 'illusory' in the sense that it existed only as a convenient tool for analysis. He quoted the pioneer animal ecologist Charles Elton, who affirmed that ' "The balance of nature" hardly exists, except in the minds of scientists. It seems that animal numbers are always tending to settle down into a smooth and harmonious working mechanism but something always happens before this happy state is reached'.[51] Similarly, in human societies, the natural operation of the competitive process, insofar as it brought about an ever finer division of labor, tended to diminish the intensity of competition and produce a certain degree of stability. But this potential for equilibrium was, like the meeting of parallel lines in infinity, only a logical culmination; in practice some new development always interrupted the process and set in motion another cycle of what Park, borrowing from plant ecology, called 'succession' – another period of instability, followed by a cycle of patterned serial developments, 'an irreversible series in which each succeeding event is more or less completely determined by the one that preceded it'.[52] Succession was most readily visible in spatial terms in the great cities in the changing ethnic distribution of population. Immigrant groups would first settle in or near the 'centers of cities, in the so-called areas of transition. From there they are likely to move by stages ... from an area of first to areas of second and third settlement, generally in the direction of the periphery of the city and eventually into the suburban area – in any case, from a less to a more stable section of the metropolitan region'.[53] The movement was irreversible and was accompanied by other changes, economic, cultural, and psychological, in the immigrant group itself. On a grander scale, he thought, the same process could be seen in the settlement of South Africa: a procession of peoples from bushman, to Hottentot, to Bantu, Boers, and finally the English, each one more sophisticated and economically efficient than the last, and the whole thing representing to Park 'not a sequence of events but the consequences of an inexorable historical process'.[54]

An example of the unity and simplicity of explanation beneath the dense texture of Park's sociology is the way in which the broad processual concept of 'natural history' seems to be formally related to the specific ecological concept of 'succession', to be an effort to generalize the model of a predictable sequence of events to much larger historical phenomena. 'Succession' applied to the sequence of peoples and uses on a particular bit of turf, or the sequential location of a single group, while 'natural history' was an effort to organize any data involving change over time, by seeing them as part of an 'orderly and irreversible series of events' and 'correlated with other less obvious and more fundamental social changes' so that 'they may be used as indices of these changes'. Patterned historical phenomena, which had been grouped together by common sense through the use of a classifying term such as 'revolution', might be expected to go through a typical cycle of stages; so might a series of institutions having a similar function, such as communication, or a single institution within this historical continuum, like the newspaper.[55] A particular, isolable type of human interaction, like the contact of diverse human cultures and races, might also be expected to reveal common patterns of change when studied comparatively. All these phenomena might be organized in terms of succession, or as Park put it when thinking in broader terms, in terms of a natural history. 'What is needed is not so much a history as a natural history of the press – not a record of the fortunes of individual newspapers, but an account of the evolution of the newspaper as a social institution'.[56]

The stimulus to this standard pattern of explanation seems to have been Park's desire to reinforce and illustrate the usual German distinction between microscopic history and comparative, generalizing social science, which discussed institutions as types, but not particular examples in isolation. The conceptual root-metaphor, however, seems to be a deduction from Aristotelian logic.[57] It conceived of the development of institutions or processes as the evolutionary working-out of potentialities present in the 'thing' under study from its inception, just as the oak tree was present in the acorn. The potentialities were not all fore-ordained for successful development, since the fate of the organism was affected by the peculiar historical and environmental circumstances in which it grew. In the language of twentieth century social science, 'natural history' was an ideal-typical process, similar to the ideal-typical structure of a society or belief system advanced by Max Weber. The emphasis on analyzing and categorizing processes rather than structures was, as we have said, characteristic of Park's sociology, in part as a result of the influence of Simmel. Several of Park's students employed the model of natural history to organize and explain sequential phenomena. Emory S. Bogardus applied Park's general cycle of group interaction to the ethnic conflict on the Pacific Coast, Lyford Edwards offered a set of typical stages in the progress of revolutions, Everett Stonequist applied the model to the development of the 'marginal' personality type.[58]

Park himself applied the natural history approach to his old interest in crowd psychology to produce a new approach to the study of social order which he termed 'collective behavior'.[59] Crowds, social movements, and other manifestations of unrest should not be regarded as pathological disruptions of natural social order. They were merely temporary heightenings of a cyclical process by which society was continually changing; like earthquakes, they were sudden visible shifts in processes which were always going on. Every institution was the temporary end product of an on-going process which began with discontent with previously crystallized institutions and moved through upheaval or even revolution to stabilization. 'There is at first a vague general discontent and distress. Then a violent, confused, and disorderly, but enthusiastic and popular movement arises. Finally the movement takes form; develops leadership, organization; formulates doctrines and dogma. Eventually it is accepted, established, legalized. The movement dies, but the institution remains'.[60] These processes of collective behavior involved different mechanisms of social control. Within the crowd social control is complete, the individual has lost himself in the mass excitement; on the other hand the tension required to sustain this excitement is difficult to maintain over long periods. In a stable society, social control has become objectified in institutions, in ritual, law, and public opinion, and internalized in the conscience of individuals. This type of social control had the advantage of long term stability, but it was never total and complete, since it allowed individuality to flourish and because conscience is always an untrustworthy tool of conformity.[61] Park was always particularly interested in the phenomenon of sects, conflict groups which managed to sustain the tension and the total unanimity and subordination of the individual to the whole over a long period of time. Their revolutionary potential was thus considerable and Park thought that any really thorough-going revolution was likely to have its origin in a sect, either political or religious. Often however the success of the sect was blocked and the group remained frozen in an arrested state out of the mainstream of the social process.[62]

The natural history of an institution or interaction-cycle was closely allied to the ecological order of human phenomena, since both involved large-scale determination of events by forces beyond human intention. No human institution, Park insisted, could be understood unless it were analyzed as the result of a competitive market, as the unintended product of impersonal forces, as well as of conflicting human desires. 'The press, as it exists, is not, as our moralists sometimes seem to assume, the willful product of any little group of living men. On the contrary, it is the outcome of an historic process in which many individuals participated without forseeing what the ultimate product of their labors was to be'.[63]

Ecology and the Analysis of Urban Communities

The most important dualism in Park's sociology was his distinction between the ecological and the moral orders, between the symbiotic interaction of human beings based on the competition for scarce resources, and the social relations influenced by values not specifically derived from the quest for survival. This highly arbitrary and abstract division, which would prove so difficult to apply, was developed by Park from his readings in classical economic theory and post-Darwinian biology, apparently as an effort to do justice to the radically different philosophies, approaches and orders of knowledge — Aristotle and Hobbes, *Verstehen* and behaviorism, subjective understanding and external constraint — which he felt essential to an adequate theory. 'Man and society present themselves in a double aspect. They are at the same time products of nature and of human artifice. ... the conflict between Hobbes and Aristotle is not absolute. Society is a product both of nature and of design, of instinct and of reason.'[64]

As a metaphor for organizing the data of the 'Hobbesian' side of his analysis, Park turned to the developing sciences of plant and animal ecology.

From the 1870s plant geographers and others had used Darwinian ideas to develop a special study of the interdependence of plants within a functional zone, or 'community', whose borders were defined by observation. After 1900 a similar approach was applied to the study of animals. Both of these gradually differentiating studies adopted the title 'oecology' or 'ecology', which had been coined by the German zoologist and philosopher of science, Ernst Haeckel, in the 1860s, and which was apparently discovered by Park in the translation of the work of the Dane, Eugenius Warming.[65]

Park's essay of 1915 on 'The City' shows that he was already thinking along the lines which would later produce the explicit category of human ecology; however, he did not use the exact words, or make overt comparisons of human with plant and animal communities, until 1921. By the time 'The City' was reprinted in 1925, Park had inserted a specific mention:

There are forces at work within the limits of the urban community – within the limits of any natural area of human habitation, in fact, – which tend to bring about an orderly and typical grouping of its population and institutions. The science which seeks to isolate these factors and to describe the typical constellations of persons and institutions which the cooperation of these forces produces, is what we call human, as distinguished from plant and animal, ecology.[66]

In the *Introduction to the Science of Sociology* of 1921, he had made use of the analogy between plant, animal, and human communities to offer a metaphor on which to order the distribution of and relations among disparate human populations. The studies of plant communities by the American ecologist Frank E.Clements, Park suggested, 'might well serve as a model for similar studies in human ecology'. In both the 1921 and 1924 editions of the *Introduction*, however, the presentation of human ecology was still subordinate to the organization based on Park's cycle of human interaction; the work of Clements and J.Arthur Thomson on ecological themes appeared in the chapter upon the first of Park's processes of interaction, 'Competition'.[67] Indeed, Park's original attraction to ecology may have come from a realization that it gave strong support to his feeling that 'Competition is universal in the world of living things'. Plant and animal ecology exhibited the process of competition in pure form, as in W.M.Wheeler's account of 'Social Symbiosis' among ants and aphids, without the distorting effect of human processes like communication or inhibition imposed by values. Park defined pure competition as 'interaction without social contact' and insisted that this 'character of externality in human relations' was a 'fundamental aspect of society and social life'.[68]

The suggestion is irresistible that this definition of competition, together with the ecological analogies which supported it, was a theodicy as well as a means of ordering objective data. Like Darwin's tangled bank from which it derives, the ecological analogy offered by Park was on one level an assertion of fatalism, a means of affirming the natural limits set upon the realization of human desires, the inevitable frustration which external 'conditions' assured for every idealist, reformer, and planner. Indeed, Park's eco-theodicy went back behind Darwin to a more frankly legislative realist, Thomas Hobbes. The scientific prestige of ecology would reinforce the partial but vital truth of Hobbes' 'war of each against all'. Here as often in Park's theories, the reader feels uneasy at the blurring of two concepts, in this case the equation of the Hobbesian state of nature with strictly symbiotic 'competition'. Surely the former belongs to Park's second form or process of interaction, 'conflict'? Perhaps the confusion is understandable, given the tendency of ecology itself to employ such bellicose terms as 'invasion' and 'dominance'. Park himself noted that among human beings competition was usually made conscious and thus converted into conflict.[69]

Indeed, to judge from the content and footnotes of the *Introduction* and Park's earlier ecological essays, plant and animal ecology was largely a source of expansive metaphors within which to assemble data from the long tradition of philosophy, population theory, and political economy, a tradition from which ecology itself had descended via Darwin. Park's borrowing of the term 'ecology' from biology was thus the terminus of a conceptual round-trip, since natural science had earlier taken from political economy the root-metaphor of competition for scarce resources leading to a temporary equilibrium, in order to describe the interdependence of species within a self-sufficient natural habitat or 'community'.

Applying this root-idea to his favorite subject, Park wrote: 'The Metropolis is ... a great sifting and sorting mechanism, which, in ways that are not yet wholly understood, infallibly selects out of the population as a whole the individuals best suited to live in a particular region and a particular milieu. ... The city grows by expansion, but it gets its character by the selection and segregation of its population, so that every individual finds eventually, either the place where he can, or the place where he must, live'.[70] In this egoistic interaction of individuals and groups within a territorial unit, an Invisible Hand sorted out the competing units, without their conscious co-operation, into a functioning system. There is more than a hint of Spencerian functionalism in the idea that individuals sometimes serve collective ends unconsciously; through this statement we may see that Park's 'human ecology' was a substitute for overtly functional analysis, based on classical economic theory (mediated through plant ecology) rather than directly on biology — but a substitute directed to the same end as Spencerian functionalism and all utilitarian theories, that of explaining social coherence as the resultant of individual actions devoted consciously to the furthering of private ends. After 1930, as some of his own students and other sociologists took up the analogy with subhuman interaction more seriously, Park deepened his own knowledge of the field and attempted to carry the analogies further than he had in the twenties.[71] This later elaboration may have been stimulated by direct conversations with the student of termites, Alfred Emerson, who joined the Chicago faculty in 1929.[72]

Park's determination to teach the hard utilitarian lesson of symbiosis was reflected in his use of the ecological definition of 'community'. The relation between the organisms in an ecological community was one of 'competitive co-operation', or a struggle for existence which resulted in a series of adaptations and accommodations, providing the survivors with enough soil, light, and air to reproduce, thus making them a system sustained by the mutual utility of its parts. Park adopted this ecological meaning of 'community' despite the risk of confusion with the more customary 'soft' usage in which a community was characterized by stability, moral consensus, and face-to-face relations. 'Plant life, in fact, offers an illustration of a *community* which is *not a society* ... because it is an organization of individuals whose relations, if not wholly external, are, at any rate, "unsocial", in so far as there is no consensus'.[73] This redefinition of 'community' reflected Park's desire to avoid a static and consensual model of society; the mere definition serves to remind the student that stable social relations may often be based on utility rather than love or agreement. Though Park recognized consensus of conscious belief as an important source of unity, his experience of the fluid contemporary world had convinced him that social cohesion did not necessarily rest on consensus. 'People live together on the whole, not because they are alike, but because they are useful to one another.'[74] Societies are composed of 'individuals who act independently of one another, who compete and struggle with one another for mere existence, and treat one another, as far as possible as utilities'. What made them a society was not 'like-mindedness, but corporate action ... consciously or unconsciously, directed to a common end'.[75]

On the level of applied urban ecology, the unconscious social process of competition was responsible for the shape of the city. The Chicago school saw the city as always developing according to pattern, a pattern which invariably turned out to be 'a constellation of typical urban areas, all of which can be geographically located and spatially defined'. These areas Park designated as 'natural' because they came into existence without design, tended to go through typical cycles of development and performed each its specific function in the urban community as a whole 'though the function, as in the case of the slum, may be contrary to anybody's desire'. Each natural area had its characteristic population, with its own moral climate and universe of discourse: areas in which there were few children, or a disproportionately high number, areas with particularly high incidence of crime, divorce, or juvenile delinquency, areas which were the turf of particular ethnic groups, red light districts, and Bohemias.[76]

In the analysis of natural areas, however, it was necessary to move beyond the strictly ecological level to that of culture, of subjective values and perceptions. At this point, Park's social psychology meshed with his ecological interest in 'natural areas'. These areas were in fact 'worlds' with differing codes of conduct; each particular milieu would offer a distinct set of roles and criteria for status. 'Character and habit were formed under the influence of environment' and whether this environment was the Gold Coast or the slum it embodied an interlocking complex of physical, cultural, and psychological limits and expectations. The personality was so plastic that it continued to be shaped by its various milieux throughout life — so much so that behavior patterns could actually be changed 'by transferring the individual from an environment in which he behaved badly to one in which he behaves well'.[77]

Though they were all part of the larger community of the city, relations between the natural areas were symbiotic — they coexisted without much sympathy, empathy, or even communication. Here again, the closeness to direct observation of Chicago sociology can be seen: this purely symbiotic relation of groups was difficult to avoid noting in the ghettoized Chicago of the early twentieth century. Casual commentators noted the ethnic fragmentation which made the city a congeries of isolated communities existing in a state of watchful antagonism. 'Each race is organized, each is separate, each is antagonistic to all the others, and the racketeers invade them all, crashing with armoured cars and machine guns through the frontiers that are marked by railway bridges and tram lines'.[78]

The study of 'natural areas' performed a vital function for the sociologist by providing him with a ' "frame of reference", a conceptual order within which statistical facts gain a new and more general significance'. Further, because the areas were 'natural and typical', an explication of the social processes in one would be applicable to similar areas in other modern cities.

Every city, every great city, has its more or less exclusive residential areas or suburbs; its areas of light and of heavy industry, satellite cities and casual labor mart. ... Every American city has its slums; its ghettoes; its immigrant colonies, regions which maintain more or less alien and exotic cultures. Nearly every large city has its bohemias and hobohemias, where life is freer, more adventurous and lonely than it is elsewhere. These are the so-called natural areas of the city.[79]

Thus, the plotting and analysis of natural areas was to be not simply an exercise in local color reporting but a series of case studies to demonstrate basic sociological processes. The natural-area study, conceived as a joint examination of the spatial pattern of a *milieu* and the 'mentality' of its denizens, became a hallmark of the Chicago school. Park described one of the earliest studies to be completed, Nels Anderson's *The Hobo*, as investigating 'the casual laborer in his habitat, that is to say in the region of the city where the interests and habits of the casual laborer have been, so to speak, institutionalized'.[80] In the later 1920s came Louis Wirth's *The Ghetto*, which studied the Jewish community of Chicago in the light of European ghetto life, and Harvey Zorbaugh's *The Gold Coast and the Slum*, a study of the diverse subcultures clustered together on the Lower North Side.[81]

One important result of this emphasis on the milieu was the development of an approach to crime – especially juvenile crime – as the product of the particular urban environment rather than of ethnic or individual predisposition. Delinquency was most likely to appear, the investigators discovered, in those areas of a city which had a high rate of transiency, recent immigration, poverty, and breakdown of communal norms: the slums. Data on Chicago demonstrated not only that the central slum areas of the city had the highest rate of juvenile delinquency, but that they continued so, even through successive occupation by different ethnic groups. Delinquency thus seemed to be a characteristic of the area, the *milieu* and its persistent social traits, rather than of particular ethnic groups or personality types. Frederic Thrasher's study of boys' gangs in Chicago found that the gang was 'primarily a phenomenon of the children of foreign-born immigrants', who escaped parental control and became superficially Americanized. 'The normally directing institutions of family, school, church and recreation break down on the intramural frontier of gangland and the gang arises as a sort of substitute organization'. Thrasher described the gang as a spontaneous primary group, characterized by face-to-face relations, 'the development of tradition, unreflective internal structure, esprit de corps, solidarity, morale, group awareness and attachment to a local territory'.[82] Thus, the juvenile gang could be seen as an unconscious defense mechanism against the disintegration of personality threatened by the decline of the traditional primary groups in the slums; it was the weakness of community forces controlling behavior which allowed the gangs to become criminal.

As Park and his students investigated Chicago they found that the natural areas of the city tended to distribute themselves throughout the urban area in a discernible pattern, a pattern which, because of Chicago's relative lack of physical barriers to the free play of market forces, they assumed would be typical of cities in general, though somewhat modified by local topography and history. The city's center was always occupied by a complex of highest-value uses:

Within this central downtown area itself certain forms of business, the shops, the hotels, theaters, wholesale houses, office buildings, and banks, all tend to fall into definite and characteristic patterns, as if the position of every form of business and building in the area were somehow fixed and determined by its relation to every other.

Out on the periphery of the city ... industrial and residential suburbs, dormitory towns, and satellite cities seem to find, in some natural and inevitable manner, their predetermined places.

Between these two extreme zones of the metropolitan area, 'the city tends to take the form of a series of concentric circles. These different regions, located at different relative distances from the center, are characterized by different degrees of mobility of the population'.[83] For Park, the typical city radiated out from a shifting, opulent, unstable center through zones of specialized human types, to a ring of dull, solid bourgeois virtue and stability. The elaboration of this concentric zone theory of cities — a theoretical pattern which was both spatial and moral in two senses, the result of market forces but also producing unique patterns of self-consciousness — was the specialty of Park's closest colleague, Ernest Burgess, who developed it into a zonal hypothesis to describe the ideal-type of the industrial city, unhindered by any obstructing or deflecting geographic features.[84]

Mobility and Social Change

In his discussion of the pattern of the city, Park introduces a new variable, which is both description and explanation — *mobility*. The crucial variable which both *distinguishes* and in a sense *causes* the difference between 'natural areas' is the degree of in- and out-migration among the population of each area. As often in Park's writings, there is more than one crucial ambiguity in the use of a word. In addition to the conflation of cause with distinctive feature, we are not sure whether 'mobility' is to be read in its most literal sense, as any kind of movement in space, or in its sociological sense, as a relatively permanent change of place or location in either physical or social space. The 'mobility' of the central city is of both types — the movement of commuters to and fro, and the large transient population which inhabits hotels high and low. Yet while Park's ambiguity here is frustrating, it may also be pregnant — one wonders whether there may not be some 'deeper' connection between the commuter and the transient which was obvious to Park's middle-border sensibility and standard of comparison, but has been lost to later generations who are themselves all commuters of spirit if not of body. Mobility served as a mediating concept between the external and internal, as cause and/or index of changes in consciousness, tending 'not merely to undermine the existing social order, but progressively to complicate social relations, and by so doing, release and emancipate the social units of which society is composed'.[85] Technical facilitations of mobility such as railways, automobiles, airplanes 'have literally plowed up the ancient landmarks, undermined the influence of the traditional social order in every part of the world, and released immense social forces which are now seeking everywhere a new equilibrium'.[86]

Park was most fascinated by the effect of mobility on human personality. For the individual, change in status was invariably accompanied by a change in location, 'up to the Gold Coast, or down to the slum', and the change in milieu not only registered a change of status, but in turn produced a change in habits and self-conception.[87] Park's Jamesian-Deweyan view of intelligence led to the proposition that the human mind itself was essentially an 'incident of locomotion' and an 'organ of control' which mobilized the organism for action, disposed it *towards* something. At a more rarefied level, mobility produced the intellectual, for physical wandering emancipated the individual from the mores in which he had been reared, showed him the relativity of human conduct and made him both a stranger and a 'cosmopolitan'.[88]

Mobility had this effect because it provided the individual with a wide variety of stimuli; it was not merely that the individual moved but that as he moved the scenery changed, and each new set of impressions added another layer of images to the mural inside the mind. Mobility was to be measured

not merely by change of location, but rather by the number and variety of the stimulations to which the individual or the populace responds.

Spatial movement and occupational mobility are sociologically significant mainly ... so far as they serve as indices for measuring the 'contacts', i.e., the shocks, clashes and the incidental interruptions and breakdowns of customary modes of thought and action which these new personal encounters inevitably produce.[89]

Thus external behavior merges with states of consciousness, and the explanatory categories of Park's sociology reveal themselves again as rephrasings of the concerns of literature and social theory since at least the eighteenth century, in this case the fear that sophistication destroyed the civic virtue, the stolid 'sincerity', that was based on an acceptance of the givens of one's existence. Park's role in this ongoing discussion was not so much innovative as translative, taking categories and concerns from the humanist elite of the nineteenth century and transmitting them to the technical elite of twentieth century social science.[90]

As an index of social change, mobility was valuable because quantifiable, but there was considerable confusion as to the causal weight to be accorded his two 'orders'. At times Park seemed to say that the basic determinants of change must be sought through social psychology. These changes on the cultural level would then be reflected on the material plane, since 'the physical or ecological organization of the community, in the long run, responds to and reflects the occupational and the cultural'.[91] Yet elsewhere he states categorically that 'Changes in ... the less material culture always and inevitably reflect changes in the more material culture ... technique and the mores are so related that any changes in the former inevitably bring corresponding changes in the latter. The relation is, however, probably not reversible'.[92] The location of the independent variable thus shifted; Park immersed in social psychology plumped for attitudes, but Park concentrating on ecology, and perhaps registering an indirect protest against W.I. Thomas' excessive 'softness', insisted that 'the origin of social change, if one could trace it to its source, would be found in the struggle for existence and in the growth, the migration, the mobility and the territorial and occupational distribution of peoples which this struggle has brought about'.[93] A measure of broad consistency existed beneath the verbal contradictions, in that the processes of migration and of competition for scarce resources were central. Ecological position was symptomatic, and perhaps molded the behavior of individuals trapped on their turf, while culture was at least intermediately causal, though Park could not decide how much flexibility of response resided in the 'social order'.

The Moral Order: Communication and Social Psychology

The ecological order of human relations was only one aspect; a society could be understood only if viewed in double perspective, as a symbiotic association of competing individuals and a self-conscious realm of communicated meanings, in which the messages and the media mutually affected one another. Although Park, at least in his later essays, seems to have seen the ecological order not only as an infrastructure but also as more determinative of human behavior, he found the 'superstructure' of communicated meanings more interesting. The element of personal philosophy is crucial here as elsewhere in Park's thought: while he wished to do justice to the limits on human choice set by external forces, he was more fascinated by the frail, idiosyncratic traits and cultural products men developed while struggling against constraint.

Park divided the superstructure in various ways; often it was characterized only as the 'moral' or 'social' order, but in its most differentiated form it was divided into three suborders, each more distant from the order of impersonal ecology — the economic, political, and moral orders. He was perfectly aware that the notion of a division into orders was a classificatory abstraction, since in any actual human situation the natural relations of symbiosis and competition, characteristic of plant communities, were modified by laws, customs, convictions — by the forms and products of human self-consciousness. But Park, unlike critics then and since, felt that behavior could be understood more fully through his expansive set of categories than through a more specialized and limited system of explanation.[94] Of the three cultural orders, even the economic, which was nearest to a Darwinian struggle for existence, was still modified by law and convention — trade, as Simmel had pointed out, was one of the later and more sophisticated of human relationships. Each of these layers of social life was characterized by a greater degree of conscious control over human destiny and of conscious awareness — and thus, in a typical Parkian paradox, by both more and less freedom. On the economic level, men were limited only by their capacities and the conflicting actions of other men, but on the political level they were hedged round by laws and police, while the moral order provided man with the most exacting of tyrants, conscience.[95]

Just as the mechanism of the ecological order was competition, the mechanism of the social or cultural superstructure was communication. Park was fond of quoting John Dewey to the effect that 'Society exists in and through communication'.[96] Communication was the process through which self-conscious individuals tried to bridge the gap between themselves and others, by objectifying their personal experience and projecting it as symbols into a public universe of discourse where all could meet. From this process emerged the traditional values and patterns of behavior which constituted a society.

Not only does communication involve the creation, out of experiences that are individual and private, of an experience that is common and public but such a common experience becomes the basis for a common and public existence in which every individual, to a greater or less extent, participates and is himself a part. Furthermore, as a part of this common life, there grows up a body of custom, convention, tradition, ceremonial, language, social ritual, public opinion, in short all that Sumner includes under the term 'mores' and all that ethnologists include under the term 'culture'.[97]

Thus communication operated as the 'integrating and socializing principle'.[98]

However, as the equilibrium towards which the ecological order tended was never wholly achieved, so the process of communication, which bound men together on the cultural level, could never be complete or total. The same quality which made communication necessary and possible – self-consciousness—also made it inevitably partial and imperfect. 'The final obstacle to communication is self-consciousness'.[99] Further, the effect of communication on the individual involved a frustrating or self-limiting effect, since increasing awareness of others increased the individual's awareness of his own uniqueness and separateness. As the intensity and variety of communication increased, for an individual or a public, shades and intensities of attitude and opinion were revealed which made the individual more aware of his own uniqueness, and set him further apart from his fellows. Referring to his favorite essay by James, 'A Certain Blindness in Human Beings', Park noted that 'Literature has been able to express for us sentiments and attitudes which we would otherwise have been wholly unable to discover or communicate. One of the consequences of all these changes seems to have been to intensify the subjectivity of individual man and at the same time increase his moral isolation'.[100] This view of communication as paradoxical was reflected in Park's comments on the social role of 'news', i.e., information which 'had or seemed to have some importance for the community concerned' and 'the significance of which was still under discussion'.[101] The circulation of 'news' enabled the members of a society to participate in political acts, i.e., the concerted action of society 'in accordance with some considered purpose and in furtherance of some rational end'.[102] However, the prime function of news was not to create a consensus, but to start people talking by knocking an existing consensus off center, showing its definition of the situation as inadequate to encompass the new information being transmitted. News was thus initially disruptive, since it fostered a sense of inadequacy and a need to arrive at a new consensus in the public which received it. Like so many other models in Park's sociology, this one assumes a 'natural history', an inner tendency toward a new equilibrium, as the process of discussion incorporates the news into a revised consensus on proper action. However, for Park, this revised equilibrium was not inevitable within the existing universe of discourse. Discussion, like competition on the ecological level, would lead to a new consensus if the previous one had been strong and the disruptive news was not so fragmenting as to defeat efforts to contain it. Discussion, however, was inherently a divisive process; Park, in his later years, lacked the progressive faith that increased communication by itself led to the reduction of conflict. On the contrary:

Discussions not only make public opinion, they sometimes make war. But as far as my observation goes, they rarely ever make peace. That does not seem to be their function. ... The outcome of discussion is usually to lay bare the submerged hypotheses, not to say submerged complexes, on which divergent opinions are based. This sometimes leads to an agreement, but it sometimes reveals differences so profound and so charged with emotion and sentiment that further discussion appears unprofitable, if not impossible. When that happens to individuals there seems to be no way of carrying on the controversy except by fighting.[103]

Thus Park's theory of communication displayed his characteristic irony and duality. He tried to combine the Deweyan concept of communication as integrative, implying an 'I — Thou' relation which was moral in its closeness and honesty, with his own personal perception of communication as an *invasion* of the integrity of another mind or culture, of every connection as potentially a collision. In a late essay, 'Communication and Culture' (1938), he resolved the problem by employing his model of the interaction cycle.

It is true ... that when new forms of communication have brought about more intimate associations among individuals or peoples who have been culturally isolated, the first consequence may be to intensify competition. Furthermore, under the influence of communication, competition tends to assume a new character. It becomes conflict. In that case the struggle for existence is likely to be intensified by fears, animosities, and jealousies, which the presence of the competitor and the knowledge of his purpose arouse. Under such circumstances a competitor becomes an enemy.

On the other hand, it is always possible to come to terms with an enemy whom one knows and with whom one can communicate, and, in the long run, greater intimacy inevitably brings with it a more profound understanding, the result of which is to humanize social relations and to substitute a moral order for one that is fundamentally symbiotic rather than social. ... [104]

However, because communication had this divisive potential, its tendency was always to crumble the cake of custom; thus it played a vital role in the process of social change. In this sense, communication on the 'moral' level was the equivalent of mobility on the biotic or ecological level, and Park's transformational definition of 'mobility' had indeed conflated the two. Both mobility and communication involved a transformation of the individuals concerned and both contributed to the development and differentiation of personality by exposing the individual to a variety of different stimuli.[105]

Park was always concerned with the effects of social processes on the individual and particularly the 'emancipated' individual, and worked out for himself and his students a simple usable theory of human personality developed through interaction with others. His work in this field was largely a simplification of the American interactional theory associated with William James, Josiah Royce, James Mark Baldwin, Charles H. Cooley, John Dewey, and his own colleagues at Chicago, Thomas and George Herbert Mead, plus a direct dose of Hegel's dialectical theory of consciousness which had helped to shape the older theorists. The discussion of psychological concepts in his pamphlet of 1915, *Principles of Human Behavior*, was with his customary humility largely a review of current theories and came to no very closely articulated new statement. However, an underlying set of propositions was present, and the work of men such as Freud and Jacques Loeb was collated to give possible depth and detail to a simple, almost traditional statement of human volition in terms of mental 'faculties'. The pamphlet is interesting to later readers as the attempt of a mind trained in traditional categories of philosophical psychology to absorb psychoanalysis and behaviorism, and also for displaying the extent to which this effort could be superficially successful, because these revolutionary theories retained the contours, if not the content, stamped on psychology by Thomas Reid and Dugald Stewart in the late eighteenth century.[106] Park was concerned to modify the over-rationalistic accounts of psychology stemming from Descartes, which made cognition the central faculty; but, following William James in this effort, he still conceived of the argument in traditional terms, as the need to give greater stress to 'emotion' as against 'reason'. Park followed James very closely in describing human nature as 'a superstructure founded on instincts, disposition, and tendencies, inherited from a long line of human and animal ancestors'.[107]

Park's speculations about 'original nature', or the eternal nature/nurture question, which still bulked large in *Principles of Human Behavior*, were to be rendered at least temporarily obsolete by the revolt against explanations which departed from the specifically social level of analysis. Sociologists rejected not only the various psychologies based on classifications of 'instincts', but even the idea that the human animal had any specific tendencies to action which are not transmitted from society through the family and primary group.[108] This rejection of 'instinct' during the 1920s was technically a process of linguistic clarification, a growing conviction that instinct psychology was word-magic. The process was hastened by the reception of behaviorism and the absorption of Chicago social psychology by the next generation of scholars, who came to believe that there was no need to rely on concepts borrowed from another discipline, especially when younger men in that discipline had rejected them. Thus the shedding of instinct theory was part of an assertion of disciplinary autonomy by younger sociologists. The result, however, was a temporary isolation of sociological theory from the progress of cognate disciplines, and was one source of the sense of stagnation which would later cause some sociologists to revolt against Chicago domination of their discipline. This isolation from other studies and the 'over-socialized' theory of personality it produced, would later be countered by the efforts of Talcott Parsons and others to integrate psychoanalytic personality theory into a functional theory of society. However, critics continued to point to the extreme environmentalism of sociology, its tendency to make the individual a passive vessel filled with norms and roles by an all-embracing society, as one of its major weaknesses.[109]

At the same time that he struggled with the problem of original nature, Park also developed the Chicago analysis of the social formation of personality. The concept of the self as a social structure arising out of interaction with others and social experience worked out over many years in his courses in the department of philosophy and psychology by George Herbert Mead had an immediate appeal to the sociologists. By 1915 Park had absorbed much of the approach of Mead as well as the earlier work of Dewey and Charles H. Cooley.[110] In *The Principles of Human Behavior* he pointed out that the distinctively human qualities of the individual were acquired through social interaction, which superimposed on and developed out of the original repertoire of instincts that unique possession of the human being, upon which philosophy and psychology had always insisted — self-consciousness. Man became human by reflecting upon his behavior, modifying action in the light of standards which he developed to judge himself. 'When these thoughts about our actions or the actions of others get themselves formulated they react back upon and control us'. The animal psychology of Lloyd Morgan and Edward L. Thorndike was valuable as a beginning in the study of human behavior, but it must remain always incomplete, since

there is in all distinctively human activities a conventional, one might almost say a contractual, element which is absent in the action of other animals. Human actions are more often than not controlled by a sense of understanding of what they look like or appear to be to others, this sense and understanding gets itself embodied in some custom or ceremonial observance. In this form it is transmitted from generation to generation, becomes an object of sentimental respect, gets itself embodied in definite formulas, is an object not only of respect and reverence but of *reflection and speculation as well*. As such it constitutes the mores, or moral customs, of a group, and is no longer ... an individual possession.[111]

This passage, with its effort to fuse the Cooley—Thomas tradition of social psychology with the larger cultural overview of Spencer and Sumner, is characteristic of Park's writings on the relation of individual to society. The insistence that customary formulas are objects of 'reflection and speculation' as well as 'respect and reverence' displays the pragmatic, voluntarist manner in which Park reworked his extensive borrowings from Sumner, who had stressed that mores could not be made the object of rational discussion.[112]

Park built his discussion of human nature around the twofold concept of 'personality' as developed by individual and social psychology. In the analysis of individual consciousness, 'personality' could be viewed both in the Jamesian manner as 'the memories of the individual and his stream of consciousness', and in a psychoanalytic manner as 'the characteristic organization of mental complexes and trends which may be thought of as a supercomplex' or structure of complexes forming the relatively permanent tendencies-to-action of the individual.[113]

The third aspect of personality was social: the individual personality was a resultant of the action of the social group working upon the raw materials of inherited instincts and 'certain undefined capacities for learning other forms of behavior' with which each individual was born.[114] Each society would mold out of this raw material the kind of personalities which were useful and appropriate to it:

The sociological conception of personality ... may be said to take its departure from the observations of Thomas and Znaniecki that 'personality is the subjective aspect of culture'. The customs of the community inevitably become the habits of the individuals who compose it. The individual invariably incorporates, in his own personality, the purposes and aims that find expression in the institutions by which the individuals conduct is controlled.[115]

However, of equal importance to Park was the function of conflict, of competition with and reaction against other persons, in creating and maintaining the personality. When competition and conflict became conscious, especially in the case of cultural groups, they helped to develop and expand the personality of the group member faced with an 'other', by heightening introspection and self-definition and bringing 'into the light of understanding impulses and attitudes of which we would otherwise remain unconscious. ... ' Park's language may seem Hegelian, but the citation is not to Hegel but to William James' doctrine of the 'vital secret' possessed by each personality, composed of repressed attitudes and desires.[116]

The primary way in which the individual became a person was by finding a role to play and being assigned a status in various social groups within the larger society, first in the family and local community, later 'in the larger, freer, and more impersonal world of politics and of professional and business affairs'.[117] Social man is naturally and spontaneously an 'actor':

We are parents and children, masters and servants, teachers and students, clients and professional men, Gentiles and Jews. It is in these roles that we know each other; it is in these roles that we know ourselves.

One thing that distinguishes man from the lower animals is the fact that he has a conception of himself, and once he has defined his role he strives to live up to it. He not only acts, but he dresses the part, assumes quite spontaneously all the manners and attitudes that he conceives as proper to it.[118]

With his customary emphasis on the rational bases of identity, Park assumed that in the modern urban world the most important of roles was one's job or profession which would entail its own particular subculture. Park was always interested in the effects which one's particular niche in the division of labor would have in shaping the character. To what extent was intelligence largely a function of the continuing demands or lack of them of one's job? To what extent were social and political creeds largely a product of the occupation? Questions of this sort, which Park raised in his early essay on 'The City', would in later years lead to fruitful work on the part of some of his students and grand-students.[119]

A man's role was related to a set of behavior patterns and also to a *status*, a position, in society which was an essential component of his personality. At one point in the *Introduction* Park and Burgess used the term 'status' in the same sense that Sir Henry Maine had used it, to refer to an inherited fixed position in society, in contrast to a position which resulted from the competition among individuals for place and prestige. In the same work, however, and usually thereafter, Park used the term in its more modern sense, as designating the position of any person in a particular group, whether fixed or acquired:

We come into the world as individuals. We acquire status and become persons. Status means position in society. The individual inevitably has some status in every social group of which he is a member. In a given group the status of every member is determined by his relation to every other member of that group. Every smaller group, likewise, has a status in some larger group of which it is a part and this is determined by its relation to all the other members of the larger group.[120]

This relationship is a product of the kind of recognition that the group is prepared to give the individual and can often be measured in terms of the social distance or degree of intimacy between the individual and other members of the group.[121]

Park's concept of status, like his ecological concern with location in 'social space', can be seen as one aspect of the American liberal, pluralist search for a non-Marxian − perhaps more important, a non-rigid and non-reductive − theory of social position. The concept of status accepts the phenomenon of social stratification, but tends to undercut the study of this stratification in terms of class. As T.H.Marshall has pointed out, 'status', as it has entered into the mainstream of American sociology, 'has no direct or necessary reference to position on a scale or in a hierarchy. It embraces all relationships, not only those of superiority and inferiority'.[122] The individual may have several statuses in the different groups with which he is associated and they rest not only on the hard realities of economic function or power but also on religion, ethnicity, even personal taste and the shifting consensus of significant group opinions.

As Park pointed out, the word 'personality' is derived from the Latin *persona*, a mask used by actors in the Roman theatre.[123] The social scenario provided the limits to the flexibility and viability of the human personality − the more associational groups it offered for the individual to be part of, the more selves that individual might have. But though a man might play many parts, he could not escape from the play; his conception of himself must conform more or less to the status held within his group or groups. 'The completely isolated individual, whose conception of himself is in no sense an adequate reflection of his status, is probably insane'.[124]

Still, Park could not temperamentally accept a concept of the individual which was totally that of the 'looking-glass' self, a passive absorption of the conceptions and expectations of society. If humanity and personality could only be *achieved* through interaction with society, they could only be *maintained* by a certain conscious isolation from society: 'for a certain isolation and a certain resistance to social influence and social suggestion is just as much a condition of sound personal existence as of a wholesome society'.[125] Citing such divergent examples as the deliberate isolation of mystics, the value which Rousseau found in true solitude, and the desire of kings, officers, and other manipulators of prestige to preserve necessary distance, Park argued that personality depended not only on interaction but upon distance and privacy.[126]

Considering that man lives so largely in the minds of other men, and is so responsive to the attitudes and emotions of those about him, it is nevertheless true that he is rather less dependent upon his environment, that is to say, the world to which he is oriented, than other animals. He maintains, as over against other individuals − their attitudes and their claims − a certain degree of reserve. It is only in states of exultation and of ecstasy that he lets himself go completely, and yields himself wholly to the occasion and to the influences of the persons about him.[127]

Further, Park exploited the ambiguity contained in the popular analogy of 'playing a role' to emphasize the 'duplicity', the conscious, self-protective dissembling, involved in all reciprocal behavior. We conform deliberately to the stereotyped expectations of behavior proper to our status, both to preserve inner freedom from prying eyes and to win the approval due to a good performance. Man is able most of the time 'by means of his rationalizations, his cynicisms, and his casuistry, to defend himself against the psychic assaults which the presence of other persons makes upon him. He can, when he chooses, make his manners a cloak and his face a mask, behind which he is able to preserve a certain amount of inner freedom even while mingling freely with other persons'. It would be tempting to reduce this misanthropic usage of role theory to a function of Park's personality, but whatever its origins it offers an intriguing alternative to the common contemporary readings that see the 'normal' human being either as the sum of his customary roles or as an innocent natural creature warped by the dirty tricks of an alien 'society' or 'establishment'. In his stimulating review of role theories, Peter Berger quoted the Christian humanist query of Erasmus, 'What else is the whole life of mortals but a sort of comedy, in which the various actors, disguised by various costumes and masks, walk on and play each one his part, until the manager waves them off the stage?'[128] The contemporary critical use of role theory as evidence of the hollowness and inauthenticity of modern life has a certain kinship with the Erasmian usage, but here as in other transformations of traditional concepts, the loss of faith in transhuman categories and a real after-life has transmuted a stoic sense of human limits into nascent revolutionary frustration. Park's idiosyncratic reading will seem too stoic for meliorists, but points to a possible path between the facile expectations of easy adjustment or automatic alienation.

The concept of role playing as the 'crucial link between the individual and the social structure' has become one of the central concerns of modern, and specifically modern American, sociology, and Park played a crucial role in the diffusion of this concept from psychology into sociology. Dennis Wrong attributes to role theory part of the blame for what he calls the 'oversocialized conception of man' among modern sociologists.[129] It is true that the role is the method through which the individual's activities are channeled into acceptable, or at least tolerable because predictable, patterns. The role carries with it 'both certain actions and the emotions and attitudes that belong to these actions', the actor through playing his role over a long period, may grow into it and eventually become it.[130]

On the other hand, the concept of society as drama, and of individuals as role players, can offer considerable scope for individual autonomy. Even the most Method-oriented actor must preserve a certain distance between his own sense of self and the role he chooses to play. To Park this distance was crucial and constituted the individual's *self-consciousness*. Because man is mobile in space and time he always plays more than one role and it is difficult for habits to become totally assimilated and unconscious.

The fact that every individual is capable of movement in space insures him an experience that is private and peculiar to himself, and this experience, which the individual acquires in the course of his adventure in space, affords him, in so far as it is unique, a point of view for independent and individual action. ... Our self-consciousness is just our consciousness of these individual differences of experience, together with a sense of their ultimate incommunicability.[131]

Thus every individual has a mystery — a secret — whose 'ultimate incommunicability' is both his freedom and his tragedy.

The more modern and sophisticated the society, the greater the variety of unique experience offered to the individual, therefore the greater his self-consciousness, the greater the distance between his sense of identity and his roles, and the greater the problem of social control. Life for man in society, and particularly for modern man, must inevitably involve a degree of estrangement and frustration. In an article on juvenile delinquency Park stated quite baldly that the 'natural condition of the individual in society is one of conflict ... with the conventions and regulations of the social group'. Here he speaks with obvious personal passion and in almost Freudian terms, of man as by nature at odds with civilization:

So ill-adapted is the natural, undomesticated man to the social order into which he is born, so out of harmony are all the native impulses of the ordinary healthy human with the demands which society imposes, that it is hardly an exaggeration to say that if his childhood is spent mainly in learning what he must not do, his youth will be devoted mainly to rebelling. As to the remainder of his life, his recreations will very likely turn out to be some sort of vacation and escape from this same social order to which he has finally learned to accommodate, but not wholly reconcile himself.[132]

While this outburst seems to pose a total opposition between the individual and any society, the more general implication of Park's theories, particularly his speculations on urban life, was rather that this friction is a product of the process of modernization, that modern urban, industrialized society produces people who, because of their very individuality, feel the inevitable disciplines and frictions of social life ever more keenly. The increasing pressure of society against the resistance of the individual was responsible for both the strengths and the weakness of civilized man. It produced, for example, 'his sophistication and his introversion', which enables him to cope with and find refuge from the demands of society. 'It is responsible for the fact that he has a conscience, and a divided self; and for many, if not most of his mental and functional diseases. Mental and not sexual are, it seems, the true social diseases'.[133]

Park's essays on personality reveal a complexity and sense of tragedy which, like Freudianism, resist easy translation into clear hypothesis. Thus, out of Park's wide speculations on personality, the most influential was his restatement of the Jamesian 'social self' into a formula suitable for use in field research. 'The person is an individual who has status ... status means position in society. The individual inevitably has some status in every social group of which he is a member'.[134] In this more straightforward form, with the Parkian ambiguities excised, Park presented the Chicago theory of personality in a manner which proved abundantly serviceable as a vehicle for empirical research. However, perhaps because Park's sense of inevitable tension was too pessimistic to appeal to a manipulative discipline, perhaps from a behaviorist reluctance to grant their subjects a capacity for irony, the subtlety and sense of paradox in Park's own role theory was not fully developed for decades, until the work of Everett Hughes and his student Erving Goffman realized the range of contradictions Park had adumbrated. While Park knew and influenced the psychiatrist Harry Stack Sullivan, whose subtle interactional, almost historicist, concept of personality and norms was one of the great legacies of Chicago theory in the next generation, it is more difficult to find the peculiar Parkian ironies reflected in the work of the meliorist, politicized Sullivan. Here again, Park seems to have served as impresario, intermediary, more than as concrete intellectual influence. It is a tempting, perhaps unanswerable question whether Park's dialectical ironies were filtered out because they were unsuitable for testing or because their aura of enclosedness, of frozen frustration, made them unpalatable to an audience whose scholarly identity still entailed problem-solving if not overt moralistic exhortation.[135] At the very least, Park's complex restatement of the 'social self' theory, with its dialectical emphasis on the necessary and creative role of conflict and its awareness of the frustrations transmitted by 'significant others', refutes any necessary connection between an environmentalist theory of personality and a meliorist faith in human perfection through the production of euphonious, adjusted personalities free of inner conflict.

It is perhaps more possible in the longer perspective of the 1970s to recover the often inchoate conceptual richness of Park's thinking, which was masked for many in the intervening generations by its unwelcome overtones of German antipositivism as well as by its over-optimistic abstractions of commonsensical links between antinomies − large historical process and intimate milieu, natural area and human type, social space and social face. Perhaps most damaging was the retrospective labeling of Chicago sociology as a theory of 'social disorganization', which facilitated its dismissal as passé in that relentless critique of unexamined bourgeois remnants which became a permanent prism of the sociological mentality after the arrival of the sociology of knowledge in the 1930s. The criticism not only blocked appreciation of the varied insights available in Park's writings, but by assuming the possibility of a pure theory untainted by value commitments it inhibited the realization that theoretical and moral dilemmas are imposed by the need to mediate and perhaps choose among the varying reference groups to which the scholar responds.

The Chicago school's own choice of concepts to contain the changes that crowded around it had certainly reflected the dilemmas faced by the social expert who must be member and observer of a society, must attempt to do justice both to clients and subjects. 'Social disorganization', a term that implies the existence of objective observers able to appraise the health of the organism they view, embodied the worldview of agencies charged with diagnosing and curing perceived threats to accepted values and social efficiency, and probably of the educated lay public which digested this expert diagnosis in texts and magazine articles. The concern with deviant social types and their 'mentalities' would later provide the ground for a theory of deviance-as-stigmatization, as the result of definition and labelling by the lay or expert carriers of normative authority. Park, however, assumed that the social norms and consequent spontaneous reactions of any group and era carried psychological and therefore moral force on majority and minority, normal and deviant, even though better 'acquaintance with' at least some minorities would slowly alter attitudes. Thus, while the conceptual roots of the relativist, interactional sociology of deviance associated with Howard S.Becker, Erving Goffman, and others can be found in the Chicago studies of the 1920s, the flowering of the field had to await greater intellectual distance of the observer from 'majority' norms. Nevertheless, as David Matza's brilliant *Becoming Deviant* demonstrates, the issues formulated in the Chicago theory of disorganization have reappeared more reflexively in recent discussions of the extent to which expert analyses of social deviance and mental health are, or can be, independent of the ethical values of the analysts.[136]

Appropriately in view of his long and direct 'acquaintance with' the area, Robert Park probably contributed more ideas of lasting value in the field of 'racial' or intergroup relations than in any other area of sociology. In a series of essays sometimes neglected by later students of the subject, he adumbrated a sophisticated theory of ethnic encounters – arguably one more sophisticated at some points than much later work. Aside from this substantive intellectual contribution, Park has considerable historical importance in a crucial phase of 'racial' study. While less directly influential on the general intellectual milieu than a man like Franz Boas, Park was a leading figure in the transition from a 'biological' to a 'cultural' point of view in the study of group conflict. He played a vital role in that crucial three-fold shift of scholarly attention: first, away from the description of racial traits to an examination of the changing relations between different ethnic groups; second, the redefinition of the ideas of 'race' and 'racial differences' as themselves subjective and problematic; and third, to the treatment of ethnic prejudice as a function of group and status conflict rather than an automatic reaction to perceived differentness.[1]

The early twentieth century had witnessed the high tide of popular and scholarly concern with problems of 'race' relations, that is, with the eternal question of conflict among distinguishable and self-conscious groups, which was now typically defined as the result of biological differences among human types. The political questions of the assimilation and/or restriction of European immigrants, the rights and 'place' of Negroes, and Oriental exclusion were topics of absorbing importance, and workers in the budding social sciences naturally turned their attention toward them. The formation of new and more heterogeneous polities needing automatic loyalty had earlier stimulated theories of 'racial' unity based on language and history, but the prestige of the biological sciences, the rise of eugenics and the legacy of Darwinism pushed toward the definition of race in biological terms, and the attribution of observed differences in character and culture to inheritance rather than environment. As one academic observer pointed out in 1903, the rise of biological racism sprang from 'the post-Darwinian, more especially the post-Weismannian ... perception, whether real or imagined, of the lordship of heredity in history and in life. ... Modern science proclaims "blood will tell".'[2]

Social scientists responded not only to these theoretical developments but to the widespread *fin de siècle* fear of degeneration, especially of the alleged decline in the quality of American moral character and political life which accompanied the growth of crowded and ethnically mixed cities. This *nativist* fear of cultural decline made social thinkers more willing to adopt a technically *racist* explanation of differences in ethnic character, but it is important to realize that the two were theoretically quite distinct. If one believed, with a sociologist like Franklin H.Giddings of Columbia or Edward A.Ross of Wisconsin, that social cohesion rested upon 'like-mindedness' or 'consciousness of kind', then the presence of culturally distinct peoples might be seen as disruptive without resort to a racial theory of character. In practice, many sociologists combined elements of both cultural and biological theories into a messy amalgam which they dubbed 'racial traits' or 'racial differences'. Indeed, it may be impossible to make a clear distinction between a trait which was 'racial' or 'biological' and one which was 'cultural' or 'environmental', since the vague social theory of the early twentieth century did not consider a clear distinction important. As George W.Stocking has shown, the neo-Lamarckian strain which characterized much American writing on race relations assumed that habits acquired through the struggle for survival could become 'instincts', but that such culturally acquired 'instincts' could then be broken down by changed conditions.[3]

However, even sociologists like William Graham Sumner or Charles H.Cooley, who avoided biological explanations, could come to pessimistic conclusions about the possibility of eliminating racial conflict which would earn them the title 'racist' in the loose polemic usage of the late twentieth century. Cooley, the Michigan sociologist who attributed human personality to the effects of interpersonal relations rather than to any innate traits, still concluded that Oriental exclusion was justified due to the existence of prejudice and the basis for it in contrasting 'mentalities' formed through social interaction within separate communities.[4] Sumner's Burkean discussion of *ethnocentrism* as a natural reaction, preserving morale and cohesion in the in-group, provided a functional legitimation of prejudice even if one did not accept that the groups rejected were biologically or culturally inferior or even distinct. If hatred for the outsider was indeed an 'instinct', as William I.Thomas said in 1904, then it was reasonable to assume that it was not totally curable by education or other therapy, and contact among diverse 'races' would inevitably lead either to segregation or to serious conflict. It was this non-biological theory of permanent group conflict which offered the greatest challenge to a meliorist approach to ethnic relations. Robert Park's great service was to transform this theory from within, as it were, accepting its partial truth while supplying it with a dynamic of historical change which allowed greater optimism about the possibility of improvement in group relations.[5]

The whole subject of the parameters of thought which can be considered 'racist' has become a controversial one in the late twentieth century, and involves a dialogue between the assumptions of social theory in the 1900s and 1970s. The distinction offered here, between racial, cultural, and purely sociological theories of group solidarity and conflict, seems essential for clear thinking, though certainly 'race' and 'culture' had often been synonymous in earlier nationalist thought and many writers of the early 1900s muddied the waters with a Lamarckian effort to ascribe environmental influences to 'race'. In the late twentieth century it has become common practice, especially but not only in radical circles, to consider any conflict theory to be 'racist' in implication if not in technical detail. The redefinition arises partly from Orwellian semantics — a theory that does not ascribe total responsibility for the existence of inequality to the 'establishment' or 'dominant class' can be seen as 'blaming' the oppressed, therefore 'racist' — but more profoundly from a shift in ethical paradigm, from a naturalistic, environmentalist, 'Darwinian' theory to one based on a kind of existential egalitarianism. In the environmentalist ethics, current perhaps from the eighteenth to the mid or late twentieth century, groups and individuals derived legitimacy from the ability to mesh with a 'natural' environment which included human factors beyond their own control. In the emerging ethical context, all self-conscious beings are equal and legitimate, and moral discriminations that would undercut this existential equality are invidious or 'racist'. Whatever the merit or logical consistency of the new ethical framework, it makes the study of past ideas difficult by collapsing the distinctions that were significant to historical actors into a generalized category of insignificance due to invalidity. The presentist and polemical basis of definition here is probably so obvious as to be self-defeating so long as the community of scholars values intellectual precision over ethical modernity.[6]

Racialist or sociological pessimism, however, was not the only intellectual source on which Americans at the turn of the century could draw to discuss ethnic relations. The eighteenth century tradition of liberal environmentalism, with its assumption of human plasticity, remained powerful, and received political expression in the great 'Americanization' campaigns of the first two decades of the twentieth century.[7] By the turn of the twentieth century, a laissez-faire attitude was becoming more difficult to maintain due both to changes in theory and in the situations which students of ethnicity faced. More commentators began to believe that if assimilation were still possible, it could no longer be taken for granted as the inevitable work of time. Conscious and immediate efforts must be made to 'make over' the immigrant, and to provide the physical and moral conditions in which the second generation could grow up 'wholesomely'. The *Annals* for July-December 1909, devoted to the question of 'Race Improvement in the United States', still displayed a majority faith that such 'improvement' would depend upon intelligent social amelioration rather than on blind exclusion of new-comers. The minority was present, however: two contributors stated that only whites were assimilable. It remained unclear, as through most of the immigration debates, just what cultural or psychic changes were entailed by 'assimilation'.[8]

These confusions over the feasibility and even the meaning of assimilation form the background of Robert Park's theory of ethnic relations as it developed in the 1910s and 1920s. Over the same period, new developments in anthropology and psychology divorced the study of culture from biological and overtly 'racial' considerations, thus removing the clearest conceptual support given racial and ethnic oppression by the community of social scientists. The most important single individual was the Columbia anthropologist Franz Boas, that explicit and tireless opponent of racial theories of character. The essential approach of the 'Chicago school' in psychology and social psychology was also important in shifting scholarly attention away from the biological roots to the cultural and environmental determinants of personality, and, on the level of psychological concepts, the replacement of 'instincts' by 'attitudes', which were products of experience and interaction, and therefore changeable to a degree.[9] In particular, W.I.Thomas' discussion of the Polish peasant in America in terms of the disorganizing impact of a new environment upon traditional attitudes was to have considerable impact upon Robert Park's own work both on the adjustment of European immigrants and on the relations between black and white. Park noted that Thomas and Znaniecki in *The Polish Peasant* (1918-20) showed how the concept of 'social attitudes ... could be used in characterizing local cultures as well as in measuring, in some fashion, cultural and institutional changes', and also called 'attention to the fact that the situation of the European immigrant in the United States can be defined in terms that imply its logical relation to that of the Negro'.[10] This perception formed the framework of all Park's work in the field of race relations and ethnic adjustment: the relations between Negroes and whites in the South, Orientals and whites on the West Coast, Poles and Anglo-Saxons in Chicago, were all to be seen in interactional terms, as examples of the contact and collision of cultures, a process which was one of the most important energizing forces in human history, and which had become one of the major characteristics of the modern order.

Indeed, perhaps the best-known and most influential of Park's efforts to offer a coherent theory of social process through the 'natural history' was the interaction cycle, or cycle of group interaction, developed in his attempt to organize the data of ethnic encounters and memorized by two generations of undergraduates in scattered universities and even high school where Chicago doctors and concepts had come to rest. The relations among groups of persons could be classified into a four-stage cycle arranged according to the amount of conscious, willed, symbolic communication which took place during the interaction.[11] Human contacts tend to move through a series of states, each corresponding to a social process, from the most universal and elementary — 'competition', — to the most sophisticated and equilibriated — 'assimilation'. 'Competition' was the most elementary process because it involved the contact of individuals unaware of one another, through the organizing power of the market place.

Competition is the process through which the distribution and ecological organization of society is created. Competition determines the distribution of population territorially and vocationally. The division of labor and all the vast organized economic interdependence of individuals and groups of individuals characteristic of modern life are a product of competition. On the other hand, the moral and political order, which imposes itself upon this competitive organization is a product of conflict, accommodation, and assimilation.[12]

'Conflict' involved the bringing to self-consciousness, and therefore the politicization, of a competition among individuals or peoples which had gone on without awareness, but now became intense and hostile due to the sense of distinctness and threat engendered by increasing communication and awareness of difference. Until biotic competition was raised to the higher plane of conscious conflict there could be no creation of a new moral order. Conflict was thus essentially a 'settling' process — although the settlement need not be either just or equal. This could be seen best in the extreme case of conflict — war. Historically the function of war had been 'to extend the area over which it is possible to maintain peace' by imposing a new political, social, and moral order upon the vanquished.[13]

'Accommodation', the third stage, resulted from the unstable equilibrium achieved by conflicting parties who became weary of the struggle for self-protective dominance, and agreed (overtly or tacitly) to limit their claims and co-exist with potential rivals, or who had their respective positions defined for them by force. Park seems to have derived this notion of accommodation from such historical sequences as the growth of religious toleration after a century of principled slaughter in the name of truth.[14] Conflict and accommodation were intermediate categories, characterized by greater instability than those at either end of the cycle. The final stage was 'assimilation', in which differences among individuals or groups were eroded and finally reduced to triviality by the mutual introjection of alien values and attitudes: 'a process of interpenetration and fusion in which persons and groups acquire the memories and sentiments and attitudes of other persons and groups, and, by sharing their experience and history, are incorporated with them in a common cultural life'. Assimilation was more stabilizing than accommodation because it was not a rational compromise of conflicting elements which retained their distinctness, but a gradual homogenizing of traits which led to easier relations until once-disparate elements blended into a looser, imperfect yet viable new community characterized not by complete uniformity but by easy intercourse and agreement on values sufficient to insure stable relationships. Assimilation followed accommodation in the interaction cycle presumably because Park saw it as the 'natural' result of a workable accommodation which produced increasing communication, curiosity, and empathy among initial strangers.[15]

It is important to see that the interaction cycle can be stated in formal terms, as above, without reference to race or nationality. However, it is also vital to note that it was developed in the light of Park's experience of race relations in the South, and from his involvement in a study of European immigrants commissioned by the Carnegie Foundation in 1917. The Survey of Race Relations on the Pacific Coast in 1924 was then conducted in consciousness of the cycle.[16] While working on the Carnegie study Park lived for several months in Greenwich Village, observing immigrant life in Manhattan, and consulted closely with W.I.Thomas, then recently dismissed from Chicago and ostracized from the community of academic sociologists. Thomas supplied many of the ideas and apparently even the text for the book published as Robert E.Park and Herbert A.Miller, *Old World Traits Transplanted*.[17]

As the title suggests, *Old World Traits* generalized the interpretation offered first by Thomas and Znaniecki in *The Polish Peasant*, and traced the dynamic processes involved in the breakdown and reformation of personality involved in the course of accommodation to American life. The methods used in both the Carnegie and West Coast studies were also indebted to Thomas, particularly in a heavy reliance on the collecting of personal histories of immigrants – a technique Thomas had pioneered in *The Polish Peasant*. These became for Park perhaps the central tool of the sociologist because they revealed the subjective inner life of 'mental and imaginative behavior'.[18] Life histories were particularly useful in the study of race relations because they revealed the way in which attitudes were formed and changed. Park urged his students to record these autobiographies in the individual's own words and frame questions so as to reveal the organization and disorganization of attitudes as 'the result of changes in fortune, and their incorporation and expression through and their regulation by the organizations of which the individual was a member'. In particular, the interviewer should treasure and ponder the 'naive utterances', i.e., those unself-conscious statements of value which revealed what the subject assumed was 'generally understood and taken for granted'.[19] For the purpose of a race relations study a 'life-history' would be the account given by an individual of his 'own first-hand encounter, in a problematic situation, with members of another race', including '(a) first contacts and impressions, (b) early impressions, particularly those formed before the age of reflective thought and formal opinion, (c) later opinions and attitudes, particularly those based on experiences, (d) conclusions and reflections which these experiences have enforced'. The ideal life-history would be 'anecdotal, a record of first-hand experience, and like the Padre's description of a confession, it should be "sudden, bitter and complete".'[20] A 'life-history' questionnaire used by Park and his assistants reveals his idea of the individual as a creature in constant process, comprehensible only in relation to the goals he had set and his own understanding of his life's progress.

At what age did you first begin to think of a vocation? What was your first choice of a vocation and which books, persons, experiences or necessities determined you in that choice? What interests and ambitions have been sacrificed to your vocation or to your personal ideals of right, duty, etc.? How far, thus far, does your life seem to you a consistent whole? How far do you regard its progress as haphazard and its achievements fragmentary?[21]

For all Park's distaste for a directly utilitarian sociology, there was still a therapeutic intent behind this method, though a quietist, meliorist one, consistent with Park's philosophy of life: the life-history method should work a quiet catharsis of comprehension. Bringing out the inner life of immigrants, and of natives, would ease the passage of racial conflict toward understanding and therefore assimilation. Changes in his own opinions, he recalled, had come from more 'intimate acquaintance with the problem itself and the people involved' through 'sudden flashes of insight'. The best stimulus to insight was the personal document. There was 'no other technique for improvement of race relations in which I have any confidence whatever'.[22] If the sociologist should not be a reformer, he could be a midwife of adjustment.

My own experiences prove that there is nothing which has so completely transformed the attitudes of people towards each other as these intimate life histories, of which Booker Washington's *Up From Slavery* is the most striking example. For this reason, we have put more emphasis on the collection of materials of this kind, than we have put on formal statistics. ... Such a study ... will achieve the ends for which this investigation was undertaken without the necessity of making any appeal, argument, or special plea for anyone.[23]

Two major conclusions emerged from the Carnegie and Pacific Coast race relations studies. The first was a confirmation of the earlier insight of Thomas and others, including Franz Boas, that differences in human behavior could be explained better by studying the environment and especially the culture of a group, than by resorting to biological explanations. The other major insight was one which has since become hackneyed in studies of immigration — the crucial importance of the second generation, the children of immigrant parents who grew up in the United States.[24] Most seemed to become almost wholly Americanized in attitude and outlook, though at the cost of inner conflict. This painful transformation suggested the strong conditioning power of *secondary* groups and contacts, like schools, popular entertainment, and the press, as against the primary group, notably the family. The crucial role of secondary groups, in turn, showed that human character was extensively modifiable by environment. As Thomas wrote to Park: 'One feature of my work is to show that the differences in attitude between generations of the same people is as profound as the contemporaneous differences between races ... One of the Chinese-American letters in "Old World Traits" shows how completely the Chinese girl in America is assimilated to our personal sentiments'.[25] Writing two years later in an issue of *Survey Graphic* devoted to the results of the Pacific Coast Survey, Park concluded that the most significant finding was the change taking place in 'the manners and character of the younger generation of Orientals'. This reinforced 'a growing conviction among students of human nature that the most important, if not the most fundamental, difference between nations and peoples, aside from physical characteristics, are reflected in their manners, in their etiquette, and in the conception which they form of themselves. The characteristic traits of people are, in other words, not so much innate qualities as conventions'.[26] And these conventions could change, if not as the result of social engineering, at least from the impact of outside forces on the symbiotic and subjective life of the individual

To Park, race and ethnic relations in America could only be understood in the context of the universal interaction cycle which was set in motion whenever diverse ethnic groups were brought into long-term contact. Various stages of this cycle could be observed in operation throughout the world. The dynamic expansion of Europe and of industrialism had created a world society which was potentially a vast melting-pot; no ethnic group could resist indefinitely the pressures bringing all the peoples of the world into one interdependent economic framework, and superficially at least into one civilization.[27] The first contact of 'races', in the modern world at least, was in the market-place; the relationship was the symbiotic one of mutual utility and impersonal competition. Such a relation enabled different races and cultures to meet and even to live side by side, but they did not at once become sufficiently homogenized to be considered members of a single society, in the Parkian sense of that term which implied mutual awareness and a degree of empathy. There was no conscious consensus, except on the rules which allowed them to trade with or employ one another. The situation of the Jews in Medieval Europe, or that of the Gypsies down to the nineteenth century, were examples of this symbiotic relation. Such an accommodation could last for centuries, so long as it did not prove intolerable to either side. However, to Park, such an indefinite freezing of the 'natural' progression of the cycle was unusual: mere contact through the market-place tended to increase knowledge and sensitivity, and thus to initiate a cycle of assimilation which might prove complex and gradual, but was rarely reversed. In a generalization which may have been based too much on American idealism, if not American experience, Park insisted that:

The relations of races and peoples are never for very long merely economic and utilitarian, and no efforts to conceive them in this way have ever been permanently successful. We have imported labor as if it were mere commodity, and sometimes we have been disappointed to find, as we invariably do, that the laborers were human like ourselves. In this way it comes about that race relations which were economic become later political and cultural. The struggle for existence terminates in a struggle for status, for recognition, for position and prestige, within an existing political and moral order. Where such a political and moral order does not exist, war, which is the most elementary expression of political forces, creates one.[28]

Thus the crucial stage in the movement from competition to a more profound assimilation was the development of conflict. Once the minority was no longer content with living in but not being part of a wider society, their efforts to break their way in would activate hostility among the dominant groups, resulting in conflict. This conflict was not only inevitable but creative, producing among the minority a solidarity and self-consciousness which might not have existed, and therefore creating one precondition for successful assimilation – the sensitizing of groups to the differences among them. Both symbiosis (or 'competition', the stage of impersonal co-existence based on economic relations), and socialization, the stage of assimilation at the end of the race relations cycle, were relatively lacking in conflict, but the first could not be transformed into the second except through the catalyst of conflict. Park pointed out that there was a tendency to fear that the growth of immigrant institutions and of ethnic feeling among minorities would become permanent barriers to Americanization. This fear was mistaken, since the establishment of immigrant institutions was a sign that the interaction cycle had been activated. The national solidarity which peasants from European villages learned to feel, the creation in them by America of Poles or Italians, was the necessary intermediate step which brought them out of their folk isolation and prepared them to become citizens of a modern civilization.

It is an interesting fact that as first step in Americanization the immigrant ceases to be a provincial and becomes a nationalist. The Wurtemburgers and the Westphalians become Germans; the Sicilians and Neapolitans become Italians, and the Jews become Zionists. The ambition of the immigrant to gain recognition in the American community, 'to represent' the national name 'well in America', as Agaton Giller says, is one of the first characteristic manifestations of national consciousness and it is because he has been unable to get that recognition as an individual that he seeks it as a member of a nationality. One reason immigrants live in a colony is that they cannot get out, and one reason they establish nationalist societies which seek among other things to represent the old country well in this, is that in this way they can participate in American life. If the immigrant chooses to remain a hyphenated American it is frequently because, only through an organization of his own language group, can he get status and recognition in the larger American world outside. As a leader in an immigrant community he and the community are enabled to participate in American life in ways which they could not as individuals, unacquainted with the language and with the customs of the country as they are.[29]

The immigrant foreign language press, though its intention was to maintain the ties between the immigrant and the home land, in fact inadvertently acted as an agency of assimilation, through providing its readers with American news, and because it was read by people who in Europe would seldom if ever have looked at a newspaper. In this way, the immigrant was drawn out of his state of symbiotic isolation into a 'public'. Assimilation should be regarded essentially as a group process; the 'defense' organizations thrown up by immigrant groups for self help and the salving of wounded pride were essential tools in the gradual process of assimilation.

The organization as a whole is influenced, modified, Americanized by its efforts to adjust itself to American conditions. This happened, for example, when the immigrant athletic organizations recently joined the American Amateur Athletic Association; for this alliance implies acceptance by the immigrant of all the American athletic standards. Similarly, the immigrant who penetrates American society as a member of an immigrant group forms a bond between this group and American society.[30]

The attitude of the majority toward the consolidation of immigrant communities and the inevitable development of ethnic self-consciousness should be one of tolerance: the immigrant institution was 'so necessary and inevitable a part of the life of the immigrant in this country that, rather than destroy it, as has been so frequently proposed, we should seek to cooperate with and use it'.[31]

Not only did these community organizations provide functional links with the majority of society but the ethnic pride and self-consciousness which they fostered had the valuable psychological effect of countering the disintegration of personality which cultural conflict tended to produce in the individual caught in the middle. The secondary community institution, like the religious sect or the slum gang, was a necessary substitute for the solidarity of the stable community. Park suggested that cultural conflicts, when they failed to provoke mass solidarity and nationalist institutions, were likely to 'manifest themselves in family disorganization, in delinquency and in functional derangement of the individual psyche'. 'The rise of nationalist and racial movements within the limits of a state, like the rise of sects and religious orders within the limits of a church, strike me as a natural and wholesome disturbance of the social routine, the effect of which is to arouse in those involved a lively sense of common purpose and to give those who feel themselves oppressed the inspiration of a common cause'.[32] Thus, Park's interaction cycle served in short-run political terms as a compelling argument for tolerance toward minorities.

Assimilation, Prejudice, and Tolerance

Despite (or because of) its centrality in their ideology, the exponents of Americanization were never quite clear exactly what was meant by 'assimilation'. Many took rather literally the melting pot metaphor and saw the process of assimilating immigrants in strict dictionary terms, 'to make or be like', 'to absorb or incorporate'.[33] To be an American meant a total and deliberate repudiation of one's past. Assimilation was only complete, said one commentator, 'when the individuals or ethnic groups are emotionally dead to all their varied past'.[34] Park, here as elsewhere trying to create a scientific category from a polemical one, always insisted that assimilation did not entail the total absorption of the immigrant into some pre-existing national type, without effect on it. Nor did the melting pot produce a new fully merged national type.

It has sometimes been assumed that the creation of a national type is the specific function of assimilation and that national solidarity is based upon national homogeneity and 'like-mindedness'. The extent and importance of the kind of homogeneity that the individuals of the same nationality exhibit have been greatly exaggerated. ... The growth of modern states exhibits the progressive merging of smaller, mutually exclusive, into larger and more inclusive social groups. ... The immigrant readily takes over the language, manners, the social ritual, and outward forms of his adopted country. ... What one actually finds in cosmopolitan groups ... is a superficial uniformity, a homogeneity in manners and fashion, associated with relatively profound differences in individual opinions, sentiments, and beliefs.[35]

There may be a fundamental level of attitudes which remain unmodified, but this deep level does not necessarily affect ethnic relations. 'It is probably true ... that in the process of Americanization only superficial traits are modified, but *most of the racial traits that determine race relations are superficial*'.[36] Park and Miller's example of the immigrant athletic leagues joining the American Amateur Athletic Association suggests what was involved in this process of just-sufficient assimilation. The immigrant group adopted the outward conventions of the host society, including those values (in this case, accepting the umpire's decision without great retaliatory violence) which would enable them to cooperate in joint though still limited action.[37] Once there was sufficient honing away of obvious differences and relaxation of hostilities to allow different cultural groups to act together when necessary, then this joint action itself would generate feelings of loyalty and sentiment towards the wider community. 'Men must live and work and fight together in order to create that community of interest and sentiment which will enable them to meet the common crises of life with a common will. At the very least there must be such a consciousness of common interest that differences can be discussed, and out of the conflict of interests a genuine public opinion may be formed'.[38] The level of consensus required, however, was strictly limited to certain norms of procedure; cooperative action, like discussion, permitted great differences to exist in values, attitudes, behavior, so long as they did not seriously inhibit joint action.

Thus, Park's optimistic view of assimilation came from a narrower redefinition of its scope, and a rejection of any simple theory of identity based on 'like-mindedness'. The redefinition was related to the distinction he made between culture and civilization, and the shift from a world of *Gemeinschaft* or 'sacred' societies to a *Gesellschaft* order of interrelated diversity within unity.

Civilization ... is not a local phenomenon in the same sense in which that is true of culture. ... It is not a term which describes what is individual and unique in the life of races or peoples. Civilization is the term we apply to those aspects of culture which have been generalized, rationalized, and are generally intelligible. ... Civilization emphasizes technique as culture emphasizes mores.[39]

Successful and fairly quick assimilation was possible at the more complex and alienated level of civilization, where a variety of roles and greater social distance made the degree of conformity required for acceptance much less than in a more homogeneous and insular community. So the city in particular has been the melting pot of races and cultures: it breaks down the old sacred cultures, replacing them with a mosaic of half-gelled subcultures, each aware of its own lack of total claim on the individual. The United States, in this sense, was uniquely 'urban': America had a 'civilization', but not a 'culture' shared by all its diverse inhabitants.

In modern society, then, like-mindedness or even mutual trust were less important than tolerance and mutual utility. Park's most concentrated theoretical discussion of assimilation, published in 1935, discussed the process in these hardheaded terms as entailing only that degree of 'cultural solidarity' sufficient at least to sustain a nation's existence. This was a crucial redefinition of Americanization, which required of the immigrant merely that he acquire such traits, in particular the language and social ritual, as would enable him to 'get on in the country'. 'This implies among other things that in all the ordinary affairs of life he is able to find a place in the community on the basis of his individual merits without invidious or qualifying reference to his racial origin or to his cultural inheritance'. However, it also required that he lose such visible stigmata of foreignness as made him conspicuous and thus likely to arouse the fear or hostility of the dominant group. 'Assimilation may in some senses and to a certain degree be described as a function of visibility';

it did not require the immigrant to change his soul, merely to wear the same conventional mask as everyone else.[40] This superficial homogeneity of attitude and behavior then mobilized the individual, permitted him to move without restriction and find whatever level his talents allowed. 'It realizes for the individual the principle of laissez-faire, laissez-aller' by substituting 'personal for racial competition'.[41]

Once the level of 'personal competition' had been reached then the way was open for individuals to reach out to one another and form the surest solvent of racial tension — personal friendship. Personal relationships would stabilize the multi-cultural accommodations of modern society, which without them would tend to remain fragile and inherently volatile. Above the level of tolerance and a live and let live attitude, an imaginative effort to understand the deeper lives of others was needed. 'We are very likely to attribute something sinister to conduct the motive for which we do not understand. In fact, it is only to the extent that we are able to enter imaginatively into the lives and experience of others that we regard them as human like ourselves'.[42]

Park was not a naive environmentalist or assimilationist, like some enthusiasts for the melting pot. He certainly believed that cultural change was inevitable, and not necessarily harmful to the people involved; he was never a pessimist like Horace M.Kallen, the philosopher of pluralism, who argued along lines parallel to Park's sociology but concluded that any assimilation beyond the most perfunctory must be harmful to the immigrant.[43] Still, the formal similarity of some themes in Park's writings to the uncompromising doctrines of Kallen is important; whether or not the direct influence was large, Park did stress the importance of the immigrant *group*, not the individual, and assumed that in the short run 'race' relations must be understood as relations among groups. The anxious or opportunistic individual who tried to assimilate too rapidly, who cut himself off from his heritage and attempted to 'make it' socially and economically, caused himself much inner stress and guilt, and would have great difficulty winning complete acceptance in the society toward which he aimed. In a statement paralleling pluralist rhetoric of the early twentieth century, and prophetic of its revival after 1960, Park insisted that 'the renegade is never fully received by the new group and never gets complete recognition. ... His position resembles that of the parvenu. The only means of securing respect in America is to be identified with a group which provokes respect'.[44] Thus Park helped inject into the study of ethnic relations the concept of the organic group and its role in maintaining the morale and self-respect of group members.[45]

Even if complete absorption were desirable, the invisibility which allowed it was possible only for the European. The African or Asian displayed an irreducible 'visibility' which offended the prejudices of the dominant group. If those who controlled the institution that inculcated values, like schools and media of communication, were sensitive to physical differences among men, then the greatest exercise of will by a racially-stigmatized immigrant would not be sufficient. The Oriental immigrant, Park discovered in the course of his Pacific Coast Survey, may experience 'a profound transfiguration in sentiment and attitude', but 'he is still constrained to wear his racial uniform; he cannot, much as he may sometimes like to do so, cast aside the racial mask', and so he is usually perceived not as an individual but as an example of a type.[46] 'This, in turn, accounts for the fact that competition between Oriental and Occidental ceases to be individual and personal and becomes impersonal and racial'.[47] Similarly, the Negro after three hundred years in America had still not been assimilated, 'not because he has preserved in America a foreign culture and an alien tradition, for with the exceptions of the Indian and the Appalachian mountaineer no man in America is so entirely native to the soil, but because he is still regarded as in some sense a stranger, a representative of an alien race'. This lack of acceptance is based 'not upon cultural traits but upon physical and racial characteristics'.[48]

Thus Park was fully aware that the position of the Oriental or Negro in the U.S. was not identical with that of the European immigrant. However, the basis of difference was not racial traits as such but people's sensitivity to them. He made the crucial assumption that relations between black and white, or Anglo-Saxon and Chinese, must be studied not solely in the historically unique context of contemporary race relations in America but in the context of sociological process and comparability, as a particular case of the interactional pattern most fully expressed in the interaction cycle.[49] From this perspective what is important is less the innate qualities of the different racial groups than the terms and stages of their interaction and the attitudes which are produced therein. Park's tolerance was as much a function of his sociological theory as his personal character and experience. His model of society was a market one which assumed change, competition, and conflict as inevitable. Men like Edward A.Ross and Henry Pratt Fairchild, who assumed a more consensual model of society, tended to be more hostile to blacks and Asian immigrants.[50]

Park's earliest sociological writings disavowed any effort to rank races in a hierarchy of superiority and inferiority. In *Principles of Human Behavior*, published in 1915, Park asserted that 'the differences between the civilization of Central Africa and that of Western Europe is due, not to the differences in native abilities of the individuals and the peoples who have created them, but rather to the form which the association and interaction between those individuals and groups of individuals has taken'.[51] In 1918, he found the psychological experiments designed to measure the intelligence of races 'inconclusive', and concluded that 'the average native intelligence in the races is about the same'.[52] Similarly, Park's interest in the 'hybrid', or 'marginal man', the product of racial intermixture, was based on his usual fascination with the exotic – the mentality, in this case, produced by the contact of two cultures. The very term he used, 'marginal', suggests the way in which he preserved yet transformed a traditional subject, away from the study of mulattoes as degenerates embodying the worst traits of both races, to a study which still assumed them 'special', but now assumed their uniqueness to be due to an unusually complex and contradictory process of socialization and a divided identity. Thus he assimilated under the rubric of 'marginal man' not only the mulatto but the 'emancipated Jew', the eternal 'stranger'.[53] In Park's formulation the marginal man took on something of the character of a romantic hero: intelligent, ironic, detached, his personal anguish was the price he paid for his progressive function.

The marginal man is a personality type that arises at a time and a place where, out of the conflict of races and cultures, new societies, new peoples and cultures are coming into existence. The fate which condemns him to live, at the same time in two worlds is the same which compels him to assume, in relation to the worlds in which he lives, the role of a cosmopolitan and a stranger. Inevitably he becomes, relatively to his cultural milieu, the individual with a wider horizon, the keener intelligence, the more detached and rational view-point. The marginal man is always relatively the more civilized human being.[54]

Park considered the mulatto the natural leader of the American blacks in their upward struggle and thought him 'more restless, aggressive, and ambitious' and more intelligent. This was not due to the admixture of 'superior' white blood, but rather to his marginal status and the greater stimulation which it entailed. Caught between two 'unassimilated races', the mulatto found himself in a situation 'at once anomalous and untenable' which imposed upon him 'foremostly and before all others the task of finding a solution'. 'This task, which is for the mixed blood, so intimate and personal a matter, is at the same time difficult enough to call into action all his energies'.[55]

However, Park's persistent dualism did manifest itself in his ethnic theory, and he seems always to have preserved, quite separate from the dominant interactional side of his thought, a sense that races did have 'temperaments' which, once acquired, were relatively resistant to rapid change in response to new situations. Writing in 1918, he assumed that races possessed special aptitudes or 'temperaments' − 'a few elementary but distinctive characteristics, determined by physical organizations and transmitted biologically'. The distinctive racial temperament determined the 'run of attention', the subjects which most members of a race would be interested in, it directed their attention to particular spheres of activity. 'Fundamental temperamental qualities which are the basis of interest and attention, act as selective agencies and as such determine what elements in the cultural environment each race will select; in what region it will seek and find its location in the larger social organization'.[56]

Thus, Park's dualistic analysis of racial traits was the counterpart of his individual psychology: while the prime molding power was cultural, in both the person and the racial group there were inborn tendencies toward certain kinds of expression, which enable both to have a peculiar vocation. And Park did tend to personalize groups for more than literary convenience – he discussed the history of 'the Negro' in America as a process of absorbing such cultural forms from the surrounding white society as were necessary and useful for its survival, but the race had

put into these relatively external things ... such concrete meanings as its changing experience and its unchanging racial individuality demanded. Everywhere and always it has been interested rather in expression than in action; interested in life itself rather than in its reconstruction or reformation. The Negro is, by natural disposition, neither an intellectual nor an idealist, like the Jew; nor a brooding introspective, like the East African, nor a pioneer and frontiersman, like the Anglo-Saxon. He is primarily an artist, loving life for its own sake. His *metier* is expression rather than action. He is, so to speak, the lady among the races.[57]

The phrase 'lady among the races' offended blacks raised in the era of liberal faith that groups had no common 'character', at least if that character displayed traits less than wholly admirable. In a heartfelt cry which shows how 'American' some black Americans were, and are, Ralph Ellison recalled that 'I had undergone, not too many months before taking the path which led to writing, the humiliation of being taught in a class in sociology at a Negro college (from Park and Burgess, the leading textbook in the field) that Negroes represented the 'lady of the races'. This contention the Negro instructor passed blandly along to us without even bothering to wash his hands, much less his teeth'.[58]

However, Park's belief in distinctive 'racial temperaments' was shared by militant Negroes of the early twentieth century, including W.E.B. DuBois, who stressed the emotional, expressive nature of 'the Negro'.[59] DuBois seems to have seen Negro 'rhythm' as something more than a cultural response to a restricted repertoire of opportunities for expression and achievement. Indeed, with the romantic rejection of liberal individualism and rationality as especially Anglo-Saxon traits which ascended after 1960, Park's formulation might almost seem once more fashionable, were it not for the unfortunate phrase 'lady among the races'.[60] Even for Ellison, it appears not so much the idea of racial temperament as the characterization of Negroes as 'feminine' which gave offense.

At any rate, whatever the varying fashionability of Park's theory of racial temperament, it was logically separate from the fresher interactional theories which his students would carry forward. Here, for once, there is a positive effect resulting from Park's usual theoretical expansiveness and lack of close logical articulation.[61] While Park never repudiated the notion of 'racial temperament', it drops out of his later published works on race and culture.

Even in the 1910s, Park saw this temperament as little more than a crystallization of habit, so adaptable that it did not preclude eventual accommodation among groups or the adaptability of individuals to changing circumstances.[62]

While anxious to maintain a balance between objective and subjective influences on ethnic encounters, Park did much to encourage what later became the dominant mode of analysis, the study of 'prejudice' among dominant or 'majority' groups. Park approached the analysis of racial prejudice by establishing a distinction between two types of negative attitude, racial 'antipathy' and 'prejudice' defined with etymological precision. 'Antipathy', he felt, was an unfocused universal response to new experience which was seen as strange and potentially threatening. Men are fascinated by novelty, but they are also made tense and insecure by it. 'We may define the situation in which races meet, as one of vague apprehension tinged with and qualified by curiosity'. The situation of first encounter is open and unpredictable; men may decide that strangers are less than fully human, but also more than human, godlike, as in the first Aztec reactions to the Spaniards. However, Park assumed both that our intuitive responses include a strong fund of fear, and that the ecological situation in which groups come together often gives objective basis for an arousal of hostility. Thus, it would be easy for the strangers' behavior to arouse distrust or disgust, leading to an antipathy which would crystallize into a relatively stable attitude. The ensuing attitude was then likely to persist and pass into the culture of the group, especially in a situation like the conflict of life-styles and of material interests which Park saw on the Pacific Coast in the 1920s. 'Prejudice' was the term for this relatively stable group of judgments made in advance of direct personal encounter, which became part of the culture of a community. While these were usually negative pre-judgments used for defensive purposes, in a formal sense a 'prejudice' was a convenient shorthand used to classify and predict behavior of members of any distinguishable group.[63] In studying the development of racial attitudes during the Pacific Coast Survey, Park tried to employ this distinction between antipathy and prejudice by urging his field workers to discover whether informants' attitudes had developed as a result of personal encounter or passive acceptance of group stereotypes, and whether there were contradictions between attitude and direct experience.[64]

To view this limited topic through the categories of Park's general system, prejudice was a means by which the moral order restricted pure competition among individuals for wealth and status.[65] Groups identifiable by culture or physical type were denied access to positions to which their talent and energy might entitle them in a free market. Prejudice, then, was a psychological force with the objective social function of maintaining existing social distances, and with them the existing social equilibrium. As long as this equilibrium was preserved by acceptance of the unequal situation by both sides, there was little need for overt hostility or force, and certain contacts could be carried on smoothly and even with good will across the caste barrier. 'The Negro is "all right in his place" and the same is probably true of every other race, class or category of persons towards whom our attitudes have become fixed, customary, and conventionalized. Every one, it seems, is capable of getting on with every one else, provided each preserved his proper distance.'[66]

Park followed Herbert Spencer in pointing to the 'etiquette' governing behavior in social situations as one of the most vital means of social control. Only when this 'etiquette' becomes problematic in a fluid situation, through the arrival of newcomers, deliberate challenge, or changing external conditions which undermine it, do specific legal restrictions, like the Southern segregation laws of the 1890s, become necessary. Like other social rituals, the etiquette of race relations was a means by which the individual preserved a degree of inner autonomy, serving as 'the masque behind which one controls and conceals his emotions rather than reveals them. Etiquette in that case becomes a kind of social device by which one does the expected thing but preserves his inner freedom.'[67]

Perhaps the best brief statement of the subtle refinement of a conservative's common sense which was Park's racial theory, together with his application of it to contemporary America, was one he made in 1928.

Prejudice — that is caste, class and race prejudice — in its more naive and innocent manifestations, is merely the resistance of the social order to change. Every effort of the Negro ... to move, to rise and improve his status, rather than his condition, has invariably met with opposition, aroused prejudice, and stimulated racial animosities. Race prejudice, so conceived, is merely an elementary expression of conservatism ... The Negro is rising in America and the measure of the antagonism he encounters is, in some very real sense, the measure of his progress.[68]

The Sociologist in the World

Park had never wanted to be a secluded scholar and his desire for involvement had encouraged the Chicago school's pushing the sociologist out of the study into the streets to watch and observe at first-hand. With his global perspective on race relations in the United States, Park wanted to observe the process of culture contacts all over the world, and from the late 1920s through the late 1930s he was extraordinarily peripatetic. Between 1929 and 1934 he travelled and studied in Japan, Hawaii, China, India, Africa, and Brazil, serving as resident professor at the University of Hawaii from 1931 to 1932 and visiting lecturer at Yenching University in Peking from 1933 to 1934. At Yenching as at Chicago, he urged scholars towards a mixture of introspection and field work. He did not use a text-book in his year there but instead forced his students to write their own text 'by answering ... observation-and-thought provoking questions'.[69] In Brazil, where he was fascinated by what seemed to be a unique absence of racial tension, he sought out a gifted American student, Donald Pierson, supervised his studies and eventually recommended him for a professorship at the University of Sao Paulo where he built up a pioneer school in the social sciences.[70] Park found Hawaii particularly congenial as an exotic and colorful collection of races. As he told the audience at a University of Hawaii commencement, some people enjoy cosmopolitan and colorful communities 'where the processes of civilization are so visibly going on around them as they are here. The existence of cosmopolitanism makes life problematic, of course, but it makes it interesting.'[71]

The Orient held a special fascination for Park, partly from his professional contact with marginal Chinese and Japanese immigrants on the West Coast, partly because it was a region in the throes of rapid and visible modernization and Westernization. The year before he died, he wrote to a Chinese friend who was occupying his old office in Chicago that Peiping was the 'most interesting city in the world today' and that what China needed was its own Domesday Book which would be 'the most complete and most momentous social survey that has ever been made anywhere'.[72] A decade and a half earlier, a trip to Japan had confronted him with startling visual evidence of the crumbling of traditional cultures under the juggernaut of Western cultural and economic expansion.

On the corner of the Ginza, I am suddenly aware of familiar music, and recognize the thrilling notes of 'Onward Christian Soldiers' which is being broadcasted from a building across the street. I am standing in front of an English book store, its windows filled with English books, mostly of a religious character. ... Down the street is a brand new very modern and elegant cinema theatre, where they are presenting an Irish melodrama, made in America of course.

There was a shop selling pictures of American actresses

... most of them chorus girls, scandalously draped or undraped from the traditional Japanese point of view. ... And in the midst of all this visual and audible turmoil the notes of 'Onward Christian Soldiers' roll out into the street and dominate the scene. This scene is a symbol of the turmoil in Japanese life and culture which one notes everywhere, on the street and in the newspaper. ... It is all bewildering, fantastic and thrilling. The visible and audible confusion is merely a symbol and index of the incredible and silent tumult in the minds of the people and particularly is this true of those not numerous but still significant individuals of European and Asiatic origin who have intermarried.[73]

This unpublished diary entry suggests both that Park's old Sunday-supplement style came to the fore again as he neared retirement, and the way in which the themes of his sociology came to dominate his raw perceptions. For all his injunctions to empathy and careful observation, Park could clamp his broad conceptual categories on the available data without much restraint.

At home, Park was influential in making the study of race relations a central concern of sociology and developing the field as part of the college curriculum. Projects with which he was involved such as the Pacific Coast Survey had the effect of stimulating the working up of race relations courses in colleges and even high schools.[74] More important, many people who were later to do distinguished work in the field of race and 'minority' relations were his graduate students, in particular Donald Pierson, Edgar T. Thompson, Louis Wirth, Charles S.Johnson, later President of Fisk, and E.Franklin Frazier. Frazier and Johnson, who were to have a profound effect on the study of the Negro in the United States, took from Park not only basic organizing concepts, such as social disorganization, social distance, and marginality, but converted the old man's tough attitude into the belief that the Negro intellectual must be a hardheaded realist providing not moral uplift but objective information and useful categories of analysis.[75]

Park was in an ideal position to study race relations at a bitter and explosive point in their cycle in the great Chicago race riot of 1919. He had indeed predicted that the mobility of Negro troops during the war would unsettle their attitudes, resulting in conflict on their return home. In view of his interest in conflict, it is curious that he did not do any personal study of the riot or even discuss it in his essays on race relations. However, because of his position and interests, Park could not. but be involved. He was appointed chairman of a Joint Emergency Committee, set up by the Urban League, the NAACP, the Negro YMCA, and other groups to look after the interests of Negroes arrested during the riots. As might be expected, given his old relation to Booker T.Washington, his relations with the NAACP were not entirely cordial. Mary White Ovington, chairman of the national organization, thought that Park was a 'slow going conservative, the astute political kind', that he had 'never been aggressive' and 'would dally and fail'. Park was more fully involved in the attempts to make sense of the riots since several of his students were employed on the investigating commission. Of the seven people hired to compile the data collected and write drafts for the final report, three had studied under Park and the chief researchers in the sub-study on public opinion were students in his class on 'The Crowd and the Public'. In particular, his graduate student, the black former soldier, Charles S.Johnson, was appointed associate executive secretary of the Commission. According to Johnson's recollections and those of a research worker, Park gave considerable time and assistance to the research team in organizing the research and analyzing its findings. The finished report does seem to reflect Parkian interests and also Parkian limitations — for example, in its lack of any analysis of the political structure of Chicago or 'the connections between the political system and various urban economic interests as they affected race relations', and the emphasis on public opinion and attitudes and the role of the newspapers in shaping them.[76]

Mary Ovington's complaint that Park had 'never been aggressive' in the field of race relations could be defended, but her implication of political cowardice seems the blind judgment of an enthusiastic progressive activist upon an Olympian Social Darwinist. Park was involved in 'practical' ways in race relations, though never as 'reformer' or social engineer. The projects which interested Park were those which practised indirect therapy through increased communication and the gathering of information. The Chicago Urban League, of which he was a founder, married Park's interest in a vigorous city life with his concern for the Negro and combined the outlook of a research agency with the philosophy of Booker T. Washington. The main purpose of the league was to help Chicago Negroes, particularly those recently migrated from the South, to adjust to life in a Northern city, to mediate between them and regular city welfare boards and particularly to help broaden industrial opportunities for the Negro man and woman. During the first two years of the league's existence, while Park was president (1916-18), the basic stress of the league was upon research, on the assumption that 'efficiency rests in the long run, upon knowledge'.[77] The self awareness brought about by the feeling of racial solidarity which participation in the league might stimulate, together with the objective awareness of his situation which the research done by the league would provide, would enable the Negro to carry out Booker T. Washington's philosophy in the more complicated surroundings of the urban North and pull himself up by his own bootstraps. 'The most important service that one individual or group of individuals can perform for others is to give them the means of helping themselves. It is this service which the Urban League, through its department of records and research, is seeking to render to the Negro of Chicago.'[78] A Bureau of Investigations and Records was set up with a grant from the University of Chicago and the first employee was Charles S. Johnson, then a student at Chicago. The bureau assembled a file of clippings, surveys, and reports which would provide a fund of information for agencies interested in the race question. Park felt that one result of the league work was that 'there is a tendency everywhere to establish social work among Negroes on a sound basis of fact and take the problem of Negro welfare out of the realm of controversy.'[79] Park also hoped that the league would be able to convert the race feeling and hostility of the Chicago Negro, inspired by white prejudice, into 'constructive channels'. So the league organized block clubs and community improvement societies to encourage Negroes to keep their houses well and improve their neighborhoods, to show whites that blacks did not inevitably depreciate property values.[80]

The other 'philanthropic' projects with which Park was associated involved much the same mixture of self-help, constructed community and therapy through increased communication and understanding. He was president of the National Community Center Association (1922-24), an organization aimed at increasing awareness and democratic participation in urban life. He was also one of the founding members of Park House, a center established in the late spring of 1934 on the Near North Side of Chicago, to meet 'the needs of young persons ... who needed some stabilizing influence in their lives' and at the same time act as the focus for a research project to study the 'changes in American "morals" ... what was happening to the American home ... the neighborhood and the church'.[81] The initial idea for the house seems to have come from Park, although it was elaborated by others. As a member of the advisory board, Park spent a good deal of time there: it had for him the attraction that 'doing good' was combined with, or possibly masked by, an intellectual rationale and the opportunity to meet interesting people of a mildly bohemian character. Park thought of the center as a place of adjustment to the difficulties of urban life for the youth from the country or small town 'who goes to the city to seek his fortune'. In particular it would combat the 'two types of malaise that are widely prevalent in every Bohemia ... nostalgia and cynicism'. The homelike atmosphere and the opportunity for making friends would deal with the nostalgia, while Friday night anecdotal talks by guest speakers who had 'achieved a career' would mitigate the incipient cynicism by demonstrating that one could become at home in the bewildering world of the city.[82] The center met with a good deal of initial resistance as an agent of the University of Chicago, but it was eventually fairly successful – although not quite in the way Park had intended. Some people came from as far as Evanston and the South Side to take advantage of its facilities and between 300 and 350 a year were actively associated with the house, most of them white, Protestant, native born, white collar workers or struggling artists or writers. The majority were not in fact from the country, but were natives of Chicago or at least fairly long term residents. The main attraction of the center seems to have been the opportunity to make friendships; the most successful activity was folk dancing, which seems to have served the same function as a T group in lowering the inhibitions and defenses of middle-class males.[83]

Park's practical commitment to the improvement of race relations, and its particular mode of expression, are perhaps best revealed in his decision, after his teaching at Chicago finally ceased in 1934, to teach at Fisk University. He spent the last nine years of his life there (1935-44). At Fisk University Park came into contact, in the words of its president, Charles S. Johnson, with 'students out of a critically marginal population who were unaware of the process of which they were a part'.[84] Park anguished over them and tried as the first essential step in education to draw them into the world – to make them aware.[85] For this, the opening wedge was not so much technical sociology as literature and the habit of reading for pleasure. His daughter recalls that Park 'took to reading aloud amusing books' to students who had no conception of reading except class texts. 'One student I remember told him that it was the first time she ever knew books could be fun.'[86] His impact in a fairly brief time was considerable and some years after his death a new building on the campus was named Park Hall in his memory (after the death of Charles S. Johnson, it was renamed Park-Johnson Hall).

The Decline of the Chicago School

While Park, from his outpost at Fisk, tried to guide and encourage his former students in sustaining the type of sociology that Chicago had made its own, by the mid-1930s the Chicago department's and 'school's' ascendancy in American sociology was rapidly waning. This shift in institutional and intellectual position was due to a complex network of forces, which can only be adumbrated here along with more detail on Park's awareness of and response to them. Simply stated, they were: an increasing concern with the scientific status of the field, reflected in a preoccupation with methodology; the rise of other sociology departments as centers of research and graduate instruction; the absorption of major European sociological theories; and changing concepts of the proper role of the sociologist in relation to the society he studied.

Without either Thomas or Park to provide a dominant personal force and inspiration, the deficiences of Chicago's theories and methods became more apparent. By 1930 methodology — even at Chicago itself, with the arrival of the statistical sociologist William Fielding Ogburn from Columbia — was becoming more self-conscious, precise, statistical, and determined to exclude the random insight and unassimilated if revealing anecdote. Although Park had spoken for a more 'scientific' sociology, his implicit definition of 'science' seems to have been adequate explanation of external reality through direct observation and then classification within a set of interrelated concepts; the 'adequacy' of explanation would be measured subjectively, not through a very explicit and precise method of inference and verification. Writing in the mid-twenties for the Pacific Coast Survey, he had said

The question of methods of investigation is important, but it is distinctly secondary. I think we should assume that we can study anything in regard to which we need knowledge. It is important that we employ the best methods such as they are ... if we succeed in getting a more accurate, objective, intelligible statement about the matter than anyone else, we may count the results of our investigations as science. Science is not a ceremonial matter, as some reverent souls seem to think.[87]

Their orientation toward the analysis of complex situations in terms of the subjective perceptions of actors pushed Park and the 'Chicago school' away from statistics. More intensely as he grew older and the demand for statistics grew, Park came to despise it as 'parlor magic', partly because, as he told his class on 'The Crowd and the Public', statistics did not allow for the subjective sense of identity, the 'conception of the group as an entity: that is to say as an object whose behavior is defined by its internal reaction', but also, one suspects, because statistics squeezed out the idiosyncratic and peculiar which to Park were the prime fascination in the study of society.[88] This aversion to statistics, however, meant that as sociological research became more quantitative in the late twenties, the development isolated Park himself as an exotic. Gradually, 'research' came to mean 'quantifiable results', though more slowly at Chicago where Park maintained the methods of natural history and the case study. Statistics did not immediately adapt themselves to what for Park and his students remained the ultimate purpose of sociology: 'to establish a knowledge of social processes and social causation, formulated in general, i.e., generalized terms, ... social causation takes place primarily on the psychic level, on the level of the action and interaction of organisms, each acting as a total.'[89]

In many ways, the Parkian approach, though less exact, may have offered a greater respect for the complexities of human behavior. For many modern sociologists, the 'gross', quantifiable, and standardizable traits which people have in common seem to be given total weight in explaining and predicting their behavior − except insofar as psychological peculiarities are invoked to explain 'deviance' from behavior proper to their 'class', whatever that might be (race, sex, age group, educational or regional category, social class, etc.). The method seems often to entail a moral preference for people to conform to type: there is a certain style of behavior proper to members of each verifiable class of person, deviance from which is problematic and indeed 'deviant' in a sense which seems to imply psychological and moral inferiority. The classification in terms of statistical types, often combined with a functional theory of group coherence, may tend to degrade the individual's autonomy and encourage conscious conformity to the norms defined by the sociologist. Sociology itself, especially the functional approach joined to statistical definition of categories, may become a method of social control; its mere existence becomes a normative tool, if its results are widely diffused and accepted. Whether this tendency is not inherent in any effort to classify human types and behavior is a difficult question, but it may be less likely to result from Park's interactional conflict theory and intense concern for the variety of subjective understandings.

While other centers outstripped Chicago in methodological sophistication and power within the discipline, the attention of younger sociologists was also shifting away from Parkian categories like 'The City'. The classic formulation of the Parkian approach came in 1938 with Louis Wirth's essay, 'Urbanism as a Way of Life', but younger sociologists, searching for tools to comprehend a new historical era and adapting a Weberian and Marxian emphasis on class structure as the basic analytic category, found Park's approach less and less useful.[90] Moreover, the 'hard' side of Park's dualistic system, human ecology, or social ecology, was coming under specific attack. As developed by a number of Chicago students, most notably Roderick

McKenzie of the University of Michigan, ecology had become an influential method of approach, because it seemed to offer a natural-science or behavioral theory which sought causation 'outside the sphere of consciousness'. However, it tended to become a preoccupation with the spatial distribution of urban phenomena and plotting them on maps, together with the correlation of behavior with location and external conditions — of crime with type of housing, for example. As a later ecologist said, this development of ecology independent of Park's balancing social psychology became a 'statistical study in psychological behaviorism. ... One of the techniques employed in ecological research — mapping — has been mistaken for the discipline itself.'[91]

In 1938 the attack on Chicago's dominance produced a book-length critique of ecology. Milla Aissa Alihan, a ph.d. from Columbia, attacked what she saw as the fatalism implicit in Park's emphasis on the determining power of impersonal forces and even of areas; she argued that since in practice the symbiotic relations of men were so enmeshed with their cultural life, to attempt to divide them for analytic purposes could only lead to confusion and theoretical sterility.[92] Perhaps Chicago's vulnerability and defensiveness were reflected most vividly in the letter sent to Alihan by Nels Anderson, one of Park's earliest students. No one, Anderson told the critic, could adequately appraise Park's theories who had not, like him, 'walked the highways and byways ... gone out among the people where they live'. He also pointed out more calmly that Park's own interpretations had been more tentative, he had claimed less for ecology than Alihan assumed for polemical purposes. 'Park is merely trying to think of people as mobile in space, in social contact with their feet on the ground. It makes a difference where the ground is and who lives next door.'[93] Park himself took the book calmly, writing to a friend that while it contained 'malicious interpretations', 'on the whole' the criticisms were just.[94]

Within a decade after World War ii, a revival of the ecological method was under way, retaining Park's stress on adaptation to environment but relying less on spatial expression, and still fueled by a desire to check the persistent tendency of American sociology to study subjective states of mind and cultural values while neglecting external and especially economic imperatives on behavior. Leo Schnore in 1961 defined postwar ecology as concerned with the organization of a society to sustain itself; its ultimate goal was to describe 'the patterning of social relationships within the population that are manifested in sustenance activities' from an external viewpoint. In a manner reminiscent of Park's hearty encouragement of a method, the goal seemed to be to see how far the sociologist could go with a behavioral-economic approach.[95]

The hegemony of the University of Chicago over the field stimulated resentment among sociology departments in other centers. This resentment tended to center on the fact that the official journal of the American Sociological Society, the *American Journal of Sociology*, had always been owned by the University of Chicago and edited by a member of its faculty. At the 1935 convention of the society a long brewing revolt climaxed in the election of a non-Chicago secretary and in the establishment of a separate official journal – the *American Sociological Review*.[96] This palace revolt signalled the fact that other centers of influence were emerging strongly enough to challenge Chicago's long held role of leadership. The most important of these were Columbia and Harvard.

The Columbia department developed a more highly rationalized, efficient, and large scale organization of research than Chicago had ever been able to do. As the latest historian of these developments has pointed out 'the research for which Columbia graduate students were trained could be done without personal inspiration: it was easily reproduced and multiplied'.[97] The kind of study for which Chicago was known, on the other hand, seems to have been much more dependent on the inspiration of a great teacher and the personal flair of the researcher.

The ascendancy of Harvard was based mainly on the dynamic and productive Talcott Parsons whose own system by-passed earlier American theories and drew directly from the great continental masters, Durkheim, Pareto, Weber, and Freud.[98] Park was certainly familiar with these men and used them sometimes in his teaching. Everett Hughes recalls that Park had his graduate students at Chicago read Durkheim in the original.[99] In the thirties too, under the influence of L.J.Henderson of Harvard, whom he had known as a fellow student in Strassburg, Park began to absorb Pareto.[100] Perhaps under this stimulus, as well as that of his advancing years and the trend of his own opinions, Park's work in the 1930s sometimes shows a greater sensitivity to social equilibrium.[101] Yet the theories of Pareto, like those of Freud, Durkheim, and Weber, played a major role at Harvard, and later in the profession generally, without ever penetrating beyond the horizon of Park's intellectual spectrum.

The supersession of Parkian sociology by the next theoretical generation was in great part the technical progress of a developing academic discipline, which from both introspection and clients' impatience will move toward methodological sophistication and the articulation of concepts that mesh with empirical data to the satisfaction of its customers both internal and external. Still, there was more than immanent and logical development involved; the change also entailed a shift of metaphor and sensibility, of ideological context. In this case it entailed the replacement of one general model of the normal society by a radically different one. Park's own model may be seen as an effort to blend the individualistic liberalism of traditional American social thought with the organicism of early European sociology by using the ideas of Simmel as the foundation of a system that stressed process, conflict, and the limitations upon human will imposed by external conditions and competitive forces. To simplify a far larger and more diverse theoretical universe, the generation that succeeded in the 1930s, in both general sociology and such special fields as race relations, offered relatively static models, stressing structure, equilibrium at least as theoretical norm, consensus on values, and the psychological explanation of what was seen as problematic and disequilibrating. This shift entailed, perhaps was caused by, a parallel transformation of the attitude toward change and the ability of individuals to cope with it. Park's system assumed that conflict was natural and sometimes creative, and that men were tough enough to adapt to changing circumstances in many cases. Later treatments, however, were more sensitive to human frailty, to the limits on adaptation and the need for stability, sometimes to the point of stressing the old romantic analogy between men or cultures and plants, whose very survival was threatened by 'uprooting'.[102]

Further, the two paradigms bear a striking, if perhaps superficial, resemblance to the major models of 'liberal' political theory prominent between 1910 and 1940. The change from Parkian to 'equilibrium' sociology seems to parallel the changing context of political liberalism from Woodrow Wilson to Franklin Roosevelt, from the New Freedom's affirmation of competition as ethical norm to the static, therapeutic view of society as 'a patient etherized upon a table' offered by the younger and more original theorists of the New Deal.[103]

Finally, the academic climate of the thirties was unfriendly to Park's determinedly detached, apolitical approach to research. The number of sociologists working in public agencies increased, and many came to consider their role as that of manipulative elite, consultants to a powerful state rather than an active, rational public. As they became involved in the practical problems of the depression era and the challenge of Fascism from abroad, an open commitment to social engineering and political involvement replaced the Parkian image of the concerned scholar as detached observer and midwife to attitude change.[104] Park, of course, was upset by this Comtean tendency. His own politics were conservative in the American sense: he believed in limited government and competition. While granting that the state must adapt to changing conditions, his pessimism and anarchistic streak generated skepticism toward what seemed the elitism of the New Deal. Although voting Republican, he referred to himself as a 'Jeffersonian Democrat'. 'I am, therefore, against dictatorship and regimentation and centralization on principle.'[105] He disliked personal involvement with politics beyond the act of voting and was always resisting the efforts of interested people to get him to sign petitions of various kinds.[106] His skepticism about the success of planning on anything but the most local and small scale level continued unabated throughout the thirties. At this time when sociologists were drawn more than ever into practical affairs he strove to prevent institutes of research from becoming political or propaganda agencies. 'I shall be interested in learning more about the Institute of Race Relations', he wrote to Charles S.Johnson who had just become a co-director, but added rather sharply 'I hope it will not take, under the influence of New York University, the character of an Institute of Anti-Nazi Propaganda.'[107]

Several of Park's colleagues at Chicago were also concerned about the trend in sociology in the thirties and in particular what they regarded as the turning away of the American Sociological Society 'from its traditional scholarly research character toward an active participation in national political and social controversy'. The outcome of conversations on this topic between Park, Herbert Blumer, R.D. McKenzie, E.W. Burgess, Ellsworth Faris, and others was the setting up of a separate Sociological Research Association, as a small group to keep alight the flame of pure research and objectivity. However, since the main society did not in the judgment of most professionals become politicized, the new association soon became an almost purely social organization.[108]

The sharpest contrast between Park's perspective and that of the next generation came in the field of race relations. Park had a strikingly 'Olympian' quality of mind. He strove to 'feel' and comprehend the full range of the *comédie humaine*, and this personal passion, joined to the ideal of scientific scholarship, precluded taking an active role. This ideal of rigid objectivity was perhaps always a minority one in American sociology, but it flourished in the 1920s, as later in the 1950s, both in their own ways periods of disillusionment. But it was this very Olympian manner which disturbed the younger sociologists of the late 1930s and 1940s, who tended to interpret it as callousness or hide-bound conservatism. The Swedish economist Gunnar Myrdal was one of the best-known of the Europeans who exerted direct influence on American social science at the end of the '30s; in race relations he may be taken as representative of the activist, manipulative stance of the new generation. His *American Dilemma*, the summation of a project staffed largely by younger Americans and building partly on the data of the 'Chicago school', became the most influential study of American race relations.[109] It concluded by dismissing Park and his students as having transmitted a 'naturalistic and, therefore, fatalistic philosophy' with the implication that 'man can and should make no effort to change the "natural" outcome of the specific forces observed. This is the old do-nothing (laissez-faire) bias of "realistic" social science.' Myrdal saw the sociologist as a social engineer, who must use his research and his theory as instruments 'in planning controlled social change'; in a sense he was going back to the American tradition in sociology of the early twentieth century, to a rationalist Enlightenment approach to the improvement of society.[110] Park was certainly opposed to this whole orientation, but it is a misunderstanding of his attitude to think that he was complacent or that he particularly valued stability. In a letter to Myrdal himself Park not only stated that he thought the race situation in the

South was being 'completely altered' by the rise of a black middle class, but he urged Myrdal to study the Negro as the 'focus for studying a changing America'. Park's essential divergence from Myrdal was not that he thought change must necessarily be slow or evolutionary (in the classic conservative evasion) but that the *mechanism* would not be that of social engineering – rather, it would be largely through the struggle and transformation of the peoples concerned.[111]

Edward Shils has recently deplored what he considers a decline in sociological interest in the Negro after the passing of the 'Chicago school', until the actions of blacks themselves forced renewed attention in the 1960s.[112] Certainly, the publication of the massive Myrdal volume seems to have been followed by a decisive shift in interest in race relations studies away from the consideration of dynamic inter-actional patterns towards the psychodynamic study of 'majority' prejudice. The focus shifted away from Negroes, or other minorities, who tended to become background factors, shadowy, passive victims whose own identity was often seen as a projection of the psychic needs of their oppressors. Park had certainly been interested in the subjective dimension of ethnic encounter, had encouraged both Harry Stack Sullivan and Myrdal himself to study them. His letter to Myrdal reveals the generational difference, however; characteristically in light of his dualistic and situational theory, Park was concerned not only with the oppressors but with the oppressed and particularly with the phenomenology of the rising Negro, intensely self-conscious and uneasy in a 'less than caste situation', feeling as Booker T. Washington had once said like 'a gold fish in a glass bowl'.[113]

Clearly the shift from historical and situational to psychodynamic study as the most influential mode of analyzing race relations had complex sources, including the rise of a professional generation more sensitive to psychoanalysis than to the Parkian phenomenology, and, perhaps, the sheer sense of exhaustion and lack of clear policy directive left by the Myrdal summation. Still, the rise of the new approach seems closely linked to the new definitions and felt necessities of social scientists. While the criteria for selecting theories are often complex and obscure, in the sociology of race relations since the 1930s the crucial standard has been immediate utility. The most influential work embodying the exploration of the psychodynamics of prejudice was *The Authoritarian Personality*, result of a collaboration between the emigré Frankfurt school and native psychologists, commissioned and financed by the American Jewish Committee. The book afforded a striking contrast with the Myrdal summation a half-decade earlier. Almost as massive but intellectually introverted toward self-conscious research design and experimental results, quite divorced from previous work, it seemed to embody the shift from scholarship to science that Robert Merton and others called for, quoting Whitehead's dictum that 'a science that hesitates to forget its founders is lost.'[114] In the full context of the Frankfurt school's own history this impression was ironically misleading; as Martin Jay has shown, the Frankfurt theorists suppressed their own post-Marxian historical sociology in order to present a rigorous (if controversial) account of psychodynamics whose categories were deduced from their philosophy of modern history but were designed to stand separately. While Jay ascribes this to ideological caution in an alien environment, the imperative of effective 'action research' demands causal simplicity and emotional impact. In the American context, what more effective indictment of prejudice could be made than supplying it with an etiology of mental illness?[115]

Another cause of the decline of Parkian racial theory was the acceptance of cultural pluralism as an ethical norm that should underpin sound scholarship. Park's dynamic situational approach assumed that assimilation entailed attitude and behavior change in both majority and minority, dominant and suppressed, while the later stance assumed that only powerful groups need to be or should be altered in the pluralistic society that scholars now took as the norm. Park's perspective was not overtly ethical, but a theoretical assumption based upon impressionistic observation and study of history; for the generation after the 1930s only active ethical commitment to pluralism allowed valuable contributions. Cultural pluralism is a complex and arguably, at least in its American manifestation, an internally inconsistent doctrine; there is as yet no thorough study of its rise to dominate educated opinion on social questions. I have argued elsewhere that its early rise in academic circles was due to the self-conscious alienation from bourgeois normality that began to spread from Bohemia and unattached intellectuals into the ranks of university teachers. Hostility toward the culture and character of the 'majority' — until recently seen as a 'public' — logically translated itself into sympathy for other victims, and beyond that into a fellow-feeling based upon victimization by a pervasive Other, the bourgeois and self-estranged 'majority'. This sense of membership in a gifted but victimized outcaste seems to have penetrated the ranks of professional sociology later than it did anthropology or literary criticism; some of Robert Park's anger over the diversion of the discipline from his true path seems to result from a sense that scholars were being replaced by intellectuals, men of wisdom, knowledge, and balance by men with a drive for maximum conceptual abstraction and an outcaste sensibility. He was more inclined to denounce the intelligentsia and exalt the value of 'common sense': 'I have found very few people among my colleagues in the university or elsewhere in the intelligentsia ... who seem to me to understand or appreciate the importance of wisdom and common sense as a form of knowledge.' While this can be read as an old man's resentment of greater specialization, that very process of specialization and abstraction may be seen as involved with the 'radicalization' of the social scientist and his move to a more elitist and activist role, consciously separate from the society he studied.[116]

Another hint that a massive shift in the position and ideology of social scientists was involved may be found in the later career of Park's notion of 'marginality'. To Park, marginality was a liberating, if perilous, opportunity and in a sense an exalted status; but as David Riesman noted as early as 1951, marginality had become linked with the study of social mobility and a generally apprehensive view of its effects.

The implication is, even among thinkers who feel in the abstract that an open society is a good thing, that such mobility is hard on those who strive for it; they would be happier if they stayed put. And of course this view operates much more strongly among those increasingly active voices who sing the charms of the static society. Here it is thought that marginality can be eliminated largely by operations on the social structure, to ensure its rigidity ... , though there will also be operations on psychic structure to eliminate the 'anal' motivations which impel to climbing.[117]

Thus a rather paradoxical ideology of pluralism, combined with an organicist stress on community, made Park's treatment of marginality seem dated. The degree to which research verified or resulted from the pluralist organicism of the new sociology is a subject deserving study.

While Park's own earlier work had helped prepare for the new pluralist perspective, his awareness of race conflict as a product of clashes of material interest, social change, and rising expectations led him away even from the more traditional moralism of Myrdal. The latter, in a classically Progressive vein, asserted the primacy of values and thought that change could be achieved by the inducement of guilt over the way in which 'official values' were being violated.[118] Park's own belief in the gradual resolution of racial conflict through the growth of understanding and then of intimacy between individuals did not depend upon the moral conversion of the prejudiced, but rather upon all concerned reaching a more detailed and complex understanding of themselves and their situation. Attitudes could be changed, not by pointing out their moral iniquity, but by the achievement of a 'more accurate and interesting statement of the problem itself'.[119]

Park's vision of conflicting races as independent actors in a complex drama is expressed in his reply, a year before his death, to a statement by the Southern Conference for Human Welfare that 'a carefully planned conspiracy exists to deliberately exploit racial differences.' 'There is a great deal of opposition in the South against the government's efforts to give the Negro a "fair deal" but it seems to me it was the result of quite spontaneous resentment by the masses of the Southern people to the presence of large numbers of Negro soldiers who were ignorant of racial etiquette in the South and were, in any case, not disposed to conform to it.'[120] Park's preference for studying the blacks in such a situation came from his conviction that their psychic changes were more important, and also more moving, not because they were victims but because they were 'not disposed to conform'. With his sociological skepticism of the formal political process and his specific dislike of reformers, Park assumed that changes were not *granted* but *won;* the dynamic force must come from the oppressed themselves. Racial self-consciousness and willingness to struggle were phenomena of the Negro community; the blacks were essentially heroic, the whites, whether obstinately resisting or acting as 'sympathetic spectators, sharing vicariously in his struggles but never really able to make his cause whole-heartedly our own', were not. Black self-consciousness was a healthy ethnocentrism, which would contribute to individual discipline and self-respect in good Tuskegee fashion; the blacks' struggle would eventually gain for them 'the moral concentration and discipline that fit them to share, on anything like equal terms in the conscious life of the civilized world'. Racial consciousness and solidarity, therefore, would produce the aptitudes and dignity that would then lead to the breakdown of prejudice. Unlike the 'dominant and comfortable classes', the struggling minority came to have no problem of morale, it appealed to Park by virtue of its sense of purpose which ennobled the daily round, the being 'merely good', into the higher realm of historical significance. 'It seems to me the Negro, like all the other disinherited peoples, is more fortunate than the dominant races. He is restless, but he knows what he wants. The issues in his case at least, are clearly defined.' Thus conflict among groups was a permanent part of the historical process, and its phenomena should not be regarded as abnormal or even as necessarily damaging or undesirable.[121]

The conception 'oppression psychosis' seems a little over-worked at times, particularly as it involves the tacit assumption that conflict in some form — not necessarily war — is something less than the normal relation of social groups. As a matter of fact, nationalities, like political parties, exist for the purpose of conflict. There is no other way of maintaining the disinterestedness which we call 'idealism' in individuals, nor the discipline which we call 'morale' in social groups. The struggle to rise of the peoples who are down is one of the most wholesome exercises in which human beings have ever engaged.[122]

In an address at Fisk towards the end of his career, Park noted that the Negro career in America was an 'epic'. American Negroes had been forced

to vindicate and justify — so far as they ever have been or ever can be vindicated — the Declaration of Independence, the Bill of Rights and all the principles on which our government was founded. The Negro people have been, whether they willed it or not, the representatives and the protagonists in the last three centuries of the world's history of all the peoples who have striven to rise and achieve the dignity and independence of free people.[123]

Park tended to be rather contemptuous of those well meaning individuals who approved the ends but shuddered at the conflict bound to arrive in the process of achieving them. 'I think the liberals realize now', he wrote to Horace Cayton in 1943, that the Negroes cause must in the long run win. The only thing is, they don't want it to win too soon and they don't want the change to be so rapid as to result in the disorders that we have had. Personally I don't agree with these liberals. In fact I've never been a liberal. If conflicts arise as a result of the efforts to get their place it will be because the white people started them. These conflicts will probably occur and are more or less inevitable but conditions will be better after they are over. In any case this is my conviction.[124]

One of Park's last letters was to his former assistant Winifred Raushenbush, who had sent him a pamphlet on 'How to Prevent a Race Riot',

... I am not quite clear in my mind that I am opposed to race riots. The thing that I am opposed to is that the Negro should always lose. If they had a fair chance of winning once in a while I don't know but what I would be in favor of them. I am in favor of winning the present war and this seems to be merely one aspect of the war — war on the home front. ... I am sure that one way to expedite change in racial ideology, which is after all back of all public opinion, may not be expedited by these conflicts ... on the home front.[125]

Everett Hughes recalled that not long before he died Park 'shocked a young political scientist by asking why there should be racial peace before there was racial justice'.[126]

Thus Park's 'conservative' approach to racial activism was rooted firmly in a conflict theory of social change and a sensitivity to the nuances of ethnic encounter, which often make it a more powerful tool of analysis than the rather one-dimensional psychological approach which succeeded it. And if Park and Myrdal are compared as prophets of change, an observer from the 1970s may conclude that Park's tough-minded approach and concern with the sources of change in the minority group itself have proved of greater prophetic value.

Conclusion: Sociology as Moral Equivalent

Park's global curiosity remained with him to the end. In 1942 he was writing to his granddaughter that Peiping was 'one of the most marvelous cities in the world' and that he had an 'immense desire to extend his acquaintance with it'. Yet he realized that his days of exploring strange cities were over, for he continued: 'The trouble is there is "so little time." I am reading a book by J.P. Marquand entitled "So Little Time." He keeps reiterating that phrase and I find myself uttering it or thinking it every day, almost every hour, "so little time".'[127]

As Park grew older, he came to value more highly those things which drew him closely into the common life of the community. 'I do not at present', he wrote to a friend, 'cherish as I once did, my right to dissent. On the contrary, I am inclined to accept Santayana's dictum that, finally and fundamentally, orthodoxy is always right and heterodoxy is always wrong.'[128] By the end of his life, Park seems to have decided that modern society needed to become in some measure sacred once more. To live together in harmony, diverse peoples needed more than rote copying of techniques or rational adaptation of advantageous behavior patterns; they needed 'a body of common customs and fundamental beliefs in accordance with which they sought to direct their individual and collective lives – that is to say, a common culture and a common religion'.[129]

At the end of 1943 Park suffered a slight stroke; though his mind remained active and he still loved to receive letters from his numerous friends and former students, those near him realized that it was only a matter of time. As one wrote, they hated to think they were soon to lose 'such a *good* man'. A week before his eightieth birthday, Park died of a cerebral thrombosis at his home in Nashville.[130]

Perhaps the most remarkable thing about Park was the extraordinary imprint he placed upon his students, the permanent shaping force of the formed personality upon the plastic, like Mark Hopkins in Garfield's metaphor. While his theories impressed them as powerful tools for explaining their own experience, his personality was clearly of great importance. He was a solid, confident man, not smooth, not clever or elusive, but frank and obviously honest, with a sense of personal power behind his reserve. He was given to moments of impatience and anger and perhaps, to judge from his surviving correspondence, though not from students' reminiscences, to a humility bordering at times on depression. His capacity for easy relations with students, especially with members of ethnic minorities, came both from his personality and his philosophy of life. He was not anxious, humanitarian, liberal, nor a reformer; and his Social Darwinism, itself an expression of a strong if self-doubting personality with a marked respect for the mystery of others, made him, as his assistant told him, 'a natural democrat'. One Negro student and colleague recalled that Park was the 'most genuine' white man he had ever encountered. Indeed, Park's effect on his black students in particular is revealing. He inspired them to become serious, skeptical scholars, perhaps because he championed, indeed embodied, the scholarly ideal with great personal power and virility of character. It was this which imposed itself upon those with whom he came in contact. 'The moment you arrived on the scene', Winifred Raushenbush told him, 'the name and the title were unimportant. You were, as the Jews say, "ein Mensch".'[131]

As a sociologist, Park combined a stubborn optimism about the toughness and adaptability of the human personality, an avid curiosity about and appreciation of the dizzying multiplicity of the modern world, with a deep and stoic sense of the tragedy of human history. 'Park used to tell a story of an old ex-slave whom he met in Alabama. The old man was poor, and undoubtedly worse off in all material respects than under slavery. In fact, he used to boast about what a good life he had had under his old master. Park asked him whether he was not sorry about having been emancipated, and the old man replied that, no, he liked freedom — for, he said, "There's a kind of looseness about this here freedom".'

This appreciation of change and possibility was combined with 'a very fine sense for the limitations of the human animal'. The sense of limits permeated especially his urban theories, which were pervaded by a brooding sense that man's most splendid artifact, the city, continually escaped his control and became once again a natural force which he must battle. The city was man's most successful effort to escape from nature and 'remake the world he lives in more after his heart's desire. But if the city is the world which man has created, it is the world in which he is henceforth condemned to live.'[132] Further, as we have seen, the city symbolized the interlocking forces that produced the modern chaos. Park did not employ either Durkheim's term *anomie* or Marx's *alienation*, words whose semantic baggage summarizes the major efforts to comprehend and conceptualize the threatening aspects of modern society from 'liberal' or 'radical' viewpoints, that is, in terms either of Durkheim's acceptance or Marx's rejection of the division of labor. Still, Park's theories display the family resemblance imposed by the impact of modern mobility and specialization on a mind steeped in the classical tradition of Western philosophy and its assumption of fundamental human essences in which ethical categories were anchored. Park's own theories have historical interest and, perhaps, the power to generate new ideas, because of his own special intellectual marginality, the conflict between deductive and environmental theories in a single mind. Park's own vacillations, the loose dialectical oppositions, can be seen as an effort to keep open the question of theory and description, to juxtapose the two without embracing the kind of dogmatism involved in Marx's insistence that the divsion of labor 'alienates' basic human properties. To adapt a comment of T.W. Adorno, the greatest obstacle to progress in social science is the tendency for theories to be either trivial and verifiable or profound and tautological. Park's loose dialectic of theory and data was an effort to place the questions raised by the confrontation of classical theory and modern experience in a problematic context, where premises would not dictate answers.[133]

On some of the issues raised by classical theory and urban conditions, Park's answers changed over time, but always reflected a sense of the way in which different contexts might still furnish the psychic security prerequisite to a viable society. Thus, while the mobile and iconoclastic world of the modern city could never provide village *Gemeinschaft*, in some ways the decline of local ties had already been balanced by the forging of new ones, based on vocational and occupational interests rather than 'contiguity, personal association and the common ties of humanity'.[134] Fashion, public opinion, even advertising replaced custom and tradition as means of social control. Similarly, 'the extraordinary means of communication that characterize modern society — the newspaper, the radio and the telephone' were means of supplying a specious closeness, a fictitious 'locality and local association' which are necessary for all forms of human association, and of combining this with 'the greatest possible mobility and freedom of its members'.[135] But the community thus produced was curiously disembodied, it lacked a territorial rootedness and sense of place. Toward the end of his life, Park seems to have doubted that without this visible, containing space, the stability necessary to vital social relationships could be maintained, yet the sufficiency of the local community had been fundamentally undermined. This was due not only to ecological developments but also to the Faustian hubris of man, with his romantic straining against limits and yearning for escape. The local community organizations, he warned, must encourage a 'new parochialism', seek 'to initiate a movement that will run counter to the current romanticism with its eye always on the horizon, one which will recognize limits and work within them. Our problem is to encourage men to seek God in their own villages and to see the social problem in their own neighborhoods.' Park's concern for community was connected with his tragic sense of modern life; like his contemporary, Frank Lloyd Wright, he saw the modern flux as liberating, but potentially destructive, needing to be contained within limits, social or architectural. As he told a commencement audience, 'Life is like a sonnet. Its quality and charm consist in what it is possible to achieve within rigorous limitations.'[136]

Park saw his own profession in traditional terms, as part of the modern re-creation of moral community. While much of Park's significance lies in his advocacy of value neutrality in the pursuit of truth, in a broader sense the purpose of sociology was deeply moral: knowledge was not only enriching but integrative. The civilized sensibility must now supply the bonds previously forged by habit and propinquity. Louis Wirth recalled that Park sometimes liked to say that sociology was essentially 'a pedagogical discipline, meaning ... to suggest that the significance of its propositions, and perhaps even something of their truth value, lay in their communicability'.[137] By revealing the long term forces underlying the scattered events of the day, it would realize the promise of the abortive *Thought News* — make the world intelligible to the educated public, if not necessarily any more controllable. Moreover sociology would provide modern, urban, individualistic man not only knowledge about but more importantly 'acquaintance with' his fellows, particularly those of other races and life styles, so that they would become less strange to him, more 'real' or individuated, and therefore less threatening. As he said of race relations: 'the problem now is to bring all these people who are so intimately bound together in the economic nexus in the same moral universe. This can only be done so far as we learn to know one another not merely externally as races but know each other intimately as persons. This is the task of the social sciences.'[138]

Sociology for Park was thus a humanistic and healing study, a 'science' in the older sense, a body of knowledge and insight that made man more at home in his world, by showing him its limits and imperatives but also by affording that understanding of the range of subjective experience that constituted 'wisdom'.

Chapter 1

1 August Meier, *Negro Thought in America, 1880-1915. Racial Ideologies in the Age of Booker T.Washington* (Ann Arbor, 1963), p. 202.

2 Program of the International Conference on the Negro, Tuskegee, Alabama, 19 April 1912, in Park-Hughes.

3 Note attached to Robert E.Park, 'Autobiographical Fragment' in file 'Robert Ezra Park: Recollections and Letters', Park-Hughes.

4 Ellsworth Faris, 'Robert E.Park, 1864-1944', *American Sociological Review* 9 (1944): 322-25.

5 Robert E.Park, 'Autobiographical Fragment'.

6 See Lionel Trilling, *The Liberal Imagination* (New York, 1950). The common sources of literary and sociological 'realism' in journalism and a 'romantic' dissatisfaction with the modern world are adumbrated by John A.Jackson, 'The Map of Society: America in the 1890s', and Malcolm Bradbury, 'Romance and Reality in Maggie', *Journal of American Studies* 3 (July, 1969): 103-10, 111-21.

7 See the discussion of 'the immediately useful and the practical' as Midwestern ideology in Lewis Atherton, *Main Street on the Middle Border* (Bloomington, Indiana, 1954), pp. 109-19.

8 Robert E.Park, 'Curriculum Vitae' in *Masse Und Publikum: Eine Methodologische Und Soziologische Untersuchung* (Bern, 1904), p. 111; 'Park, Robert Ezra', *Dictionary of American Biography*, Supplement Three, 1941-45 (New York, 1973), pp. 577-80.

9 Norman S.Hayner and Una M.Hayner, Diary, 1921, entry for 7 January 1922. Ms in possession of Professor Hayner, University of Washington. Robert E.Park, 'Methods of Teaching: Impressions and a Verdict', *Social Forces*, 20 (1941): 36-46.

10 Interview with Professor Everett C.Hughes of Brandeis University, 21 May 1965.

11 Interview with Mrs. Robert Redfield, 23 October 1963.

12 Ibid.

13 Ernest W.Burgess, 'The contribution of Robert E.Park', *Sociology and Social Research*, 29 (March-April 1945): 255-61. Milla Aissa Alihan, *Social Ecology: A Critical Analysis* (New York, 1938), pp. 3-4. Park's memory of this and the

comment by his close associate, Burgess, are significant at least for his own adult view of his childhood. It is more difficult to discern whether the Park family really existed socially on the 'wrong side of the tracks'. It is possible either that Robert's romantic rebellion from convention distorted his memory, or that the struggling merchant booster, Hiram Park, and his family were regarded as somewhat inferior by the Yankee settlers.

14   Interview with Mrs. Redfield; Winifred Raushenbush, 'Robert Park, 1864-1944. A Memoir'. Unpublished Ms. in possession of the author.

15   Alihan, *Social Ecology*, p. 3, assumes that Park was inspired to a life-long interest in immigrants by growing up in a Scandinavian community, but Park's own reminiscences make no mention of this.

16   Robert E.Park, 'Methods of Teaching'. See also, Orvin Larson, *American Infidel: Robert G.Ingersoll* (New York, 1962), pp. 139-40.

17   Robert E.Park, 'Methods of Teaching'. Larson, *American Infidel*, pp. 77-79.

18   Interview with Everett C.Hughes.

19   Ibid. Edwin E.Slosson, *Great American Universities* (New York, 1910), p. 253.

20   Interview with Everett C.Hughes. Professor Hughes remembers Park having told him this. Robert E.Park, 'Transcript', Registrar's Records, University of Michigan.

21   Slosson, *Great American Universities*, p. 182. Charles B.Pearson, 'The University of Michigan as I knew it sixty years ago', University of Michigan Historical Collections, University of Michigan, Ann Arbor.

22   George Dykhuizen, 'John Dewey and the University of Michigan', *Journal of the History of Ideas*, 33 (1962): 513-44. In 1868-69 there were 1,114 students, in 1881-82, 1,834; by 1888-89 there were 1,882 students; ten years later the number had risen to 3,059. Slosson, *Great American Universities*, p. 209. For a general account, see Howard H.Peckham, *The Making of the University of Michigan 1817-1967* (Ann Arbor, 1967), pp. 69-88.

23   Dykhuizen, 'John Dewey', pp. 513-14. Elizabeth M.Farrand, *History of the University of Michigan* (Ann Arbor, 1885), pp. 211-12.

24   Frederick Rudolph, *The American College and University. A History* (New York 1962), p. 143.

25   Farrand, *University of Michigan*, p. 262; University of Michigan *Catalog*, 1885-86.

26   Farrand, *University of Michigan*, p. 262; Interview with Everett C.Hughes.

27   *Michigan Argonaut*, 5 number 7, 20 November 1886.

28   Arthur M.Taub, 'After Thirty Years Absence, Park returns to his Alma Mater', *The Michigan Daily* (Ann Arbor), 22 March 1934; Farrand, *University of Michigan*, p. 284.

29   Farrand, *University of Michigan*, pp. 284-85. On the style of political loyalty and action in the 1880s, see Richard Jensen, *The Winning of the Midwest: Social and Political Conflict 1885-1896* (Chicago, 1971).

30 Edwin E.Slosson, *Great American Universities*, p. 192; Farrand, *University of Michigan*, p. 287.

31 Taub, 'After Thirty Years'. *Michigan Argonaut*, 7 May 1887; *L.S.A. Faculty Minutes*, 5 (1886-96), 63 (Michigan Historical Collections, University of Michigan, Ann Arbor).

32 Laurence R.Veysey, *The Emergence of the American University, 1865-1910* (Chicago, 1965), pp. 294-301.

33 Taub, 'After Thirty years'.

34 Park, 'Methods of Teaching', pp. 36-37.

35 *Dictionary of American Biography*, ed. Dumas Malone (New York, 1928-36), 18: 422-23, 'Calvin Thomas'.

36 Henry A. Pochmann, *German Culture in America* (Madison, Wisc., 1957), p. 654.

37 Park, 'Methods of Teaching', pp. 36-37.

38 Robert E.Park, Transcript, Registrar's Records, University of Michigan, Ann Arbor; University of Michigan, *Catalog, 1885-86, 1886-87,* in Michigan Historical Collections, University of Michigan, Ann Arbor; George Dykhuizen, 'John Dewey', pp. 514-18.

39 Park, 'Methods of Teaching', pp. 39-40.

40 The reconciliation of the claims of the state and the claims of the individual was a common concern of German trained sociologists and economists. Henry Carter Adams, the economist, for example, found, like Dewey, that this reconciliation could be made through the concept of society as an organism. Jurgen Herbst, *The German Historical School in American Scholarship. A Study in the Transfer of Culture* (Ithaca, New York, 1965), p. 150.

41 John Dewey, 'Ethics of Democracy', *University of Michigan Philosophical Papers*, 2nd series, 1888, pp. 1-28, quoted in George Dykhuizen, 'John Dewey', p. 522.

42 Robert E.Park, 'An Autobiographical Note', in Robert E.Park, *Race and Culture*, (Glencoe, Ill.: Free Press, 1950), p. 6. Park referred to a later shift from academy to 'Real World', but the impatience with the career choices imposed by the era's unnatural opposition of values and energy is visible throughout his career.

43 Frank Luther Mott, *American Journalism. A History 1690-1960.* (3rd ed. New York, 1962; first revised ed. 1950), pp. 488-89.

44 Park, 'Autobiographical Note', p. 5.

45 Taub, 'After Thirty Years'. For a later variation on this eternal theme, see Robert Benchley, 'My Untold Story' in *My Ten Years in a Quandary, and How They Grew* (Harper and Row, New York, 1936).

46 Park, 'Autobiographical Note', p. 8. F.L.Mott, *American Journalism,* pp. 480-82. Frank Foxcroft, 'The American Sunday Newspaper', *The Nineteenth Century*, 62, no. 368 (October 1970): 609-15.

47 Taub, 'After Thirty Years'.

48 Park, 'Autobiographical Note', p. 8.

49 Robert E.Park, 'Walt Whitman', unpublished Ms. in possession of Everett C.Hughes.

50 Park, 'Autobiographical Note', p. 8.

51 Ibid., p. 5. On the short life of a New York reporter see Frederic C.Howe, *Confessions of a Reformer* (New York, 1925), pp. 40-49. It was a common fear that the logical end was the East River at age forty-five.

52 Manuscript chronology of Park's career, in Park-Raushenbush. Box C, Folder Misc. cont.

53 Bernard A.Weisberger, *The American Newspaper* (Chicago, 1961), p. 156.

54 These comments are stimulated by Park's own interpretative remarks in 'The Natural History of the Newspaper' and 'News and the Human Interest Story', written in 1923 and 1940 respectively, and reprinted in Robert E.Park, *Society* (Glencoe, Ill.: Free Press, 1955), pp. 97-98, 105-107. Technical and economic changes, notably a drop in the cost of newsprint, certainly facilitated the' expansion of newspaper space and scope which allowed the reporter to play this social role. See Peter Lyon, *Success Story: The Life and Times of S.S.McClure* (New York, 1963), pp. 72-74.

55 Weisberger, *The American Newspaper*, pp. 159-60.

56 'Robert E.Park, Recollections and Letters', Park-Hughes.

57 Interview with Edgar T.Thompson, Montreal, 2 September 1964.

58 Taub, 'After Thirty Years'.

59 Obituary of Mrs. Robert E.Park, *Freeport Journal-Standard,* Illinois, 29 October 1951. Clipping in Park-Raushenbush, folder, 'What other people have said about Park'. Interview with Mrs. Redfield.

60 Park to Clara Cahill, n.d. 1893. Park-Raushenbush.

61 Ibid.

62 Scrapbook of newspaper clippings from Detroit, 1893, Park-Raushenbush.

63 Park to Clara, Detroit, May 1893. Park-Raushenbush.

64 Park to Clara, Detroit, 20 July 1893. Park-Raushenbush.

65 Park to Clara, Detroit, 26 June 1892. Park-Raushenbush.

66 For the stifling quality of the 1880s in Europe and the desire of youth for liberation and idealism see H.Stuart Hughes, *Consciousness and Society. The Reorientation of European Social Thought 1890-1930* (New York, 1958), ch. 2. The intellectual malaise of the 1890s in America is dealt with in Henry Steele Commager, *The American Mind. An Interpretation of American Thought and Character since the 1880s* (New Haven, 1950), pp. 47-50.

67 Park to Clara, Detroit, 30 May 1893. Park-Raushenbush.

68 Sherwood Anderson, *Marching Men* (New York, 1917).

69 Commager, *The American Mind,* ch. 2. Richard Hofstadter, 'Manifest Destiny and the Philippines', in Daniel Aaron, ed. *America in Crisis* (New York, 1952),

pp. 173-200. For evidence that Shaw remains a potent figure for liberal jeremiads by middle-aged Yankees, see Robert Lowell, 'For the Union Dead', *Selected Poems* (London, 1965), pp. 62-64.

70 Park to Clara, Detroit, 14 March 1893. Park-Raushenbush.

71 John Higham, *Strangers in the Land* (New Brunswick, N.J., 1955), ch. 3; Barbara Solomon, *Ancestors and Immigrants* (Cambridge, Mass., 1956); Lewis S.Feuer, 'John Dewey and the Back to the People Movement in American Thought', *Journal of the History of Ideas,* 20 (1959): 545-68; Jill Conway, 'Jane Addams: An American Heroine', *Daedalus, Proceedings of the American Academy of Arts and Sciences,* 93, no. 2 (Spring 1964); for the widespread influence of Tolstoy, see Feuer, 'John Dewey', and the Introduction by Tony Tanner to William Dean Howells, *A Hazard of New Fortunes* (Oxford, 1965, first pub. 1890), especially xi and xvii; Van Wyck Brooks, *Howells, His Life and World* (London, 1959), pp. 175-86.

72 Park to Clara, Detroit, 14 March 1893. Park-Raushenbush.

73 Interview with Winifred Raushenbush, Peterborough, New Hampshire, 14 March 1965.

74 The quotations are from Park, 'Writings of Ibsen. Professor Boyesen's Exposition of the Literary Rebel', a review in Scrapbook of Detroit press clippings, 1893-95, Park-Raushenbush. On the Ibsenite faith, especially as propounded by Georg Brandes from whom these expressions are taken, see Michael Meyer, *Ibsen: A Biography* (New York, 1971), pp. 330, 338-39, 348-49, 361, 592. Meyer notes the similarity of the Ibsenite and Marxian utopias.

75 'Psyche Dressed Up', undated press-cutting, Detroit Press Clippings.

76 Robert E.Park, 'Walt Whitman'.

77 Robert E.Park, 'A City of Paupers. Wayne City House and Asylum', clipping of 1895 in Scrapbook of Detroit Press Clippings.

78 Robert E.Park, Detroit Press Clippings, n.d.

79 Robert E.Park, 'That Intolerable Widow', drama review, Detroit Press Clippings, 1893.

80 Robert Park to Clara, Detroit, n.d., Park-Raushenbush.

81 *Chicago Daily News*, editorial, February 1944. It is difficult for a historian raised with the depth-psychological mentality of the twentieth century to avoid concluding that Park's persistent hostility to activist idealists was a projection of the guilt incurred by his own turn from idealism to realism.

82 Robert Park to Clara, Detroit, n.d., Park-Raushenbush.

83 F.M.Barnard, *Herder's Social and Political Thought: from Enlightenment to Nationalism* (Oxford, 1965), pp. 73-74. Christopher Lasch, *The New Radicalism in America* (New York, 1964), *passim.*

84 Robert Park to Clara, Detroit, n.d., 1893, Park-Raushenbush. He was also very fond of 'The Man with the Hoe', and wanted a copy in his ideal library, along with busts of his other heroes, Goethe, Carlyle, Whitman, Emerson, Wagner, Chopin, Hegel, Savonarola, Jesus, Lincoln, George Eliot, Bernhardt, Ibsen, Zola, Tolstoy, Turgenev, Napoleon, Heine, and Plato. Ibid.

85 Robert E. Park, 'Some Personal Opinions upon Music, Literature and other things', *The Song Journal*, March 1895, in Scrapbook of Detroit press clippings, 1893-5.

86 Robert Park to Clara, Detroit, 14 March 1893. Park-Raushenbush.

87 Commager, *The American Mind*, p. 231.

88 In the article about a visit to an insane asylum, written for a Detroit newspaper in 1893, there is an interested fatalism about the phenomenon of madness and an off the cuff observation that pauperism often led to insanity, but this did not induce him to any railing at the universe or even at society. Robert E. Park, 'A City of Paupers'.

89 Park to Clara, Detroit, 21 April 1893. Park-Raushenbush. For the 'cash-value' idea of success in the midwest see Lewis Atherton, *Main Street on the Middle Border* (Bloomington, Ind., 1954), pp. 116-18.

90 Robert Park to Clara, London, Ontario, 16 May 1893. Park-Raushenbush.

91 Theodore Dreiser, *The Titan* (New York, 1914). This novel is based on the life of Yerkes.

92 Herbert Spencer, *Social Statics* (New York, 1908, first pub. 1850), pp. 150-55. Richard Hofstadter, *Social Darwinism in American Thought* (rev. ed., Boston, 1955), pp. 31-50, first pub. 1944. J.D.Y.Peel, *Herbert Spencer. The Evolution of a Sociologist* (New York, 1971).

93 See the article which Park wrote for Booker T. Washington in 1914, published under Washington's name, 'Inferior and Superior Races', *North American Review*, 201 (April 1915): 538-42; and his address at Tuskegee in 1942, 'Founder's Day Address, Tuskegee Institute, April 12, 1942', unpublished Ms., Park Papers, Fisk University, Nashville, Tenn.

94 Charles Darwin, *The Origin of Species* (London, 1859, reprinted 1950), pp. 414-15. J.D.Y.Peel notes the function of Spencer's theory as theodicy for a secular age that still needed total comprehension to feel comfortable in the universe. Jack London's Martin Eden was 'drunken with comprehension' after a study of Spencer. It is a difficult question to what degree later sociology evolved away from theodicy into self-correcting problem solving, as Peel seems to argue; certainly one line of criticism of each theoretical generation in turn is that it is not self testing, but functions, at least on the psychological level, as a justification of the standing order. J.D.Y.Peel, *Herbert Spencer*, p. 2.

95 'Aubobiographical Fragment', in Park-Hughes, file 'Robert E. Park: Recollections and Letters'.

96 George Dykuizen, 'John Dewey', pp. 513-44.

97 John Dewey, 'Christianity and Democracy', a lecture given March 1892, quoted in Feuer, 'John Dewey', pp. 554-55.

98 John Dewey, 'The Ethics of Democracy', *University of Michigan Philosophical Papers, Second Series* (Ann Arbor, 1888): 1-28.

99 Feuer, 'John Dewey', p. 546. Feuer's article is useful and generally persuasive, except on one point, which unfortunately seems to have been the central intention of the whole. He tries to show that Dewey, Ford, and others of the

'back to the people' persuasion were socialists, or syndicalists, in the explicit sense of demanding public ownership and control of the means of production. For evidence to the contrary, see Dykhuizen, 'John Dewey', Dewey's letters to James cited below, and even many of the quotations in Feuer's essay.

100   For all quotations in the previous paragraph, Dewey to James, 3 June 1891 in Ralph Barton Perry, *Thought and Character of William James* (London, [1935]), 2: 518-19.

101   Feuer, 'John Dewey', pp. 548 ff. Willinda Savage, 'John Dewey and "Thought News" at the University of Michigan', *Michigan Alumni Quarterly Review* 56 (May 1950): 204-207. On Ford, see Mark De Wolfe Howe, ed. *Holmes-Laski Letters* (Cambridge, Mass., 1953).

102   Robert E.Park, 'Autobiographical Note', p. 9.

103   Feuer, 'John Dewey', p. 549.

104   Dewey to James, 3 June 1891.

105   Ibid.

106   John Dewey in the *Detroit Tribune*, 15 April 1892, quoted in Savage, 'John Dewey and "Thought News",' p. 207.

107   From a circular reprinted in the *Michigan Daily*, 16 March 1892, quoted in Savage, 'John Dewey and "Thought News",' pp. 204-205.

108   Robert E.Park, 'Autobiographical Fragment'.

109   Dewey to Willinda Savage quoted in Savage, 'John Dewey and "Thought News",' p. 209.

110   Dewey, quoted in *Detroit Tribune*, in Savage, 'John Dewey and "Thought News",' p. 207.

111   Circular in *Michigan Daily*, in Savage, 'John Dewey and "Thought News",' pp. 204-205.

112   The influence of Franklin Ford (1848-1918) on Dewey is discussed in Corydon Ford, *The Child of Democracy* (Ann Arbor, 1894), p. 174, quoted in Savage, 'John Dewey and "Thought News",' p. 206.

113   The phrase is Corydon Ford's quoted in Savage, 'John Dewey and "Thought News",' p. 206; the idea constantly appears in Park's work as an explanation of the modern world; see, for example, Robert E. Park, 'Human Nature and Collective Behavior' and 'Sociology and the Social Sciences', reprinted in Robert E.Park, *Society* (Glencoe, Ill.: Free Press, 1955), pp. 13-21, 187-242.

114   On the relation between the vitality of sociological theory and the history to which it responds, see Robert A.Nisbet, *The Sociological Tradition* (London, 1967; first pub. 1966), pp. 315-19; Maurice Stein, *The Eclipse of Community: an Interpretation of American Studies* (Princeton, N.J., 1960).

115   Hedda Gabler noted of her scholar husband: 'Tesman is a specialist ... and specialists are not at all amusing to travel with. Not in the long run, at any rate'. Cited in the perceptive essay by Leo Lowenthal, 'Henrik Ibsen: Motifs in the Realistic Plays', in Rolf Fjelde, ed., *Ibsen: a Collection of Critical Essays* (Englewood Cliffs, N.J., 1965), pp. 146-47.

116 The background of this interpretation will be found in Raymond Williams, *Culture and Society 1780-1950* (New York, 1958), Martin Green, *The Problem of Boston* (London, 1966), esp. ch. 9, and Stow Persons, *The Decline of American Gentility* (New York, 1973), but the precise formulation should not be blamed on them.

117 Laurence R.Veysey, *The Emergence of the American University* (Chicago, 1965), ch. 2.

118 Feuer, 'John Dewey', p. 552.

119 Veysey, *The Emergence of the American University*, pp. 188-91.

120 Morton White, *Social Thought in America* (Boston, second ed. 1957; first ed., 1947), pp. 191-92.

121 Louis Hartz, *The Liberal Tradition in America* (New York, 1955), ch. 1.

122 David F.Bowers, 'Hegel, Darwin and the American Tradition', in David F.Bowers, ed. *Foreign Influences in American Life*, (Princeton, N.J., 1944), pp. 146-71, especially, pp. 152-53, 163.

123 The idea of the functional interrelation of society is one that goes back to Plato; see George H.Sabine, *A History of Political Theory* (third ed. New York, 1961; first pub. 1937), pp. 49-50. On modern uses of the term see Robert K Merton, *Social Theory and Social Structure* (second ed. New York, 1957), pp. 20-54.

124 Herbert Spencer, *The Principles of Sociology* (New York, 1898), 2nd Section pp. 214-17, 223, 270-71.

125 Charles Darwin, *The Origin of Species* (1859) quoted in John C.Green, *The Death of Adam* (Ames, Iowa, 1959), p. 248.

126 For example, Eric F.Goldman, *Rendezvous with Destiny* (Rev. ed., New York, 1956; first pub. 1952), pp. 70-74.

127 William Graham Sumner, *What Social Classes Owe to Each Other* (New York, 1884), pp. 17-19.

128 Perry Miller notes that pragmatists like James and Dewey had much in common with Sumner's method, though nothing with his temperament. Perry Miller, *American Thought: Civil War to World War I* (New York, 1954), Introduction, xxviii.

129 Charles H.Cooley, Notes on Lectures by John Dewey at Michigan. University of Michigan Historical Collections.

130 Ibid.

131 Robert E.Park 'Autobiographical Fragment'. Feuer, in contrast, compares *Thought News* with the later New York radical publication, *PM* (1940-1948), Feuer, 'John Dewey', p. 522.

132 Robert Park to Clara, Detroit, 26 February 1893. Park-Raushenbush.

133 Ibid.

134 Robert Park to Clara, Detroit, 26 March 1893. Park-Raushenbush.

135 On the 'therapeutic' ethic, see Philip Rieff, *The Triumph of the Therapeutic* (New York, 1965). This interpretation was worked out before the appearance

of John Higham's brilliant overview of the history of American identities, 'Hanging Together: Divergent Unities in American History', *Journal of American History* 61 (June 1974): 5-28. It is, however, congruent with the Spencerian progression of social ideologies which Higham offers.

136 Josiah Royce, *The Philosophy of Loyalty* (New York, 1908); Charles Horton Cooley, *Social Organization* (New York, 1909), pp. 32-57.

137 Robert Park to Clara, London, Ontario, 16 May 1893. Park-Raushenbush.

Chapter 2

1 Winifred Raushenbush, 'Robert Ezra Park 1864-1944. A Memoir', Ms. in Park-Raushenbush.

2 Robert E.Park, 'An Autobiographical Note', in Park, *Race and Culture* (Glencoe, Ill.: Free Press, 1950), p. 6; Frederick Rudolph, *The American College and University. A History* (New York, 1962), p. 535; Laurence R.Veysey *The Emergence of the American University, 1865-1910* (Chicago, 1965), pp. 227-33.

3 Norman S.Hayner and Una M.Hayner, *Diary, 1921*, Ms. in possession of Professor Hayner, University of Washington, entry for 7 January 1922.

4 Luther L.Bernard, 'The Teaching of Sociology in the U.S. in the last Fifty Years', *American Journal of Sociology*, 50 (1945): 534-48.

5 Park, 'An Autobiographical Note', p. 6.

6 Veysey, *The Emergence of the American University*, pp. 231-32.

7 Ibid., pp. 228-29; Park, 'Methods of Teaching: Impressions and a Verdict', *Social Forces*, 20 (1941): 36-46, quotations pp. 38, 39. James' behavior may not seem either bizarre or especially perceptive in the age of R.D.Laing, but it had power to shock in the century of faith in a scientific ethics founded in psychiatry.

8 Ralph Barton Perry, *The Thought and Character of William James* (London, [1935]): 2, 266.

9 William James, 'A Certain Blindness in Human Being', *Selected Papers on Philosophy* (London, 1917), p. 4.

10 Park, 'Methods of Teaching', p. 39.

11 James, 'A Certain Blindness in Human Beings', p. 7. Park, 'Autobiographical Note', p. 6. At least one other graduate at Harvard in the late nineties was deeply impressed by 'A Certain Blindness'. The future industrial consultant and prime minister of Canada saw James' pluralism as evidence of a realizable millenium in which universal empathy would eliminate war. W.L.MacKenzie King, *Industry and Humanity* (Toronto, 1973; first pub., 1918), p. 19.

12 Park, 'Methods of Teaching', pp. 38-39.

13 Bliss Perry, *And Gladly Teach* (Boston, 1935), pp. 88-89, quoted in Jurgen

Herbst, *The German Historical School in American Scholarship. A Study in the Transfer of Culture* (Ithaca, N.Y., 1965), p. 3.

14 Winifred Raushenbush, 'Robert Ezra Park 1864-1944. A Memoir'.

15 Herbst, *The German Historical School*, p. 16.

16 Ralph Barton Perry, *William James*, 2: 469.

17 Interview with Mrs. Robert Redfield, 23 October 1963. The three children were Edward Cahill, Theodosia Warner, and Margaret Lucy; a fourth child, Robert Hiram, was born later, *Dictionary of American Biography, Supplement Three*, p. 577.

18 Park, Course notes for 'The Crowd and the Public', 13 February 1920, Park-Hughes.

19 See Park's letters to Clara, ch. 1, pp. 13-14, 18-19.

20 Park, 'The German Army. The Most Perfect Military Organization in the World', *Munsey's Magazine*, 24, no. 3 (December, 1900): 386-405, quotations from page 405. This article was the second in a series on 'great secular organizations of the world'; the first (October, 1900) was on Tammany Hall. For the value which progressive thinkers placed on the military virtues see William James, 'The Moral Equivalent for War', *Memories and Studies (New York, 1911)*, pp. 267-06. It is significant that Park was rather more conservative than his mentor was to become.

21 H.Stuart Hughes, *Consciousness and Society. The Reorientation of European Social Thought 1890-1930* (New York, 1958), pp. 45-46.

22 John Theodore Merz, *A History of European Thought in the Nineteenth Century* (Edinburgh and London, 1903-1914; reissued New York, 1965), 4: 52-53.

23 Park, 'An Autobiographical Note', p. vi.

24 George Santayana to William James, 28 January 1888, quoted in Ralph Barton Perry, *William James*, 1: 404.

25 Park, 'An Autobiographical Note', p. vi.

26 Gerhard Masur, *Prophets of Yesterday. Studies in European Culture, 1890-1914* (London, 1963), pp. 173-75; Heinz Maus, *A Short History of Sociology* (London, 1962; first pub. in Germany 1956), pp. 70-71; Don Martindale, *The Nature and Types of Sociological Theory* (London, 1961), p. 378. Fritz K.Ringer, *The Decline of the German Mandarins. The German Academic Community 1890-1933* (Cambridge, Mass., 1969), pp. 310-12.

27 Park, 'Methods of Teaching', p. 37.

28 John Theodore Merz, *European Thought*, 2: 565-66.

29 Park, 'Methods of Teaching', p. 37; George L.Mosse, *The Crisis of German Ideology. Intellectual Origins of the Third Reich* (New York, 1964), p. 27.

30 Park, 'Methods of Teaching', p. 37. Curiously, Park never showed much interest in the American Indians. It seems likely that Park's stereotype of 'the people' as residue of virtue contained a strong personal sense of submissiveness,

the ability to bear adversity with passive dignity, which he did not associate with the American Indians. The latter did not adapt to conditions, did not prove themselves in the Darwinian struggle as the Negroes who followed Booker T.Washington were trying to do. For Park, as for Rousseau, the golden mean of human virtue was found in the simple farming society, not that of heroic nomadic hunters. See Robert E.Park, 'Founder's Day Address, Tuskegee Institute, 12 April 1942', Park Papers, Social Science Research Institute, Fisk University, and Mozell C.Hill, 'Some Early Notes of Robert E.Park', *Phylon: the Atlanta University review of Race and Culture,* 14, no. 1, (1st quarter, 1953): 88.

31   Robert E.Park, *Masse und Publikum. Eine Methodologische und Soziologische Untersuchung.* Inaugural-Dissertation zur Erlangung der Doktorwürde der Hohen Philosophischen Fakultät der Ruprecht-Karls-Universität zu Heidelberg. Vorgelegt von Robert E.Park aus Watertown, S.D. USA. (Bern, 1904). This has recently been translated by Charlotte Elsner, *The Crowd and the Public, and other Essays,* ed. with an Introduction by Henry Elsner Jr., (Chicago: University of Chicago Press, 1972).

32   Robert A.Nisbet, 'Conservatism and Sociology', *American Journal of Sociology,* 58 (1952-53): 167-75.

33   Ibid. See also Leon Bramson, *The Political Context of Sociology* (Princeton, N.J., 1961), pp. 27-32.

34   Edward Shils, *The Present State of American Sociology* (Glencoe, Ill., 1948), p. 6.

35   Nisbet, 'Conservatism and Sociology', pp. 169-70.

36   Frank E.Manuel, 'From Equality to Organicism', *Journal of the History of Ideas,* 17, no. 1 (January, 1956): 54-69. The quotation is from Jacques Necker, *De la Révolution Française* (Paris, 1797), 2: 116, quoted in Manuel, 'From Equality to Organicism', p. 63.

37   Manuel, 'From Equality to Organicism', pp. 64-67.

38   Heinz Maus, *A Short History of Sociology* (London, 1962; first pub. in German 1956), pp. 12-13.

39   Martindale, *Types of Sociological Theory,* pp. 62-63.

40   Frank E.Manuel, *The Prophets of Paris: Turgot, Condorcet, Saint-Simon, Fourier, and Comte* (Cambridge, Mass., 1962), p. 286.

41   Ibid., pp. 288-90.

42   Quoted in Gerhard Masur, *Prophets of Yesterday: Studies in European Culture, 1890-1914* (London, 1963), p. 52.

43   Auguste Comte, *Positive Philosophy,* trans. Harriet Martineau, (London, 1853), I: p. 3.

44   Herbert Spencer, *The Principles of Sociology* (London, 1877, first ed. 1876), I: p. 475. Since this chapter was written an excellent treatment of Spencer's thought and heritage has appeared: J.D.Y. Peel, *Herbert Spencer: The Evolution of a Sociologist* (New York, 1971). Peel has made Spencer *terra cognita* for the

first time in sixty years, if not ever; the present formulation may at least suggest the perils of the independent ascent.

45 Ibid., p. 469.

46 Herbert Spencer, *The Principles of Sociology* (London, 1893), pp. 449-50, cited in Park, *Society: Collective Behavior, News and Opinion, Sociology and Modern Society* (Free Press, Glencoe, Ill., 1955), p. 212.

47 Herbert Spencer, *The Study of Sociology* (New York, 1874), p. 329.

48 Henry Maine, *Ancient Law* (London, 1861); J.W.Burrow, *Evolution and Society: a Study in Victorian Social Theory* (Cambridge, 1966), pp. 137-78; Werner Stark, *The Fundamental Forms of Social Thought* (London, 1962), pp. 209-12. Park does not cite Tönnies' *Gemeinschaft und Gesellschaft* in his and Ernest Burgess' *Introduction to the Science of Sociology* (University of Chicago Press, 1921); his treatment of historical change and penchant for dualistic interpretations of social development reflect his use of general ideas which were in the air and given classic treatment by Tönnies, rather than any direct influence. Maine's *Ancient Law* and *Village Communities in the East and West* (London, 1871) were more direct influences, the latter used to support some of Park's generalization about the process of 'competition'. Park and Burgess, *Introduction*, pp. 556, 565.

49 Steven Lukes, *Emile Durkheim. His Life and Work.* (London, 1973), pp. 147-67; Martindale, *Types of Sociological Theory*, pp. 86-92; Nicholas S.Timasheff, *Sociological Theory. Its Nature and Growth* (rev. ed., New York, 1964; first pub. 1955), pp. 106-18. While Park quoted Durkheim in the *Introduction to the Science of Society* and had his students read his works, his own theories seem little affected by the French master's writings, except in the sense that sociological theories of the period, as responses to commonly perceived problems, had a family resemblance. Indeed, one of the major events in the supersession of Parkean sociology after 1930 was the 'rediscovery' and translation of Durkheim's writings.

50 Georg Simmel, *Soziologie, Untersuchungen Uber die Formen der Vergesellschaftung* (Leipzig, 1908); a number of translations of part of Simmel's work appeared in the *American Journal of Sociology* between 1896 and 1910; for a complete list see Kurt H.Wolff, *The Sociology of Georg Simmel* (Glencoe, Ill., 1950), pp. lix-lxi.

51 Robert E.Park and Ernest W.Burgess, *Introduction to the Science of Sociology* (University of Chicago Press, 1921; 2nd ed. 1924).

52 Georg Simmel, *Die Grossstadte und das Geistesleben* (The Metropolis and Mental Life), *Die Grossstadt*. Vorträge und Aufsätze zur Stadteausstellung von K. Bücher, F.Ratzel, G.V. Mayr, H.Waentig, G.Simmel, Th.Petermann und D.Schafer. Gehe-Stiftung Zu Dresden, *Jarhbuch der Gehe-Stiftung Zu Dresden* (Winter, 1902-3): 185-206; Park, 'The City: Suggestions for the Investigation of Human Behavior in the City Environment', *American Journal of Sociology*, 20, no. 5 (March, 1915): 577-612; also in Park, Burgess and McKenzie, *The City* (Chicago: University of Chicago Press, 1925), pp. 1-46.

53 Georg Simmel, *Soziologie*, quoted in Wolff, *Georg Simmel*, pp. 22-23; and Wolff's Introduction, xxxi-xl; Fritz Ringer, *The Decline of the German Mandarins*, pp. 171-73.

54 Georg Simmel, 'The Problem of Sociology', translated by Albion W.Small from *Soziologie*, ch. 1, *American Journal of Sociology*, 15, no. 3 (November 1909): 289-320.

55 Donald N.Levine, 'The Structure of Simmel's Social Thought', in Kurt H.Wolff, ed., *Georg Simmel*, pp. 9-32, especially, 22.

56 Albion W.Small in a footnote to his translation of 'The Problem of Sociology', p. 302, criticized as untenable Simmel's attempt to divorce the '*form* of socialization', from 'the more fundamental consideration of the "motives and interests" which produced the forms'. More recently, Raymond Aron has described Simmel's formalism as 'dazzling exercises' which often seem 'like an elaborate game' and thus *Soziologie* has 'brought its author many admirers, but few disciples'. Raymond Aron, *German Sociology* (tr. Mary and Thomas Bottomore, Glencoe, Ill., 1957), p. 6.

57 Georg Simmel, 'The Problem of Sociology', pp. 299-301; Georg Simmel, 'The Number of Members as Determining the Sociological Form of the Group', tr. Albion W.Small, *American Journal of Sociology*, 8 (July-September 1902): 1-46, 158-96.

58 The characteristic point of departure, the common-sense modes of organizing the normal stimuli presented to us, is notable; this lack of scientific abstraction in the choice of categories was to become a weapon in the attack on Simmel's and Park's sociology, and still later in their revival under the banner of phenomenology.

59 Kurt Wolff, ed., *Georg Simmel*, p. 87.

60 Ibid., p. 88.

61 Ibid., pp. 89-90.

62 Park and Burgess, *Introduction*. For John Dewey's role in diffusing this concept, see John W.Petras, 'John Dewey and the Rise of Interactionism in American Social Theory', *Journal of the History of the Behavioral Sciences* 4 (January 1968), 18-27.

63 Levine, 'The Structure of Simmel's Social Thought', pp. 24-26.

64 Ibid., pp. 13-14.

65 Martindale, *Types of Sociological Theory*, p. 239.

66 Levine, 'The Structure of Simmel's Social Thought', pp. 14-15. For example, changes in the size of the membership will lead to changes in the institution itself.

67 Nicholas J.Spykman, *The Social Theory of Georg Simmel* (Chicago, 1925), pp. 4-10.

68 Talcott Parsons, *Structure of Social Action* (Glencoe, Ill., 1949; first ed. New York, 1937), pp. 473-74; Hugh Dalziel Duncan, 'Simmel's Image of Society', in Wolff ed., *Georg Simmel*, pp. 110-18; esp. 110-13.

69   Park, 'The Urban Community' (1925), in Park, *Human Communities. The City and Human Ecology* (Glencoe, Ill., Free Press, 1952), pp. 165-77.

70   Levine, 'Structure of Simmel's Social Thought', pp. 27-28.

71   Martindale, *Types of Sociological Theory,* p. 246.

72   Georg Simmel, 'The Sociology of Sociability' (*Soziologie der Geselligkeit* 1910), *American Journal of Sociology,* 55 (1949-50): 254-61, quotation from p. 254.

73   Martindale, *Types of Sociological Theory*, pp. 239-40.

74   Park, 'An Autobiographical Note', p. vi. Park said that his earliest conception of a sociologist was as 'a kind of super-reporter'. Ibid. p. x.

75   Levine, 'Structure of Simmel's Social Thought', p. 16.

76   Ibid., p. 17.

77   Ibid., pp. 17-18.

78   See Leon Bramson, *The Political Context of Sociology* (Princeton, New Jersey, 1961), ch. 3. The assumption by early American sociologists that the individual was the basic unit of action and analysis is surveyed in John W.Petras, 'Images of Man in Early American Sociology, Part 1: The Individualistic Perspective in Motivation', *Journal of the History of the Behavioral Sciences* 6 (July 1970), 231-40. Simmel's work was made available to Americans quite early through Albion W.Small's translations in the *American Journal of Sociology* from 1896 on. On the variant meanings of the term 'individualism', see Steven Lukes, *Individualism* (New York, 1973).

79   'Robert Park – Chronology', Ms. in Park-Raushenbush, Box C, folder Misc. cont.

80   Park, *Masse und Publikum.*

81   Park defined collective behavior as each individual acting 'under the influence of a mood or a state of mind in which each shares, and in accordance with conventions which all quite unconsciously accept, and which the presence of each enforces upon the others'. Park and Burgess, *Introduction*, p. 865.

82   Park, 'Autobiographical Fragment', Park-Hughes.

83   Many of the ideas in *Masse und Publikum* reappear in the chapter on collective behavior in Park's *Introduction*.

84   Gustave Le Bon, *The Crowd. A Study of the Popular Mind,* (London, 1896, p. 15. (First pub. Paris, 1895, as *La Psychologie des Foules.*)

85   Bramson, *The Political Context*, pp. 53-56.

86   Scipio Sighele, *Psychologie des sectes* (Paris, 1895); *La Foule criminelle* (Paris, 1901); Gabriel Tarde, *L'Opinion et la Foule* (Paris, 1901).

87   Le Bon, *The Crowd*, p. 21.

88   For the conservatism of the crowd psychology school of European sociologists, see Bramson, *The Political Context*, ch. 3. A sophisticated specification of the

'conservative' tendency of American functionalism is in Paul F.Kress, *Social Science and the Idea of Process* (Urbana, Ill., 1970), pp. 198-201.

89 Park, *Masse und Publikum*, p. 108.

90 Le Bon, *The Crowd*, p. 57, p. 156. The crowd also has a certain creativity — language, for example, is a product of 'the unconscious genius of crowds', ibid., p. 6. Another evidence that irrationality was a central concern of this school is given by comparing their work with the recent historical studies of George Rudé, who tends, with much evidence, to see his documented crowds as rational in the sense of purposive, deliberate, and self-controlled. George Rudé, *The Crowd in History* (New York, 1964); *The Crowd in the French Revolution* (London, 1959).

91 Robert K.Merton, Introduction to the Viking Press edition of Le Bon, *The Crowd* (New York, 1960).

92 Le Bon, *The Crowd*, p. 27; Martindale, *Types of Sociological Theory*, p. 310.

93 Robert E. Park, 'Course Notes for "The Crowd and the Public",' Park-Hughes.

94 Bosanquet's *Philosophical Theory of the State* (1899) was frequently cited in *Masse und Publikum*. An excellent discussion of the theories and especially the historical background of British neo-idealism is Melvin Richter, *The Politics of Conscience: T.H.Green and his Age* (London, 1964).

95 William James, *Psychology* (New York, 1900), pp. 179-80.

96 Josiah Royce, *The World and the Individual* (New York, 1899), 2: 261; see also James Harry Cotton, *Royce on the Human Self* (Cambridge, Mass., 1954), pp. 46-47.

97 Gabriel Tarde, *Social Laws, An Outline of Sociology*, tr. Howard C.Warren (New York, 1899), pp. 38-39.

98 Martindale, *Types of Sociological Theory*, p. 314. A perceptive treatment of Baldwin and others of his intellectual generation in America, published after this chapter was written, is R.Jackson Wilson *In Quest of Community: Social Philosophy in the United States, 1860-1920* (New York, 1968), esp. pp. 60-86.

99 James M.Baldwin, *Social and Ethical Interpretations in Mental Development* (1897), p. 27, quoted in Fay B.Karpf, *American Social Psychology* (New York, 1932), p. 281.

100 James M.Baldwin, *Mental Development in the Child and the Race* (1895), p. 335, quoted in Park, *Masse und Publikum*, p. 73.

101 Karpf, *American Social Psychology*, p. 280, pp. 287-88.

102 Park, *Masse und Publikum*, p. 100; like Simmel, Park recognized the role which conflict played in producing consensus; he noted that a custom becomes elevated into a norm only when some individual or group sets himself against it. *Masse und Publikum*, pp. 100-101.

103 On the idea of 'sympathy', and Hume's treatment of it, see Philip Mercer, *Sympathy and Ethics* (Oxford, 1972); Park used the term in the sense of 'fellow-feeling', i.e., the slightly later coinage, 'empathy', plus a desire to

achieve belonging through conformity. For a discussion of 'empathy', see below, ch. 4, note 164. *Masse und Publikum*, p. 102; also, Lester Frank Ward, 'Contemporary Sociology', Part 2, *American Journal of Sociology*, 7 (March 1902): 629-658, esp. 647.

104 *Masse und Publikum*, pp. 104-106.

105 Gabriel Tarde, L'Opinion et la Foule (Paris, 1901), pp. 6-7.

106 Park, *Masse und Publikum*, pp. 107-108. 'Wo das Publikum aufhört Kritisch zu sein, da geht es auseinander oder wandelt sich in eine Masse um'. Park expresses the same ideas in Park and Burgess, *Introduction*, p. 869.

107 Park, *Masse und Publikum*, p. 108.

Chapter 3

1 'Robert Park – Chronology', Park-Raushenbush, Box C, Folder, 'Misc. cont.'

2 Park, 'Autobiographical fragment', in 'Robert E. Park: Recollections and Letters', Park-Hughes.

3 Professor Hughes remembers Park having told him this. Interview with Everett C. Hughes, Cambridge, Mass., 26 September 1963.

4 Park, 'Autobiographical Fragment.'

5 Interview with Everett C. Hughes.

6 Obituary of Robert E. Park, *American Sociological Review*, 9 (1944): 322-25.

7 Park, 'Autobiographical Fragment.'

8 Ruth Slade, *King Leopold's Congo* (London, New York and Accra, 1962), esp. pp. 178-90; George Martelli, *Leopold to Lumumba: a History of the Belgian Congo, 1877-1960* (London, 1962), esp. pp. 161-74.

9 Park, 'Autobiographical Fragment.' For *Everybody's* see Louis Filler, *Crusaders for American Liberalism* (Yellow Springs, Ohio, 1939), p. 85.

10 Slade, *King Leopold's Congo*, pp. 189-90; Park, 'A King in Business. Leopold II of Belgium, Autocrat of the Congo and International Broker', *Everybody's Magazine*, 15 (November 1906): 624-33; Park, 'The Terrible Story of the Congo', ibid., 15 (December 1906): 763-72; Park, 'The Blood Money of the Congo', ibid., 16 (January 1907): 60-70.

11 Park, 'Founders Day Address, Tuskegee Institute, April 12, 1942;' Park Papers, Social Science Research Institute, Fisk University.

12 Park, 'Autobiographical Fragment.'

13 Park, 'A King in Business', p. 624.

14 Park, 'The Blood Money of the Congo', p. 61.

15 An article which appeared in the same issue of *Everybody's* as Park's own, a sympathetic account of prize fighting, neatly stated an attitude which was very close to Park's. The article was intended to provide the respectable reader with

'a glimpse of man's nature of which you are ignorant. ...It is the author's province to observe, and perhaps to analyse a bit. I question his right to moralize much. It is the duty of us to know the thing we condemn, to see it as it is, if not with out own, then with another's eyes. We are a strong race, willing to face truth, to know conditions.' Rex Beach, 'The Fight at Tonopah', *Everybody's Magazine*, 16 (April 1907): 464-74, quotation p. 466.

16 Park, 'Methods of Teaching: Impressions and a Verdict', *Social Forces*, 20 (October 1941): 36-46, quotation, p. 41.

17 Andrew W. Lind, Ed. *Race Relations in World Perspectives. Papers read at the Conference on Race Relations in World Perspective. Honolulu 1954* (Honolulu 1955). This volume was dedicated to Park. E. T. Thompson and E. C. Hughes, eds., *Race: Individual and Collective Behavior* (Glencoe, Ill., 1958).

18 Park, 'Founder's Day Address', p. 3.

19 Ibid., Park to Washington, 25 September 1905, Booker T. Washington Papers, Library of Congress. Later Park said that Washington was not particularly interested in the Congo or in anything except the American Negro and Tuskegee, 'Autobiographical Fragment'.

20 Louis R. Harlan, 'Booker T. Washington and the White Man's Burden', *American Historical Review*, 71 (January 1966): 441-67.

21 Booker T. Washington, with the collaboration of Robert E. Park, *The Man Farthest Down: A Record of Observation and Study in Europe* (Garden City, N.Y., 1912), p. 14.

22 Park, 'Founder's Day Address', p. 5.

23 Ibid.

24 Park to Washington, 16 April 1911, Booker T. Washington Papers, Library of Congress. Robert E. Park, 'Booker T. Washington', Ms. of interview with Dr. Thompson, 1942, Park papers, Fisk University.

25 Park, 'Autobiographical Fragment.' See also Park to Emmett J. Scott (Washington's secretary), 18 April 1904 (1905), Booker T. Washington Papers, Library of Congress: 'I distrust my ability to perform any great original task in the world but I believe that I can do good work as a lieutenant and have no other ambition except that of doing the best that lies in me under the direction of some first class man.'

26 Park, 'Founder's Day Address.'

27 *Order of Parade during the visit of President Theodore Roosevelt*, Tuskegee Normal and Industrial Institute, Tuesday, October 24, 1905 (Tuskegee Institute Steam Print).

28 Washington to R. C. Ogden, 31 May 1906, Washington Papers.

29 August Meier, *Negro Thought in America, 1880-1915* (Ann Arbor, Michigan, 1963), p. 112. Meier's treatment of Washington is the most perceptive known to me; a brief, competent life is Samuel R. Spencer Jr., *Booker T. Washington and the Negro's place in American Life* (Boston, 1955). A more detailed and generally admiring account is Basil Mathews, *Booker T. Washington: Educator and Inter-racial Interpreter* (Cambridge, Mass., 1948).

30 Robert E. Park, 'Booker T. Washington', Ms. of interview with Dr. Thompson, Fisk University, 1942, Park Papers, Fisk University.

31 Park To Washington, 3 December 1905; and two letters of June 1906, Booker T. Washington Papers, Box 33, Library of Congress.

32 Washington to Park, 31 July 1912, Booker T. Washington Papers, Box 61, Library of Congress.

33 Park, notes on an article by William H. Baldwin, with suggestions for articles to be written under Washington's name. Washington Papers, Box 37.

34 Booker T. Washington, *The Story of the Negro* (New York, 1909); Mathews, *Booker T. Washington,* p. 225.

35 Park to Washington, 14 December 1908, Washington Papers, Box 42.

36 See, however, August Meier, *Negro Thought in America,* part 4.

37 Park to Washington, n.d. probably June 1906, Washington Papers, Box 33.

38 Park to Washington, 12 September 1908, Washington Papers, Box 42.

39 Washington, *The Man Farthest Down,* p. 16.

40 Park to Washington, 13 September 1908, Washington Papers, Box 42.

41 Park to Washington, 6 July 1910. Booker T. Washington Papers, Box 51.

42 Washington, *The Man Farthest Down,* pp. 15-16.

43 Park, 'Booker T. Washington', Ms. of interview with Dr. Thompson, Fisk University, 1942.

44 Washington, *The Man Farthest Down,* p. 13.

45 Ibid., p. 19.

46 Park, 'Booker T. Washington', p. 5.

47 Washington to Park, 2 December 1910, Washington Papers, Box 54.

48 Washington to Park, 2 October 1906, Ibid., Box 33. Park to Emmett Scott, 12 January 1906. Park to Emmett Scott, n.d. (1906), Ibid., Box 33. Park to Villard, 1 October 1908, Ibid., Box 42. Washington to Park, 24 January 1908, Ibid.

49 Park to Washington, 10 December 1908, Washington Papers, Box 42.

50 Park to Washington, 13 January 1906, Ibid., Box 33.

51 *Springfield Daily Republican,* Monday, 29 November 1909, p. 7.

52 Washington Papers, Box 30, Box 77.

53 Merle Curti, *The Social Ideas of American Educators* (Second ed. Paterson, N.J., 1959; First ed. pub. 1935), p. 289.

54 Booker T. Washington, *My Larger Education* (New York, 1911), p. 133; Curti, *Social Ideas of American Educators,* p. 29.

55 Park, 'Methods of Teaching; Impressions and a Verdict', *Social Forces,* 20 (October 1941): 36-46; quotation from p. 45.

56 Park, 'Education by Cultural Groups', *The Tuskegee Student,* 24, no. 18 (4 May 1912): 6.

57 Park, 'Methods of Teaching', p. 44. Modern accusations of the irrelevance of the education given at Tuskegee seem somewhat exaggerated. Besides instruc-

tion in blacksmithing and carriage trimming there were also classes in electrical crafts, machinery, printing, plumbing, and mechanical drawing. See the *Order of Parade during the Visit of President Theodore Roosevelt.*

58 Park to Emmett J. Scott, 27 May 1907, Washington Papers, Box 37.

59 Park-Washington Ms. 'What the Carnegie Library does for Tuskegee students', Washington Papers, Box 30.

60 Park, 'Methods of Teaching', p. 43.

61 Report of the 21st Annual Tuskegee Negro Conference, *The Tuskegee Student*, 24, no. 3 (20 January 1912).

62 Park, 'Founder's Day Address', p. 9.

63 Park, '57 Books Every Tuskegee Graduate Should Know', reprint from *The Tuskegee Student*, 9 April 1910, Washington Papers, Box 77.

64 Robert E. Park, 'Founder's Day Address', p. 11. See also Merle Curti, *The Social Ideas of American Educators*, pp. 289-90. The phrase 'character and a career' was borrowed from Samuel C. Armstrong, q.v. 15.

65 Park, Notes on an article.

66 Park to Washington, 13 September 1908, Washington Papers, Box 42. See also an article written by Park for Washington, 'Inferior and Superior Races', *North American Review*, 101 (April 1915): 538-72.

67 Park, 'Founder's Day Address', p. 12.

68 *Springfield Daily Republican*, 29 November 1909, p. 7. The Ms. is in Park-Hughes, folder labelled 'Booker T. Washington'. For the harmful effect of Washington's caution, see Meier, *Negro Thought in America*, pp. 117-18. This chapter is heavily indebted to Meier's excellent interpretation, pp. 100-18.

69 Park, 'Founder's Day Address', p. 14.

70 Park, 'Methods of Teaching', p. 38.

71 Reminiscences of Jessie Bernard in a letter to the author, 8 December 1964.

72 Interview with Norman Hayner, Montreal, 3 September 1964.

73 Park, 'Founder's Day Address', p. 10.

74 Washington to George Foster Peabody, 15 April 1909, Washington Papers, Box 47. Robert R. Moton succeeded Washington at Tuskegee in 1915.

75 Telegram from Washington to Park, 9 January 1906, Washington Papers, Box 33.

76 Park mentions Washington's habit of using dialect stories 'to convey profound truths', in 'Founder's Day Address'. The interpretation is not explicitly stated, but strongly implied in Park's account of Tuskegee.

77 Meier, *Negro Thought in America*, p. 105. Washington's position was put neatly by a Negro interviewed in the observation car of the Oriental Ltd. The Negro is happiest in the South where he knows what he can and can't do. He should stay on the 'farm as a producer, not in the city as a parasite'.

78 Booker T. Washington, *The Future of the American Negro* (Boston 1899) pp. 202-203.

79   Peabody wrote to Washington opposing buying an organ for the dining hall at
      Tuskegee on the grounds that it would be 'apt to hinder your hold on your
      plantation melodies which seem to me of the first importance for the great
      masses of your people for two or three generations yet'. Peabody to Washing-
      ton, 4 January 1905, Washington Papers, Box 30. However, Washington also
      liked hardware, the visible sign of affluence.

80   Quoted in P. Sorokin, *Principles of Rural Sociology* (New York, 1929), p. 308.

81   Robert E. Park and Ernest W. Burgess, *Introduction to the Science of Sociology*
      (Chicago: University of Chicago Press, 1921), p. 929. Isaiah Berlin, 'Herder and
      the Enlightenment', in *Aspects of the Eighteenth Century* (Baltimore and Lon-
      don, 1965), pp. 47-104.

82   Werner J. Cahnman, 'Max Weber and the methodological controversy in the
      social sciences', in Werner J. Cahnman and Alvin Boskoff, eds. *Sociology and
      History: Theory and research*. (New York, 1964), pp. 103-27. Quotation p.
      105.

83   See ch. 2, at note 52 on Tönnies; Seymour M. Lipset, *Political Man. The Social
      Basis of Politics* (London, 1960), p. 25 on Marx and Engels' response to the cult
      of the peasant. Another tradition of thought which overlaps this one — the
      concern with the sociological prerequisites of a self-governing society, em-
      phasizing the rural smallholder as backbone of democracy — may have been in
      the background of Park's thought, but the overt romantic imagery is more
      salient.

84   Horace M. Kallen, *Culture and Democracy in the United States: Studies in the
      Group Psychology of the American Peoples* (New York, 1924), p. 101. Freud
      suggested that all these ideal formulations of the primitive community are a
      generalized 'other' based on the revulsion from civilized inhibition which is
      especially strong among intellectuals. If Freud was right, the particular content
      of the civilization which repressed them should show a mirror image relation to
      the qualities which the Utopian theorists regard as ideal. Sigmund Freud,
      Civilization and its Discontents. James Strachey tr. (New York, 1962; first
      published Vienna, 1930), pp. 34, 42-43. For the related yet distinct idea of the
      'Noble Savage', see the succinct discussion in J. W. Burrows, *Evolution and
      Society: a Study in Victorian Social Theory* (Cambridge, 1966), pp. 1-6.

85   Mozell C. Hill, 'Some Early Notes of Robert E, Park', *Phylon: the Atlanta
      University Review of Race and Culture*, 14, no. 1 (1st quarter, 1953): 88.

86   For evidence that this reaction was common, see, for example, William James,
      'A Certain Blindness in Human Beings', *Selected Papers on Philosophy* (Lon-
      don, 1917), pp. 17-18. First published in *Talks to Teachers in Psychology: and
      to students on some of Life's Ideals*, (1915). Mary Austin, *Earth Horizon* (New
      York, 1931), p. 365. In a letter to William James, Rudyard Kipling diagnosed
      the malaise of the American intellectual as boredom with the comfort of
      civilized life, Kipling to James, 31 August 1896, quoted in Ralph Barton Perry,
      The Thought and Character of William James (London, 1935), 2: 276. The
      feeling that American life lacked the variety and vividness provided by more
      static and stratified societies was of long standing. James Fenimore Cooper for

example, deplored the absence of an American peasantry. See Harry Levin, *The Power of Blackness* (New York, 1958), p. 241. Emerson contrasted the sterility of the mercantile life with the rich 'wilderness' of Negro life. William H. Gilman and J.E. Parsons, ed., *The Journals and Miscellaneous Notebooks of Ralph Waldo Emerson* 8 (Cambridge, Mass., 1970): 88.

87 Park, 'The Land of Darkness', Ms. in Park-Hughes.

88 Ibid.

89 Park, 'Negro home life and Standards of living', *The Annals* 49 (September,1913): 158-59.

90 Park, 'The Land of Darkness.'

91 Ibid.

92 Untitled manuscript in Park's hand, Park-Hughes.

93 Washington to Park, 6 October 1912, Washington Papers, Box 61.

94 Park to Washington, 29 May 1913, Washington Papers, Box 61.

95 Park later called the Negro on the plantation 'the only peasant class America has produced, and his is the only native folk culture that America possesses'. Park, 'Assimilation, Social', *Encyclopedia of the Social Sciences*, 2 (1935): 281-83.

96 Meier, *Negro Thought in America*, pp. 171-89.

97 Park to Emmett J. Scott, 13 March 1907, Washington Papers, Box 37.

98 See, for example, Oswald Garrison Villard to Washington, 13 April 1913 and Washington to Villard, 7 September 1913, Washington Papers, Box 42.

99 Park, 'Booker T. Washington', p. 4.

100 Ibid., pp. 11, 7, 4.

101 Park, 'Founder's Day Address', p. 18.

102 August Meier, *Negro Thought in America*, pp. 110-14.

103 Robert E. Park, 'Negro Race Consciousness as Reflected in Race Literature', *American Review*, 1 (September-October, 1923): 505-16, reprinted in Park, *Race and Culture* (Glencoe, Illinois: Free Press, 1950), pp. 284-300, see especially pp. 298-99.

104 Park, 'Founder's Day Address', p. 7.

105 Ibid., p. 9.

106 Park, 'Immigrant Heritages', *Proceedings of National Conference of Social Work, 1921* (Chicago, 1921), pp. 492-97.

107 Park, 'Founder's Day Address', p. 5.

108 Ibid., p. 6.

109 Ibid.

110 'Natural Science, History and the Negro. An address to the Scientific Society of the Tuskegee Institute by Robert E. Park, Friday, February 18, 1905', Washington Papers, Box 30.

111 Gunnar Myrdal noted the tragic irony of Bertram W. Doyle's fatalism, since Doyle, one of Park's students at Chicago, was himself Negro. See Gunnar Myrdal, with the assistance of Richard Sterner, *An American Dilemma, The Negro Problem and Modern Democracy* (New York, 1962; first pub., 1944), p. 1362n. It is true, as S. P. Fullinwinder points out in his perceptive *The Mind and Mood of Black America* (Homewood, Ill., 1969), pp. 100-15, that some of Park's Negro students later employed the thorough, tough-minded scholarship which he inculcated for more activist purposes. Such activity came in most cases after 1940 and the waning of the master's influence. St. Clair Drake and Horace Cayton in 1962 noted this contrast in the writings of E. Franklin Frazier, and wrote of their own *Black Metropolis* (dedicated to Park) that in it they 'were trying to combine the roles of "Negro", which society imposed on them, and social scientist, which they themselves had chosen'. Drake and Cayton, *Black Metropolis: a study of Negro Life in a Northern City* (Rev. ed., New York, 1962), 2: x. Myrdal's note on Park is in *American Dilemma,* 1049-50. The argument here is not that whites or anyone else should never try to interpret the experience of other groups but that the conceptual framework within which data is interpreted will have implications for action. But see also James E. Blackwell and Morris Janowitz, eds. *Black Sociologists* (Chicago, 1975), which arrived too late for use here.

112 Washington to Park, 27 February 1911, expressing sympathy on the death of his father. Washington Papers, Box 54. Clara Park to Washington while Park was ill, complaining that his salary was months behind. Clara Park to Washington, 12 July 1907. Washington Papers, Box 37.

113 Theodosia Park to Park, 21 February 1913, Park-Raushenbush, Box C.

114 Ms. in Park-Raushenbush, Folder, 'REP', letters from his children.

115 Margaret Park Redfield to the author, 19 June 1964. Clara Park wrote an article on the plight of widows with children and was appointed by the governor of Massachusetts to a three man commission on the subject which led to a law providing for widows' pensions. Mrs. Donald L. Breed to the author, 4 March 1975.

116 Park to Washington, Wollaston, Mass. 28 July 1909, Washington Papers, Box 47. Park, 'Autobiographical Fragment', Park-Hughes.

117 Park to Washington, 10 April 1912, Washington Papers.

118 Washington to Park, 31 July 1912, Washington Papers.

119 Park, 'Methods of Teaching', p. 41.

120 For Park's meeting with Thomas see above, chapter 1.

121 See, for example, Park to Scott, 16 March 1914 (complaining that someone had stolen his electric light bulb and asking for a replacement), Washington Papers, Box 72. In the summer of 1914, Park and Washington were planning a second tour of Europe for the next spring. Writing on 24 July, Park optimistically recommended to Washington that if war did break out in Europe the trip should be postponed until the fall of 1915. Park to Washington, 24 July and 1 August 1915, ibid., Box 72.

122 Washington to Park, 15 August 1914, Ibid., Box 72; Park to Washington, 15 April 1915, ibid., Box 77; Park to Scott, 1 October 1913,ibid., Box 66. While drawing the Tuskegee salary Park remitted $300.00 of his Chicago salary to the Institute.

123 See, for example the letter from Park to William E. Holmes of Macon, Georgia, 13 November 1913, ibid., box 66.

124 Park to Scott, 19 January 1915, still from Wollaston, Mass., ibid., container 13.

Chapter 4

1 Park to Emmett Scott, 1 October 1913, Booker T. Washington Papers, Library of Congress, Box 66.

2 Park to Booker T. Washington, 20 June 1914. Ibid., Box 72.

3 Park to Scott, 19 January 1915. Ibid., container 13.

4. Park to Booker T. Washington, 21 December 1913. Ibid., Box 66; Park, 'Racial Assimilation in Secondary Groups with particular reference to the Negro', *American Journal of Sociology* 19 (1913): 606-623.

5 University of Chicago, *Course Catalog,* 1915 (Chicago, 1915), p. 40.

6 Ellsworth Faris, 'Robert E. Park, 1864-1944', *American Sociological Review*, 9 (June 1944): 322-25, quotation from p. 323.

7 Albion W. Small to President E.D. Burton, 23 March 1923, Presidential Papers, University of Chicago, Sociology. Small pointed out to the president that as Park was already 58 years old he 'cannot become a charge on the retiring fund.'.

8 Interview with Edgar T. Thompson, Montreal, 9 September 1964; letter from Jessie Bernard, Pennsylvania State University, to the writer, 8 December 1964.

9 See for example, Park's relations with his employers on the California Race Relations Survey, discussed below. This paragraph develops a point made by Barbara Klose Bowdery, 'The Sociology of Robert E. Park', Ph.D. dissertation, Columbia University, 1951, p. 7.

10 Winifred Raushenbush, 'Robert Ezra Park, 1864-1944: a memoir', Park-Raushenbush.

11 Interview with Edgar T. Thompson, Montreal, 2 September 1964; Nels Anderson to the writer, Bonn, West Germany, 9 June 1964; interview with Everett C. Hughes, Cambridge, Mass., 21 May 1965, and note to the writer, 1964.

12 Park felt that men go to church essentially to 'revive a sense of their social solidarity and of their participation in common destiny'. R.E. Park, 'The Nature of Race Relations,' in Edgar T. Thompson (ed.) *Race Relations and The Race Problem* (Durham, N.C., 1939), pp. 3-45, reprinted in R.E. Park, *Race and Culture*, (Glencoe, Ill, Free Press, 1950), pp. 81-116, quotation, p. 89.

13 The idea of Chicago as archetype was almost a cliché by 1913 and is discussed together with Park's urban sociology in chapter 5. Edward Shils, *The Present State of American Sociology* (Glencoe, Ill., 1948), p. 2.

14 Edwin E. Slosson, *Great American Universities* (New York, 1910), p. 406; Thomas Wakefield Goodspeed, *The Story of the University of Chicago, 1890-1925* (Chicago, 1925), p. 205. Richard J. Storr, *Harper's University. The Beginnings* (Chicago and London, 1966).

15 Goodspeed, *The University of Chicago*, pp. 203-204. Laurence R. Veysey, *The Emergence of the American University* (Chicago, 1955), pp. 273, 286.

16 Slosson, *Great American Universities*, pp. 410-11. There were 3253 students in summer, against 2339 in the autumn of 1909; in 1908-9 there were 5659 summer students, of whom 1416 were graduates. The total number of Ph.D.s produced by Chicago 1896-1908 was 448, against 436 for Columbia and 418 for Harvard. Ibid., pp. 423-33.

17 Nels Anderson, *The Hobo* (Chicago, 1923); Frederic Thrasher, *The Gang* (Chicago, 1927); Everett C. Hughes, 'Robert Park', *New Society*, 118 (31 December 1964): 18-19; Robert E. L. Faris, *Chicago Sociology 1920-32* (San Francisco, 1967), pp. 65-66.

18 Veysey, *Emergence of the American University*, p. 374.

19 Ames of the divinity school gave a course on the 'Psychology of Religion' in the sociology department in 1914. University of Chicago, *Course Catalog, 1914*, 45. Alvin W. Gouldner, *The Coming Crisis of Western Sociology* (New York, 1970), p. 24, points out that as late as 1964, 27.6 percent of 3,441 members of the American Sociological Society who responded to a poll had thought, at *one time or another*, of becoming clergymen. A close tie between the divinity school and the developing social sciences was quite common. For the situation at Harvard, see Robert Church et al., edited with an introduction by Paul H. Buck, *Social Science at Harvard, 1860-1920; from Inculcation to the Open Mind* (Cambridge, Mass., 1965), esp. David B. Potts, 'Social Ethics at Harvard, 1881-1931', pp. 92ff.

20 Slosson, *Great American Universities*, pp. 431, 437; Veysey, *Emergence of the American University*, p. 368n. This *was* true after the 1895 Bemis case, when fear of adverse criticism hurting the university assured this freedom, though the anxious search for professional neutrality described in the text may be seen as the internalization of trustees' hostility to scholarly agitation. See Mary O. Furner, *Advocacy and Objectivity* (Lexington, Kentucky, 1975).

21 A case could be made that Franklin H. Giddings and his department at Columbia were more direct ancestors of the discipline's concerns and methods after 1935 than were Small, Thomas, and Park at Chicago. But Chicago was dominant during the early, formative period and has continued to dominate the professional memory of sociologists. H.E.Barnes, ed., *An Introduction to the History of Sociology* (Chicago, 1948), p. 763.

22 L. L. and Jessie Bernard, *Origins of American Sociology : the Social Science Movement in the United States* (New York, 1943), p. 611; George Fitzhugh, *Sociology for the South* (Richmond, Va., 1854); Harris E. Starr, *William Graham Sumner* (New York, 1925), p. 172.

23 Jessie Bernard, 'The History and Prospects of Sociology in the United States' in George A. Lundberg, Read Bain, Nels Anderson ed., *Trends in American*

Sociology (New York, 1929), pp. 1-71, references pp. 1-5. As a subject within established departments, courses were instituted at Boston University in 1883, William Penn College in 1885, Indiana University a year later, and the University of Wyoming in 1887. Jessie Bernard, 'The Teaching of Sociology in the U.S. in the last fifty years', *American Journal of Sociology,* 50 (1945): 534-48. Whether Small's innovation at Colby was much more than a significant change of title would make an interesting inquiry for a student of the early period of academic social science. Colby itself changed its title from College to University in 1867, and then, in a remarkable display of the New England conscience, back to College in 1899. *Encyclopedia Americana* (New York, 1970), 6: 218.

24 Veysey, *Emergence of the American University,* p. 62.

25 In 1870 about one-fifth of the population lived in cities and towns over 8,000; by 1890 about one-third of a much larger population lived in such places and the population of New York, Chicago, and Philadelphia was over a million, John A. Garraty, *The New Commonwealth, 1877-1890* (New York, 1968), p. 179.

26 Donald Fleming, 'Social Darwinism', Arthur M. Schlesinger, Jr., and Morton White, eds., *Paths of American Thought* (Boston, 1963), pp. 123-46. For evidence of the co-existence of social concern with a decline in religious belief among university students in the late nineteenth century see George Dykhuizen, 'John Dewey and the University of Michigan', *Journal of the History of Ideas,* 23 (1962): 513-44. See also Church *et al., Social Science at Harvard,* esp. pp. 92ff.

27 L. L. and Jessie Bernard, *Origins of American Sociology,* p. 579.

28 The quoted phrase is from the announcement of the founding of the Columbia sociology department. Jessie Bernard, 'History and Prospects of Sociology', p. 13. The census of 1880, directed by F.A. Walker, had used the phrase to categorize challenges to social norms.

29 Charles A. Ellwood, 'The Science of Sociology: A Reply', *American Journal of Sociology,* 15 (1909): 105-10.

30 Small, quoted in Jessie Bernard, 'History and Prospects of Sociology', p. 21. Alvin Gouldner, in his eccentric and often perceptive *The Coming Crisis of American Sociology* (New York and London, 1970), pp. 91-92, has also made this point; the formulation here was reached independently.

31 For a general interpretation of the reform impulse in this vein see Clifford Griffin, *Their Brothers' Keepers: Moral Stewardship in the United States, 1800-65* (New Brunswick, N.J., 1960), an important work which is weakened by the author's distaste for his subjects and resulting tendency to reduce their motives to an attempt to preserve the power of their class. It is a book which demonstrates the close affinities between hard-boiled twentieth century pluralist liberalism and William Grahan Sumner.

32 Robert H. Wiebe, *The Search for Order, 1877-1920* (New York, 1967), p. 139; Henry F. May, *Protestant Churches and Industrial America* (New York, 1949), pp. 114 ff., 122-23, 170 ff; C. Howard Hopkins, *The Rise of the Social Gospel in American Protestantism 1865-1915* (New Haven, 1940), pp. 75-77, 108-12.

For the corresponding movement in Canada, and its interest in 'sociology', see William Magney, 'The Methodist Church and the National Gospel, 1884-1914', Committee on Archives of the United Church of Canada, *Bulletin, no. 20, 1968* (Toronto, 1968), esp. pp. 32-36.

33 Partly this was due to the sheer growth of the United States; Society was becoming more complicated and the land was filling up. See for example William Graham Sumner, 'Earth Hunger and the Philosophy of Land Grabbing' (1896), in *Earth Hunger and Other Essays* (New Haven, 1933), pp. 31-64, esp. pp. 42-43; also 'Economics and Politics' (1905), pp. 318-33, esp. p. 332. James Bryce, *The American Commonwealth*, vol 2. New Rev. ed. (New York, 1913; first pub. 1893), pp. 912-13, 932.

34 Josiah Strong, *Our Country*, ed. Jurgen Herbst (John Harvard Library, Cambridge, Mass., 1963; first pub., 1885), pp. ix, 218, xxi. 'The city', said Strong, 'has become a serious menace to our civilization, because in it, excepting Mormonism, each of the dangers we have discussed is enhanced, and all are focalized'. p. 172. May, *Protestant Churches*, p. 116, calls *Our Country* 'the *Uncle Tom's Cabin* of city reform', 175,000 copies had been sold by 1915.

35 Henry Adams, *The Education of Henry Adams* (Boston, 1918). An interesting effort to relate social change to the development of social criticism, Stow Persons' *Decline of American Gentility* (New York, 1973), came too late to influence this treatment. Persons' work tends to the hard-boiled reduction of ideas to status-defenses noted in the case of Clifford Griffin; however fashionable, this reduction denatures the power of ideal constructs of the common good to mold men's behavior.

36 Wiebe, *The Search for Order*, pp. 140 ff. David W. Noble, 'The Paradox of Progressive Thought', *American Quarterly*, 5 (Fall 1953): 201-12.

37 Albion W. Small, *Adam Smith and Modern Sociology* (Chicago, 1907), p. 22. See also, Small, 'The Era of Sociology', *American Journal of Sociology,* 1 (February 1895): 13-14. 'It is possible to so far increase our present intelligence about social utilities that there may be much more effective combinations for the promotion of the general welfare.' On the early dominance, decline, and rebirth of meliorism in American sociology, see now Robert W. Friedrichs, *A Sociology of Sociology* (New York, 1970).

38 C.R. Henderson, *The Social Spirit in America* (Meadville, Pa., 1897), p. 9.

39 Lester F. Ward, *Dynamic Sociology*, 2 vols. (New York, 1883); for Ward see Henry Steele Commager, *The American Mind* (New Haven, 1950), pp. 199-210. The quotation is from Ward, *Applied Sociology* (Boston, 1906), p. 6. Ward recognized that although Malthus had been rejected by most Americans in his original guise, his ideas and attitudes had slipped in through the medium of his intellectual heirs, Darwin, Spencer, and Sumner. See Bernard Crick, *The American Science of Politics. Its Origin and Conditions* (London, 1959), p. 56. An independent source of meliorist sociology, who had some influence on future political leaders but apparently little or none on future sociologists, was the philosopher and president of the University of Wisconsin, John Bascom (1827-1911). Bascom transmitted the voluntarism and intuitionism of Scottish

and Kantian ideas down past the Darwinian era to such students as Robert LaFollette. See the excellent analysis, Robert A. Jones, 'John Bascom 1827-1911', *American Quarterly*, 24, no. 4 (October 1972): 501-22. See also Charlotte G. O'Kelly and John W. Petras, 'Images of Man in Early American Sociology, II: The Changing Concept of Social Reform', *Journal of the History of The Behavioral Sciences* 6 (October 1970); 317-34.

40 Dumas Malone ed., *Dictionary of American Biography* (New York, 1963; first pub. 1935), vol. 4, pp. 524-25; Louise C. Wade, *Graham Taylor, Pioneer for Social Justice 1815-1938* (Chicago, 1964), pp. 99, 165-67; Roy Lubove, *The Professional Altruist* (Cambridge, Mass., 1965 pp. 1-2, 140-41.

41 Wade, *Graham Taylor*, pp. 170 ff, p. 81; Lubove, *Professional Altruist*, p. 144; Hopkins, *Rise of the Social Gospel*, p. 157.

42 As is well known and as Darnell Rucker, *The Chicago Pragmatists* (Minneapolis, Minn., 1969) has conveniently summarized, there were 'Chicago schools' of philosophy, psychology, and theology, all of them influencing, and to a much lesser extent influenced by, the Chicago brand of sociology. Sociology, the most empirical of the Chicago social sciences, reached its high point of activity and influence later than the others, under the leadership of Park and Ellsworth Faris in the 1920s and the early '30s. It was the last flowering of Chicago's pre-eminent position in American intellectual life, which had declined earlier in other areas. For a broader view of the 'Chicago' perspective at the turn of the twentieth century, including architecture, see Hugh D. Duncan, *Culture and Democracy; the struggle for form in society and architecture in Chicago and the middle West during the life and times of Louis H. Sullivan* (Totowa, N.J., 1965).

43 *Dictionary of American Biography*, vol. 9, pp. 221-22; H.E.Barnes, ed., *An Introduction to the History of Sociology* (Chicago, 1948), pp. 766-67.

44 See Albion W. Small, *Adam Smith and Modern Sociology*, and *The Meaning of Social Science* (Chicago, 1910). For 'sociological imperialism', see the excellent (if mistitled) essay by Charles H. Page, 'Sociology as a teaching enterprise', in Robert K. Merton, Leonard Broom, L.S.Cottrell Jr., eds., *Sociology Today: Problems and Prospects* (New York, 1959), pp. 579-99. Page insists that sociology still assumes that it is the *essential* social science, with others developing specialized theories to account for limited areas of human behavior.

45 Barnes, *Introduction to the History of Sociology*, p. 768; Faris, *Chicago Sociology*, pp. 12, 33; *Dictionary of American Biography*, vol. 9, pp. 221-22.

46 He left his estate to the University of Chicago to found a journal devoted to the application of moral and Christian principles to society. Ibid., Small, 'The Era of Sociology', *American Journal of Sociology*, 1 (July, 1895): 13-14.

47 Albion W. Small and George E. Vincent, *Introduction to the Study of Society* (Chicago, 1894), p. 38.

48 Small to William R. Harper, 25 April 1895, University of Chicago Special Collections, Presidential File, Sociology Department, University of Chicago.

49 Macmillan, the publisher of Ross, Giddings, and Veblen, on the dust jackets of

its publications, lumped together advertisements for 'sociology' and 'socialism' as of 'related interest'. Lewis A Coser, 'Toward a Sociology of Social Conflict', Ph.D. dissertation, Columbia University, 1954; Magney, 'Methodist Church', p. 34. The lumping of sociology and socialism seemed not only embarrassing but confused to the early sociologists. From a distance, however, a link may be established, in that the popular teaching of sociology eroded individualism by inculcating a sense of the whole, a sensitivity to others, and often a guilt at denying their expectations.

50 Don Martindale, *The Nature and Types of Sociological Theory* (London, 1961), pp. 185, 194; on the history of the idea of 'process' in American social science, see Paul F. Kress, *Social Science and the Idea of Process* (Urbana, Ill., 1970), esp. pp. 89-105 on Small. Behind the more limited formulations of the late-nineteenth century was the stress on process and principles of change in the philosophy of Hegel. Sidney Hook, *From Hegel to Marx* (New York, [1936]), pp. 54-55.

51 Jurgen Herbst, *The German Historical School in American Scholarship. A Study in the Transfer of Culture* (Ithaca, N.Y., 1965), p. 156. For the creative importance of the paradigm see Thomas Kuhn, *The Structure of Scientific Revolutions* (Chicago, 1961). Morton White, *Social Thought in America: The Revolt against Formalism* (Second ed., Boston, 1957, first ed. 1947).

52 Albion W. Small, *General Sociology* (Chicago, 1905), p. 677, quoted in Herbst, *The German Historical School*, p. 157.

53 Herbst, *The German Historical School*, p. 155.

54 Robert E. L. Faris thought that little of the content of Small's sociology was found useful by other sociologists. *Chicago Sociology 1920-1932* (San Francisco, 1967), p. 12. However, for a more favorable view of Small's influence see Cynthia Eagle Russett, *The Concept of Equilibrium in Social Thought* (New Haven and London, 1966), pp. 70-75. The quotation is from Small, *General Sociology*, p. 209, quoted in Russett, p. 73.

55 Barnes, *Introduction to the History of Sociology*, p. 793.

56 Ibid., p. 794; Martindale, *Types of Sociological Theory*, pp. 347-48; Faris, *Chicago Sociology*, pp. 135, 16.

57 Martindale, *Types of Sociological Theory*, pp. 347-49; Barnes, *Introduction to the History of Sociology*, p. 793; John W. Petras, 'Changes of Emphasis in the Sociology of W.I. Thomas', *Journal of the History of the Behavioral Sciences*, 6 (January 1970) 70-79.

58 W.I.Thomas and Florian Znaniecki, *The Polish Peasant in Europe and America* (5 vols., Chicago, 1918-20). R.E.Park, 'Notes on the Origin of the Social Forces Social Research', *Bulletin of the Society for Social Research* (August 1939), quoted in Edmund H. Volkart ed., *Social Behavior and Personality: Contributions of W.I.Thomas to Theory and Social Research* (New York, 1951), p. 84n.

59 Martindale, *Types of Sociological Theory*, pp. 348-49; for a discussion of functional psychology see Edwin G. Boring, *A History of Experimental Psychology* (New York, 1950), pp. 552-59; Park, 'Course Notes for "Crowd and Public",' Park-Hughes.

60 W.I.Thomas, *Source Book for Social Origins* (Chicago, 1909), p. 16. Bruce Kuklick argues that the distinction between pragmatism and neo-kantianism is largely a result of the ignorance of intellectual historians. *Josiah Royce, An Intellectual Biography* (Indianapolis, 1972), pp. 1-2.

61 Ibid., pp. 13-15.

62 Ibid., pp. 16-17. See William James, *Psychology: Briefer Course* (New York, 1892), ch. 13.

63 Thomas, *Source Book,* pp. 16-17.

64 See Charles S. Peirce. 'How to make our ideas clear', in *Collected Papers of Charles Sanders Peirce,* ed. Charles Hartshorne and Paul Weiss (Cambridge, Mass., 1934), vol. 5, pp. 248-71. Originally published 1878.

65 'To say that language, reflection, discussion, logical analysis, abstraction, mechanical invention, magic, religion and science are developed in the effort of the attention to meet different situations through a readjustment of habit, is simply to say that the mind itself is the product of crisis.' Thomas, *Source Book*, p. 17.

66 Ibid., pp. 13-21; quotation p. 20.

67 Thomas' basic concepts underwent considerable development away from function toward a kind of phenomenology, during the course of his career. By the time he wrote *The Polish Peasant*, 'control' had become 'value' and 'attention', 'attitude'; and by 1923 both were taking second place to what Thomas called the 'definition of the situation'.

68 Thomas and Znaniecki, *The Polish Peasant*, p. 1127. The concept of 'social disorganization' was popularized into a textbook truism that 'explained' phenomena that seemed 'deviant' in terms of the moral perspective of the explainers. In turn, succeeding generations subjected it to relentless critique which reflects both its own ambiguities and the shift of scholars from a majoritarian, or middle-class, to a pluralist point of view. Probably the most influential attack was C. Wright Mills, 'The Professional Ideology of Social Pathologists', American Journal of Sociology 49 (September, 1942): 165-80; a recent comment is in Tamara K. Hareven, 'The History of the Family as an Interdisciplinary Field', *Journal of Interdisciplinary History,* 2 (Autumn, 1971); 410-11. Without denying the weaknesses of the concept, it seems clear that the attack upon it draws from ethical sources, notably from a resentment that lifestyles deviant from those of the bourgeoisie should be classed as 'disorganized'. Most of the critics, however, retain the Darwinian assumption that organized lives are superior to unorganized, that survival is a prime test of value. See note 136 to chapter five and works cited there.

69 Roscoe C. Hinkle, Jr., and Gisela J. Hinkle, *The Development of Modern Sociology* (New York, 1954), p. 14.

70 Thomas and Znaniecki, *The Polish Peasant*, p. 1127.

71 Martindale, *Types of Sociological Theory*, p. 348. 'The individual develops his attitudes and makes his selection of the values that a situation offers on the basis of a general pattern of wishes', p. 351. Martindale suggests that Thomas' wishes were modeled on what Ratzenhofer and Small had named 'interests'. The

change of name seems to represent a move away from the nineteenth century assumption of rationality.

72 John Madge, *The Origins of Scientific Sociology* (Glencoe, Ill., 1962), p. 66; Donald Fleming, 'Attitude: the history of a concept', *Perspectives in American History, I* (1967): 286-365, esp. pp. 326-27.

73 W.I.Thomas, *The Unadjusted Girl* (Boston, 1923), p. 42, as quoted in Martindale, *Types of Sociological Theory*, p. 348.

74 W.I.Thomas, 'The persistence of primary group norms in present day society and their influence in our educational system', Herbert S. Jennings, J.B. Watson, Adolf Meyer, and W.I.Thomas, *Suggestions of Modern Science Concerning Education* (New York, 1920, first ed. published 1917), pp. 157-97, esp. p. 168; Peter L. Berger, *Invitation to Sociology* (Harmondsworth, Middx., England, 1966; first ed. published Garden City, N .Y., 1963), pp. 100-101.

75 Edmund H. Volkart, ed., *Social Behavior and Personality*, pp. 28-30.

76 Fleming, 'Attitude', p. 331; Park, 'A Race Relations Survey', p. 164.

77 Park to Emory S. Bogardus, 4 February 1925, Park-Raushenbush, Box A, Folder 'Emory S. Bogardus.' Most further development in this area, beyond the social distance scale which Bogardus developed at Park's suggestion, came from the psychologists, in particular one at the University of Chicago who seems to have become active only as Park disengaged in the late 1920s. L.L.Thurstone published his important article, 'Attitudes can be measured', in 1928. See Fleming, 'Attitudes', pp. 340-47.

78 H.J.Wells to President Judson, 17 August 1906, Iowa, University of Chicago Special Collections, Newspapers 11.

79 The quotation shows that sociologists had already developed their fatal ability to denature the fascinating. *New York Times,* 22 April 1918, 9:2. The Thomas affair is reported in the New York Times, 13 April 18:6; 14April 19:6; 16April 11:2; 17April 13:3; 20 April 13:5, 1918.

80 Interview with Everett C. Hughes, Cambridge, Mass., 26 September 1963.

81 Coser, 'Sociology of Social Conflict', p. 92.

82 Robert E. Park, 'Sociology and the Social Sciences', *American Journal of Sociology*, 26 (1120-21): 401-24; 27 (1921-22): 1-21; 169-83; reprinted in Park, *Society* (Glencoe, Ill.: Free Press) pp. 187-242. The reference is to pp. 229-31.

83 Pauline V. Young (with Calvin F. Schmid), *Scientific Social Surveys and Research. An Introduction to the Background, Content, Methods and Analysis of Social Studies* (New York, 1939), p. 26; the quotation is from Paul U. Kellogg, *The Pittsburgh District: Civic Frontage*, vol. 1, p. 493, quoted in Young, p. 22.

84 Paul U. Kellogg, 'Spread of the Survey Idea', *Proceedings of the Academy of Political and Social Sciences*, (July 1912), See Young, *Scientific Social Surveys*, p. 23.

85 Kellogg, *The Pittsburgh District*, p. 495, quoted in Young, *Scientific Social Surveys*, p. 22; Robert E. Park, 'Sociology and the Social Sciences', p. 231.

86 Ernest W. Burgess, 'The Social Survey: a field for constructive service by departments of sociology', *American Journal of Sociology*, 21 (January 1916): 492, quoted in Young, *Scientific Social Surveys*, p. 50.

87 Mary K. Simkovitch, quoted in Young, *Scientific Social Surveys*, p. 3.

88 Small quoted in Barnes, Introduction to the History of Sociology, p. 777. Two years earlier he had written to Judson that social science was at the cross roads 'going through the motions of research' but 'no one seems to have any vision of a function for social science as a whole,' Small to Judson, 3 November 1922, University of Chicago Presidential Files, 'Social Science', University of Chicago.

89 Park, 'Sociology and the Social Sciences', p. 229.

90 Howard Odum, *American Sociology. The Story of Sociology in the U.S. Through 1950* (New York, 1951), p. 292. Lee Davids, 'Franklin Henry Giddings: Overview of a Forgotten Pioneer', *Journal of the History of the Behavioral Sciences* 4 (January 1968) 62-73. See, for example, T. J. Jones, *The Sociology of a New York City Block* (1904).

91 Robert L. Faris, *Chicago Sociology, 1920-1932* (San Francisco, 1967) pp. 30-31.

92 Ibid., pp. 26-27; Odum, *American Sociology*, p. 168.

93 Ernest W. Burgess and Donald J. Bogue, *Contributions to Urban Sociology*, p. 3.

94 Interview with Walter C. Reckless, Montreal, 3 September 1964. Interview with Everett C. Hughes, Cambridge, Mass., 21 May 1965.

95 Interview with Winifred Raushenbush, 14 March 1965; Winifred Raushenbush, 'Robert Ezra Park, 1864 -1944: a memoir', Park-Raushenbush; Faris, *Chicago Sociology*, p. 29; Norman Hayner and Una M. Hayner, Diary 1921, 10, 11 October 1921, in possession of Professor Norman Hayner, University of Washington.

96 Nels Anderson to the writer; Harold D. Lasswell, Yale University Law School, to the writer, 9 December 1965.

97 Hayner and Hayner, Diary, 22 June 1922; Erle F. Young, 'A Sociological explorer: Robert E. Park', *Sociology and Social Research*, 27, no. 6 (July-August, 1944): 436-39.

98 Ellsworth Faris, "Robert E. Park, 1864-1944," *American Sociological Review*, 9, no. 3 (June 1944): 322-25.

99 Park's autobiographical note in Odum, *American Sociology*, p. 132.

100 Herbert Blumer to the writer, Department of Sociology, University of California at Berkeley, 13 December 1963.

101 Norman Hayner, Diary, entry for 10 January 1922.

102 Leslie A. White to the writer, 15 November, 1964.

103 Herbert Blumer to the writer, 13 December 1963; Erle F. Young, 'A Sociological Explorer: Robert E. Park', *Sociology and Social Research*, 27 (July-August, 1944): 436-39.

104 Robert E. Park, 'Understanding a Folk Culture', introduction to *The Shadow of the Plantation* by Charles S. Johnson (Chicago, 1934) reprinted in Robert E. Park, *On Social Control and Collective Behavior* edited by Ralph H. Turner (Chicago and London, University of Chicago Press, 1967) pp. 19-32, quotations pp. 23, 25.

105 Nels Anderson, quoted by Everett C. Hughes, interview in Cambridge, Mass., 26 September 1963.

106 For example, Everett C. Hughes, *Men and their Work* (Glencoe, Ill., 1958); Erving Goffman, *The Presentation of Self in Everyday Life* (Edinburgh, 1956).

107 Saul Alinsky to the writer, Chicago [1965].

108 Interview with Everett Hughes, Cambridge, Mass., 21 May 1965. Everett C. Hughes, 'A Study of a Secular Institution: the Chicago Real Estate Board', Ph.D. dissertation, Chicago, 1928.

109 Leonard D. White, 'The Local Community Research Committee and the Social Science Research Building', in T.B. Smith and Leonard D. White eds., *Chicago: an Experiment in Social Science Research* (Chicago, 1929), pp. 20-32; Leonard D. White, 'Cooperation with Civic and Social Agencies', ibid., pp. 33-46. Robert E. L. Faris, *Chicago Sociology*, pp. 53-54; *1923 Report of the Local Community Research Committee: The Social Science Group, The University of Chicago* (University of Chicago Files, 'Social Science',) p. 111.

110 Faris, *Chicago Sociology*, p. 52; Everett C. Hughes, 'Plan for a book on Robert E. Park', Ms. in possession of the author; Ernest W. Burgess, 'The Contribution of Robert E. Park', *Sociology and Social Research*, 29 (March-April 1945): 255-61, especially pp. 260-61.

111 Ernest W. Burgess and Donald J. Bogue, 'Research in Urban Society: A Long View', in Burgess and Bogue eds., *Contributions to Urban Sociology* (Chicago, 1964), p. 6; 'Robert Park Material on the Use of Life Histories', Park-Raushenbush, Box B. Rural sociology had an initial advantage over urban sociology since much research into rural conditions was undertaken by the land grant colleges and subsidized by the government.

112 T.V. Smith and Leonard D. White, eds. *Chicago: an Experiment in Social Science Research* (Chicago 1929), pp. 36-37. Burgess and Bogue, *Contributions to Urban Sociology*, pp. 6-7.

113 *Report of the Laura Spelman Rockefeller Memorial, 1927-8* (New York, 1929), pp. 17-18; Raymond B. Fosdick, *The Story of the Rockefeller Foundation* (New York, 1952), p. 199.

114 *Report of the Laura Spelman Rockefeller Memorial, 1932* (New York, 1933), pp. 10, 14.

115 Raymond B, Fosdick, *Story of the Rockefeller Foundation*, p. 194.

116 *Report of the Laura Spelman Rockefeller Memorial*, p. 11.

117 Fosdick, *Story of the Rockefeller Foundation*, p. 196; *Report of the Laura Spelman Rockefeller Memorial 1932*, p. 12.

118 See for example the complaints in *The Institute of Social and Religious Research 1921-34* (New York, 1934), p. 29.

119   Smith and White, *Chicago: an Experiment*, p. 42.

120   Fosdick, *Story of the Rockefeller Foundation*, p. 202.

121   Ibid., p. 207.

122   Beardsley Ruml, 'Recent Trends in Social Science', in Leonard D. White, ed., *The New Social Science* (Chicago, 1930), p. 105.

123   Fosdick, *Story of the Rockefeller Foundation*, p. 197.

124   'Basis of Survey of Race Relations on the Pacific Coast; adopted by the regular committee on the Pacific Coast and the Institute of Social and Religious Research after negotiations during July, August and September, 1923', Folder: 'The Oriental Study. Correspondence File', 4 October 1923, Park-Raushenbush.

125   Interview with Winifred Raushenbush, 14 March 1965.

126   Emory S. Bogardus, *The New Social Research* (Los Angeles, 1926), p. 29.

127   Park to Ruth H. Grenier, 7 May 1924, Park-Raushenbush, Box A, Folder, 'Race Relations, Miscellaneous.' Park to Eliot G. Mears, 9 December 1924, ibid., Box A, Folder, 'Eliot G. Mears.'

128   Emory S. Bogardus, *The New Social Research*, pp. 16-17. It is an indication of how far Park's associates incorporated his ideas into their own work that the above is actually a direct quotation from a letter of Park to Bogardus, 4 February 1925, Park-Raushenbush, Box A, Folder, 'Emory S. Bogardus', although it is not acknowledged as such.

129   Park to William C. Smith, University of Southern California, 10 November 1924, Park-Raushenbush, Box A, Folder, 'Race Relations, Miscellaneous.' He added that the Institute however realized that the project would be much cheaper if done by the universities. Park to Mears, 24 April 1925, ibid., Box A, Folder 'Eliot G. Mears.'

130   Galen Fisher to Eliot Mears, telegram 4 April 1925, Park-Raushenbush, Box A, Galen Fisher File.

131   Winifred Raushenbush to the writer 15 January 1975.

132   Interview with Winifred Raushenbush, 9 April 1965, Peterborough, N.H. *Tentative Findings of the Survey of Race Relations* (Stanford, Calif., 1925), p. 18.

133   Interview with Winifred Raushenbush, 9 April 1965.

134   Park to Galen Fisher, 21 April 1925, Park-Raushenbush, Box A, Galen Fisher File.

135   Emory S. Bogardus to the writer, 12 September 1963.

136   Erle F. Young, 'A Sociological Explorer.'

137   'What other people have said about Park', Park-Raushenbush, Box C. Park himself did not empoy the term 'empathy', defined as a 'power of projecting one's personality into, and so fully understanding, the object of contemplation' which yet did not involve sympathy or agreement with the object; its first use in English, as an equivalent of the German *einfuhlung*, came as late of 1912. (*Shorter Oxford English Dictionary* (Oxford, 1946), II, 2110.) However, the

term clearly sums up his effort to transmit an understanding both intimate and detached. The student's inability to make this distinction in practice suggests the difficulty of transmitting a scholarly attitude, and the way in which a word like *empathy* (or that other verbal cornerstone of the scholarly attitude, *disinterested*) may come to seem meaningless, contradictory, or unhealthy as the mental climate of the intelligentsia moves toward a demand that the scholar join some tribe of faith. See Gouldner, *The Coming Crisis*, p. 103.

138 Gouldner, *The Coming Crisis*, p. 103. Friedrichs's *A Sociology of Sociology*, esp. pp. 104-109, 206-12, explores the multiple meanings that have given the concept of 'objectivity' much of its power. It is used here in the sense of value-neutrality and universal empathy. Friedrichs sees the Chicago doctrine of value-neutrality as stemming from the work of G.H.Mead, but while Mead may have given a more refined statement, Park's position seems to stem from personal temperament and the intellectual sources, German and American, which he shared with Mead.

139 Ernest W. Burgess, quoted in the Introduction by Ralph H. Turner, to Robert E. Park, *On Social Control and Collective Behavior*, p. xvi.

140 Park to M. van der Veer of the *Birmingham News*, 23 April 1937, Park Collection, Fisk University; interview with Everett Hughes, Cambridge, Mass., 21 May 1965.

141 See Walter Kaufmann, *Hegel* (London, 1966; first pub., 1965), section 28, esp. pp. 133-135.

142 Robert E. Park, 'The Nature of Race Relations', in Edgar T. Thompson ed., *Race Relations and the Race Problem (1939)* reprinted in Park, *Race and Culture* (Glencoe, Ill., Free Press, 1950) pp. 81-116, quotation p. 90.

143 James Q. Wilson, 'Crime and the Criminologists', *Commentary*, 58 (July 1974): 47-53. On objectivity as a component of the ideology of modern scholarship, see Richard Hofstadter and Walter P. Metzger, *The Development of Academic Freedom in the United States* (New York, 1955), passim., esp. Metzger's chapters on 'Darwinism' and 'The German Influence', Also Veysey, *Emergence of the American University* (Chicago, 1965), pp. 132-49.

144 'To Robert E. Park', 12 February 1938, Park-Rausehnbush, Box C or XXX, folder, 'What other people have said about Park.'

145 Emory S. Bogardus to the writer, 12 September 1963; William J. Goode and Paul K. Hatt, *Methods in Social Research* (New York, 1952), p. 243.

146 Helen MacGill Hughes, 'Park, Robert E. ', *International Encyclopedia of the Social Sciences,* vol. 2, pp. 416-19; interview with Winifred Raushenbush, 14 March 1965.

147 Ralph H. Turner, Introduction to Park, *On Social Control*, p. x.

148 Ibid., xvii; Edward Shils, *The Present State of American Sociology* (Glencoe, Ill., 1948), p. 11.

149 Harold D. Lasswell to the writer, Yale University Law School, 9 December 1965.

150 Shils, *Present State*, pp. 10-11.

151 See, for example, R. Heberle, review of Park's *Society; American Journal of Sociology*, 62 (July 1956): 97-98; J. Milton Yinger, review of *Society; Annals of the American Academy of Political and Social Science*, 305 (May 1956): 196-97; Oliver C. Cox, 'The Racial Theories of Robert E. Park and Ruth Benedict', *Journal of Negro Education*, 13 (Fall 1944): 452-63. The phrase 'kaleidoscopic intellectual style' is from p. 458 of Cox.

152 Herbert Blumer to the writer, University of California, Berkeley, 13 December 1963.

Chapter 5

1 Ralph H.Turner, Introduction to Robert E.Park, *On Social Control and Collective Behavior* (Chicago: University of Chicago Press, 1967), p. xxv.

2 Robert E.Park, 'Human Migration and the Marginal Man', *American Journal of Sociology*, 33 (May 1928): 881-93, reprinted in Park, *Race and Culture* (Glencoe, Ill.: Free Press, 1950), pp. 345-56, quotation, p. 353.

3 Robert E.Park, 'Politics and "The Man Farthest Down" ' Introduction to Harold F.Gosnell, *Negro Politicians* (Chicago, 1935), pp. xiii-xxv, reprinted in Park, *Race and Culture*, pp. 166-76, quotation p. 167.

4 William Wordsworth, *Prelude*, Book 7.

5 The phrase is Charles Dickens' in *Dombey and Son*, quoted in Raymond Williams, 'Literature and the City', *Listener*, 23 November 1967, p. 655. Irving Howe points out that Dickens was particularly important in fashioning a set of categories with which to approach the city. He was 'the first to write the novel of the city as some enormous, spreading creature that has gotten out of control, an Other apart from the men living within it'. Irving Howe, 'The City in Literature', *Commentary*, 51, no. 5 (May 1971): 61-68. Another source for people seeking imagery to express their concern for the degeneration of modern life was Ruskin, whose theories often paralleled those of Marx noted later. A brief account of Ruskin's influence on the first generation of American social settlement workers is in Allen F.Davis, *Spearheads for Reform: the Social Settlements and the Progressive Movement, 1890-1914* (New York, 1967), pp. 3-7, 29, 38, 41, 47. Steven Marcus has pointed out the conceptual transfer from Victorian literature to American sociology on a more abstract level in an important article, 'Human Nature, Social Orders, and 19th Century Systems of Explanation: Starting In With George Eliot', *Salmagundi*, no. 28 (Winter 1975), pp. 20-42.

6 On the social origins of the early American sociologists, see C.Wright Mills, 'The Professional Ideology of Social Pathologists', *American Journal of Sociology* 49 (September 1942): 165-80; Fred H.Matthews, 'White Community and "Yellow Peril",' *Mississippi Valley Historical Review* (March 1964): 612-33; Howard W.Odum, *American Sociology* (New York 1951). The most celebrated thinker to employ a political category was of course Tocqueville, who ascribed among other traits the 'loneliness' of modern man not to 'indus-

trialism' or 'the City', but to 'democracy'. Alexis de Tocqueville, *Democracy in America*, vol. 2, Book 2, (Philips Bradley ed., New York, 1951; first pub. 1840): pp. 98-99.

7 Adrienne Koch and William Peden, eds., *The Life and Selected Writings of Thomas Jefferson* (Garden City, N.Y., 1944), p. 280 (*Notes on Virginia*, 1784, Query xix). William W.Freehling, 'Spoilsmen and Interests in the Thought and Career of John C.Calhoun', *Journal of American History*, 52 (June 1965): 25-42. Lois W.Banner, 'Religious Benevolence as Social Control', *Journal of American History*, 60 (June 1973): 23-41. The fear that opulence, concentration, and the corruption of politics by special interests would undermine the civic virtue of a healthy society is a major theme of Robert Kelley's important study, *The Transatlantic Persuasion: the Liberal-Democratic Mind in the Age of Gladstone* (New York, 1969), esp. pp. 329-34 on Grover Cleveland and pp. 386-98 on the Canadian, Alexander Mackenzie. J.G.A. Pocock, *The Machiavellian Moment* (Princeton, 1975), is a magisterial treatment of the concept of political virtue through the eighteenth century.

8 Gaillard Hunt, ed., *The Writings of James Madison* (New York, 1900-1910), vol. 6, p. 96; Aristotle, *Politics*, Book 1; Koch and Peden, eds., *Selected Writings of Jefferson*; for the continuance of the tradition into early sociology see Albert L.Anderson, *The Country Town. A Study in Rural Evolution* (New York, 1906), especially the introduction by Josiah Strong. Leo Marx, *The Machine in the Garden: Technology and the Pastoral Ideal in America* (New York, 1964), pp. 124-27.

9 Henry Thoreau, 'Sounds' (1854), Philip Van Doren Stern, ed., *The Annotated Walden* (New York, 1970), p. 248; James Fenimore Cooper, *Home as Found* (New York, 1896, first ed. 1838), *passim*, esp. ch. 2; Harry Levin, *The Power of Blackness* (New York, 1958), p. 241; Anselm Strauss, *Images of the American City* (New York, 1961), p. 106; Anderson, *Country Town*, pp. 204-205; Henry F.May, *Protestant Churches and Industrial America* (New York, 1949), pp. 112-24; Morton and Lucia White, *The Intellectual versus the City; Thomas Jefferson to Frank Lloyd Wright* (Cambridge, Mass., 1962), *passim*, esp. pp. 95-138 and pp. 155-78 on Park and Dewey. Oscar Handlin and John Burchard, ed., *The Historian and the City* (Cambridge, Mass., 1963), especially the essays of Morton White and Frank Friedel, pp. 84-94 and pp. 115-20. While the Whites' critique of 'romanticism' as the source of American hostility to the city was salutary, it may have discouraged the perception that another single (though internally complex) ideological tradition, the classic theory of the conditions of a self-governing society, does underlie urbanist writings both 'amateur' and 'professional' from the 1780s through the 1930s, if not beyond. Further, and understandably due to the merging of categories in the subject itself, the Whites, like many of the urban critics they discuss, tend to conflate the effects of urbanism, industrialism, and the division of labor, as well as oversimplifying Park's ambivalent and differentiated reaction to the city. Richard Wohl, 'The "Rags to Riches Story": an episode of secular idealism', in Reinhard Bendix and Seymour Martin Lipset, ed., *Class, Status and Power* (Glencoe, Ill., 1953), pp. 388-95.

10   W.I.Thomas and F.Znaniecki, *The Polish Peasant in Europe and America*
     (Boston, 1918), vol. 3, pp. 63-64, quoted in Robert E.Park and Ernest
     W.Burgess, *Introduction to the Science of Sociology* (Chicago: University of
     Chicago Press, 1921), p. 58. C.Wright Mills, 'Professional Ideology of Social
     Pathologists', has made a related point about the moral implication of Ameri-
     can social psychology. Whether middlewestern common sense was ultimately
     indebted to Locke and early nineteenth century Christian thought for its
     categories is one of those questions that haunts the border between formal ideas
     and prejudices or 'mentalities'. John L.Thomas' masterly account of 'Romantic
     Reform in America 1815-1865', *American Quarterly* 17 (Winter 1965):
     656-81, certainly suggests greater continuity between the popular and even the
     academic psychology of the 1830s and early 1900s than is often assumed. And,
     if one concentrates on the model of personal and social health offered,
     B.F.Skinner's *Walden Two* (New York, 1948) may be seen as a late, defensive
     version of this ideal, without the ideological faith in 'freedom' which persis-
     tently frustrated its actual realization.

11   Karl Marx, *The German Ideology,* quoted in David McLellan, *Karl Marx. His
     Life and Thought* (New York, 1973), pp. 147-48. An excellent 'placing' of this
     cornerstone of modern radical analysis in its original intellectual context is in
     McLellan, pp. 104-28, 142-50. The desirability of a more complex division of
     labor was a subject of American political discussion. See Herbert Croly, *The
     Promise of American Life* (New York, 1909), pp. 62-65, 102-103, 138-40,
     427-41; and the review of the Progressive debates in Richard Hofstadter, *The
     Age of Reform* (New York, 1955).

12   Milton M.Gordon, *Social Class in American Sociology* (Durham, N.C., 1958),
     ch. 2, esp. pp. 25-32. Harold M.Hodges Jr., *Social Stratification* (Cambridge,
     Mass., 1964), pp. 57-58. The American preference for an 'urban' explanation is
     probably tied closely to the special development of sociology as a 'residual'
     field, and perhaps more loosely to the special status and outlook of the
     bourgeois 'intelligentsia' coming to self-consciousness, with their romantic and
     non-Marxist, almost non-political, style of radicalism. See Christopher Lasch,
     The New Radicalism in America: the Intellectual as a Social Type (New York,
     1964). A stimulating comparison of the Parkian approach to the presented
     pattern of urban segregation with that of Friedrich Engels, which came to hand
     after this section was written, is in David Harvey, *Social Justice and the City*
     (London, 1973), pp. 130-36. On Park's development of 'mobility' as a concept,
     see below at notes 85ff. E.Foxwell and T.C.Farrer, *Express Trains English and
     Foreign. Being a Statistical Account of All the Express Trains of the World with
     Railway Maps of Great Britain and Europe* (London, 1889), esp. 'Some Effects
     of Express Speed', pp. 70-73. These authors do not use the term 'mobility' in
     their ingenious argument for the railway as the source of economic, social, and
     cultural change, but do employ the word 'locomotion', which was later used by
     Park in similar context.

13   Michel Foucault, *Madness and Civilization,* tr. David Cooper (London, 1967),
     pp. 212-14; George Rosen, *Madness in Society* (New York, 1969; first pub.
     1968), pp. 181-82.

14 Philip Wiener, 'George M.Beard and Freud on American Nervousness', *Journal of the History of Ideas,* 17 (April 1956): 269-74. On the frequent laments during the nineteenth century that the advance of civilization led to a greater incidence of mental illness, see Rosen, *Madness,* ch. 6, pp. 172-94; Norman Dain, *Concepts of Insanity in the United States 1789-1865* (New Brunswick, N.J., 1964), pp. 88-95, 234-36.

15 While the response delineated here was dominant among 'serious' thinkers, on both sides of the Atlantic, there was also a tradition of celebration of urban traits that went beyond the self-congratulation of Chambers of Commerce and journalists who reported growth trends. B.I.Coleman in *The Idea of the City in 19th Century Britain* (London, 1973), pp. 227-30, notes the persistence of a celebratory mood in such writers as Conan Doyle. Sherlock Holmes' famous defense of urban density as facilitating the rule of law was an expression of an anti-pastoral mode of analysis that would find sympathy in Park if not in all the Chicago monographs:

> It is my belief, Watson, founded upon my experience, that the lowest and vilest alleys in London do not present a more dreadful record of sin than does the smiling and beautiful countryside. ... The pressure of public opinion can do in the town what the law cannot accomplish. There is no lane so vile that the scream of a tortured child, or the thud of a drunkard's blow, does not beget sympathy and indignation among the neighbours, and then the whole machinery of justice is ever so close that a word of complaint can set it going, and there is but a step between the crime and the dock.

Arthur Conan Doyle, 'The Adventure of the Copper Beeches', *The Complete Sherlock Holmes* (Garden City, N.Y., n.d.) p. 369. For a parallel response in the U.S., see Morton and Lucia White's discussion of William James in *The Intellectual versus the City,* ch. 9. The perceptive essay by Donald J. Olsen, 'Victorian London: Specialization, Segregation and Privacy', *Victorian Studies* 17 (March 1974): 265-78, fuels the generalization that the actual development of the nineteenth century city was a working-out of classical-liberal ideology and expectations, while the critical tradition expressed the fears of organicists about the viability of a privatistic, segmented society.

16 Robert E.Park, 'The City: Suggestions for the Investigation of Human Behavior in the City Environment', *American Journal of Sociology,* 20 (March 1915): 577-612, quotation p. 608; also in Park, Burgess and McKenzie, *The City* (Chicago: University of Chicago Press, 1925), pp. 1-46. Henry D.Thoreau, *Walden or Life in the Woods* (Boston 1856), especially the opening chapter, 'Economy'.

17 Park, notes for his course on the 'Crowd and the Public', Park-Hughes.

18 Mary Borden, 'Chicago Revisited', *Harper's,* 162 (April 1931): 541-47, reprinted in Bessie Pierce, ed., *As Others See Chicago* (Chicago, 1933), p. 490.

19 Edward Wagenknecht, 'The Hog Butcher to the world was home to many writers', *New York Times Book Review* (23 February 1964), p. 4.

20 Theodore Dreiser, *Sister Carrie* (New York, 1965; first pub. 1900), pp. 13-14. Dreiser's vivid impression stressed a quality of Chicago less noted by urban ecologists, its self-feeding dependence for activity on the expectation of further growth. 'Its population was not so much thriving upon established commerce as

upon the industries which prepared for the arrival of others', a statement of dubious literal accuracy but powerful perception. Ibid.

21   Jean Gottmann, *Megalopolis* (Cambridge, Mass., 1961), pp. 188, 163; Bessie Pierce, *As Others See Chicago* (Chicago, 1933), p. 370. For the wild extrapolations of growth made in the 1920s, see Mel Scott, *American City Planning* (Berkeley, Calif., 1969), pp. 212-13.

22   William T.Stead, *If Christ Came to Chicago* (London, 1894), p. 110.

23   Bessie Pierce, *As Others See Chicago*, pp. 376-77; Mary Borden, 'Chicago Revisited', pp. 488-89. The best literary impression of this facet of Chicago is Saul Bellow's *Adventures of Augie March* (New York, 1953).

24   Jean S.Gottmann, *Megalopolis*, p. 19.

25   Norman Hayner and Una M.Hayner, Diary (17 June 1922); Mary Borden, 'Chicago Revisited', p. 489.

26   Floyd Dell, 'Chicago in Fiction', Part 1, *Bookman*, 37 (November 1913): 275; Blanche H.Gelfant, *The American City Novel* (Norman, Okla., 1954), pp. 6-9, 21, notes this as a trait of 'urban' novels generally, but there is an obvious problem of circularity of definition here, reflecting that of urban sociology, which would result in denying James' *Bostonians* the status of 'urban novel'. Dell did admit that Frank Norris and Theodore Dreiser had rather more appreciation of the nuances of locality. Whether this power of specific description is helpful or misleading to the historian has become the subject of a minor scholarly controversy. See Richard Sennett, *Families Against the City* (Cambridge, Mass., 1970); Mark H.Haller, 'Family Fictions', *Reviews in American History* 1 (March 1973): 113-19.

27   Robert E.Park, 'The City as a Social Laboratory', in T.V.Smith and L.White, eds. *Chicago: an Experiment in Social Science Research* (Chicago, 1929), pp. 1-19, reprinted in *The Collected Papers of Robert Ezra Park*, ed. Everett C.Hughes, vol. 2, *Human Communities: the City and Human Ecology* (Glencoe, Ill.: Free Press, 1952), pp. 73-84, quotation p. 78; see also Maurice Stein *The Eclipse of Community* (Princeton, 1960), p. 94.

28   Leonard D.White, 'The Local Community Research Committee and the Social Science Research Building', in Smith and White eds., *Chicago*, pp. 20-32, quotation, p. 20. It may also be that different scholarly generations respond to different styles of theoretical abstraction, that the spatial symbolism of the 'Chicago school' belongs to the same intellectual generation as that of Park's regional contemporary, Frederick Jackson Turner. See Richard Hofstadter, *The Progressive Historians* (New York 1970; first pub. 1968), pp. 100-14. Certainly the expression of what later eras would see as class conflicts in concrete geographical terms was common; Al Smith in the 1880s thought of Central Park as a natural habitat of 'uptowners', the prosperous who could afford to live near the Park. Robert A.Caro, *The Power Broker* (New York, 1974), p. 114. The conceptual gentility involved may be an indication of the strength of egalitarian ideas in nineteenth century America which converted the 'vertical' picture of a class system into the 'horizontal', and less claustrophobic, picture of distribution in space.

29 Hayner and Hayner, Diary, entry for 22 June 1922. The general point is well stated by Maurice R.Stein, *The Eclipse of Community: an Interpretation of American Studies* (Princeton, N.J., 1960), p. 15.

30 Ernest Burgess, 'Basic Social Data', in Smith and White eds., *Chicago*, pp. 47-66, quotation p. 57.

31 Interview with Norman Hayner, Montreal, September 1964; 'Sociology 1917-1930', *Encyclopedia of the Social Sciences*, vol. 1, p. 204.

32 Robert E.L.Faris, *Chicago Sociology, 1920-1932* (San Francisco, 1967), Appendix A, pp. 135-36; Park, 'The City', *American Journal of Sociology*, 20 (March 1915): 577-612; reprinted with revisions in Robert E.Park, Ernest W.Burgess, and Roderick D.McKenzie, *The City* (Chicago, 1925), pp. 1-46.

33 Park, 'The City', reprinted in Park, *Human Communities*, pp. 13-51, quotation p. 14.

34 Cf. Georg Simmel, 'The Metropolis and Mental Life', in Kurt Wolff, ed., *The Sociology of Georg Simmel* (Glencoe, Ill., 1964, first pub. 1950), pp. 409-24. Park, 'The City as a Social Laboratory', p. 84.

35 Park, untitled Ms. in Park Collection, Social Science Institute, Fisk University, p. 7. Ralf Darhrendorf criticises much modern sociology, particularly that of Talcott Parsons, as not growing out of 'puzzlement over specific, concrete ... riddles of experience'; 'Out of Utopia: toward a Reorientation of Sociological Analysis', *American Journal of Sociology*, 64 (September 1958): 115-17.

36 Park, *The Principles of Human Behavior* (Chicago, Zalas Corp., 1915). Robert E.Park and Ernest W. Burgess, *Introduction to the Science of Sociology* (Chicago, 1924).

37 Howard Odum, *American Sociology* (New York, 1951), p. 169; sales figures are from Morris Janowitz's preface to the latest reissue of Park and Burgess (Chicago, 1969), p. vii; Saul Bellow, in his novel *Herzog*, pictures a typical Chicago student of the 1930s as clutching the 'grimy texts — Park and Burgess, Ogburn and Nimkoff'. Saul Bellow, *Herzog* (New York, 1961); paperback edition, p. 157.

38 Robert E.L.Faris, *Chicago Sociology 1920-1932* (San Francisco, 1967), p. 38; Morris Janowitz, preface to Park and Burgess, *Introduction* (Chicago, 1969).

39 Albion W.Small to President Judson, 6 May 1921, Small Papers, University of Chicago Library. The *Introduction* was used at Chicago for both the introductory course for sophomores and for graduate students. Faris, *Chicago Sociology*, p. 41.

40 Don Martindale, *The Nature and Types of Sociological Theory* (London, 1961), p. 256.

41 Park, 'The Problem of Cultural Differences', Preliminary paper prepared for the Institute of Pacific Relations, Hangchow, China, 1931. Reprinted in Park, *Race and Culture*, pp. 3-14; quotation p. 12.

42 Park, 'Community Organization and Juvenile Delinquency', in Park, Burgess and McKenzie, *The City*; reprinted in Park, *Human Communities*, pp. 52-63; quotations pp. 59,60.

43 Park, 'Culture and Civilization', previously unpublished paper, in Park, *Race and Culture*, pp. 15-23, reference p. 22; Everett C.Hughes, Preface to *Human Communities*, p. 6.

44 Park, 'Missions and the Modern World', *American Journal of Sociology*, 50 (November 1944): 177-83, reprinted in Park, *Race and Culture*, pp. 331-41, reference pp. 338-39.

45 Park passed easily from specific observation to broader sociological observation and then on to philosophical speculation, as can be seen in the following extract from a letter to Roderick D.McKenzie.

> This distinction [between ecological and economic organization] connects up, in my mind, with a number of other things that strike me as interesting and important. For example, I think of the division of labor as being largely responsible for science and for the type of society which we have achieved through the division of labor and the application of science. Cultural organization, however, represented by culture, tradition and public opinion, is a control organization. You see you get the contrast between intelligence and will. I think that has great possibilities of elaboration.

Park to Roderick D.McKenzie, 31 January 1925, Park-Raushenbush, Box C, Folder 'Letters about the Pacific Coast Survey, etc.'

46 Wilhelm Windelband, *Geschichte und Naturwissenschaft*, (Strassburg, 1900) quoted in Park, 'Sociology and the Social Science', *Society* (Glencoe, Ill., Free Press, 1955), pp. 187-242, quotation p. 195. This is a reprinting of chapter 1 in the *Introduction to the Science of Sociology*.

47 Park, 'Sociology and the Social Sciences', p. 209.

48 Park and Burgess, *Introduction*, p. 11.

49 Interview with Everett C.Hughes, Cambridge, Mass, 21 May 1965.

50 Ralph Turner, Introduction to Park, *On Social Control and Collective Behavior*, p. xxii. For a discussion of the importance of the ideas of organic equilibrium in the social sciences see Cynthia Eagle Russett, *The Concept of Equilibrium in American Social Thought* (New Haven and London, 1966).

51 Robert E.Park, 'Human Ecology', *American Journal of Sociology*, 42 (July 1936): 1-15, reprinted in Park, *On Social Control and Collective Behavior*, pp. 69-84; the quotation from Charles Elton's article on 'Animal Ecology', from *Encyclopaedia Britannica* (14th ed.), appears on p. 73.

52 Robert E.Park, 'Succession, an Ecological Concept', *American Sociological Review*, 1 (April 1936): 171-79, reprinted in Park, *On Social Control and Collective Behavior*, pp. 85-94, quotation p. 87.

53 Ibid., p. 85.

54 Ibid., p. 89.

55 Park, 'Human Ecology', p. 86. Park was here generalizing the concept of 'succession' to apply to the phenomena he elsewhere subsumed under the rubric 'natural history', though he does not use the words 'natural history' at this point. See also Park, 'The Natural History of the Newspaper', *American Journal of Sociology*, 29 (November 1923): 273-89, reprinted in Park, *On Social Control*, pp. 97-113.

56 Park, 'The American Newspaper', *American Journal of Sociology*, 32 (March 1927): 806, quoted in Ralph Turner, Introduction to Park, *On Social Control*, p. xxiii.

57 Stanford Lyman has developed this point in his searching *The Black American in Sociological Thought* (New York, 1972), esp. pp. 29-35. It seems to me that the formal rigidities which Lyman finds in the Aristotelianism of Park's thought are less crippling in actual application, perhaps just because theoretical consistency was less important to him than a flexible search for insight.

58 Emory S.Bogardus, *Immigration and Race Attitudes* (New York, 1928); Lyford Edwards, *The Natural History of Revolution* (Chicago, 1927); Everett Stonequist, *The Marginal Man* (New York, 1937).

59 Ralph H.Turner, Introduction to Park, *On Social Control*, p. xli.

60 Park and Burgess, *Introduction*, p. 875.

61 Park, Course notes for 'The Crowd and the Public', Park-Hughes. For an alternative way of organizing the data of collective behavior see Neil J.Smelser, *Theory of Collective Behavior* (London, 1962).

62 Robert E.Park, Introduction to *The Pilgrims of Russian-Town*, by Pauline V.Young (Chicago, 1932), pp. xi-xx, reprinted in Park, *On Social Control*, pp. 240-48; see also the Introduction to this volume by Ralph H.Turner, p. xliii.

63 Park, 'The Natural History of the Newspaper', p. 97,

64 Park and Burgess, *Introduction*, pp. 29-30.

65 Eugenius Warming, *Plantesamfund* (1895), translated as *Oecology of Plants* (Oxford, 1909). For Park's use of Warming, see Park and Burgess, *Introduction*, pp. 175-82, p. 218, p. 555; Park, 'The Urban Community as a Spatial Pattern and a Moral Order' (1925), in *Human Communities* (Glencoe, Ill., Free Press, 1952), p. 165; and 'Symbiosis and Socialization' (1939), ibid., pp. 250-51.

For the early history of plant and animal ecology, see W.C.Allee, Alfred E.Emerson, Orlando Park, Thomas Park and Karl P.Schmidt, *Principles of Animal Ecology* (Philadelphia and London, 1949), pp. 13-72; J.Richard Carpenter, *An Ecological Glossary* (New York, 1962; first pub. Norman, Okla., 1938), pp. 1-8; Amos H.Hawley, *Human Ecology: a Theory of Community Structure* (New York, 1950), pp. 3-10.

Any attempt to reconstruct the exact lines of influence upon Park's development of 'human ecology' is largely circumstantial since the memories of his surviving students did not include the late 1910s. We know that Park was an omnivorous reader, and that his work in 'crowd psychology' had sensitized him to analogies between animal and human behavior of the type which were common at the time. See, for example, the essay by the entomologist William Morton Wheeler, 'The Ant Colony as an Organism', *J.Morphology*, 22 (1911): 307-25, and the excerpts from other work by Wheeler along similar lines in Park and Burgess, *Introduction*, pp. 169-72, 182-84. At the zenith of faith in natural science, the desire to explain human behavior by analogy would be powerful. Beyond that, the intricate and easily moralized systemness of ecology makes it a perfect model for secular theodices, as has been witnessed in the last decade. See Donald Fleming, 'Origins of the New Conservation Movement', *Perspectives in American History*, 6 (1972): 7-91.

66 Park, 'The City: Suggestions for the Investigation of Human Behavior in the Urban Environment', in Park, Burgess, McKenzie, *The City* (Chicago, 1925; second ed., ed. Morris Janowitz, Chicago, 1967).

67 Park and Burgess, *Introduction*, pp. 555, 504-44. On the differences between 1921 and 1924 editions, see the 'Preface to the Second Edition', ibid., p. ix.

68 Ibid., pp. 509, 508. The fragment on symbiosis from Wheeler's *Ants* is at pp. 182-84.

69 Ibid., pp. 511-12. On the same page Park moved from definition to political speculation about the virtues and vices of a competitive society.

70 Park, 'The City as a Social Laboratory', Smith and White, *Chicago* (1929), p. 10. Park's thinly disguished fatalism, together with his willingness to dilute his theory by attempting to accommodate common-sense reality, appear in the phrase, 'or the place where he *must*, live'.

71 On Darwin's sources, Park, 'Human Ecology', *Human Communities*, p. 146. Compare Park's references to ecology in Park and Burgess, *Introduction; 'The Urban Community as a Spatial Pattern and a Moral Order'*, and *'Sociology, Community and Society'*, of 1925 and 1929 respectively, in *Human Communities*, pp. 165-209, with the more formal essays of the next decade: 'Dominance' (1934), 'Succession: an Ecological Concept' (1936), and 'Human Ecology' (1936), ibid., pp. 159-164, 223-232, 145-158.
    Even these later essays tend to offer a relatively modest use of specifically ecological concepts to provide a very loose and general theoretical crust over a mass of data and interpretation from political economy and contemporary applied work in urban geography, land values, and descriptive sociology, the latter often the work of Park's own students. The reader is left with the feeling that while a more subtle student might be able to explain the data of urban change through such ideas as 'succession' and 'natural area', Park's loose usage often remained at the level of dramatic metaphor rather than closely articulated theory. As noted earlier, Park often 'bequeathed' a special topic to a student. The inheritor of ecological theory was Roderick D.McKenzie, later of the University of Michigan, whose early formulation, 'The Ecological Approach to the Study of the Human Community', Park, Burgess and McKenzie, *The City*, pp. 63-79, shows a sharper focus than Park then gave but otherwise the same traits as described above.

72 Interviews with Everett C.Hughes, Cambridge, Mass., 26 September 1963, and 21 May 1965. *American Men of Science. A Biographical Directory*, ed. Jacques Cattell Press, 11th ed. (New York, 1965), p. 1410.

73 Park and Burgess, *Introduction*, p. 165; Park, 'Human Ecology', *Human Communities*, pp. 147-48. The boundaries of a community were to be established by observing the limits of the competitive process. Ibid., p. 156.

74 Park, 'The City as Social Laboratory', Smith and White, *Chicago*, p. 11; also in *Human Communities*, p. 80.

75 Park, 'Sociology', Wilson Gee, ed., *Research in the Social Sciences* (New York, 1929), p. 6. This emphasis on individuality and competition reflected Park's strong preference for a 'liberal' sociology which recognized the importance of traits often overlooked by the central tradition of European and post-1935 American sociology. See above, chapter 2.

76 Park, 'The Urban Community as a spatial Pattern and a Moral Order' in Ernest W.Burgess ed., *The Urban Community* (Chicago, 1926), pp. 3-18, reprinted in *Human Communities*, pp. 165-77, 'The City as a Social Laboratory', Smith and White, *Chicago*, pp. 9-10, 'The City' (1925), Park, Burgess, McKenzie, *The City*, pp. 9-12.
   This definition of 'natural areas' created a scholarly debate (with strong resonance into local politics and general intellectual history) that has persisted ever since at varying levels of activity and passion. The most famous name is of course Jane Jacobs, but perhaps the most stimulating clarification of the complex issues is Gerald D.Suttles, *The Social Construction of Communities* (Chicago, 1972). Suttles feels that Park and Burgess misled later commentary by overstressing the homogeneity of ethnic areas, indeed the importance of ethnicity as a definer of natural areas, seeing instead a 'natural' defensive tendency to wall off the local community against heterogenous intruders. But this still leaves the original recruitment of the area to other agencies, though often the projections of the promoter or builder would anticipate the later fears of the residents. See Sam B.Warner, Jr., *Streetcar Suburbs: the Process of Growth in Boston 1870-1900* (Cambridge, Mass., 1962).

77 Park, 'The City as a Social Laboratory', p. 11.

78 Borden, 'Chicago Revisited', p. 495. The classic novelistic accounts of ethnic segregation and hostility in Chicago during the years that Park studied the city are James T.Farrell's *Studs Lonigan* and Richard Wright's *Native Son*. Suttles, *Social Construction*, p. 27, criticizes this formulation as exaggerated because no discoverable zone, except some black areas later, was ethnically homogenous. But the 'ghetto' could be mental, a screening-out of the familiar outsiders, or an adoption of them into the ethnic group.

79 Park, 'Sociology, Community and Society', in Wilson Gee ed., *Research in the Social Sciences* (New York, 1929), pp. 3-49, reprinted in Park, *Human Communities*, pp. 178-209, quotations from pp. 198, 196.

80 Park, 'The City as a Social Laboratory', p. 9.

81 Nels Anderson, *The Hobo: The Sociology of the Homeless Man* (Chicago, 1923); Louis Wirth, *The Ghetto* (Chicago, 1928); Harvey W.Zorbaugh, *The Gold Coast and the Slum* (Chicago, 1929). A complete list of Chicago Ph.D. dissertations in sociology appears in Faris, *Chicago Sociology* pp. 135-40.

82 Frederic C.Thrasher, Abstract of 1926 Ph.D. dissertation, 'The Gang: A Study of 1,313 Gangs in Chicago', quoted in Faris, *Chicago Sociology*, pp. 73-74; See also, Faris, pp. 73-79 and Burgess and Bogue, *Contributions to Urban Sociology*, p. 488.

83 Park, 'The Urban Community as a Spatial Pattern and a Moral Order', p. 61. Researchers in Chicago quickly noticed that a high degree of mobility coincided

with a high degree of 'social disorganization' as defined by rates of alcoholism, suicide, crime, and other quantifiable pathologies. This connection between mobility and pathology was developed by Ernest Burgess, who attempted to correlate social disorganization with changes in city life that could be measured in terms of mobility, and by other Park students such as Harvey W.Zorbaugh, and Robert E.L.Faris and H.Warren Dunham in *Mental Disorders in Urban Areas* (Chicago, 1939), all of whom made much of the connection between social problems and a constantly shifting population. A criticism of the Burgess approach appears in C.Wright Mills 'The Professional Ideology of Social Pathologists', *American Journal of Sociology*, 49 (September 1942): 165-80.

84 Ernest W.Burgess, 'The Growth of the City', in Park, Burgess and McKenzie, *The City*, pp. 50-51. A brief contemporary appraisal of the theory and the alternative formulations it provoked is in Raymond E.Murphy, *The American City* (New York, 1972), pp. 293-309. Jacob Spelt probably speaks for most would-be users when he notes of Toronto that 'the various theoretical concepts ... such as concentric, sectorial, or multiple-nuclei, apply in varying degrees, without any of them providing adequate representation by itself. They are far too generalized'. Spelt, *Toronto* (Don Mills, Ont., 1973), p. 102. David Harvey's *Social Justice and the City* (London, 1973), pp. 130ff, 160ff, contains an ambitious effort to assimilate Parkian ecology to the Marxian framework by specifying the market mechanisms through which spatial distribution expresses class power. An extensive review of the literature of urban location theory is in R.J.Johnston, *Urban Residential Patterns. An Introductory Review* (New York, 1972).

85 Park, 'The Problem of Cultural Differences', *Race and Culture*, p. 15, pp. 12-13. See also Barbara Klose Bowdery, 'The Sociology of Robert E.Park', Ph.D. dissertation, Columbia University, 1951, pp. 48-49.

86 Park, 'Succession, an ecological concept', *American Sociological Review*, 1 (April, 1936): 171-79; reprinted in Park, *Human Communities*, pp. 222-32, quotation p. 232. One notices here Park's awareness of the way in which changes impelled by technology and market forces erode the effect of conscious human control over behavior. The railway, automobile, etc., were all artifacts of human ingenuity, as was the city in a sense, but were not conscious agents of control, and so created unforeseen consequences, unleashed forces which circumvent previous expressions of human will.

87 Park, 'The City as Social Laboratory', p. 79; the classic literary exposition of this process is the fall of Hurstwood in Theodore Dreiser's *Sister Carrie* – another example of the closeness of Park's sociology to literary imagery. One should note that Park uses the concept of mobility in at least three ways: 1. as *cause* of social change, 2. as *index* of social change, 3. as a way of *classifying* social changes.

88 Park, 'The Mind of the Hobo, reflections upon the relation between mentality and locomotion', in Park, Burgess, McKenzie, *The City*, pp. 156-60, reprinted in Park, *Human Communities*, pp. 91-95, reference p. 92. Park, 'Human Migration and the Marginal Man', *American Journal of Sociology*, 33 (May, 1928): 881-93, reprinted in Park, *On Social Control and Collective*

Behavior, pp. 194-106. The source of this idea in Thomas is shown by Park in 'The City', *Human Communities*, pp. 25-29.

89 Park, Burgess, McKenzie, *The City*, p. 27; Park, 'Sociology, Community and Society', in Wilson Gee ed., *Research in the Social Sciences* (New York, 1929), pp. 3-49, reprinted in Park, *Human Communities*, pp. 178-209, quotation p. 189. A fascinating hypothesis to connect the urban experience with modern art forms via the notion of 'mobility' is in Raymond Williams, *The Country and the City* (London, 1973), p. 242.

90 Stow Persons, *Decline of American Gentility* (New York, 1973), outlines a parallel line of descent. The possible literature is vast, but two titles may suggest the continuity. Lionel Trilling's *Sincerity and Authenticity* (Cambridge, Mass., 1972) traces the moral concern with human personality that underlies the sociological study of mobility and its effects; and Bruno Bettelheim and Morris Janowitz, *Social Change and Prejudice* (New York, 1963), exemplifies the concern with mobility in the mid-twentieth century liberal-pluralist context that stressed tolerance as the most fundamental human virtue in a heterogeneous society.

91 Park, 'The Problem of Cultural Differences', *Race and Culture*, pp. 10-11; 'Concept of Position in Sociology', (1925); reprinted under the title, 'The Urban Community as a spatial Pattern and a Moral Order', *Human Communities*, 165-77.

92 Park, 'Culture and Cultural Trends', *Publications American Sociological Society*, 19 (1924): 35.

93 Park, 'Succession, an Ecological Concept', *On Social Control*, p. 93. For the 'softer' view of Thomas, see William I.Thomas and Florian Znaniecki, *The Polish Peasant in Europe and America*, 4 (Boston, 1920): 8-9; 'Change of conditions is a factor, but not a cause of social happenings; it merely furnishes influences which will produce definite effects only when combined with preexisting attitudes and is a cause only together with the latter'. See also ibid., 1 (Boston, 1918): 13. Park, however, usually saw the substructural changes forcing an ultimate reorganization of values, attitudes, and institutions on the cultural level. This reorganization, whose outcome varied with the specific values and institutions of the pre-existing society, could be classified according to his cycle of types of interaction. Since attitudes and institutions had a certain inertia, a period of maladjustment would occur. This model, which Park shared with others of his generation, was codified by William Fielding Ogburn, later a colleague at Chicago, in *Social Change: With Respect to Culture and Original Nature* (New York, 1922). Ogburn coined the phrase 'cultural lag' which has since stuck to the theory. For evidence of its general acceptance, see Stow Persons, *American Minds. A History of Ideas* (New York, 1958), pp. 232-35.

94 Park, 'Human Ecology', *Human Communities*, p. 157. A very late reclassification of orders – territorial, economic, or competitive, cultural – is in 'The City as a Natural Phenomenon', ibid., pp. 118-27.

95 Park, 'Succession, An Ecological Concept', *On Social Control*, pp. 85-94, reference p. 91; Park, 'Human Ecology', ibid., p. 80 *Human Communities*, p. 155.

96 John Dewey, *Democracy and Education* (New York, 1916), p. 5; Robert E.Park, 'The Urban Community as a Spatial Pattern and a Moral Order', *Human Communities*, p. 173; Park, 'Sociology and the Social Sciences', first three chapters of *The Introduction to the Science of Sociology*, reprinted in Park, *Society*, pp. 187-242, reference p. 222.

97 Park, 'Sociology and the Social Sciences', p. 222.

98 Park, 'Reflections on Communication and Culture', *American Journal of Sociology*, 44 (September 1938): 187-205, reprinted in Park, *Race and Culture*, pp. 36-52, quotation, p. 43.

99 Park, 'The Urban Community as a Spatial Pattern and a Moral Order', *Human Communities*, p. 176.

100 Park, 'Human Nature, Attitudes and Mores', in Kimball Young, ed., *Social Attitudes* (New York, 1931), pp. 17-45, reprinted in Park, *Society*, pp. 267-92, quotation p. 284.

101 Park, 'A Memorandum on Rote Learning', *American Journal of Sociology*, 43 (July 1937): 23-36, reprinted in Park, *Race and Culture*, pp. 53-65, quotation p. 63.

102 Park, 'News as a Form of Knowledge', *American Journal of Sociology*, 45 (March 1940): 669-86, reprinted in Park, *Society*, pp. 71-88, quotation p. 79.

103 Park, 'Morale and the News', *American Journal of Sociology*, 47 (November 1941): 360-77, reprinted in Park, *On Social Control*, pp. 249-67, quotation, pp. 253-54. See also Introduction to this volume by Ralph H.Turner, p. xlv.

104 Park, 'Reflections on Communication and Culture'. It may be significant that the anecdote Park chose in this essay to illustrate what transformed a physical fact into a communication involved his being hit on the head by a falling brick and looking up to find a face grinning down at him 'maliciously'. Ibid., p. 38.

105 'The Urban Community as a Spatial Pattern. ... ' Park's reflections upon communication and its varying media are apparently one ancestor of the work of Marshall McLuhan. For the influence of Park on the work of the Canadian economist and historian Harold A.Innis, who had taken his Ph.D. at Chicago, see McLuhan's introduction to the second edition of Innis' *The Bias of Communication* (Toronto, 1971; first ed., 1951).

106 Edwin G.Boring, *A History of Experimental Psychology* (New York, 1950), pp. 205-208; for the development of the 'Chicago school' of psychology see R.E.Faris, *Chicago School of Sociology*, pp. 88-89; Darnell Rucker, *The Chicago Pragmatists* (Minneapolis, 1969), pp. 57-82; Also, two articles by John W.Petras: 'John Dewey and the Rise of Interactionism in American Social Theory' and 'Psychological Antecedents of Sociological Theory in America: William James and James Mark Baldwin', *Journal of the History of the Behavioral Sciences*, 4 (1968), pp. 18-27, 132-42; and, in more detail, Fay B.Karpf, *American Social Psychology* (New York, 1932).

107 Park and Burgess, *Introduction*, p. 76.

108 Luther L.Bernard, *Instinct: A Study in Social Psychology* (Chicago, 1924); Ellsworth Faris, *The Nature of Human Nature* (New York, 1937); Robert E.L.Faris, *Chicago School of Sociology*, pp. 93-97; Donald Fleming, 'Attitude:

The History of a Concept', *Perspectives in American History*, 1 (1967): 287-365.

109 Dennis Wrong, 'The Oversocialized Conception of Man in Modern Sociology', *American Sociological Review*, 26 (April 1961): 183-93. Park was aware of Freud in 1915 and incorporated some of his ideas into his own scheme, e.g., to demonstrate how emotional conflicts can be caused by the suppression of certain memories which then tend to find expression in hysteria or mental illness. *Principles of Human Behavior*, pp. 30-31.

110 George Herbert Mead, *Mind, Self and Society* (Chicago, 1934); R.E.Faris, *Chicago School of Sociology*, pp. 96-99.

111 Park and Burgess, *Introduction to the Science of Sociology*, pp. 188-89. Italics added.

112 William Graham Sumner, *Folkways* (Boston, 1906), chapters 1 and 2.

113 Park and Burgess, *Introduction*, pp. 69-70.

114 Park, 'Sociology and the Social Sciences', p. 240.

115 Park, 'Personality and Cultural Conflict', *Publications, American Sociological Society*, 25 (May 1931): 95-110, reprinted in Park, *Race and Culture*, pp. 357-71, quotation, p. 358.

116 Park, 'Reflections on Communication and Culture', p. 50. In his emphasis on the self-revelatory, therapeutic value of conflict, Park was both Victorian and hyper-modern; his absorption of nineteenth century German philosophy would make his work of at least passing interest with the revival of an interest in dialectical theories after 1960. For Simmel's similar formulation see Don Martindale, *The Nature and Types of Sociological Theory* (London, 1961), p. 245.

117 Park, 'Personality and Cultural Conflict', pp. 358-59.

118 Park, 'Human Nature and Collective Behavior', *American Journal of Sociology*, 32 (March 1927): 695-703, reprinted in Park, *Society*, pp. 13-21, quotation p. 18.

119 Park, 'The City', p. 25; One of Park's most distinguished students, Everett C.Hughes, has done much work on the sociology of professions; see for example, *Men and their Work* (Glencoe, Ill., 1958). For an important trend of thought contemporary with Park arguing that the non-rational basis of identity was most important see Fred H.Matthews, 'The Revolt against Americanism. Cultural Pluralism and Cultural Relativism as an Ideology of Liberation', *Canadian Review of American Studies*, 1, no. 1 (Spring 1970): 4-31.

120 Park and Burgess, *Introduction*, p. 709, and chapter 1, reprinted as 'Sociology and the Social Sciences' in Park, *Society*, pp. 187-242, quotation p. 240. See also Lewis A.Coser and Bernard Rosenberg, *Sociological Theory: a Book of Readings* (New York, 1957), p. 351.

121 Park, 'Human Nature, Attitudes and Mores', pp. 285-86. Park, 'The Concept of Position in Sociology', p. 16.

122 T.H.Marshall, *Sociology at the Crossroads and Other Essays* (London, 1963), p. 214.

123 Park and Burgess, *Introduction*, p. 70.

124 Robert E.Park, 'Sociology and the Social Sciences', p. 240. It is not entirely clear from this brief reference to insanity whether Park considered insanity and sanity as purely social definitions or whether he meant that the personality could not be maintained without continuous reinforcement by society.

125 Park, 'The Urban Community as a Spatial Pattern and a Moral Order', *Human Communities*, p. 176.

126 Park and Burgess, *Introduction*, p. 231. Here again Park owes much to Simmel; see his discussion of 'Discretion', in Kurt H.Wolff, ed., *The Sociology of Georg Simmel* (Glencoe, Ill., 1950), p. 321.

127 Park, 'Personality and Cultural Conflict', *Publications American Sociological Society*, 25 (May 1931): 95-110, reprinted in *Race and Culture*, pp. 357-71, quotation p. 361.

128 The Park quotation, Ibid; Peter L.Berger, *The Precarious Vision* (Garden City, N.Y., 1961), pp. 48-67.

129 Dennis Wrong, 'The Oversocialized Conception of Man in Modern Sociology', p. 118. Ralph H.Turner, Introduction to Park, *On Social Control*, p. xxxix.

130 Peter L.Berger, *Invitation to Sociology* (Harmondsworth, England, 1966; first pub. 1963), pp. 111, 113. This is the sense in which Stanley Elkins has used the theory to explain what he considers the development of a Sambo personality type among Negro slaves. Stanley Elkins, *Slavery: A Problem in American Institutional and Intellectual Life* (Chicago, 1959).

131 Park, 'The Urban Community as a Spatial Pattern and a Moral Order', *Human Communities*, p. 175.

132 Park, 'Community Organization and Juvenile Delinquency', Park, Burgess and McKenzie, *The City*, pp. 99-112, reprinted in Park, *Human Communities*, pp. 52-63, quotation p. 57.

133 Park, 'Human Nature, Attitudes and Mores', p. 291.

134 Park, 'Sociology and the Social Sciences', p. 240.

135 Everett C.Hughes, *Men and Their Work*; Erving Goffman, *The Presentation of Self in Everyday Life* (Edinburgh, 1956). See Helen Swick Perry, 'Introduction', Sullivan, *The Fusion of Psychiatry and Social Science* (New York, 1964), esp. pp. xix-xxvii.

136 Thomas's formulation of 'social disorganization' was discussed in chapter 4 above. Orrin E.Klapp, a later Chicago doctor, has developed the theory of social types in *Heroes, Villains and Fools* (Englewood Cliffs, N.J., 1963); *Symbolic Leaders* (Chicago, 1964). The incisive classification of theories of deviance by Earl Rubington and Martin S.Weinberg — Rubington and Weinberg, *The Study of Social Problems: Five Perspectives* (New York, 1971); Weinberg and Rubington, ed., *The Solution of Social Problems* (New York, 1973) — separates the models of social pathology and social disorganization more thoroughly than those who used the models may have done. There are sufficient similarities between Chicago's 'Lockean' model, in which individual and collectivity are analagous structures of crystallized reactions to experience, and the 'medical' model which sees the healthy organism as one capable of

recovering equilibrium, to make it seem plausible to treat a unit manifesting inner conflict or instability as pathological. David Matza, *Becoming Deviant* (Englewood Cliffs, N.J., 1969), offers the subtlest appraisal of the relation of Chicago sociology to the 'neo-Chicago' studies of such grandstudents as Becker and Goffman. The 'historicizing' of psychiatry, the effort to reinterpret its medical norms as expressions of the ideology of dominant social groups, is especially associated with Thomas S.Szasz in America and Michel Foucault in France; a vigorous summary and attempt at refutation is by Peter Sedgwick, 'Mental Illness *Is* Illness', *Salmagundi* no. 20 (Summer-Fall, 1972), pp. 196-224.

Chapter 6

1 Peter I.Rose, *The Subject is Race: Traditional Ideologies and the teaching of Race Relations* (New York, 1968), pp. 67, 72-73; S.P.Fullinwinder, *The Mind and Mood of Black America* (Homewood, Ill., 1969), p. 101; Fred H.Matthews, 'White Community and "Yellow Peril"', *Mississippi Valley Historical Review* (March 1964); pp. 612-33. One wonders if even his own students grasped Park's interactional view of 'race' relations completely, since when they collected his essays, one important piece dealing with European immigrant groups, 'Immigrant Community and Immigrant Press', was included in Park, *Society: Collective Behavior, News and Opinion, Sociology and Modern Society* (Glencoe, Ill., Free Press, 1955), pp. 152-64, rather than the volume titled *Race and Culture* (Glencoe, Ill., Free Press, 1950).

2 William B.Smith of Tulane University, in *The Nation* 76(5 March 1903): 191. Bruno Bettelheim and Morris Janowitz, *Social Change and Prejudice, including Dynamics of Prejudice* (New York, 1964), p. 247. See also Thomas F.Gossett, *Race: the History of an Idea in America*, (Dallas, 1963), esp. pp. 144-75, and George W.Stocking, Jr., 'Lamarckianism in American Social Science: 1890-1915', *Journal of the History of Ideas*, 23 (April 1962): 239-56. Stocking's collected essays, *Race, Culture and Evolution* (New York, 1968), provide invaluable background. For an effort to clarify the environmentalist and biological streams of thought within the muddy river of 'racial' thinking, see Matthews, 'White Community', esp. pp. 619-25.

3 Stocking, 'Lamarckianism', p. 247.

4 Rose, *The Subject is Race*, p. 65; for Charles H.Cooley's view of the Negro see *Social Process* (New York, 1922), pp. 268-80.

5 William G. Sumner, *Folkways* (Boston, 1911), chapter 1; William I.Thomas, 'The Psychology of Race Prejudice', *American Journal of Sociology,* 9 (March 1904): 609, quoted in Rose, *The Subject is Race*, p. 62. Thomas did, however, believe that 'people prejudiced against one another could learn to live in harmony', ibid.

6 Stocking, 'Lamarckianism'. The current semantic explosion of the term 'racist' is best seen in the disputes over the work of Edward Banfield, *The Unheavenly*

City (Boston, 1970), but is a broader manifestation, not confined to political radicals. Gossett's valuable *Race* comes close to ascribing 'racism' to the conflict theories of Ward, Gumplowicz, and Ratzenhofer. On environmentalist ethics, Gertrude Himmelfarb, *Darwin and the Darwinian Revolution* (Garden City, N.Y., 1959), pp. 379-80; Stow Persons, *American Minds* (New York, 1958), pp. 76, 357-59. A striking expression is in Michel Foucault, *Madness and Civilization*, tr. David Cooper (London, 1967), pp. 217-20.

7 Edward G.Hartmann, *The Movement to Americanize the Immigrant* (New York, 1948). For an essay at appraising the significance of this campaign and its aftermath, cf. Fred H.Matthews, 'The Revolt against Americanism: Cultural Pluralism and Cultural Relativism as Ideologies of Liberation', *Canadian Review of American Studies,* 1 (Spring 1970): 4-31.

8 For representative contemporary opinions, see John Mitchell, 'Immigration and the American Laboring Class', *Annals*, 34 (1909): 125-29; William Z.Ripley, 'Race Progress and Immigration', Ibid., pp. 130-38. A schematic treatment of the general subject is Milton M.Gordon, *Assimilation in American Life* (New York, 1964).

9 Gossett, *Race*, pp. 418-24; Matthews, 'The Revolt Against Americanism', pp. 16-17; George W.Stocking, Jr., 'Franz Boas and the Culture Concept in Historical Perspective', *American Anthropologist*, 68 (August 1966): 867-82; Donald Fleming, 'Attitude: the History of a Concept', *Perspectives in American History*, 1 (1967): 287-365, esp. pp. 328-29.

10 Park, 'The Career of the Africans in Brazil', Introduction to Donald Pierson, *Negroes in Brazil* (Chicago, 1942), pp. xi-xxi, reprinted in *Race and Culture*, pp. 196-203, quotation pp. 198-99.

11 Robert E.Park and Ernest W.Burgess, *Introduction to the Science of Sociology* (Chicago, 1921), p. 505; Barbara Klose Bowdery, 'The Sociology of Robert E.Park', Ph.D. dissertation, Columbia University, 1951.

12 Park and Burgess, *Introduction*, p. 508.

13 Park, 'War and Politics', *American Journal of Sociology* (January 1941), pp. 551-70; reprinted in *Society*, pp. 50-68, quotation p. 68.

14 The exposition here follows closely that of Bowdery, 'Sociology of Park', although I do not agree that Park's theory can apply only to modern western society; it may not be universal, but the status of metics in Greek city states and the Imperial Roman approach to religious diversity as it relates to political authority would suggest it was a more widespread phenomenon.

15 Park and Burgess, *Introduction*, p. 735. For an analysis and critique of this cyclical explanation of human contacts and its later intellectual career, see Stanford M.Lyman, *The Black American in Sociological Thought* (New York, 1972), pp. 27-70.

16 See chapter 4.

17 Park and Miller, *Old World Traits Transplanted* (New York, Harper, 1921). The source for the large role Thomas played in the production of this book is Helen MacGill Hughes, 'Park, Robert E.', *International Encyclopedia of the Social Sciences*, vol. 11, pp. 416-19. Park's book, *The Immigrant Press and its*

Control (New York, Harper, 1922), a study of the role of the foreign language newspapers in the assimilation process, also grew out of his work on the Carnegie study.

18 *Social Science: A Case Book* (Chicago, 1931), pp. 154-75, reprinted in Park, *Society*, pp. 243-66, quotation p. 257.

19 Park, 'Americanization Study, Division of Immigrant Heritages, Life Histories: standpoint and questionnaire', Ms., Park-Raushenbush, Box C or XXX, Folder, 'Letters ... Pacific Coast Survey'.

20 Park, 'A Race Relations Survey', *Journal of Applied Sociology*, 8 (1923): 195-205, reprinted in *Race and Culture*, pp. 158-65, quotations pp. 163-64.

21 'Robert Park material on the use of life histories', Park-Raushenbush, Box B. The great advantage of the personal document approach, particularly in the form of life histories, was that it added a temporal dimension to the spatial dimension of Chicago sociology and forced the investigator to remember that the individual must be studied not merely as a role player, but also as a self-conscious creature who could range in imagination over past and future and thus make his life 'as he projects it ahead of him in imagination, a project'. Park, 'The Sociological Methods of William Graham Sumner, ... ' p. 262.

22 Park to William M.Cooper, 16 February 1938, Park Collection, Fisk University.

23 Park to Galen Fisher, Institute for Social and Religious Research, 21 April 1925, Park-Raushenbush, Box A. File: Race Relations Survey, Galen Fisher.

24 For the conflict of loyalties and identities faced by the second generation see, for example, Park, 'Behind Our Masks', *Survey Graphic*, 56 (May 1926): 135-39, reprinted in *Race and Culture*, pp. 244-55. See also, Oscar Handlin, *The Uprooted* (Boston, 1952), ch. 9; Milton M.Gordon, *Assimilation in American Life*, pp. 112-13.

25 William I.Thomas to Park, 9 June 1924; Park-Raushenbush, Box B, correspondence folder.

26 Park, 'Behind Our Masks', p. 251.

27 Park, 'Our Racial Frontiers on the Pacific', *Survey Graphic*, 9 (May 1926): 192-96, reprinted in *Race and Culture*, pp. 138-51, ref. p. 149; 'Missions and the Modern World', *American Journal of Sociology*, 50 (1944), reprinted in *Race and Culture*, pp. 331-41, ref. p. 333.

28 Park, 'Our Racial Frontier on the Pacific', p. 150.

29 Park, 'Immigrant Heritages', *Proceedings of the National Conference of Social Work, 1921* (Chicago, 1921), pp. 492-97, quotation p. 495; Park and Miller, *Old World Traits Transplanted*, pp. 135-39.

30 Park and Miller, *Old World Traits*, p. 289; Park, 'Immigrant Heritages'; Park *The Immigrant Press* pp. 448-49, 467; Bowdery, 'Sociology of Park'. This interpretation gained classical status over the years, and was later employed extensively by historians. Since the middle 1960s Timothy Smith and his students, and other scholars like Rudolph J.Vecoli and Robert Harney, have complicated what became a stereotype by showing the great degree of 'moder-

nization' through which many immigrants had gone before crossing the Atlantic. As a subject of intellectual history, the theory shows how an evolutionary, determinist, 'conflict' theory could function to combat nativist intolerance at a time when the dominant trend of popular thought was xenophobic.

31 Park, 'Immigrant Heritages', p. 497.

32 Park, 'Personality and Cultural Conflict', *Publications of the American Sociological Society*, 25 (May 1931): 95-110, reprinted in *Race and Culture*, pp. 357-71, quotation pp. 368-69.

33 *Oxford Universal Dictionary on Historical Principles*, third ed. (Oxford, 1955) p. 11.

34 Albert E. Jenks, 'Assimilation in the Philippines as Interpreted in Terms of Assimilation in America', *American Journal of Sociology*, 19 (May 1914): 773.

35 Park, 'Racial Assimilation in Secondary Groups', *Publications of the American Sociological Society*, 8 (1913): 66-83, reprinted in *Race and Culture*, pp. 204-20, quotation pp. 204-205. Park here characteristically neglects the simple act, or faith, of political loyalty.

36 Park, 'Behind Our Masks', p. 251. Italics in original, deservedly so. For all the legitimate objections that can be made to Park's theories, one must also note that his insights have been too sophisticated for their academic audience.

37 This, after all was Park's definition of society: 'the touchstone of society, the thing that distinguishes a mere collection of individuals from a society is not like-mindedness, but corporate action.' 'Sociology and the Social Sciences', *American Journal of Sociology*, 26 (1920-21): 401-24; 27 (1921-22): 1-21; 169-83; reprinted in *Society*, pp. 187-242, quotation p. 227.

38 Park, 'Assimilation, Social', *Encyclopedia of the Social Sciences*, 11 (1935): 281-83, quotation p. 283. Muzafer Sherif concluded from experiments in a boys' camp that while mere social contacts between hostile groups did not necessarily diminish hostility – might indeed intensify it – working together to achieve a necessary common goal in an emergency situation did decisively reduce hostility. 'Hostility gives way when groups pull together to achieve overriding goals which are real and compelling to all concerned.' Muzafer Sherif, 'Experiments in Group Conflict', *Scientific American* (November 1956). The often observed cessation of racial hostility in a battle situation and its increase during 'rest and recreation' seems to confirm this generalization. Park's assumptions here are also very close to those of Booker T. Washington's 'Atlanta Address' (1895): 'In all things that are purely social we can be as separate as the fingers, yet one as the hand in all things essential to mutual progress', Booker T. Washington, *Up From Slavery* (1901): Basil Mathews, *Booker T. Washington: Educator and Interracial Interpreter* (Cambridge, Mass., 1948), p. 87.

39 Park, 'Culture and Cultural Trends', *Publications of the American Sociological Society*, 19 (December 1925): 24-36; reprinted in *Race and Culture*, pp. 24-35, quotation p. 29.

40 Park, 'Assimilation, Social', *Encyclopedia of the Social Sciences*, 2 (1935): 281-83.

41 Park, 'Racial Assimilation in Secondary Groups', pp. 205, 206.

42 Park, 'Behind Our Masks', pp. 254, 253. While working on the Pacific Coast survey, Park not only studied the sociological aspects of Japanese immigrant life – he also read Japanese poetry. Park to Ruth H.Grenier, 7 May 1924, Park-Raushenbush, Box A, Race Relations Survey, Correspondence 1924-25, Folder, 'Race Relations, Misc.'

43 Horace Kallen, 'Democracy versus the Melting-Pot', *Nation*, 100 (18 and 25 February 1915): 190-94, 217-20; 'A Meaning for Americanism', *Immigrants in America Review*, 1916, both reprinted in *Culture and Democracy in the United States (1924)*.

44 Park, 'Americanization Study, Division of Immigrant Heritages, life histories: standpoint and questionnaire', Park-Raushenbush, Box C or XXX, Folder, 'Letters, Pacific Coast Survey, etc', pp. 6-7.

45 Fred H.Matthews, 'White Community and Yellow Peril', p. 284. Park, though, was not an extreme organicist on the European model. Here, as elsewhere, he tried to balance liberal-individualism and organicism in the tradition of Dewey.

46 Park, 'Behind Our Masks', p. 252.

47 Park, 'A Race Relations Survey', p. 160.

48 Park, 'Assimilation Social', p. 282.

49 Ernest W. Burgess, 'Social Planning and Race Relations', Jitsuichi Masuoka and Preston Valien eds., *Race Relations Problems and Theory. Essays in Honor of Robert E.Park.* (Chapel Hill, N.C., 1961), pp. 13-25, reference to p. 17.

50 See, for example, E.A.Ross, 'The Causes of Race Superiority', *Annals, American Academy of Political and Social Science*, 28 (July 1901); *Seventy Years of It* (New York, 1936), pp. 1-25, 70, 223-26; Henry Pratt Fairchild, *Immigration: A World Movement and Its American Significance* (rev. ed., New York, 1925), pp. 100-103, 361-62; *The Melting Pot Mistake* (New York, 1926), p. 74.

   Precisely this, it seems, was the special contribution of Park, Thomas, and the Chicago approach. George Frederickson's *The Black Image in the White Mind: the Debate on Afro-American Character and Destiny 1817-1914* (New York, 1971), chapters 10 and 11, rightly notes that the general framework of Spencerian evolution characterized many theories of race and ethnic relations offered by early sociologists. Most, however, tended to place the period of harmony well in the future, and assume for the present an era of conflict based upon the strength of ingroup consciousness and the need for value-consensus in an effective and just society. Park worked with a different root-metaphor, not that of a Good Society so much as a least-intolerable society, and so could find the basis for short-run toleration.

51 Park, 'Principles of Human Behavior' (1915) reproduced in Park and Burgess, *Introduction*, p. 187.

52 Park, 'Education in its Relation to the Conflict and Fusion of Cultures', *Publications of the American Sociological Society*, 13 (1918): 38-63, reprinted in *Race and Culture*, pp. 261-83, reference p. 264.

53 Park, 'Human Migration and the Marginal Man', *American Journal of Sociology*, 33 (May 1928): 881-93, reprinted in *Race and Culture*, pp. 345-56,

reference p. 354. For Park's comment on the widely held theory of the degeneracy of mixed bloods, see 'Mentality of Racial Hybrids', *American Journal of Sociology*, 36 (January 1931): 534-51, also in *Race and Culture*, pp. 377-92.

54 Park, 'Cultural Conflict and the Marginal Man', Introduction to E.V. Stonequist, *The Marginal Man* (New York, 1937), pp. xiii-xviii, reprinted in *Race and Culture*, pp. 372-76, quotation pp. 375-76. The individual examples which Park gave of 'marginals' were all men of stature: Lewisohn, Santayana, and Heine. There is a powerful element of Romantic sensibility and sometimes of what seem like liberal transplantations from Romantic philosophy in Park's theorizing about personality types or 'mentalities'. They often seem to be 'dialectical' in a Hegelian sense — indeed, Park did use Hegel's Master/Slave paradox in a more concrete version. The resonances from German romanticism help to make Park's theories both 'backward' and 'forward-looking' at the same time, stimulating in a way that the more strictly denotative sociology of the positivist era from the 1910s to the 1960s rarely could be.

55 Park, 'Mentality of Racial Hybrids', an Address delivered at the Fourth Pacific Science Congress, Java, May 1929, published in *American Journal of Sociology*, 33 (January, 1931): 534-51, reprinted in *Race and Culture*, pp. 377-92, quotations pp. 387, 390. The most thorough development of the 'Marginal Man' concept was by Park's student Everett V.Stonequist who wrote a ph.D. dissertation on the subject in 1930, published in 1937 as *The Marginal Man: a Study in Personality and Culture Conflict* (New York, 1937). Stonequist endeavored to work out a natural history or life-cycle of the Marginal Man and define his characteristic roles. He also broadened the concept to include problems of marginality developing in situations of 'social mobility, rural-urban transition, and shifts in the traditional role of women'. Stonequist, 'The Marginal Man: a Study in Personality and Culture Conflict' (a summary of his 1930 thesis with additional comments made in 1961), in Ernest W.Burgess and Donald J.Bogue, *Contributions to Urban Sociology* (Chicago, 1963), pp. 327-45, quotation p. 328. These wider aspects of marginality were later explored by Everett Hughes, who dealt with marginality as a function of 'status-protest', i.e., the individual who belongs to a group with certain status definitions who then adopts a role which is outside this definition. Everett C.Hughes, 'Social Change and Status Protest: An Essay on the Marginal Man', *Phylon*, 10 (First quarter 1949): 58-65.

56 Park, 'Education in its Relation to the Conflict and Fusion of Cultures', p. 281. The phrase 'run of attention' had first been used by William I.Thomas in 'Race Psychology', *American Journal of Sociology*, 17 (1912): 732. Thomas did not make clear whether this group 'run of attention' was biologically or culturally determined. Park's persistence in clinging to a notion of racial temperament when it was logically quite isolated from the rest of his system is curious; a clue may come from the quotation, where 'racial temperament' allows one to explain ethnic specialization without reference to majority prejudice and the restrictions it puts on career choice. Park may have been passionately anxious to avoid any theory which encouraged a sense of injustice and pity or self-pity. *Without* this convenient survival, 'racial temperament', it would have been more difficult to avoid the kind of humanitarian indignation which irritated him so much. On the level of moral intention, it served the same function as the

ecological order in the general system, that of setting a limit to human malleability and aspirations, of warning that wishes cannot make all things possible.

57 Park, 'Education in its Relation to the Conflict and Fusion of Cultures', p. 280. A contrast is made here between 'the Negro' and 'the East African', and the title of the essay refers to the 'conflict and fusion of *cultures*'. That is, Park was talking of 'the Negro', not as a race, but as an historical type developed in the United States. His legendary vagueness confused himself and others however, and made him at this point, effectively, a 'racist'.

58 Ralph Ellison, *Shadow and Act* (New York, 1964), p. xvii. Parentheses in the original.

59 August Meier, *Negro Thought in America 1880-1915: Racial Ideologies in the Age of Booker T. Washington* (Ann Arbor, 1963), p. 267.

60 Ronald Berman, *America in the Sixties. An Intellectual History* (New York, 1968), pp. 104-109.

61 Park's two most prominent Negro students, E. Franklin Frazier and Charles S. Johnson, played a vital role in moving the study of race relations among blacks from moral uplift to an examination of the effects of a caste system. See S. P. Fullinwinder, *Mind and Mood of Black America*, pp. 100-101.

62 See, for example, Park, 'Racial Assimilation in Secondary Groups', *Publications of the American Sociological Society*, 8 (1913): 66-83. Reprinted in *Race and Culture*, pp. 204-20.

63 Park, 'The Bases of Race Prejudice', *The Annals*, 140 (November 1928): 11-20, reprinted in *Race and Culture*, pp. 230-43, quotation pp. 238-39.

64 Park, 'A Race Relations Survey', *Journal of Applied Sociology*, 8 (1923): 195-205, reprinted in *Race and Culture*, pp. 158-65. See also above, at notes 18 through 21.

65 Park, 'The Bases of Race Prejudice', p. 232.

66 Park, 'The Concept of Social Distance As Applied to the Study of Racial Attitudes and Racial Relations', *Journal of Applied Sociology*, 8 (1924): 339-44, reprinted in *Race and Culture*, pp. 256-60, quotation p. 257. Park's colleague on the Race Relations Survey on the Pacific Coast, Emory S. Bogardus, developed a scale to measure prejudice in terms of the degree of social intimacy one would allow different groups. See for example, Bogardus, 'Racial Distance Changes in The United States During The Past 30 Years', *Sociology and Social Research*, 43 (November 1958): 127-34.

67 Park, 'The Etiquette of Race Relations in the South', Introduction to Bertram W. Doyle, *The Etiquette of Race Relations in the South* (Chicago, 1937), pp. xi-xxiv, reprinted in *Race and Culture*, pp. 177-88, quotation p. 183.

While Park's treatment of the Southern racial situation was usually general and categorized, his system, freed from its deterministic framework, with its built-in allowance for the instability of all arrangements, might be applied fruitfully to the mass of historical research accumulated since his death. C. Vann Woodward's *Strange Career of Jim Crow* can be read almost as an illustration of the transition from etiquette to legal control as a minority becomes more threatening. Critics of Woodward could argue that Park's system, like Woodward's historical argument, suffers from a too-easy readiness to note trivial changes of control mechanism and neglect the primal fact of persistent 'white racism' and discrimination. But here as in all treatments of race relations, indignant simplicity is no substitute for fine analysis, and the value of both men's work has not yet been realized. For Woodward's argument, modified over time, see *The Strange Career of Jim Crow*, (first ed. New York, 1954), second ed., p. 196; *American Counterpoint* (Boston, 1971). Despite Woodward's apparent recantation in 'White Racism and Black "Emancipation",' *New York Review of Books*, 12 (27 February 1969): 5-11, an excellent article which revitalizes his earlier appreciation of contingency and variety is Lawrence C.Goodwyn, 'Populist Dreams and Negro Rights: East Texas as a Case Study', *American Historical Review*, 76 (December 1971): 1435-56.

68   Park, 'Bases of Race Prejudice', p. 233. The mainstream development of studies of prejudice will be treated below. Notice should be taken of the Marxian interpretation, since its chief American proponent in the generation of the 1940s and '50s was a black former Chicago student, Oliver Cromwell Cox. Cox's general statement is in *Caste Class and Race* (New York, 1948; reissued 1959); his detailed critique of Park's vagueness and conservative bias, first published as 'The Racial Theories of Robert E.Park and Ruth Benedict', *Journal of Negro Education* 13 (Fall 1944): 452-63, is in *Caste Class and Race*, ch. 21. While Cox exploits one of Park's weakest spots, his tendency, even while advocating a broad comparative and historical survey, to project the pattern of the recent past onto the broader canvas he has tried to paint, Cox's own brittle semantic dogmatism seems at least equally rigid and imposed, and possibly less capable of sympathetic restatement or development. The chief significance of Cox's critique, beyond what was then an isolated radical enclave, seems to have been in an area outside sociology proper. As sociology turned inward toward specialization on contemporary problems, this problem was bequeathed to historians and anthropologists, and the context of the debate was forwarded by historians like Oscar and Mary Handlin in their seminal article, 'Origins of the Southern Labor System', *William and Mary Quarterly*, 7 (April 1950): 199-222. The culmination of the strand of argument concerned with the origins of prejudice was Winthrop D.Jordan's massive *White over Black* (Chapel Hill, N.C., 1968), which represents scholarly progress in the most elemental sense, in that it shows the terms of the original dispute were too simple.

69   Bernhard L.Hörmann, University of Hawaii, to the writer, 4 January 1965; Charles S.Johnson, 'Robert E.Park: in Memoriam', *Sociology and Social Research*, 28 (May-June, 1944).

70   Donald Pierson to the writer, 7 November 1964; E.R.Faris, 'Robert E.Park', *American Sociological Review*, 9 (1944): 322-25.

71   Park, 'The University and the Community of Races', *Pacific Affairs*, 5 (August 1932): 695-703, quotation p. 703. Park saw that Hawaii would be an ideal location for a conference on 'Race Relations in World Perspective'. His students eventually organized such a conference in Honolulu in 1954. Clarence E.Glick, University of Hawaii, to the writer, 11 August 1964.

72 Park to Hsiao-Tung-Fei, 25 November 1943, Park Collection, Fisk University.

73 Park, Diary of a visit to Japan, entry for 16 November 1929, Park Collection, Fisk University.

74 Edgar Robinson and Paul C.Edwards, eds. *The Memoirs of Ray Lyman Wilbur 1875-1949* (Stanford, 1960), p. 317.

75 S.P.Fullinwinder, *Mind and Mood of Black America*, pp. 100-15. After hearing a report by Charles S.Johnson on research methods used in the study of the Chicago Race Riot of 1919, Norman Hayner noted in his diary that one 'would not know he is a Negro from his cold-blooded presentation'. Robert E.L.Faris, *Chicago Sociology, 1920-32* (San Francisco, 1967), p. 131. Other important sociologists of race who studied with Park include: Louis Wirth, Samuel A. Stouffer, chief author of *The American Soldier,* Everett C.Hughes, Helen McGill Hughes, Horace Cayton, Lewis Copeland, Bingham Dai, John Dollard, Frederick G.Detweiler, Guy B.Johnson, William H.Jones, Forrest La Violette, Andrew W.Lind, Charles Parrish, Donald Pierson, Robert Redfield, Everett V.Stonequist, Robert L.Sutherland, Edgar T.Thompson, Bertram W.Doyle; Ernest W.Burgess, 'Social Planning and Race Relations', paper read at the dedication of the Robert E.Park Building, Fisk University, March 1955, in Jitsuichi Masuoka and Preston Valien, eds. *Race Relations*, pp. 13-25, reference pp. 17-18.

76 Arthur I.Waskow, *From Race Riot to Sit-In, 1919 and the 1960s. A Study in the Connections Between Conflict and Violence* (Garden City, New York, 1966), pp. 46-47, 81-91, 98.

77 Chicago Urban League, *First Annual Report* (1916-17), 5, quoted in Arvarh E.Strickland, *History of the Chicago Urban League* (Urbana, Ill., 1966), p. 40.

78 Chicago Urban League, *Second Annual Report* (1917-18), 3-4, quoted in Strickland, *Chicago Urban League*, p. 41.

79 Park, 'Address – the Negro', given at Fisk n.d. (1936-43), Park-Hughes.

80 Chicago Urban League, *Second Annual Report* (1917-18), p. 3, quoted in Allan H.Spear, *Black Chicago. The Making of a Negro Ghetto 1890-1920* (Chicago, 1967), pp. 171-72.

81 Samuel A.Goldsmith, ed., 'The Park House: a survey, May 12, 1937', Ms., Park Collection, Fisk University.

82 Park, 'The Park House: its future', Ms., Park Collection, Fisk University.

83 'Park House. A Note on Research, 29 March, 1940' [by J.D.Nobel, the director?] Ms., Park Collection, Fisk University. Goldsmith, 'The Park House.'

84 Charles S.Johnson, 'Robert E.Park', p. 358; Mrs.Charles S.Johnson, Nashville, Tenn. to the writer, 1 October 1963.

85 Park to Dean A.A.Taylor, of Fisk, 7 December 1937, remarks on the students' ignorance of the wider world. Park Collection, Fisk University.

86 Margaret Redfield, Wallingford, Vermont, to the writer, 19 June 1964.

87 Park, 'Memorandum touching the Delimitation of the Field of Future Study of

the Institute of Social and Religious Research', Park-Raushenbush, Race Relations Survey, Folder 'Pacific Coast Survey'.

88 Park, Course notes for 'The Crowd and the Public', Park-Hughes. Park used the phrase 'parlor magic' in 'The City as a Natural Phenomenon', quoted by Ralph Turner, 'Introduction', *Robert E.Park on Social Control and Collective Behavior* (Chicago, 1967), p. xx.

89 Floyd N.House, *The Development of Sociology* (New York, 1936), pp. 393, 373-74.

90 Louis Wirth, 'Urbanism as a Way of Life', *American Journal of Sociology*, 44 (July 1938): 1-14. A critic in 1960 dismissed the rural-urban continuum as 'real but relatively unimportant', pointing out that 'many alleged urban items are common in Mid West American rural farming areas and scarce or absent in numerous cities.' Richard Dewey, 'The Rural-Urban Continuum: real but relatively unimportant', *American Journal of Sociology*, 66 (1960-1961): 60-66, quotation p. 63. Later judgments on Park's urbanism may of course reflect the viewpoint of a thoroughly urbanized society and profession; similar surveys in 1800 and 1900 would be needed before dismissing the theory. On class analysis, see Milton M.Gordon, *Social Class in American Sociology* (Durham, N.C., 1958). An important continuation of Park's ideas is in the work of his son-in-law, Robert Redfield, whose anthropological studies elaborated upon the classic *Gemeinschaft/Gesellschaft* contrast. The well-known controversy about Redfield's studies in Mexico can be recaptured in his *Tepoztlan: a Mexican Village* (Chicago, 1930), and the composite volume, *The Little Community/Peasant Society and Culture* (Chicago, 1960), which contains Redfield's late reflections on the conceptual status of his theories; the critical attack is in Oscar Lewis, *Life in a Mexican Village: Tepoztlan Restudied* (Urbana, Ill., 1951), and *Anthropological Essays* (New York, 1970), esp. pp. 35-66.

91 Amos H.Hawley, 'Ecology and Human Ecology', *Social Forces*, 22 (May 1944): 400.

92 Milla Aissa Alihan, *Social Ecology: a Critical Analysis* (New York, 1938), esp. pp. xi, 243-48.

93 Anderson to Alihan, enclosed in Anderson to Park, 11 October 1938, Park Collection, Fisk University.

94 Park to Dwight Sanderson, 17 March 1939. Park Collection, Fisk University.

95 Leo F. Schnore, 'The Myth of Human Ecology', *Sociological Inquiry*, 31 (1961): 128-39. See also Amos H.Hawley, *Human Ecology: a Theory of Community Structure* (New York, 1950), p. 69; Jack P.Gibbs and Walter T.Martin, 'Towards a Theoretical System of Human Ecology', *Pacific Sociological Review*, 2 (Spring 1959): 29-36, quotation p. 30; Otis Dudley Duncan and Leo F.Schnore, 'Cultural, Behavioral, and Ecological Perspectives in the Study of Social Organization', *The American Journal of Sociology*, 65 (September 1959): 132-46. Critical evaluations of ecology as developed by Park and the 'Chicago school' include: Walter Firey, *Land Use in Central Boston* (Cambridge, Mass., 1947); Warner Gettys, 'Human Ecology and Social Theory',

Social Forces, 18 (May 1940): 469-76; Herbert J.Gans, 'Urbanism and Suburbanism as Ways of Life: A Re-evaluation of Definitions', *Human Behavior and Social Process*, ed., Arnold Rose (Boston, 1962), pp. 625-48; Leonard Reissman, *The Urban Process: Cities in Industrial Societies* (New York, 1964); Peter Orleans, 'Robert Park and Social Area Analysis: A Convergence of Traditions in Urban Sociology', *Urban Affairs Quarterly*, 1 (June 1966).

96   Faris, *Chicago Sociology*, pp. 120-22; Jessie Bernard to author, 8 December 1964.

97   Edward Shils, 'Tradition, Ecology, and Institution in the History of Sociology', *Daedalus* (Fall 1970), pp. 760-825, ref. p. 793-94.

98   Ibid., p. 795; Talcott Parsons, 'On Building Social System Theory: A Personal History', *Daedalus* (Fall 1970), pp. 826-81, ref. pp. 827-28, 835-37. John Finley Scott, 'The Changing Foundations of the Parsonian Action Scheme', *American Sociological Review, 28* (October 1963), pp. 716-35; Robert W.Friedrichs, *A Sociology of Sociology* (New York, 1970); Alvin W.Gouldner, *The Coming Crisis of Western Sociology* (New York, 1970).

99   Interview with Everett Hughes, Cambridge, Mass., 21 May 1965.

100   Park to Henderson, 20 January 1936, Park Collection, Fisk University. See also Henderson to Park, 7 March 1935, ibid. Everett Hughes recalled spending a 'lively day' with Park and Henderson in Vermont when Henderson,

> a tremendous talker, allowed that his old friend Park was a good sociologist mainly because he had learned it for himself rather than from professionals, but maintained that all future good sociology would be done by scholars trained in the physical and biological sciences. Park, as usual, talked in his quiet, speculative – sometimes profane – way about ideas ignoring Henderson's outrageous condescension. It was clear they liked and respected each other. The strands of the sociological movement have not been so separate as we often believe.

Everett C.Hughes, 'Robert Park', *New Society, 31* (December 1964): 18-19. For the importance of Pareto in American sociology see Cynthia Eagle Russett, *The Concept of Equilibrium in American Social Thought* (New Haven and London, 1966), chapters 5 and 7.

101   See for example, Park, 'Industrial Fatigue and Group Morale', *American Journal of Sociology*, 40 (November 1934): 349-56, reprinted in *Society*, pp. 293-300.

102   On Park's paradigm and the use of Simmel, see above, chapters 2 and 5; on the romantic analogy with flora, F.M.Barnard, *Herder's Social and Political Thought: from Enlightenment to Nationalism* (Oxford, 1965), chapter 3, *passim*, esp. p. 59. On the next generation in social science, see below for a brief discussion of shifts in race relations study, and more generally Russett, *Concept of Equilibrium, passim*, and Edward Aloysius Purcell, Jr., 'The Crisis of Democratic Theory: American Thought between the Wars, 1919-1941', ph.D. dissertation, University of Wisconsin, 1968, esp. pp. 298-340.

103   The contrast adumbrated here was given classic statement by Richard Hofstadter in the final chapter of *The Age of Reform: from Bryan to F.D.R.* (New York, 1955), pp. 270-326. See also Otis L.Graham, Jr., *An Encore to Reform: the Old Progressives and the New Deal* (New York, 1967).

104 Roscoe C.Hinkle, Jr., and Gisela J.Hinkle, *The Development of Modern Sociology* (New York, 1954), p. 47. The new manipulative trend was not necessarily associated with radical politics, being offered by the industrial psychology movement as well. See Elton Mayo, *The Human Problems of an Industrial Civilization* (New York, 1935).

105 Park to Louis J.Behan, 2 November 1935, Park Collection, Fisk University. Horace Cayton, who had an office next to his at Fisk, recalled driving Park and his wife to New York one Christmas holiday and getting into a violent argument over the capitalist system.

> From an economic point of view, Park was conservative if not reactionary. The argument got hotter and hotter and finally Park told me to stop the car and get out (it was his car). I answered that it was 3 below zero and that he, Park, couldn't drive a car and that I wasn't going to get out. We continued in silence for an hour or so until the lights of New York began to appear and suddenly, without warning, he launched into a lengthy discussion of his theory of the growth of a city, and for an hour delivered one of the most brilliant lectures I've ever heard. We'd both forgotten our differences by the time we got through the Holland Tunnel and he was again the great teacher and I his humble student.

Horace Cayton, 'Robert Park. A Great Man Died, but leaves keen observation on our Democracy', *Pittsburgh Courier*, 26 February 1944.

106 Park to Franz Boas, 3 February 1938: 'I am heartily in sympathy, I think, with the motives that inspire the open letter on Culture and Democracy in Spain. I cannot at this time commit myself to the line of action it proposes.' On the other hand, he did sign a petition put out by the ACLU in favor of some imprisoned Puerto Ricans, since he had great respect for some of the other signers, including John Dewey and Felix Frankfurter, though, as he was careful to explain in a covering letter to President Roosevelt he did not 'have much interest in government by pressure groups'. Park to F.D.Roosevelt, 20 December 1938. Considering the importance he placed on group self-help activity in his race relations theory, Park had a rather irrational horror of pressure groups in politics, or perhaps of politics itself.

107 Park to Charles S.Johnson, 30 March 1938, Park Collection, Fisk University.

108 Faris, *Chicago Sociology*, pp. 121-22.

109 Shils, 'Tradition, Ecology and Institution', p. 807. Lyman, *Black American*, pp. 98-120.

110 Gunnar Myrdal, *An American Dilemma. The Negro Problem and Modern Democracy* (Twentieth Anniversary Edition, New York, 1962, first pub. 1944), p. 1052, p. 1023.

111 Park to Myrdal, 14 February 1939, Park Collection, Fisk University. In 1943 Park was much more convinced of change than other pioneer sociologists, and far less timid about acknowledging it. There is an interesting exchange in the Fisk collection in which E.A.Ross sent Park a chapter on race relations from his new textbook asking him to 'please bear in mind that I can't afford to make it something that will bar my textbook from all Southern high schools. My book aims to put over 40 times as much truth as this chapter contains. It must contain only truth, but it is too much to expect it to put over the whole truth.' Ross to Park, 31 March 1943. Park replied rather contemptuously that the book

'sounds to me, in fact, like a voice from the past. The racial situation is not nearly as static, I am convinced, as your account would suggest. Changes are taking place which have probably rendered obsolete any statement of the situation the Southern people would tolerate in their schools.' Park to Ross, 3 April 1943, Park Collection, Fisk University.

112 Shils, 'Tradition, Ecology and Institution', p. 808. Empirical data on self-definition and courses offered are given in Richard L.Simpson, 'Expanding and Declining Fields in American Sociology', *American Sociological Review, 26* (June 1961), pp. 458-66. Friedrichs, *Sociology of Sociology*, pp. 82-84, offers a different explanation of the shift in professional attention. While the influence of clients was important, it interacted with the profession's drive for theoretical sophistication and articulation and the new explanatory paradigm adumbrated here.

113 On Sullivan, see his *The Fusion of Psychiatry and Social Science* (New York, 1964), *passim*. Park to Myrdal, 14 February 1939, Fisk Collection.

114 Robert K.Merton, *Social Theory and Social Structure*, rev. ed. (Glencoe, Ill., 1957), p. 3. T.W.Adorno, Else Frenkel-Brunswick, Daniel J.Levinson and Nevitt Sanford, *The Authoritarian Personality* (New York, 1950), esp. pp. v-xv. Martin Jay, *The Dialectical Imagination: a history of the Frankfurt School and the Institute of Social Research 1923-1950* (Boston, 1973), esp. pp. 217-52; Robert Coles, 'Understanding White Racists', *New York Review of Books,* 17 (30 December 1971): 12-15. On the parallel approach of the Harvard psychologist Gordon Allport, see his widely-known *Nature of Prejudice* (New York, 1954; abridged Anchor edition, 1958), and Lyman, *Black American*, pp. 121-44. The contrast here is of course overdrawn for the sake of rhetorical clarity within limited space, and ignores the continuation of important, and in the longer term also influential, work in the Park tradition by Herbert Blumer and others. See Masuoka and Valien, eds., *Race Relations*; Blumer, 'Race Prejudice as a Sense of Group Position', *Pacific Sociological Review,* 1 (Spring 1958): 3-7; Joseph D.Lohman and Dietrich C.Reitzes, 'Note on Race Relations in Mass Society', *American Journal of Sociology, 58* (1952), pp. 240-46. Still, the polar types of approach here seem to reflect the changing spotlight of both education and scientific attention, though an extensive study of magazines, syllabi, and lecture notes would be required to document it.

115 Jay, *Dialectical Imagination*, esp. pp. 226-30, 234-52. Jay's brief discussion of the concept of 'tolerance' for the Frankfurt theorists on the one hand, and for Bruno Bettelheim and Morris Janowitz's *Social Change and Prejudice* on the other, is of central importance, since it suggests the conflation after 1945 of two strands of thought, the liberal pluralism that took toleration as a fundamental good and the radicalism that saw it as a necessary but tactical virtue of a transitional phase between bourgeois and liberated eras. See Matthews, 'Revolt againt Americanism'. Adorno's own account of *The Authoritarian Personality* is in Theodor W.Adorno, 'Scientific Experiences of a European Scholar in America', *Perspectives in American History, 2* (1968), pp. 338-70.

116 The quotation is from Park to Carl J.Friedrich, 21 November 1942, Park Collection, Fisk University. The interpretation here follows my 'Revolt against

Americanism', but on cultural pluralism see also John Higham's lucid and reflective 'Ethnic Pluralism in Modern American Thought', in *Send These to Me* (New York, 1975). On the antinomy of intellectuality and common sense, see Hannah Arendt, *The Human Condition* (Chicago, 1958), p. 187, and especially the brilliant Spenglerian repudiation of social science by John H. Schaar, 'Legitimacy in the Modern State', Philip Green and Sanford Levinson, ed., *Power and Community* (New York, 1969), pp. 276-327. Schaar's autopsy on the effort to devise an adequate science of society suggests the kaleidoscopic shifting of interpretive paradigms which plagues any effort to organize the subject historically. Christopher Lasch, *The New Radicalism in America,* and Philip Rieff, ed., *On Intellectuals* (Garden City, N.Y., 1970), provide more detail on the intellectual as American social type.

117 David Riesman, 'Some Observations concerning Marginality', *Phylon* 12 (1951): 113-27, reprinted in *Individualism Reconsidered* (Glencoe, Ill., 1954), quotation p. 162. Riesman's essay of 1951, 'The "Militant" Fight against Anti-Semitism', *Indiviualism Reconsidered*, pp. 139-52, is also valuable for the background of the shift adumbrated here, and his work of course reminds us that the tradition of the humanistic essay did not disappear from Sociology with the passing of Park's generation. A vivid portrait of a similar trend in the Hollywood films of the 1940s, to exalt familial stability and warmth and label individual striving toward ambitious goals as 'pathological', is in Barbara Deming's important book *Running Away from Myself: a Dream Portrait of America Drawn From the Films of the Forties* (New York, 1969). A recent overview of American theories of mobility is Anselm L.Strauss, *The Contexts of Social Mobility: Ideology and Theory* (Chicago, 1971).

118 Myrdal, *American Dilemna,* lxxi. See also the Marxist critique of Myrdal, Oliver C.Cox, 'An American Dilemma: A Mystical Approach to the Study of Race Relations', *The Journal of Negro Education,* 14 (Spring 1945): 132-48; *Caste Class and Race,* pp. 509-38.

119 Park to William M.Cooper, Hampton Institute, 16 February 1938, Park Papers, Fisk University.

120 Park to James A.Dombrowski, 14 January 1943, Park Papers, Fisk University. Perhaps the best embodiment of the Parkian view of race relations in the South is found in the collection of essays in his honor, Masuoka and Valien, *Race Relations: Problems and Theory. Essays in Honor of Robert E.Park.* The editors note Park's conviction that the vital events were those with 'news value', which allowed 'the student to observe changing race relations in the framework of conflict of racial movements'.

121 Park, 'Negro Race Consciousness as Reflected in Racial Literature', *American Review*, 1(September-October, 1923): 505-16, reprinted in *Race and Culture*, pp. 284-300, quotation p. 300. 'Racial Assimilation in Secondary Groups', ibid., 204-20.

122 The quotations are from 'Negro Race Consciousness', and from Park's review of Herbert J.Miller, *Races, Nations and Classes*, in *American Journal of Sociology,* 31 (January 1926): 535-37. The difference between Park and the Miller book suggests the way in which one's basic theoretical position, the root-

metaphor of one's theory, leads to different definitions of the problematic. For Park, reasoning within his conflict theory of change, the psychic effects of group struggle were likely to be desirable as well as inevitable, while his former colleague Miller accepted the common meliorist norm of tension-reduction.

123 Park, 'Address − The Negro'.

124 Park to Horace Cayton, 10 May 1943, Park Collection, Fisk University, also quoted in Horace Cayton, 'Robert Park', *Pittsburgh Courier,* 26 February 1944.

125 Park to Winifred Raushenbush, 1 November 1943, Park Collection, Fisk University.

126 Everett Hughes, 'Robert Park', p. 19.

127 Park to Lisa R.Peattie, 18 October 1942, Park Collection, Fisk University.

128 Park to Samuel Kincheloe, 12 October 1940, Park Collection, Fisk University.

129 Park, 'Missions and the Modern World', *American Journal of Sociology,* 50 (November 1944): 177-83; *Race and Culture,* pp. 331-41, quotation p. 339.

130 Martha L.Harris to Herman Burrell, 15 December 1943, Park Collection, Fisk University; 'Park, Robert Ezra (February 14, 1864 − February 7, 1944)', *Dictionary of American Biography,* Supplement 3 (New York, 1973).

131 Winifred Raushenbush to Park, 26 September 1941, Park Collection, Fisk University; Charles S.Johnson, 'The Most Genuine White Person I ever Met', clipping in Park Collection, Fisk University; Winifred Raushenbush to Park, 26 September 1941. The contention of Oliver Cromwell Cox that Park did not recognize Negroes as equals (cited by Robert L.Factor, *The Black Response to America* (Reading, Mass., 1970), p. 365) seems widely at variance with the recollections of his students, both white and black. See, e.g., Charles S.Johnson, 'Robert E.Park: in Memoriam', *Sociology and Social Research,* 28 (May-June, 1944) and especially Horace Cayton's account of Park and Richard Wright in 'Robert Park. A Great Man Died but Leaves Keen Observation on Our Democracy', *Pittsburgh Courier* (26 February 1944).

132 Riesman, *Individualism Reconsidered,* pp. 163-64. Winifred Raushenbush to Park, 25 February 1941, Park Collection, Fisk University. Park, 'The City as a . Social Laboratory', in T.V.Smith and Leonard D.White, eds., *Chicago: An Experiment in Social Science Research* (Chicago, 1929), pp. 1-19, quotation p. 1. This fatalism comes through very clearly in many of Park's students. Harvey Zorbaugh, for instance, wrote of the 'relentless succession' of types of urban areas as though he were describing the inexorable advance of soldier ants: 'the very march of the city ... encroaching upon the residential neighborhoods ... the slum eats its way into adjacent areas ... wiping out whole communities before it.' *The Gold Coast and the Slum* (Chicago, 1929), pp. 234-35.

133 On the meaning of the terms 'alienation' and 'anomie', see Steven Lukes, 'Alienation and Anomie', in Peter Laslett and W.G. Runciman, ed., *Philosophy Politics and Society, Third Series,* (Oxford, 1969), pp. 134-56; Melvin Seeman, 'On the Meaning of Alienation', *American Sociological Review,* 24 (1959):

783-91, and works cited therein. A provocative recent effort to state the circularity of much, if not all, reasoning in social science is Liam Hudson, *The Cult of the Fact* (New York, 1972). Adorno's aphorism, 'It seems to be the defect of every form of empirical sociology that it must choose between the reliability and the profundity of its findings', is in his 'Scientific Experiences of a European Scholar in America', p. 361. His sophisticated critique of the implicit value premises of the American empirical tradition must be balanced by a recognition that his own Marxian position entails basic premises about human nature and the quality of various cultural expressions.

134   Park, 'The City', p. 24. Robert Wiebe in *The Search for Order* (New York, 1967), bases his interpretation of the development of twentieth century America in the same way on this shift from a community of interest based on local ties, to a mosaic of communities based on professional identity and interest.

135   Park, 'Public Opinion and the Schools', 4 March 1916, Ms. in Park-Hughes. Park, 'The Mind of the Hobo: Reflections upon the Relation between Mentality and Locomotion', in *The City*, pp. 156-60, reprinted in Park, *Human Communities*, pp. 91-95, quotation p. 94; Park Dixon Goist, 'City and "Community": The Urban Theory of Robert Park', *American Quarterly*, 23 (Spring 1971): 46-59, ref. p. 57. For further development of Park's comments on the press as a form of social control see Jean B. Quandt's perceptive study of Park's generation of intellectuals, *From the Small Town to the Great Community. The Social Thought of Progressive Intellectuals*. (New Brunswick, N.J., 1970), esp. pp. 68-70.

136   Park, 'The Mind of the Hobo', p. 94; 'Community Organization and the Romantic Temper', *Social Forces*, 3 (May 1925): 673-77; reprinted in Park, *Human Communities; the City and Human Ecology* (Glencoe, Ill., 1952), pp. 64-72, quotation p. 72.
       Park, 'The University and the Community of Races', Commencement Address at the University of Hawaii, *Pacific Affairs*, 5 (August 1932): 695-703, quotation p. 698. For Frank Lloyd Wright see Norris Kelly Smith, *Frank Lloyd Wright: a Study in Architectural Content* (Englewood Cliffs, N.J., 1966), especially chapter 1.

137   Louis Wirth, in 'R.E.P., 1864-1944'. Appreciations read at the memorial service in the Joseph Bond Chapel of the University of Chicago, 9 February 1944.

138   Park, 'What America can learn from a study of its immigrants', Ms. in Park-Hughes.

Bibliography

Manuscripts

Robert E. Park Manuscripts in possession of Everett C.Hughes, Cambridge, Mass.

Robert E.Park Manuscripts in possession of Winifred Raushenbush (Mrs. James Rorty), Sarasota, Florida.

Robert E.Park Manuscripts. Social Science Research Institute, Fisk University, Nashville, Tenn.

Booker T.Washington Papers. Library of Congress, Washington, D.C.

Cooley, Charles H. 'Notes on Lectures by John Dewey at Michigan.' University of Michigan Historical Collections, Ann Arbor, Mich.

Hayner, Norman S. and Una M. Hayner. Diary. Manuscript in possession of Professor Hayner, University of Washington, Seattle, Wash.

Pearson, Charles B. 'The University of Michigan as I knew it sixty years ago', University of Michigan Historical Collections, University of Michigan, Ann Arbor, Mich.

Presidential File. Sociology Department, University of Chicago Special Collections, University of Chicago, Chicago, Ill.

Presidential Papers. Sociology Department, University of Chicago, Chicago, Ill.

Raushenbush, Winifred. 'Robert Park, 1864-1944. A Memoir.' Unpublished manuscript in possession of the author.

Albion W.Small Papers. University of Chicago Library, Chicago, Ill.

The Published Works of Robert E. Park.

Books

Masse und Publikum: Eine Methodologische und Soziologische Untersuchung. Bern, 1904. Translated by Charlotte Elsner as *The Crowd and The Public, and other Essays,* ed., with an Introduction by Henry Elsner Jr., Chicago: University of Chicago Press, 1972.

The Principles of Human Behavior. Chicago: The Zalaz Corporation, 1915.

The Man Farthest Down: A Record of Observation and Study in Europe by Booker T.Washington with the collaboration of Robert E.Park. Garden City, N.Y.: Doubleday, Page and Co., 1918.

Introduction to the Science of Sociology (with Ernest W.Burgess). Chicago: University of Chicago Press, 1921; 2nd edition 1924; 3rd edition 1969.

Old World Traits Transplanted (with Herbert A.Miller). New York: Harper, 1921.

The Immigrant Press and Its Control. New York: Harper, 1922.

The City (with Ernest W.Burgess and Roderick D.McKenzie, with a bibliography by Louis Wirth). Chicago: University of Chicago Press, 1925; reissued 1966.

An Outline of the Principles of Sociology (ed.). New York: Barnes and Noble, Inc., 1939.

The Collected Papers of Robert Ezra Park, ed. Everett C.Hughes, Charles S.Johnson, Kitsuichi Masuoka, Robert Redfield, and Louis Wirth. 3 vols. Glencoe, Ill.: Free Press, 1950-55. Vol. I, *Race and Culture*, 1950; Vol. II, *Human Communities: The City and Human Ecology*, 1952; Vol. III, *Society: Collective Behavior, News and Opinion, Sociology and Modern Society*, 1955.

Robert E.Park, *On Social Control and Collective Behavior. Selected Papers*. Edited and with an Introduction by Ralph H.Turner. Chicago: University of Chicago Press, 1967.

Articles and Introductions to Published Works by Other Authors

'German Army', *Munsey's Magazine*, 24 (December 1900): 386-405.

'A City of Racial Peace', *World To-Day*, 9 (August 1905): 897-99.

'King in Business', *Everybody's*, 15 (November 1906): 624-33.

'Terrible Story of the Congo', *Everybody's*, 15 (December 1906): 763-72.

'Blood-Money of the Congo', *Everybody's*, 16 (January 1907): 60-70.

'Agricultural Extension Among the Negroes', *World To-Day*, 15 (August 1908): 820-26.

'Negro Home Life and Standards of Living', *Annals of the American Academy of Political and Social Science*, 49 (September 1913): 147-63.

'Racial Assimilation in Secondary Groups with Particular Reference to the Negro', *Publications of the American Sociological Society*, 8 (1913): 66-83; also *American Journal of Sociology* (March 1914): 606-23. *Race and Culture*, pp. 204-20.

'The City: Suggestions for the Investigation of Human Behavior in the City Environment', *American Journal of Sociology*, 20 (March 1915): 577-612; revised in *The City*, by Park *et al.* (1925), pp. 1-46. *Human Communities*, pp. 13-51.

Introduction to *The Japanese Invasion* by Jesse F.Steiner, Chicago: A.C.McClurg & Co., 1917, pp. VII-XVII. *Race and Culture*, pp. 223-29.

'Methods of Forming Public Opinion Applicable to Social Welfare Publicity', *Proceedings of the National Conference of Social Work, 1918*, pp. 615-22. *Society*, pp. 143-51.

'Education in Its Relation to the Conflict and Fusion of Cultures: With Special-Reference to the Problems of the Immigrant, the Negro, and Missions', *Publications of the American Sociological Society*, 13 (1918): 38-63. *Race and Culture*, pp. 261-83.

'The Conflict and Fusion of Cultures', *Journal of Negro History*, 4: 2 (April 1919).

'Foreign Language Press and Social Progress', *Proceedings of the National Conference *of Social Work, Forty-seventh annual session, April 14-20, 1920*, pp. 493-500. *Society*, pp. 165-75.

'Immigrant Heritages', *Proceedings of National Conference of Social Work, 1921*. Chicago, 1921, pp. 492-97.

'Sociology and the Social Sciences', *American Journal of Sociology*, 26 (January 1921): 401-24; 27 (July 1921): 1-21; 27 (September 1921): 169-83; also chapter 1 in *Introduction to the Science of Sociology. Society*, pp. 187-242.

'Letters Collected by R.E.Park and Booker T.Washington', *Journal of Negro History*, 7: 2 (April 1922): 206-22.

'Negro Race Consciousness as Reflected in Race Literature', *American Review*, 1 (September 1923): 505-17. *Race and Culture*, pp. 284-300.

'The Mind of the Rover', *World Tomorrow*, 6 (September 1923): 269-70; retitled 'The Mind of the Hobo: Reflections Upon the Relation Between Mentality and Locomotion', in *The City* (1925), pp. 156-60. *Human Communities*, pp. 91-95.

'The Natural History of the Newspaper', *American Journal of Sociology*, 29 (November 1923): 273-89; also in *The City* (1925), pp. 80-98. *Society*, pp. 89-104.

'A Race Relations Survey: Suggestions for a Study of the Oriental Population of the Pacific Coast', *Journal of Applied Sociology*, 8 (March 1924): 195-205. *Race and Culture*, pp. 158-65.

'The Concept of Social Distance: As Applied to the Study of Racial Attitudes and Racial Relations', *Journal of Applied Sociology*, 8 (July 1924): 339-44. *Race and Culture*, pp. 256-60.

'Experience and Race Relations: Opinion, Attitudes, and Experience as Types of Human Behavior', *Journal of Applied Sociology*, 9 (September 1924): 18-24. *Race and Culture*, pp. 152-57.

'Play and Juvenile Delinquency', *Playground*, 18 (May 1924): 95-96.

'The Significance of Social Research in Social Service', *Journal of Applied Sociology*, 8 (May-June 1924): 263-67.

'The Concept of Position in Sociology', *Publications of the American Sociological Society*, 20 (1925): 1-14; retitled 'The Urban Community as a Spatial Pattern and a Moral Order', in *The Urban Community*, ed. Ernest W.Burgess. Chicago: University of Chicago Press, 1926, pp. 3-18. *Human Communities*, pp. 165-77.

'Community Organization and Juvenile Delinquency', in *The City* (1925), pp. 99-112. *Human Communities*, pp. 52-63.

'Magic, Mentality, and City Life', in *The City* (1925), pp. 123-41. *Human Communities*, pp. 102-17.

'Culture and Cultural Trends', *Publications of the American Sociological Society*, 19 (1925): 24-36. *Race and Culture*, pp. 24-35.

'Immigrant Community and Immigrant Press', *American Review*, 3 (March 1925): 143-52. *Society*, pp. 152-64.

'Community Organization and the Romantic Temper', *Social Forces*, 3 (May 1925): 673-77; also in *The City* (1925), pp. 113-22. *Human Communities*, pp. 64-72.

'Behind our Masks', *Survey Graphic* (1 May 1926), pp. 135-39. *Race and Culture*, pp. 244-55.

'Methods of a Race Survey', *Journal of Applied Sociology*, 10 (May-June 1926): 410-15; also in Emory S.Bogardus, *The New Social Research*. Los Angeles: 1926.

'Our Racial Frontier on the Pacific', *Survey Graphic*, 1 May 1926, pp. 192-96. *Race and Culture*, pp. 138-51.

Introduction to *The Natural History of Revolution* by Lyford P.Edwards. Chicago: University of Chicago Press, 1927, pp. ix-xiii. *Society*, pp. 34-37.

Editor's Preface to *The Gang: A Study of 1,313 Gangs in Chicago* by Frederick M.Thrasher. Chicago: University of Chicago Press, 1927, pp. ix-xii. *Human Communities*, pp. 96-98.

'Human Nature and Collective Behavior', *American Journal of Sociology*, 32 (March 1927): 733-41. *Society*, pp. 13-21.

'The Yellow Press', *Sociology and Social Research*, 12 (September-October 1927): 3-11.

'Topical Summaries of Current Literature: the American Newspaper', *American Journal of Sociology*, 32 (March 1927): 806-13. *Society*, pp. 176-84.

Introduction to *The Strike* by Ernest T.Hiller. Chicago: University of Chicago Press, 1928, pp. vii-x. *Society*, pp. 30-33.

Foreword to *The Ghetto* by Louis Wirth. Chicago: University of Chicago Press, 1928, pp. ix-xi. *Human Communities*, pp. 99-101.

'Human Migration and the Marginal Man', *American Journal of Sociology*, 33 (May 1928): 881-93. *Race and Culture*, pp. 345-56.

'The Bases of Race Prejudice', *Annals of the American Academy of Political and Social Science*, 140 (November 1928): 11-20. *Race and Culture*, pp. 230-43.

'Sociology', in *Research in the Social Sciences*, ed. Wilson Gee. New York: Macmillan, 1929, pp. 3-49. *Human Communities*, pp. 178-209.

'The City as a Social Laboratory', in *Chicago: An Experiment in Social Science Research*, ed. T.V.Smith and Leonard D.White. Chicago: University of Chicago Press, 1929, pp. 1-19. *Human Communities*, pp. 73-87.

Introduction to *The Gold Coast and the Slum* by Harvey W.Zorbaugh. Chicago: University of Chicago Press, 1929, pp. vii-x. *Human Communities*, pp. 88-90.

'Urbanization as Measured by Newspaper Circulation', *American Journal of Sociology*, 35 (July 1929): 60-79.

'Migration and the Marginal Man', in Ernest W.Burgess, ed., *Personality and the Social Group*. Chicago, 1929, chapter 6.

'Murder and the Case Study Method', *American Journal of Sociology*, 36 (November 1930): 447-54.

'The Sociological Methods of William Graham Sumner, and of William I.Thomas and Florian Znaniecki', in *Methods in Social Science: A Case Book*, ed. Stewart A.Rice. Chicago: University of Chicago Press, 1931, pp. 154-75. *Society*, pp. 243-66.

'Human Nature, Attitudes, and the Mores', in *Social Attitudes*, ed. Kimball Young. New York: Henry Holt, 1931, pp. 17-45. *Society*, pp. 267-92.

'Mentality of Racial Hybrids', *American Journal of Sociology*, 36 (January 1931): 534-51. *Race and Culture*, pp. 377-92.

'Personality and Cultural Conflict', *Publications of the American Sociological Society*, 25 (May 1931): 95-110. *Race and Culture*, pp. 357-71.

Introduction to *The Pilgrims of Russian-Town* by Pauline V.Young. Chicago: University of Chicago Press, 1932, pp. xi-xx. *Society*, pp. 22-29.

'The University and the Community of Races', *Pacific Affairs*, 5 (August 1932): 695-703.

'Abstract in Racial Contacts and Social Research', *Proceedings American Sociological Society*, 27 (1933): 101-102.

'William Graham Sumner's Conception of Society', *Chinese Social and Political Science Review*, 17 (October 1933): 430-41.

'Newspaper Circulation and Metropolitan Regions', by Robert E.Park and Charles Newcomb, in *The Metropolitan Community*, ed. Roderick D.McKenzie. New York: McGraw-Hill, 1933, pp. 98-110. *Human Communities*, pp. 210-22.

'Dominance: The Concept, Its Origin and Natural History', in *Readings in Human Ecology*, ed. Roderick D.McKenzie. Ann Arbor, Mich.: George Wahr, 1934, pp. 381-85. *Human Communities*, pp. 159-64.

'Race Relations and Certain Frontiers', *Race and Culture Contacts*, ed. Edwin B.Reuter. New York: McGraw-Hill, 1934, pp. 57-85. *Race and Culture*, pp. 117-37.

Introduction to *Shadow of the Plantation* by Charles S.Johnson. Chicago: University of Chicago Press, 1934, pp. xi-xxiv; reissued 1966. *Race and Culture*, pp. 66-78.

'Industrial Fatigue and Group Morale', *American Journal of Sociology*, 40 (November 1934): 349-56. *Society*, pp. 293-300.

Introduction to *Negro Politicians* by Harold F.Gosnell. Chicago: University of Chicago Press, 1935, pp. xiii-xxv. *Race and Culture*, pp. 166-76.

'Assimilation, Social', *Encyclopaedia of the Social Sciences*, 11 (1935), pp. 281-83.

'Social Planning and Human Nature', *Publications of the American Sociological Society*, 29 (August 1935): 19-28. *Society*, pp. 38-49.

'The City and Civilization', *Syllabus and Selected Readings*, Social Science II. University of Chicago Press, 1936, pp. 204-20. *Human Communities*, pp. 128-41.

'Succession: An Ecological Concept', *American Sociological Review*, 1 (April 1936): 171-79. *Human Communities*, pp. 223-32.

'Human Ecology', *American Journal of Sociology*, 42 (July 1936): 1-15. *Human Communities*, pp. 145-58.

Introduction to *Interracial Marriage in Hawaii* by Romanzo Adams. New York: Macmillan, 1937, pp. vii-xiv. *Race and Culture*, pp. 189-95.

Introduction to *The Etiquette of Race Relations in the South* by Bertram W.Doyle. Chicago: University of Chicago Press, 1937, pp. xi-xxiv. *Race and Culture*, pp. 177-88.

Introduction to *The Marginal Man* by Everett V.Stonequist. New York: Charles Scribner's Sons, 1937, pp. xiii-xviii. *Race and Culture*, pp. 372-76.

'A Memorandum on Rote Learning', *American Journal of Sociology*, 43 (July 1937): 23-36. *Race and Culture*, pp. 53-65.

Introduction to *An Island Community* by Andrew W.Lind. Chicago: University of Chicago Press, 1938, pp. ix-xvi. *Human Communities*, pp. 233-39.

'Reflections on Communication and Culture', *American Journal of Sociology*, 44 (September 1938): 187-205. *Race and Culture*, pp. 36-52.

'The Nature of Race Relations', in *Race Relations and the Race Problem*, ed. Edgar T.Thompson, Durham, N.C.: Duke University Press, 1939, pp. 3-45. *Race and Culture*, pp. 81-116.

'Symbiosis and Socialization: A Frame of Reference for the Study of Society', *American Journal of Sociology*, 45 (July 1939): 1-25. *Human Communities*, pp. 240-62.

'Social Contributions of Physics', *American Physics Teacher*, 7 (October 1939): 327-29.

Introduction to *News and the Human Interest Story* by Helen MacGill Hughes. Chicago: University of Chicago Press, 1940, pp. xi-xxiii. *Society*, pp. 105-14.

'News as a Form of Knowledge: A Chapter in the Sociology of Knowledge', *American Journal of Sociology*, 45 (March 1940): 669-86. *Society*, pp. 71-88.

'Physics and Society', *Canadian Journal of Economics and Political Science*, 6 (May 1940): 135-52; also in *Essays in Sociology*, ed. Clyde W.M.Hart. Toronto: University of Toronto Press, 1940, pp. 1-18. *Society*, pp. 301-21.

'The Social Function of War: Observations and Notes', *American Journal of Sociology*, 46 (January 1941): 551-70. *Society*, pp. 50-68.

'News and the Power of the Press', *American Journal of Sociology*, 47 (July 1941): 1-11. *Society*, pp. 115-25.

'Morale and the News', *American Journal of Sociology*, 47 (November 1941): 360-77. *Society*, pp. 126-42.

'Education as a Social Process', Fisk University, Nashville, Tenn., 1941. Mimeographed.

'Methods of Teaching: Impressions and a Verdict', *Social Forces*, 20 (October 1941): 36-46.

'Modern Society', *Biological Symposia*, 8 (1942): 217-40. *Society*, pp. 322-41.

Introduction to *Negroes in Brazil* by Donald Pierson. Chicago: University of Chicago Press, 1942, pp. xi-xxi. *Race and Culture*, pp. 196-203.

'Racial Ideologies', in *American Society in Wartime*, ed. William F.Ogburn. Chicago: University of Chicago Press, 1943, pp. 165-84. *Race and Culture*, pp. 301-15.

'Education and the Cultural Crisis', *American Journal of Sociology*, 48 (May 1943): 728-36. *Race and Culture*, pp. 316-30.

'Missions and the Modern World', *American Journal of Sociology*, 50 (November 1944): 177-83. *Race and Culture*, pp. 331-41.

Secondary Works

Adorno, T.W., Else Frenkel-Brunswik, Daniel J.Levinson and R.Nevitt Sanford. *The Authoritarian Personality*. New York, 1950.

Alihan, Milla Aissa. *Social Ecology: A Critical Analysis.* New York, 1938.

Allee, W.C., Alfred E.Emerson, Orlando Park, Thomas Park, and Karl P.Schmidt. *Principles of Animal Ecology.* Philadelphia, London, 1949.

Anderson, Albert L. *The Country Town: A Study in Rural Evolution.* New York, 1906.

Anderson, Nels. *The Hobo: The Sociology of the Homeless Man.* Chicago, 1923.

Aron, Raymond. *German Sociology,* tr. Mary and Thomas Bottomore. Glencoe, Ill., 1957.

Atherton, Lewis. *Main Street on the Middle Border.* Bloomington, Ind., 1954.

Barnard, F.M. *Herder's Social and Political Thought: From Enlightenment to Nationalism.* Oxford, 1965.

Barnes, H.E. (ed.). *An Introduction to the History of Sociology.* Chicago, 1948.

Bendix, Reinhard, and Seymour M.Lipset, eds. *Class Status and Power.* Glencoe, Ill., 1953.

Berger, Peter L. *Invitation to Sociology.* Garden City, N.Y., 1963.

—. *The Precarious Vision.* Garden City, N.Y., 1961.

Berlin, Isaiah. 'Herder and the Enlightenment', in *Aspects of the Eighteenth Century.* Baltimore and London, 1965, 47-104.

Berman, Ronald. *America in the Sixties. An Intellectual History.* New York, 1968.

Bernard, Jessie. 'The History and Prospects of Sociology in the United States', in George A.Lundberg, Read Bain, Nels Anderson eds., *Trends in American Sociology.* New York, 1929, 1-71.

—. 'The Teaching of Sociology in the United States in the Last Fifty Years', *American Journal of Sociology,* L (1945), 534-48.

Bernard, L.L. and Jessie Bernard. *Origins of American Sociology: The Social Science Movement in the United States.* New York, 1943.

Bernard, Luther, L. *Instinct: A Study in Social Psychology.* Chicago, 1924.

Blumenthal, Albert. *Small Town Stuff.* Chicago, 1932.

Bogardus, Emory S. *Immigration and Race Attitudes.* New York, 1928.

—. *The New Social Research.* Los Angeles, 1926.

—. 'Racial Distance Changes in the United States during the past thirty years', *Sociology and Social Research,* XLIII (November 1958).

Boring, Edwin G. *A History of Experimental Psychology.* New York, 1950.

Bowdery, Barbara Klose. *The Sociology of Robert E.Park.* Ph.D. dissertation, Columbia University, 1951, University Microfilms, Inc., Ann Arbor, Mich., 1964, pub. #2798.

Bowers, David F., ed., *Foreign Influences in American Life.* Princeton, N.J., 1944.

Bramson, Leon. *The Political Context of Sociology.* Princeton, N.J., 1961.

Burgess, Ernest W. 'The Contribution of Robert E.Park', *Sociology and Social Research,* 29 (March-April, 1945): 255-61.

—. 'Social Planning and Race Relations', in Jitsuichi Masuoka and Preston Valien, eds., *Race Relations Problems and Theory. Essays in Honor of Robert E.Park.* Chapel Hill, N.C., 1961, 13-25.

—. 'The Social Survey: a field for constructive service by departments of sociology', *American Journal of Sociology*, 21 (January 1916).

—. and Donald J.Bogue, eds. *Contributions to Urban Sociology.* Chicago, 1964.

Burrow, J.W. *Evolution and Society: A Study in Victorian Social Theory.* Cambridge, 1966.

Cahnman, Werner J. and Alvin Boskoff, eds. *Sociology and History: Theory and Research,* New York, 1964.

Carpenter, J.Richard. *An Ecological Glossary.* New York, 1962. First published Norman, Okla., 1938.

Commager, Henry Steele. *The American Mind. An Interpretation of American Thought and Character Since the 1880s.* New Haven, 1950.

Conway, Jill. 'Jane Addams: An American Heroine', *Daedalus. Proceedings of the American Academy of Arts and Sciences,* 93: 2 (Spring 1964).

Cooley, Charles Horton. *Social Organization. New York,* 1909.
—. *Social Process.* New York, 1922.

Coser, Lewis A. and Bernard Rosenberg. *Sociological Theory: A Book of Readings.* New York and London, 1957.

—. *Toward a Sociology of Social Conflict,* PH.D. dissertation, Columbia University, 1954, University Microfilms, Inc., Ann Arbor, Mich., Doctoral dissertation series, pub. #8639.

Cox, Oliver Cromwell, *Caste, Class and Race.* New York, 1948; reissued 1959.

Crick, Bernard. *The American Science of Politics, Its Origin and Conditions.* London, 1959.

Curti, Merle. *The Social Ideas of American Educators.* Second edition: Paterson, N.J., 1959. 1st ed. 1936.

Dewey, John. 'The Ethics of Democracy', *University of Michigan Philosophical Papers,* 2nd series (1888): 1-28.

Dewey, Richard. 'The Rural-Urban Continuum: real but relatively unimportant', *American Journal of Sociology,* 66 (1960-61): 60-66.

Doyle, Bertram W. *The Etiquette of Race Relations in the South.* Chicago, 1937.

Drake, St. Clair, and Horace R.Cayton, *Black Metropolis: a Study of Negro Life in a Northern City.* Rev. ed., New York, 1962.

Duncan, Hugh D. *Culture and Democracy: the struggle for form in society and architecture in Chicago and the Middle West during the life and times of Louis H.Sullivan.* Totowa, N.J., 1965.

Duncan, Otis Dudley and Leo F.Schnore. 'Cultural, Behavioral, and Ecological Perspectives in the Study of Social Organization', *American Journal of Sociology,* 65 (September 1959): 132-46.

Dykhuizen, George. 'John Dewey and the University of Michigan', *Journal of the History of Ideas,* 33 (1962): 513-44.

Edwards, Lyford. *The Natural History of Revolution*. Chicago, 1927.

Ellison, Ralph. *Shadow and Act,* New York, 1964.

Fairchild, H.P. *Immigration: A World Movement and Its American Significance,* new revised edition. New York, 1925.

—. *The Melting Pot Mistake*. New York, 1926.

Faris, Ellsworth. *The Nature of Human Nature*. New York, 1937.

—. 'Robert E.Park, 1864-1944', *American Sociological Review,* 9 (1944): 322-25.

Faris, Robert E.L. *Chicago Sociology, 1920-32*. San Francisco, 1967.

Faris, Robert E.L. and H.Warren Dunham. *Mental Disorders in Urban Areas*. Chicago, 1939.

Farrand, Elizabeth M. *History of the University of Michigan*. Ann Arbor, 1885.

Feuer, Lewis S. 'John Dewey and the Back to the People Movement in American Thought', *Journal of the History of Ideas,* 20 (1959): 545-68.

Firey, Walter. *Land Use in Central Boston*. Cambridge, Mass., 1947.

Fleming, Donald. 'Attitude: the History of a Concept', *Perspectives in American History,* I (1967): 286-365.

Fosdick, Raymond B. *The Story of the Rockefeller Foundation*. New York, 1952.

Foxcroft, Frank. 'The American Sunday Newspaper', *The Nineteenth Century*. 62: 368 (October 1970): 609-15.

Frazier, E.Franklin. *The Negro Family in Chicago*. Chicago, 1932.

Friedrichs, Robert W., *A Sociology of Sociology*. New York, 1970.

Fullinwinder, S.P. *The Mind and Mood of Black America*. Homewood, Ill., 1969.

Goffman, Erving. *The Presentation of Self in Everyday Life*. Edinburgh, 1956.

Goist, Park Dixon. 'City and "Community": the Urban Theory of Robert Park', *American Quarterly,* 23 (Spring 1971): 46-59.

Goldman, Eric F. *Rendezvous with Destiny*. Revised edition. New York, 1956, first published 1952.

Goode, William J. and Paul K.Hatt. *Methods in Social Research*. New York, 1952.

Goodspeed, Thomas Wakefield. *The Story of the University of Chicago, 1890-1925*. Chicago, 1925.

Gordon, Milton M. *Social Class in American Sociology*. Durham, N.C., 1958.

Gossett, Thomas F. *Race: The History of an Idea in America*. Dallas, 1963.

Gouldner, Alvin W. *The Coming Crisis of Western Sociology*. New York and London, 1970

Harlan, Louis R. 'Booker T.Washington and the White Man's Burden', *American Historical Review,* 71 (January 1966): 441-67.

Hawley, Amos H. *Human Ecology: A Theory of Community Structure*. New York, 1950.

Hayner, Norman. *Hotel Life*. Chicago, 1936.

Henderson, C.R. *The Social Spirit in America*. Meadville, Pa., 1897.

Herbst, Jurgen. *The German Historical School in American Scholarship. A Study in the Transfer of Culture*. Ithaca, N.Y., 1965.

Higham, John. *Strangers in the Land*. New Brunswick, N.J., 1955.

Hill, Mozell C. 'Some Early Notes of Robert E.Park', *Phylon: the Atlanta University Review of Race and Culture*, 14: 1 (First quarter, 1953).

Hinkle, Roscoe C. and Gisela J.Hinkle. *The Development of Modern Sociology*. New York, 1954.

Hofstadter, Richard, *Social Darwinism in American Thought*. Rev. ed. Boston, 1955.

Hopkins, C.Howard. *The Rise of the Social Gospel in American Protestantism, 1865-1915*. New Haven, 1940.

House, Floyd N. *The Development of Sociology*. New York, 1936.

Howe, Irving. 'The City in Literature', *Commentary*, 51: 5 (May 1971): 61-68.

Hughes, Everett C. *Men and Their Work*. Glencoe, Ill., 1958.

—. 'Robert Park', *New Society*, #118 (31 December 1964): 18-19.

—. 'Social Change and Status Protest: An Essay on the Marginal Man', *Phylon: The Atlanta University Review of Race and Culture*, x (First quarter, 1949), 58-65.

—. 'A Study of a Secular Institution: The Chicago Real Estate Board.' PH.D. dissertation. Chicago, 1928.

Hughes, H. Stuart. *Consciousness and Society. The Reorientation of European Social Thought, 1890-1930*. New York, 1958.

The Institute of Social and Religious Research 1921-34. New York, 1934.

James, William. 'A Certain Blindness in Human Beings', *Selected Papers on Philosophy*. London, 1917.

Jay, Martin, *The Dialetical Imagination. A History of the Frankfurt School and the Institute of Social Research 1923-1950*. Boston, 1973.

Johnson, Charles S. 'Robert E.Park: in Memoriam', *Sociology and Social Research*, 28 (May-June, 1944).

Johnston, R.J. *Urban Residential Patterns. An Introductory Review*. New York, 1972.

Kallen, Horace M. *Culture and Democracy in the United States: Studies in the Group Psychology of the American Peoples*. New York, 1924.

Karpf, Fay B. *American Social Psychology*. New York, 1932.

Kress, Paul F. *Social Science and the Idea of Process: The Ambiguous Legacy of Arthur F.Bentley*. Urbana, Ill., 1970.

Lasch, Christopher. *The New Radicalism in America. The Intellectual as a Social Type*. New York, 1964.

Le Bon Gustave. *The Crowd: A Study of the Popular Mind*. London, 1896, first published Paris, 1895 as *La Psychologie des Foules*. Viking edition, ed. Robert K.Merton, New York, 1960.

Lind, Andrew W. (ed.). *Race Relations in World Perspective. Papers read at the Conference on Race Relations in World Perspective, Honolulu, 1954.* Honolulu, 1955.

Lubove, Roy. *The Professional Altruist.* Cambridge, Mass., 1965.

Lukes, Steven, *Emile Durkheim. His Life and Work.* London, 1973.

—. *Individualism.* New York, 1973.

Lyman, Stanford M., *The Black American in Sociological Thought.* New York, 1972.

McKenzie, R.D. *The Neighborhood.* Chicago, 1923.

Madge, John. *The Origins of Scientific Sociology.* Glencoe, Ill., 1962.

Manuel, Frank E. 'From Equality to Organicism', *Journal of the History of Ideas,* 17: 1 (January 1956): 54-69.

—. *The Prophets of Paris: Turgot, Condorcet, Saint-Simon, Fourier, and Comte.* Cambridge, Mass., 1962.

Martindale, Don. *The Nature and Types of Sociological Theory.* London, 1961.

Masuoka, Jitsuichi and Preston Valien (eds.). *Race Relations Problems and Theory. Essays in Honor of Robert E.Park.* Chapel Hill, N.C., 1961.

Masur, Gerhard. *Prophets of Yesterday. Studies in European Culture, 1890-1914.* London, 1963.

Mathews, Basil. *Booker T.Washington: Educator and Inter-racial Interpreter.* Cambridge, Mass., 1948.

Matthews, Fred H. 'The Revolt against Americanism. Culture Pluralism and Cultural Relativism as an Ideology of Liberation.' *Canadian Review of American Studies,* 1 (Spring 1970): 4-31.

—. 'White Community and "Yellow Peril",' *Mississippi Valley Historical Review,* 50 (March 1964): 612-33.

Maus, Heinz. *A Short History of Sociology.* London, 1962.

May, Henry F. *Protestant Churches and Industrial America.* New York, 1949.

Meier, August. *Negro Thought in America, 1880-1915. Racial Ideologies in the Age of Booker T.Washington.* Ann Arbor, Mich., 1963.

Merton, Robert K. *Social Theory and Social Structure,* 2nd edition. New York, 1957; first published 1949.

—, Leonard Broom, L.S.Cottrell Jr. eds., *Sociology Today: Problems and Prospects.* New York, 1959, pp. 579-99.

Merz, John Theodore. *A History of European Thought in the Nineteenth Century,* IV. Edinburgh and London. 1903-1919; reissued, New York, 1965.

Mills, C.Wright. 'The Professional Ideology of Social Pathologists', *American Journal of Sociology,* 49 (September 1942): 165-80.

Mott, Frank Luther. *American Journalism. A History, 1690-1960,* 3rd edition. New York, 1962.

Myrdal, Gunnar, with the assistance of Richard Sterner and Arnold Rose. *An American Dilemma, The Negro Problem and Modern Democracy.* New York, 1962, first published 1944.

Nisbet, Robert A. 'Conservatism and Sociology', *American Journal of Sociology*, 58 (1952-53): 167-75.

—. *The Sociological Tradition*. London, 1967; first published 1966.

Noble, David W. 'The Paradox of Progressive Thought', *American Quarterly*, 5 (Fall 1953): 201-12.

Odum, Howard. *American Sociology. The Story of Sociology in the United States Through 1950*. New York, 1951.

Ogburn, William F. *Social Change: With Respect to Culture and Original Nature*. New York, 1922.

Orleans, Peter. 'Robert Park and Social Area Analysis: A Convergence of Traditions in Urban Sociology', *Urban Affairs Quarterly*, 1 (June 1966).

'Park, Robert Ezra', *Dictionary of American Biography*, Supplement Three 1941-45.

Parsons, Talcott. 'On Building Social System Theory: A Personal History', *Daedalus, Journal of the American Academy of Arts and Sciences* (Fall 1970): 826-81.

—. *The Structure of Social Action*. Glencoe, Ill., 1949, first published New York, 1937.

Peel, J.D.Y., *Herbert Spencer. The Evolution of a Sociologist*. New York, 1971.

Perry, Ralph Barton. *Thought and Character of William James*, vol. II. London, 1935.

Persons, Stow. *American Minds. A History of Ideas*. New York, 1958.

—. *Decline of American Gentility*. New York, 1973.

Pierson, Donald. *Negroes in Brazil*. Chicago, 1942.

Pochmann, Henry A. *German Culture in America*. Madison, Wisc., 1957.

Quandt, Jean B. *From the Small Town to the Great Community. The Social Thought of Progressive Intellectuals*. New Brunswick, N.J., 1970.

Reissman, Leonard. *The Urban Process: Cities in Industrial Societies*. New York, 1964.

Report of the Laura Spelman Rockefeller Memorial, 1927-28. New York, 1929.

Report of the Laura Spelman Rockefeller Memorial, 1932. New York, 1933.

Rieff, Philip, *The Triumph of the Therapeutic*. New York, 1965.

Riesman, David. *Individualism Reconsidered*. Glencoe, Ill., 1954.

Ripley, William Z. 'Race Progress and Immigration', *Annals*, 34 (1909): 130-38.

Rose, Peter L. *The Subject is Race: Traditional Ideologies and the Teaching of Race Relations*. New York, 1968.

Ross, Edward A. 'The Causes of Race Superiority.' *Annals, American Academy of Political and Social Science*, 28 (July 1901).

—. *Seventy Years of It*. New York, 1936.

Royce, Josiah. *The Philosophy of Loyalty*. New York, 1908.

Rucker, Darnell. *The Chicago Pragmatists*. Minneapolis, Minn., 1969.

Rudolph, Frederick. *The American College and University. A History*. New York, 1962.

Ruml, Beardsley. 'Recent Trends in Social Science', in Leonard D. White, ed., *The New Social Science*. Chicago, 1930.

Russett, Cynthia Eagle. *The Concept of Equilibrium in American Social Thought*. New Haven and London, 1966.

Savage, Willinda. 'John Dewey and "Thought News" at the University of Michigan', *Michigan Alumni Quarterly Review*, 56 (May 1950): 204-207.

Schlesinger, Arthur M. Jr. and Morton White, eds. *Paths of American Thought*. Boston, 1963.

Schnore, Leo F. 'The Myth of Human Ecology', *Sociological Inquiry*, 31 (1961): 128-39.

Shils, Edward. *The Present State of American Sociology*. Glencoe, Ill., 1948.

—. 'Tradition, Ecology, and Institution in the History of Sociology.' *Daedalus* (Fall 1970): 760-825.

Simmel, Georg. 'The Number of Members as Determining the Sociological Form of the Group', tr. Albion W. Small, *American Journal of Sociology*, 8 (July-September 1902): 1-46, 158-96.

—. 'The Problem of Sociology', tr. Albion W. Small, *American Journal of Sociology*, 15: 3 (November 1909): 289-320.

—. 'The Sociology of Sociability', *American Journal of Sociology*, 55 (1949-50): 254-61.

—. *The Sociology of Georg Simmel*, ed. Kurt Wolff. Glencoe, Ill., 1964, first published 1950.

Simpson, Richard L. 'Expanding and Declining Fields in American Sociology', *American Sociological Review* 26 (1961): 458-66.

Slosson, Edwin E. *Great American Universities*. New York, 1910.

'Small, Albion Woodbury', *Dictionary of American Biography*, Dumas Malone Ed., 9. New York, 1963, first published 1935, pp. 221-22.

Small, Albion W. *Adam Smith and Modern Sociology*. Chicago, 1907.

—. 'The Era of Sociology', *American Journal of Sociology*, 1 (February 1895).

—. *The Meaning of Social Science*. Chicago, 1910.

— and George E. Vincent. *Introduction to the Study of Society*. Chicago, 1894.

Smith, T.V. and Leonard D. White (eds.). *Chicago: An Experiment in Social Science Research*. Chicago, 1929.

'Sociology 1917-1930', *Encyclopedia of the Social Sciences*, 1: 204.

Solomon, Barbara. *Ancestors and Immigrants*. Cambridge, Mass., 1956.

Spear, Allan H. *Black Chicago. The Making of a Negro Ghetto, 1890-1920*. Chicago, 1967.

Spencer, Herbert. *The Principles of Sociology*. New York, 1898.

Spencer, Herbert. *Social Statics*. New York, 1908, first published 1850.

—. *The Study of Sociology*. New York, 1874.

Spencer, Samuel R., Jr. *Booker T. Washington and the Negro's Place in American Life*. Boston, 1955.

Spykman, Nicholas J. *The Social Theory of Georg Simmel.* Chicago, 1925.

Stark, Werner. *The Fundamental Forms of Social Thought.* London, 1962.

Starr, Harris E. *William Graham Sumner.* New York, 1925.

Stein, Maurice. *The Eclipse of Community: An Interpretation of American Studies.* Princeton, N.J., 1960.

Stocking, George W., Jr. 'Franz Boas and the Culture Concept in Historical Perspective', *American Anthropologist,* 68 (August 1966): 867-82.

—. 'Lamarckianism in American Social Science: 1890-1915', *Journal of the History of Ideas,* 23 (April 1962): 239-56.

Stonequist, Everett V. *The Marginal Man: A Study in Personality and Culture Conflict.* New York, 1937.

Storr, Richard J. *Harper's University. The Beginnings.* Chicago and London, 1966.

Strauss, Anselm. *Images of the American City.* New York, 1961.

Strickland, Arvarh E. *History of the Chicago Urban League.* Urbana, Ill., 1966.

Strong, Josiah. *Our Country.* New York, 1885; Cambridge, Mass., 1963, ed. Jugen Herbst.

Sumner, William Graham. *Earth Hunger and Other Essays.* New Haven, 1913.

—. *Folkways.* Boston, 1906.

—. *What Social Classes Owe to Each Other.* New York, 1884.

Tentative Findings of the Survey of Race Relations. Stanford, Calif., 1925.

Thomas, William I. 'Race Psychology', *American Journal of Sociology,* 17 (1912).

Thomas, W.I. *Source Book for Social Origins.* Chicago, 1909.

— and Florian Znaniecki. *The Polish Peasant in Europe and America,* 5 vols. Chicago, 1918-20.

Thompson, Edgar T. *Race Relations and the Race Problem.* Durham, N.C., 1939.

— and E.C.Hughes. *Race: Individual and Collective Behavior.* Glencoe, Ill., 1958.

Thrasher, Frederic, *The Gang.* Chicago, 1927.

Timasheff, Nicholas S. *Sociological Theory. Its Nature and Growth,* revised edition. New York, 1964, first published 1955.

'Report of the 21st Annual Tuskegee Negro Conference', *The Tuskegee Student,* 24: 3 (20 January 1912).

Veysey, Laurence R. *The Emergence of the American University, 1865-1910.* Chicago, 1965.

Volkart, Edmund H. (ed.). *Social Behavior and Personality: Contributions of W.I.Thomas to Theory and Social Research.* New York, 1951.

Wade, Louise C. *Graham Taylor, Pioneer for Social Justice, 1851-1938.* Chicago, 1964.

Ward, Lester F. *Applied Sociology.* Boston, 1906.

—. 'Contemporary Sociology', *American Journal of Sociology,* part 2, 7 (March 1902): 629-58.

—. *Dynamic Sociology*, 2 vols. New York, 1883.

Washington, Booker T. *The Future of the American Negro*. Boston, 1899.

—. 'Inferior and Superior Races', *North American Review*, 201 (April 1915): 538-42.

—. *The Man Farthest Down: A Record of Observation and Study in Europe*. Garden City, N.Y., 1912.

—. *My Larger Education*. New York, 1911.

—. *The Story of the Negro*. New York, 1909.

Waskow, Arthur L. *From Race Riot to Sit-In, 1919 and the 1960s. A Study in the Connections Between Conflict and Violence*. Garden City, N.Y., 1966.

White, Morton. *Social Thought in America: The Revolt Against Formalism*, second edition. Boston, 1957. First edition 1947.

— and Lucia. *The Intellectual Versus the City*. Thomas, first published 1962.

Wiebe, Robert H. *The Search for Order, 1877-1920*. New York, 1967.

Wiener, Philip. 'George M.Beard and Freud on American Nervousness', *Journal of the History of Ideas*, 17 (April 1956): 269-74.

Wilson, R.Jackson. *In Quest of Community: Social Philosophy in the United States 1860-1920*. New York, 1968.

Wirth, Louis. *The Ghetto*, Chicago, 1928.

—. 'Urbanism as a Way of Life', *American Journal of Sociology*, 44 (July 1938): 1-24.

Wolff, Kurt H., ed. *George Simmel, 1858-1918. A Collection of Essays, With Translations and a Bibliography*. Columbus, Ohio, 1959.

Wrong, Dennis. 'The Oversocialized Conception of Man in Modern Sociology', *American Sociological Review*, 26 (April 1961): 183-93.

Young, Pauline V. with Calvin F.Schmid. *Scientific Social Surveys and Research: An Introduction to the Background, Content, Methods and Analysis of Social Studies*. New York, 1939.

Zorbaugh, Harvey W. *The Gold Coast and the Slum*. Chicago, 1929.

Association, 58–61; work for Tuskegee Institute, 61–86; at University of Chicago, 85ff; outside activities, 176–79; after retirement, 174–76, 189–90; character and views, 12–20, 61–62, 105–107, 114–17, 125, 187–93; origins of his theories, 36–50; theories of general and urban sociology, 131–56; theories of 'race' and ethnic relations, 76–82, 159–74; relation of personality, political views, and sociological theory, 71–82, 114–17, 125, 130, 132, 134, 138–39, 152–55, 173–74, 182–83

Park House (Chicago), 178
Parsons, Talcott, 131, 149, 182
Peabody, George Foster, 72–73
Peasant, 35, 41, 71–76
People, 17, 25
Pierson, Donald, 175
Pluralism, ethnic and cultural, 79, 169, 186–87
Positivist sociology, Park's opposition to, 32–33, 179–80
Prejudice, 37, 173-74
Public, 55-56, 60

Race Relations Survey, Pacific Coast, 113–15, 162, 164, 176
Race (intergroup) relations theory, 76–81, 157–73, 184–87
Racism, 159, 170–72
Ratzenhofer, Gustav, 96, 97
Raushenbush, Winifred, 106, 118, 189
Rhodes, Cecil, 57, 58, 62
Riesman, David, 187
Role theory, 45, 152–55
Roosevelt, Franklin, 183
Roosevelt, Theodore, 61, 62, 63, 78
Ross, Edward Alsworth, 98, 158
Rousseau, 73
Royce, Josiah, 31, 33, 57, 148
Ruml, Beardsley, 110, 111

St. Simon, Henri de, 37
Schnore, Leo, 181

Shaw, Robert Gould, 14
Shils, Edward, 118, 185
Simmel, Georg, 34, 41–50, 56, 129, 134, 145; and 'American' sociology, 49–50, 182–83
Small, Albion Woodbury, 41, 57, 89, 90, 91, 93, 94–97, 104, 130
Smith, Adam, 23, 54
Social Darwinism, 27–28, 91–92, 190
Social disorganization, 99–100, 155–56, 166
Social process, 44–45, 96–97, 134–35
Social role, 152–55
Social space, 47. See also 'Ecology, human'
Social surveys, 103–104
Society, 1, 26–28, 29, 36–39
Sociology: 'American' perspective in, Park and, 47–50, 52, 55–56, 151–52, 182–83; and journalism, as modes of understanding, 10–11; and literature, inheritance of categories and images, 121–22, 125–27; as style of explanation, 80; as tool for creation of consensus, 180; emergence of, as academic subject in U.S., 89–93; goals of, Parks's view, 192; origins, in Europe, 36–39; shifts of institutional dominance in, 89, 179–87; shifts of theoretical models in, 124–25, 155–56, 159, 172–73, 179–87
Spencer, Herbert, 7, 19, 23, 26, 32, 36, 39–40, 93, 174
Status, 151–52
Stead, William T., 126–27
Stocking, George W., 158
Stonequist, Everett, 136
Strassburg (Strasbourg), University of, 35
Strong, Josiah, 92
Succession, 134–37
Sullivan, Harry Stack, 155, 185
Sumner, William Graham, 27–28, 89, 98, 129, 158

Tarde, Gabriel, 50, 52–54
Taylor, Graham, 94
Thomas, Calvin, 7, 13
Thomas, William Isaac, 1, 84, 97–103,
    118, 123, 129, 144, 148, 158, 160
Thomson, J. Arthur, 138
Thoreau, Henry David, 123, 125
Thorndike, Edward L., 149
Thought News, 20–28, 192
Thrasher, Frederic, 142
Tocqueville, Alexis de, 124
Tonnies, Ferdinand, 41, 132
Trotter, William Monroe, 76
Tuskegee Institute, 1, 60–85

Urbanism, urban interpretation.
    See 'City'
Urban League of Chicago, 176–77

Veblen, Thorstein, 89
Villard, Oswald Garrison, 77

Ward, Lester Frank, 91, 93
Warming, Eugenius, 138
Washington, Booker Taliaferro, 1,
    61–86 *passim*, 177
Weber, Max, 180, 182
Wheeler, William Morton, 138
White, Leonard, 128
White, Leslie A., 108
Whitman, Walt, 15, 17
Wilson, James Q., 117
Wilson, Woodrow, 183
Windelband, Wilhelm, 35, 133
Wirth, Louis, 141, 180, 192
Wright, Frank Lloyd, 192
Wrong, Dennis, 153

Young, Erle F., 128